Emilie Poulsson

In the Child's World

Morning Talks and sStories for Kindergartens, Primary Schools and Homes

Emilie Poulsson

In the Child's World
Morning Talks and sStories for Kindergartens, Primary Schools and Homes

ISBN/EAN: 9783744722438

Printed in Europe, USA, Canada, Australia, Japan

Cover: Foto ©Paul-Georg Meister /pixelio.de

More available books at **www.hansebooks.com**

In the Child's World

*Morning Talks and Stories for
Kindergartens, Primary
Schools and Homes*

By EMILIE POULSSON

*Author of Love and Law in Child Training, Nursery
Finger Plays, Through the Farmyard Gate,
Child Stories and Rhymes, etc.*

ILLUSTRATIONS BY L. J. BRIDGMAN

1925.

MILTON BRADLEY CO.
SPRINGFIELD, MASS.

Copyright, 1893.
BY MILTON BRADLEY COMPANY,
Springfield, Mass.

Registered at Stationers' Hall, London, England.
All Rights Reserved.

Bradley Quality Books

PRINTED IN THE UNITED STATES OF AMERICA.

FULL-PAGE ILLUSTRATIONS.

FRONTISPIECE, " O apple! Come down to me."	
BIRDS,	10
WHERE THE LOGS GO,	21
THE CARPENTER,	29
THE SUNDIAL,	35
LEAVES,	44
GETTING WELL,	55
THE WIND AT WORK,	63
THE PIGEON HOUSE,	75
THE BAKER,	83
PATTY THANKING OLD BOB,	95
POOR BUNNY,	103
LITTLE CHRISTEL,	112
SANTA CLAUS AND THE MOUSE,	123
FATHER TIME'S PROCESSION,	137
THE CAT,	143
GOING TO THE BLACKSMITH'S,	153
MILKING,	159
FIVE DOGS,	179
THE COBBLER,	185
PHILIP'S FIRST VALENTINE,	193
GEORGE WASHINGTON,	199
THE BLACKSMITH,	203
THE MINER,	211
FORMS OF WATER,	221
WATER AT WORK,	229
MR. STICKLEBACK AND HIS NEST,	249
GATHERING SAP,	261
THE BOY RAN ON THE OTHER SIDE OF THE PATH,	273

THE SUNSET WAS A FAVORITE SIGHT,	277
THE SPARROW'S HOME,	287
BALTIMORE ORIOLES AND NEST,	293
PAPILIO TURNUS,	305
ATTACUS CECROPIA,	319
THE FARMER,	327
SPECKLE AND THE SWALLOW,	339
BEES GOING MARKETING,	349
HOMES FOR THE BEES,	355
WHICH DO YOU LIKE BEST?	369
AT THE SEASHORE,	381
THE RAINBOW,	395
LITTLE LINDA,	403
A WEAVER AT HER LOOM,	411
SHEARING THE SHEEP,	415
PICKING THE COTTON,	423
FROM FLAX TO PAPER,	427
IN THE SILK FACTORY,	435

CONTENTS.

1. **FRUITS** 3
    The Sleeping Apple, *From the German.*
    Wait and see, *Josephine Jarvis.*

2. **BIRDS IN AUTUMN** 11
    Lisa and the Birds, *E. P.*
    The Crane Express, *Holmes' Third Reader.*
    Bird Thoughts.

3. **WOOD** 17
    The Logging Camp, *Josephine Jarvis.*
    The Honest Woodman, *Retold by E. P.*

4. **THE CARPENTER** 25
    Little Deeds of Kindness, *E. P.*
    An Old-fashioned Rhyme, *E. P.*

5. **THE CLOCK** 33
    What the Clock Told Dolly, *Minnie G. Clark.*
    The Discontented Pendulum, *Jane Taylor.*

6. **AUTUMN** 45
    The Baby Buds' Winter Clothes, *Josephine Jarvis.*
    An Autumn Song, *E. P.*
    The Kind Old Oak, "*Little Flower Folks.*"
    The Chestnut Boys, *Helen Towne.*

7. **SEEDS.** 51
    Five Peas in a Pod, *Hans Christian Andersen.*
    Psyche's Task, *F. H.*
    Apple-Seed John, *Lydia Maria Child.*

8. **THE WIND** 62
    How West Wind Helped Dandelion, *E. P.*
    The Dandelion Cycle, *E. P.*
    Odysseus and the Bag of Winds, *F. H.*
    North Wind at Play, *From the German, as told by Harriet Ryan.*

9. THE PIGEONS . . . .
    The Fantail Pigeon, *Mary Dendy.*
    Pearl and Her Pigeons, *Helen Keller.*
    The Constant Dove, *Celia Thaxter.*
    The Dove and the Ant, *Æsop.*
    A True Pigeon Story, *M. P.*

10. THE BAKER . . . .
    The Johnny Cake.
    The China Rabbit Family, *E. P.*
    Teddy's Birthday Cake, *E. P.*
    Nero at the Bakery, *E. P.*

11. THANKSGIVING DAY . . . . .
    A Boston Thanksgiving Story, *E. P.*
    How Patty Gave Thanks, *E. P.*

12. WINTER . . . .
    The Thrifty Squirrels, *Mary Dendy.*
    Jack Frost and His Work, *E. P.*

13. THE FLOWER BASKET, OR LOVING AND GIVING
    Little Servants, *Sidney Dayre.*
    Extract from the Dream of Little Christel.
    The Wake Up Story, *Eudora Bumstead.*
    The Go Sleep Story, *Eudora Bumstead.*

14. CHRISTMAS . . . .
    Christmas in the Barn, *Frances Arnstein.*
    Santa Claus and the Mouse, *E. P.*
    The Birds' Christmas, *F. E. Mann.*
    Piccola, *Celia Thaxter.*

15. THE NEW YEAR . . . . . .
    An All-the-Year-Round Story, *E. P.*
    The Fairy's New Year Gift, *E. P.*

16. THE CAT . . . .
    My Jet, *M. V. Gillin.*
    A Kitten Rhyme, *E. P.*
    Spotty's Family, *Josephine Jarvis.*

17. THE HORSE . . . .
    A Wise Old Horse, "*Nursery Stories.*"
    Pegasus, *F. H.*
    The Horse that Fed His Friend, "*St. Nicholas.*"

18. THE COW . . . .
    The Story the Milk Told Me, *Gertrude H. Noyes.*

The Cow that Lost Her Tail, *E. Knatchbull-Hugessen.*
Lord Cornwallis' Knee-buckles, *Holmes' Third Reader.*

19. THE DOG 174
    How Frisk Came Home, "*Nursery Stories.*"
    Cleverness of a Sheep Dog, "*Little Folks.*"
    The Dog and the Kitten.
    A True Story of a Dog.

20. THE COBBLER 181
    Goody Two Shoes, *Retold by E. P.*
    Seeing Shoes Made, *Josephine Jarvis.*
    The Cobbler and the Children, *Josephine Jarvis.*

21. ST. VALENTINE'S DAY 191
    Philip's Valentine, *E. P.*

22. WASHINGTON'S BIRTHDAY 197

23. THE BLACKSMITH 201
    Nahum Prince, *E. E. Hale.*
    Vulcan, the Mighty Smith, *F. H.*

24. THE MINER 209
    Suggestions, *A Kindergartner.*
    The Golden Touch, *E. P.*
    Coal, *Helen Keller.*

25. WATER, I 216
    To Whom shall We Give Thanks?
    Snowflakes, *Josephine Jarvis.*
    The Immortal Fountain, *Lydia Maria Child.*

26. WATER, II 227
    Stony and Rocky, *Annie E. Allen.*
    The Little Hero of Haarlem.
    Do What You Can.
    Neptune, *F. H.*
    The Brook and the Water Wheel, *Charles Foster.*

27. FISHES 239
    The Minnow's Adventure, *E. P.*
    Mr. Stickleback, *E. P.*

28. TREES 253
    The Four Apple Trees, *E. P.*
    The Story of Echo, *F. H.*
    The Tree, *B. Bjornsen.*
    The Maple Tree's Surprise, *F. E. Monr*
    Pussy Willow, *Kate L. Brown.*

29.	SPRING	263
	Spring and Her Helpers, *E. P.*	
	The Meeting of the Winds, *Charles Foster.*	
	The Little Worm that was Glad to be Alive, *Elizabeth Peabody.*	
	A Surprise, *Sue Clark Kimball.*	
30.	FRIEDRICH FROEBEL	276
	Song for Froebel's Birthday, *E. P.*	
31.	BIRDS	282
	Jack and Jenny Sparrow, *Charles Foster.*	
	Little Yellow-wing.	
	Child and Bird, *William Allingham.*	
	The Sandpipers, *Josephine Jarvis.*	
32.	BIRDS' NESTS	292
	The Scarecrow, *Celia Thaxter.*	
	The Nest of Many Colors, *E. P.*	
	The Sparrow's Nest, *Mary Howitt.*	
33.	THE BUTTERFLY	302
	Some Common Butterflies.	
	A Lesson on Faith, *Margaret Gatty.*	
34.	THE CATERPILLAR	313
	"Such a Beauty," *E. P.*	
35.	THE FARMER	321
	A Barn-yard Talk, *E. P.*	
	The Farmer and the Birds, *Josephine Jarvis.*	
	Little Gustava, *Celia Thaxter.*	
36.	THE HEN AND CHICKENS	331
	The Lost Chicken, *E. P.*	
	Pe-wee's Lesson, "*Stories for the Kindergarten and the Home.*"	
	The Story of Speckle, *E. P.*	
37.	THE BEE, I	344
	The Rhyme of the Little Idle Boy, *E. P.*	
	Edith and the Bees, *Helen Keller.*	
38.	THE BEE, II	352
	A Narrow Escape, *Maurice Noel.*	
	Solomon and the Bees, *J. G. Saxe.*	
	Mrs. Flyaway, *Ada Cook.*	
39.	FLOWERS	366
	What They Did.	
	The Plant Household, *E. P.*	

Clytie, *F. H.*
The Indian Legend of the Arbutus, *C. E. Belknap.*
The Little Plant, *Kate L. Brown.*

40. SUMMER 379
   How the Beans Came Up, *F. E. Mann.*
   Mabel on Midsummer Day, *Mary Howitt.*
   The Story of a Breeze, *Mattie McRoy.*

41. SUNSHINE 393
   The Wind and the Sun, *Retold by E. P.*
   The Sunbeams, *E. P.*
   The Story of the Morning-glory Seed, *Margaret Eytinge.*
   The Water-bloom, *Celia Thaxter.*

42. THE MOON AND THE STARS 401
   Linda and the Lights, *E. P.*

43. THE WEAVER 407
   A Visit to the Weaver, *Josephine Jarvis.*
   John's Trousers, *Josephine Jarvis.*

44. WOOL 413
   How the Little Boy Got a New Shirt, *From the German.*
      Translated by Louise Stuart.
   Molly's Lamb, "*Stories for the Kindergarten and the Home.*"
   Sequel to an Old Story, *E. P.*

45. COTTON 420
   Machinery Magic, *Holmes' Third Reader.*
   Cotton Field Stories, *E. P.*

46. LINEN 426
   The Flax, *Hans Christian Andersen*
   The Flax Flower, *Mary Howitt.*

47. SILK 434
   The Life of a Silk Worm, *Nettie Fleming.*
   The Silk Worm, *Mary Howitt.*
   The Goddess of the Silk Worm, *E. P.*

ALPHABETICAL INDEX 440

The contributors to this volume have been so cordially helpful, that it gives me pleasure to record here my sincere thanks and appreciation. For kind permission to use stories and poems specified elsewhere in the book, grateful acknowledgments are also rendered to the following publishers:—

Houghton, Mifflin & Co., Boston; The Century Co., New York; Youth's Companion, Boston; D. C. Heath & Co., Boston; Henry Holt & Co., New York; Harper Brothers, New York; The Kindergarten Publishing Co., Chicago; The Educational Publishing Co., Boston; The Charles Foster Publishing Co., Philadelphia; The University Publishing Co., New York; The Sunday School Association, London.

EMILIE POULSSON.

A PREFATORY WORD TO MOTHERS

"Isn't it nice, Mother! When we want to know about something we look in 'In the Child's World' and there it is."

Little Mary, asked to loan her copy of this same book, answered emphatically, "If you'll be sure to bring it back before bedtime." The source of her nightly story must be at hand when needed.

These are samples of children's verdicts upon this volume of talks and stories and indicate very clearly its two-fold usefulness in the home. Although owing its inception to the kindergartners' need of such material as it provides, the book has from the first, been welcomed by many mothers who have found it a "family book," one that all the children enjoy, year after year.

It contains stories for the littlest listeners, (The Wake-Up Story, The Go-Sleep Story, etc.); stories for children of kindergarten age; and a goodly number of stories (like "A Lesson of Faith") mature enough for older children. Besides this range of suitability for different ages, there is a wide variety of subjects treated in the stories, corresponding in a measure to the variety of objects, events and experiences that Life brings so richly even to little children.

But perhaps the talks in "In the Child's World" are of more specific value in the home than are the stories.

To answer a child's questions in the right way and when his interest is at white heat is to contribute materially to his education and development, to say nothing of his pleasure. Moreover, to have Mother or Father associated with this pleasure and the satisfaction of his desire for knowledge is to strengthen the bond between child and parent.

But Mother or Father is not always prepared with the simple, scientifically correct explanation which the little seeker after knowledge deserves. These talks were designed to make such explanations easily available; and they are expressed in language suited to the young child's comprehension. Through assurances of many parents that both talks and stories have proved of value to them, the author's hope that such would be the case has grown into confidence enough to warrant this special word as to the use of the book in the home.

EMILIE POULSSON.

PREFACE.

The preparation of these talks and stories was first undertaken for the kindergartens of Boston and vicinity.

With the talks especially, great freedom in the use of the material offered was always urged as essential to good results, and such freedom is urged more than ever, in submitting the collection to a wider circle of teachers and children.

The subjects follow, somewhat, the course of the kindergarten year, but selection must be exercised, since there is often under one subject more than enough for two weeks' work with the children.

The book is in no wise intended as a one-year programme.

Accuracy of fact has been assiduously sought, and in view of the pains taken, and the authorities consulted, is believed to have been obtained. Should errors be found, however, notice of them would be gratefully received.

Reading, more or less closely related to the subject, has been suggested in the hope that the lists will prove a convenience to the teacher and tempt her to avail herself of the refreshment and inspiration which poet, philosopher, scientist and story-teller are ready to give.

While most of the stories in the book are for children of the kindergarten age, whether at home, in the kindergarten, or in the lower grades of the primary school, a few stories are intended expressly for older children.

Stories of nature and child-life, of history and of mythology, have all found place, for, as the best educators tell us, all these kinds are necessary for the symmetrical development of the faculties. Like the talks, the stories are concerning those objects, activities, festivals, etc., which belong in the child's world, those with which he is in actual contact or has some relation, and of which he is eager to talk and to hear.

Whatever the kind of story, its spirit and influence have been the paramount considerations.

> "I have indited thee with care and love,
> My little book; and now I send thee forth
> On a good mission,
> In sweet homes to be a loving guest,
> And find a place in many a guileless heart."
>
> EMILIE POULSSON.

Boston, Mass., 1893

IN THE
CHILD'S WORLD

FRUITS.

To the Teacher:—

Though this talk is more upon the apple than upon fruits in general, it is better, for the sake of comparison, that the teacher should have, besides apples a pear, peach, plum and grapes and other fruits, as convenient. The best illustrative object would be a small branch bearing both fruit and leaves. A colored picture of the apple blossom will also be needed.

Let the children first name the fruits as you hold them up one by one. Question regarding the colors. Let some of the children distinguish the fruits by touch alone, following this test with questions upon the shapes. Contrast the velvety skin of the peach with the smooth skin of the apple and pear.

Let other children name the fruits by the sense of smell, and others by the sense of taste, either now or later, during the games, or at lunch time.

Take care that each of these exercises is profitable, requiring the child to discriminate by the one sense alone.

THE TALK.

Where did the fruits come from? (If the children get beyond "the fruit stand" and give the general answer "from the trees," lead them to notice that each kind of fruit comes from its own kind of tree.)

Do you think it takes the apple tree a long time to get the apples ready? Indeed it does, a long, long time. Some of the older children who were in kindergarten last year may remember the apple blossoms we saw in the springtime. (Show picture of apple blossom.)

When the pretty pink and white petals dropped off the stem, there was a tiny, hard, green knob at the end of it, and all the spring and all the summer this little green knob grew and grew and grew. Finally, late in the summer or in autumn, the apple was full-grown and ripe. (A series of quick drawings, showing the gradual enlargement of the growing apple, will interest and impress the children, if done in a spirited manner. The first figures of the series could be drawn with green crayon and the later ones with green and yellow, or whatever would best represent the ripe apple which you have shown them.)

What helped the tree to make its apples? The earth and the air, the sunshine and the rain,—nothing can grow without them.

Of what use are fruits? They are very good to eat and very wholesome when ripe and fresh, or when nicely cooked. Insects, worms and birds make many a delicious feast upon them, and even the larger animals enjoy them, too, sometimes.

I was crossing a field the other day, with a lady, when two cows walked straight to her. "Oh, yes!" said the lady, "you want some apples, don't you?" Then she explained to me that she had once given these two cows some apples and that they had since come to her every time she crossed the field, evidently expecting to be treated to fruit.

What do you find inside the apple when you eat it? What in the pear? peach? plum? grape? (Let a child cut an apple in halves vertically, and another child cut a second apple horizontally, and do the same with two pears.) How many seeds in the apple? in the pear? Are the seeds of any use? Look at the apple seeds. What a shiny brown color they are and how small! Yet each seed, if planted and cared for rightly, would grow to be a tree some day—a tree with roots and trunk and branches and leaves, and with spring blossoms and autumn fruits.

Are they not useful and wonderful, then, these little brown seeds? Would you like to have a baby apple tree growing in the kindergarten? What shall we do, then? (It will be well to plant several, to ensure the desired result.)

TEACHER'S READING.

How Plants Grow, - - - - - - - - - - Gray
Flower and Fruit - - - - - - - - Jane H. Newell
Systematic Science,
                        Edw. G. Howe, in Kindergarten Magazine, May and June, 1891
Apples, - - - - - - - - - George W. Curtis
The Apple ("Winter Sunshine"), - - - - - - Burroughs
Forest Trees and Wild Apples,
                        Thoreau, in No. 27 of Riverside Literature Series
The Planting of the Apple Tree, - - - - - - - Bryant
The Fruit Gift, - - - - - - - - - Whittier
Cellar Scene ("Bitter Sweet"), - - - - - J. G. Holland
To Autumn, - - - - - - - - - - Keats
The Orchard Lands of Long Ago, - - - - James Whitcomb Riley
August ("There Were Four Apples on the Bough"), - - Swinburne
August, - - - - - - - - - - Edwin Arnold

For the Children.

The Nut Gatherers, }
The Four Peaches. }   - - - - - - *Kindergarten Gems*

STORIES.

The Sleeping Apple.
(From the German.)

High up in a tree, among the green leaves, hung a little apple with such rosy cheeks it looked as though it might be sleeping. A little child came near, and standing under its branches, she looked up and called to the apple: "O apple! come to me; do come down to me! you do not need to sleep so long."

She called so long and begged so hard, but the apple did not waken; it did not move in its bed, but looked as though it was laughing at her in its sleep.

Then came the bright sun; high in the heavens he shone. "O Sun! lovely Sun!" said the child, "please waken the apple for me." The sun said: "O, yes; with pleasure I will." So he sent his bright beams straight in the face of the apple and kissed it kindly, but the apple did not move a bit.

Then there came a bird, and perched upon a bough of the tree and sang a beautiful song, but even that did not waken the sleeping apple. And what comes now! "I know," said the child, "he will not kiss the apple—and he cannot sing to it, he will try another way." Sure enough, the wind puffed out his cheeks and blew and blew, and shook the tree, and the little apple was so frightened that it awoke and jumped down from the tree and fell right in the apron of the little child. She was much surprised, and so glad that she said to him, "I thank you very much, Mr. Wind."

LIZZIE WILLIS.

Kindergarten Magazine.

Wait and See.

A baby beech tree was growing by the side of its mother. It said to her one day, "Mother, I wish I knew of what use I can be in the world. There is Neighbor Oak who throws down acorns for our master's pig to eat. Neighbor Birch gives him some smooth bark to make into a boat. Neighbor Spruce gives him gum to pour over the joinings of the boat to keep it from leaking, and all the others can help in some way; but what can I do?" "Wait and see," said the mother tree. So the little tree waited.

By and by some pretty flowers shaped like this (showing flower or a picture of some flowers resembling the blossoms of the beech) came upon the baby tree. Then the little tree was happy. "Oh!" it said, "now I see what good I can do. I can please our master by looking pretty."

When the blossoms fell off, the poor little tree felt badly. "O mother!" it said, "all my pretty flowers are gone, and now I cannot even look pretty any longer. What shall I do?" "Wait and see," said the mother tree. The little tree thought that waiting was a hard thing to do, but it said to itself, "Mother knows best, so I'll do what she says."

After a while some small green prickly things came where the flowers had been. These pleased the little tree as much as the flowers had done, and it was content to wait, and see if they were of any use except to look pretty.

Then the little green prickly things all turned brown and the baby beech tree thought they were not pretty any longer. "Oh, dear! mother," it said, " my little green prickly things have all turned brown, and now I cannot even look pretty any longer. What shall I do?" "Wait and see," said the mother tree. So the little tree waited.

The autumn had come, and the weather was beginning to be cold in the part of the country where the baby beech tree lived. One morning after a heavy frost, the baby beech tree found that its little brown prickly things had all fallen. "O mother!" it said, "there are my little prickly things on the ground, and now I am sure I shall never be of any use to anybody." "Do not be discouraged yet; wait and see," said the mother tree.

Just then the master's children came along. They had baskets in their hands, for they were going to pick up nuts in the woods. As they came under the baby beech, the eldest boy stopped. "O children! See!" he cried, "here are the beech nuts on the ground Mother likes them better than any other kind of nuts. Let us pick them all up and take them home to her."

As the children went away with the nuts, the mother tree said, "Now, my dear, you see what good you can do." "Yes, mother," said the little tree. And ever after it was content, even when it grew to be a big tree—as big as its mother.

JOSEPHINE JARVIS.

Cobden, Ill.

In rose time or in berry time,
 When ripe seeds fall or buds peep out,
When green the grass or white the rime,
 There's something to be glad about.

LUCY LARCOM.

BIRDS.

BIRDS IN AUTUMN.

To the Teacher:—

A closer study of birds and bird-life will be advisable in the spring, when we welcome the little travelers back. By that time the children will be prepared to observe more in detail and will have more power of expression, as well as a greater familiarity with the activities of the birds through the bird games and finger plays.

If there is a kindergarten canary, it would naturally furnish the text for this talk; but the migration of the birds and the causes which lead to it should be prominent.

THE TALK.

(Sing the Froebel finger play, "In the branches of the tree." Show a nest and enlarge somewhat upon the nest building and the family life which the song has only suggested.)

The nest is the birdie's home. A small place for a whole family to live in, is it not? The baby birds are very tiny, however, and cuddle close together under the mother bird's wings; and the father bird generally sits on a branch near the nest.

How do birds get so high in the tree? What do they use in flying? (Let the children tell all they can about birds,—their appearance and habits and songs,—and also tell what birds they know by name.)

What do birds like to eat? Fruit, grains and other seeds, and worms and insects. Where do they find them? Are the worms and insects out in the winter? Are the fruits on the trees in winter? What will the poor birds do, then, when the cold winds blow and the trees are bare and the ground is covered with snow? Poor little things! They could not live if they stayed here. They would freeze or starve in our cold land. So, some time in the autumn, when they find that the air is colder and food is getting scarce, they decide to go away. Whole flocks of them fly away together.

Where do you think they go? Far away to another part of our land where it is warm, bright, summer weather.

Is it not wonderful that they know when and where to go?— wonderful that they can find their way, sometimes across the sea even, and always a long distance? How glad they must be, after flying so far, to reach a place where they find fruit and flowers, and green trees and warm sunshine!

Do *all* the birds fly away to a warm country? Which birds stay with us all winter? Is it easy for them to find enough to eat? Would you like to help them sometimes this winter? Even if we should only give the birds the crumbs and bits from our lunch every day, it would be a help to them. Perhaps we can sometimes make quite a feast for our little feathered friends.

TEACHER'S READING.

A Popular Handbook of the Ornithology of the United
  States, Based on Nuttall's Manual, - - - - *M. Chamberlain*
Migration of Birds ("Winners in Life's Race"), - - *Arabella Buckley*
A Bird Medley ("Birds and Poets"), - - - - - *Burroughs*
November Birds ("Sharp Eyes"), - - - - - *W. H. Gibson*
The Unknown Land, - - - - - - - *Margaret Gatty*
To a Waterfowl, - - - - - - - - *Bryant*
A September Robin, - - - - - - - *D. Mulock Craik*
A Remembrance of Autumn, - - - - - *Adelaide A. Proctor*
The Flight of the Birds, - - - - - - *E. C. Stedman*
The Departure of the Swallow, - - - - - *W. Howitt*
Bird Ways, • - - - - - - - - *O. T. Miller*

For the Children

Coming and Going (Kindergarten Stories and Morning Talks), *S. E. Wiltse*

STORIES.

Lisa and the Birds.

(*From the Norwegian.*)

"Tell me," said little Lisa,
    The pretty child so sweet,
"Where do you tiny birdies
    Find all you need to eat?"
The little bird in answer
    Sang cheerily: "We know!
For us, a dainty table
    Is spread where'er we go:
The good brown earth, so kindly,
    Has scarce a single plant
Which will not feast the birdies
    When seeds or fruits they want.'
So sang the birds to Lisa;
    But Lisa, pitying, said:
" When little birds are tired
    Where can they find a bed?"
Then gaily chirped the birdies,
    "In every bush or tree
Where we may choose to build them
    We have our dwellings free.
Leaf shaded and leaf hidden
    We safely go to rest;
Was never bed more cosy
    Than is the birdie's nest."
Still questioned little Lisa:
    "But when you wish to drink,
What then?" The birdies warbled
    "We seek the brooklet's brink,
Or sip the dew of morning
    Which every leaf holds up;
Or take with joy the raindrops
    From some bright flower's cup.
And many a spring and fountain
    And many a wayside pool
Their sparkling waters offer,
    So fresh and pure and cool."

Then said the loving Lisa:
"When winter cold is here
And everything is frozen,
  Oh, you will starve, I fear!"
Again the birds chirped gaily:
"O little maiden kind,
We fly to lands of sunshine
  Where summer joys we find.
And for the birds who stay here
  Ev'n when cold winter comes,
Some child as sweet as you, dear,
  Will surely scatter crumbs."

EMILIE POULSSON.

The Crane Express.

Once upon a time there were six little birds, all fat, all fluffy, and all friendly; and they sat in a row on the shore of the Mediterranean Sea.

Said one of them to the others, "Fat and fluffy friends, let us go over to Africa. I have heard that the worms there walk into one's mouth as soon as one opens it, and that they have besides a very fine flavor."

Said the others to him, "Fluffy friend and fat, gladly would we go to Africa, but how can we get there? Our wings are short, and we are small. We never could fly so far, but should drop into the sea and be drowned."

"That is true," said the first. "Let us see if some one does not come along who will carry us over." So they all waited, sitting in a row on the sand. Soon a great fish came swimming by.

"Will you carry us to Africa, fish?" asked the six little birds.

"I will carry you to the bottom of the sea," replied the fish. "Just like this!" and, folding his fins, he darted down through the water as swift as an arrow.

"Dear! dear!" said the little birds. "How lucky that we did not go with him. We must still wait."

Soon a sheep came walking by, and as it looked very good-natured, the birds asked if it would carry them over to Africa.

"I can't," said the sheep. "I never swim, and I cannot fly. You must wait for the cranes."

"And who are the cranes?" asked the little birds.

"They are big birds," said the sheep, "with long bills, longer necks, and legs that are longer yet. Once every year they come from the north and fly to Africa, and always carry small birds like you. I wonder you have never seen them."

"We are very young," replied the fat, fluffy, little friends. "We have seen little of the world, but we thank you very much for telling us, and we will wait for the cranes."

They had not long to wait. In a few minutes they heard a rushing sound overhead, and looking up saw a flock of great birds with necks outstretched and wings spread wide, flying low over the beach.

"Will you carry us over to Africa?" called the little birds all in a flutter, as the first crane swept by.

"I am full!" replied the crane. "The fourth behind me has room for you, but you must get on quickly!"

As he flew on, the six friends saw that his back was covered with small birds, all huddled together and holding on with beaks and claws.

The second crane passed, and the third, both heavily laden. Then came the fourth. Hop! skip! flutter! scramble! and the six fat, fluffy friends were seated on his back, with a dozen or more little fellows about their own size.

"Are you all right?" said the crane. "Hold on tight!" and away he flew over the wide, blue sea.

Many other little birds came flying to the shore, to take passage on the Crane express. And many a back was covered with tiny passengers.

"All aboard! all aboard!" cried the cranes. "Twitter! chirp! twit-twit!" piped the passengers. And the whole train swept on, far away over the sea, toward the white shore of Africa.

Now, part of this story may be true, for cranes really do carry hundreds of small birds over the Mediterranean Sea every year. But whether the African worms walk into birds' mouths of their own accord or not, is quite another matter; and if I were you, I would not believe it till I saw it.

Holmes' Third Reader.

University Publishing Co., New York.

Bird Thoughts.

I lived first in a little house,
    And lived there very well,
I thought the world was small and round,
    And made of pale blue shell.

I lived next in a little nest,
    Nor needed any other,
I thought the world was made of straw,
    And brooded by my mother.

One day I fluttered from the nest
    To see what I could find.
I said: "The world is made of leaves,
    I have been very blind."

At length I flew beyond the tree,
    Quite fit for grown-up labors.
—I don't know how the world *is* made,
    And neither do my neighbors.

Unknown.

WOOD.

To the Teacher:—

(Having various familiar objects on the table, let the children tell of what they are made. Or, if the talks on fruits and seeds have been given, take the subject from the point of the tree's gifts to us.)

THE TALK.

Let us each name some kind of fruit which grows on trees. (Do not forget the different kinds of nuts, too.) Besides so many kinds of fruits, the trees give us the beautiful leaves which we have had in kindergarten this autumn, the sap of which maple sugar is made in the spring, and wood—oh! so much wood! All the wood we have to burn, and all the wood which is used in building, or in any way, comes from the trees.

(Have each child touch or tell of something made of wood. Try to have this a lively exercise. Prepare the children who you think would not be ready to mention anything, by giving them wooden objects which they can show and name. A little forethought for the backward children will often enable them to derive benefit which they would otherwise miss from an exercise.)

Our tables and chairs do not look much like the trees from, which they are made, do they? Tell me how a tree looks. What shape is the trunk—the tall, thick part? Is it rough or smooth as you touch it?

Suppose we were going to make a table out of a tree, what would be the first thing to do?

(Lead the children to trace as much of the work of preparation as possible,—the selection of a tree of the proper size and kind [choose the kind of which the table is really made,] the chopping down of the tree, and the sawing and chopping off of the branches, hauling the logs to the river, floating them to the sawmill where they are sawed into boards, piling them in the lumber yard to dry and to wait until someone comes to buy them.

Sing "Zish, zish," and let the children play that they are making a table out of some of the boards whose history they have traced.)

TEACHER'S READING.

Wood and Its Uses, - - - - - - - -	*Encyclopædia*
Pocket Key of Trees (both wild and cultivated) of Northern U. S., east of the Rocky Mts., - - - -	*Austin C. Apgar*
Drowne's Wooden Image, - - - - - - -	*Hawthorne*
Gasper Becerra, - - - - - - - - -	*Longfellow*
The Lumbermen, - - - - - - - - -	*Whittier*
A Winter Evening Hymn to My Fire, - - - - -	*Lowell*

For the Children.

The Walnut Tree that Wanted to Bear Tulips (Kindergarten Stories and Morning Talks),	*S. E. Wiltse*

STORIES.
The Logging Camp.

When my brother Russell was a little boy we lived in Maine. There were great woods near the town where our home was, and the men who lived in that part of the country used to go into these woods at the beginning of winter and stay there till spring, cutting down trees and making them ready to be sawed into boards at the sawmill.

As there were several men who went together to the same place, they built themselves a house to live in while out in the woods. This was a square house of one room, and they called it their camp. As their business was to make *logs* of the trees which they cut down, the camp was called a logging camp.

One day my uncle came to our house and said that he was going to one of his logging camps, and would stay all night. He had his little boy with him, and asked mother if Russell might go, too. Mother was willing and Russell was delighted, so off he started with his uncle and cousin.

They had several miles to go, but it was good sleighing, so the boys enjoyed it very much. When they reached the camp, late in the afternoon, the men there were delighted to see the children; for, being so far from home, none of them had seen a child for many weeks.

The boys enjoyed the supper of hot biscuit, baked pork and beans, and coffee, cooked by one of the men.

After supper they went to bed in the bunk, which was made of boards along the side of the room. The bunk was filled in with spruce boughs or hay, and covered with quilts or blankets.

The boys' feet were turned toward the fire which burned all night in the middle of the room, the smoke escaping through a square hole in the roof. Their feet being so nicely warmed, the boys did not suffer at all from cold; they slept soundly and were among the first to wake in the morning. It was very interesting to watch the cook get breakfast (which was just the same as the supper of the evening before) and after breakfast they went out to see the men at work.

They were never tired of watching the "tree-fellers," as the men who cut down the trees were called. Two tree-fellers would begin chopping at the trunk of a tree, standing on opposite sides and making the chips fly in every direction. As the gap made by each chopper came nearer and nearer to the middle, the tree would begin to shake, and, finally, down it would come! But the men, knowing in what direction it would fall, could jump out of the way.

The tree did not always fall directly to the ground, for sometimes the men would make it fall on a smaller tree to prevent the larger one from being splintered, as it might be if the force of its fall were unbroken.

When this tree was on the ground, other men would come and cut off its branches, while the two tree-fellers were cutting down another tree.

By the time the branches were cut off, a second tree would be felled and the men would pass on to cut off its branches as they had done to the other, while the tree-fellers would go back to the first tree and cut it up into different lengths. These lengths were called logs.

Then the teamsters came and loaded the logs on their sleds and hauled them to the river, down which they floated to the sawmill when the ice melted in the spring.

What do you suppose drew the sleds? "Horses?" No. They use horses in some places; but in Maine, at that time, they used oxen to haul the sleds, because oxen can move through the deep snow better than horses. The oxen were not harnessed like horses, but each pair wore a yoke* to which a ring was attached. The pole went through this ring, or a chain was fastened to it.

The visitors stayed till after dinner, and then started for home in the sleigh, so the boys had another pleasant sleighride

---

* The yoke can be represented with sticks and rings.

WHERE THE LOGS GO.

Russell brought with him one of the camp biscuits to show to mother.

"See, mother," said he eagerly, "what nice biscuits we had at the camp. I brought one home for you to taste. It is the best biscuit I ever ate." Mother and grandmother tasted it, and then looked at each other. The biscuit was yellow with saleratus, (then used instead of soda) and of course tasted strongly of it; but to the little boy, with appetite sharpened by the fresh cold air, it was delightful.

JOSEPHINE JARVIS.

Cobden, Ill.

The Honest Woodman.

Out in the green, silent woods and near a rushing river that foamed and sparkled as it hurried along, there lived a good man whose work was wood-chopping. With his strong, sharp ax over his shoulder, he started out one autumn day, and, selecting a large oak tree near the river side, was soon swinging his ax right sturdily as he hewed away at the tree trunk.

The chips flew fast at every stroke, and the sound of the ax ringing against the wood was echoed so clearly that you would have thought another wood chopper was at work not far away.

By and by the woodman thought he would rest awhile. He leaned his ax against the oak tree and turned to sit down, but tripped against his ax; and before he could catch it, it had slid down the bank and into the stream just where the water was very deep! The poor woodman gazed into the stream, which flowed on over his lost treasure as merrily as before, and then he spoke aloud in his distress. "Oh, what shall I do? My good ax! The only ax I had! I can never get it again. Even had I money to get another, I should still lament for this one,—so strong it was, and so sharp, and the stout handle worn so smooth to my hands."

The nymph or waterfairy who lived in this river (for this all happened in fairy days) heard the sad words of the woodman, and, rising to the surface, spoke to him in a voice that was like the sweet, tuneful tinkle of dropping water.

"What is your sorrow?" said she kindly. The woodman told

her of his misfortune, wondering much at the sudden appearance of this lovely creature.

"Cease your sad words," said the nymph in the same tinkling accents. "Far, far down below the reach of any mortal eyes or hands lies your lost ax; but wait and hope. Fairy eyes and fairy hands have power even in the watery depths of the stream."

> "She sank:—almost as quick as thought
> She rose again, and with her brought
> An ax of silver. The rich prize
> She held before the woodman's eyes;
> And smiling as in happy glee,
> ' Is *this* the ax you lost?' said she.
> ' Oh, no!' said he and shook his head.
> ' Well then,' the smiling naiad said,
> ' Here on the bank let this remain,
> And I'll go down and try again.
> She sank; and, instantly, behold!
> Up came she, with an ax of gold!
> Pure, solid gold—the helve, the head—
> ' Is *this* the ax you lost?' she said.
> ' Oh, no, no, no!' the man replied,
> This is not my old ax,' and sighed
> ' This is of very different ore,
> And worth, no doubt, a great deal more,
> And much more brightly does it shine,
> But 'tis not mine—no, 'tis not mine."

"Indeed!" said the fairy "Then this golden ax may lie on the bank beside the silver one, while I seek again for yours." The blue waters closed yet once more over the fairy. The woodman looked at the gold ax and at the silver ax, glittering in the grass.

"They are beautiful," said he, "and far costlier than my ax, which, though as good a one as ever hewed a tree, is naught but hardy steel; nevertheless I will not lay claim to that which is not mine, nor will I say anything but the truth."

By this time the water-nymph had again appeared above the shining waves and was holding another ax high in the air. The woodman reached forward with a shout of joy. "That is mine!" he cried. "That is surely my own old ax."

"Yes," said the fairy as she put it into his hands. "This is your ax, but it is only a plain steel one. Did you not like the silver ax and the gold ax?" "Indeed I did," answered the woodman; "but the silver ax was not mine and the gold ax was not mine. Not for them or for any other treasure will I say what is not true." "Right, honest woodman," said the fairy with a radiant smile of approval. "Truth is better than silver or gold. Truth can make you strong-hearted and happy though you lose your all. And now, farewell," she continued; "but take as a gift from me the ax of silver and the ax of gold."

So saying, she waved her white hand and disappeared. The astonished woodman gazed at the river, but it only sparkled and rippled on quite in its usual fashion; and at last with his heart full of gratitude to the fairy for her great kindness, the honest woodman gathered up the three gleaming axes and hastened home to tell of his wonderful adventure.

Retold by EMILIE POULSSON.

THE CARPENTER.

TO THE TEACHER:—

For this talk the teacher will find pieces of wood (rough and smooth, short and long, thick and thin) very useful in demonstrating the changes which the carpenter makes in his material. The carpenter's tools, too, should be shown and *used* when possible. A visit to a carpenter's shop is an excellent preparation for the teacher. If she can take the children with her or have a carpenter visit the kindergarten and show how he uses his tools, so much the better.

THE TALK.

(Question the children with regard to the origin and uses of wood as brought out in the previous talk. Let them mention again things that are made of wood,—in the schoolroom, at home, or in the street.)

Who cuts down the trees? Who makes barrels, pails, etc., out of wood? Who builds houses? What else does the carpenter build? Perhaps there are some children here whose fathers are carpenters. Let us see how many.

Suppose each one of the carpenter's children tells us of some tool his father uses in his work. Do the other children know of any more tools which the carpenter uses? (Let the children examine the tools provided, and see how many they know the name and use of. Show pieces of wood and ask for the tool by which the rough can be made smooth, the long short, holes bored, pieces fastened together, etc., etc., bringing out mention of each tool in this way.)

A man has to learn how to use all these tools and to do all these things and many more before he can be a good carpenter. Can you find places in the room where the plane must have been used? the hammer? the saw? Who has been at work here, then, to make our pleasant, comfortable room?

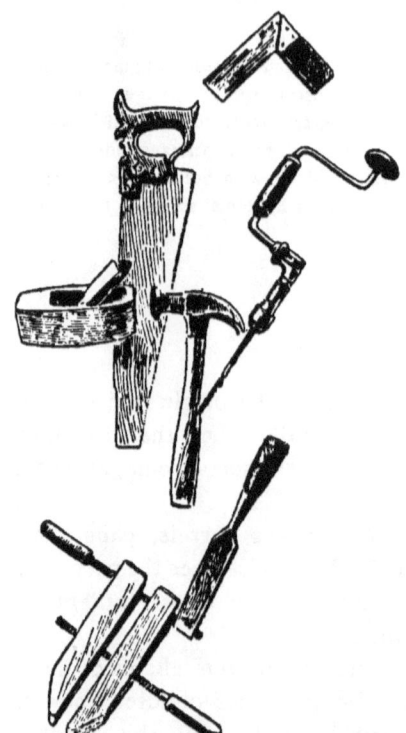

And who made the wood ready for the carpenter? The wood-chopper in the forest, and the man at the sawmill. Besides all these men, the mason and the painter and the glazier helped in building the house. The mason made the cellar and the walls, the painter painted the house, and the glazier put the glass in the windows. Think how many people we have to thank for our houses! Should we be very comfortable if we had no houses to live in? Now suppose you had a good house, nicely built,—would you like to live there alone, without mamma, and papa, and brothers and sisters? No, I am sure you would not. It is not enough to have a house,—the house needs to have a family in it—father, mother, children—those who belong to each other. Then a house, or even a part of a house, becomes a home.

TEACHER'S READING.

Frœbel's Explanation of
    The Carpenter,
    The Bridge,   *Mother's Songs, Games and Stories*
    The Joiner,
Adam Bede, - - - - - - - - - *George Eliot*
Annals of a Quiet Neighborhood, - - - - *George MacDonald*
Whittling, - - - - - - - - - - *Pierpont*
The Ship Builders, - - - - - - - - *Whittier*
The Building of the Ship, - - - - - - *Longfellow*

For the Children.

The Carpenter ("Kindergarten Stories and
    Morning Talks"), - - - - - - - *S. E. Wiltse*
Gutta Percha Willie, - - - - - - *George MacDonald*

STORIES.
Little Deeds of Kindness.

A bright red wagon with four wheels, and a long handle to pull it by, is a delightful plaything, and little Howard, who had found just such a wagon at his bedside when he awoke one morning, could scarcely wait for the time to come when he could play with it. After breakfast he hurried out as soon as he could. At first it was fun enough just to run up and down on the broad sidewalk and hear the wheels rattle on the bricks. It was interesting to practice turning, too; for the front wheels turned under the body of the wagon, just as those of a larger wagon do.

By and by his Aunt Kate came down the street, and Howard ran joyfully to meet her and to show her his new wagon.

"See the tires on the wheels, Auntie, how bright they are! And the front wheels turn, and the board at the back will come out, too!"

Aunt Kate admired everything, and, seeing the gilt letters on the side of the wagon, asked, "Is 'Star' the name of this wonderful wagon?"

"Yes," said Howard, "this is the 'Star Express.'"

"Then I will send this book to your mamma by the Star Express, for my arms are tired," said Aunt Kate. So she put the big book into the cart and Howard took it to his mamma.

After a while, Howard played that he was a milkman. He went along the walk, stopping in front of every house as if to leave the milk. By and by he came to the corner, and then turned to go back.

But something was the matter with the little wagon. Howard looked around and saw that a wheel had come off. He picked it up and then stood looking at the wagon in great distress. He felt as if he should cry. He had thought he should have such fun all day, and now his wagon was broken.

"Perhaps papa can mend it," thought Howard; "but even if he can, he will not be at home until to-night; papa is so busy, too, that he may not get time to mend it for two or three days."

Poor Howard felt very unhappy as these thoughts passed through his mind. Just then someone spoke to him. A kind voice said: "Let me take the wheel, little boy."

A man whose face was as kind as the voice stood near. He was lifting down a wooden box which he had been carrying on his shoulders.

Wondering what was going to happen, and with a sudden feeling of hope, Howard handed him the wheel. The man took some carpenter's tools from his box and went to work. Howard watched him with great interest. He saw that the man was a carpenter and knew exactly what to do.

In a very little time the wheel was on, and the gay little wagon was as good as ever.

"There!" said the carpenter, "that is strong now. I do not think it will come off again."

"Oh, thank you! Thank you!" said Howard; "I am so glad it is mended. It is a new wagon and I have such fun with it."

"Good-by," said the carpenter, as he took up his box and put it on his shoulder.

THE CARPENTER.

"Oh!" said Howard, "I wish you would let me take your box of tools for you. This is the Star Express."

"That would be a good plan," said the carpenter. "How far does this express run?"

"As far as the corner," answered Howard.

The carpenter put his box of tools into the wagon, and away went the Star Express rattling down the street.

After this Howard used to watch for his carpenter, as he called him, and run to meet him whenever he saw him in the distance; and if, as sometimes happened, the carpenter had his box of tools or a package of nails to carry, Howard always put it into the wagon and took it as far as he could.

EMILIE POULSSON.

An Old-Fashioned Rhyme.

This is the Tree of the forest.

This is the Ax whose steady blows
Cut down the Tree of the forest.

This is the Woodman, who, every one knows,
Wielded the Ax whose steady blows
Cut down the Tree of the forest.

This is the Log—to the river's side
Rolled by the Woodman, who, every one knows,
Wielded the Ax whose steady blows
Cut down the Tree of the forest.

This is the River whose flowing tide
Carried the Log that was rolled to its side,—
Rolled by the Woodman, who, every one knows
Wielded the Ax whose steady blows
Cut down the Tree of the forest.

This is the Wheel that went whirring round,
Turned by the River whose flowing tide
Carried the Log that was rolled to its side,—
Rolled by the Woodman, who, every one knows
Wielded the Ax whose steady blows
Cut down the Tree of the forest.

These are the Saws which, with buzzing sound,
Were moved by the Wheel that went whirring round
Turned by the River whose flowing tide
Carried the Log that was rolled to its side,—
Rolled by the Woodman, who, every one knows,
Wielded the Ax whose heavy blows
Cut down the Tree of the forest.

These are the Boards, so straight and long,
Cut by the Saws which, with buzzing sound,
Were moved by the Wheel that went whirring round,
Turned by the River whose flowing tide
Carried the Log that was rolled to its side,—
Rolled by the Woodman, who, every one knows,
Wielded the Ax whose heavy blows
Cut down the Tree of the forest.

This is the Carpenter, skillful and strong,
Who planed all the Boards so straight and long,
Cut by the Saws which, with buzzing sound,
Were moved by the Wheel that went whirring round,
Turned by the River whose flowing tide
Carried the Log that was rolled to its side,—
Rolled by the Woodman, who, every one knows,
Wielded the Ax whose steady blows
Cut down the Tree of the forest.

This is the House with its windows and doors
With timbers and rafters and roofs and floors,
Which was built by the Carpenter skillful and strong
Who planed all the Boards so straight and long,
Cut by the Saws which, with buzzing sound,
Were moved by the Wheel that went whirring round,
Turned by the River whose flowing tide
Carried the Log that was rolled to its side,
Rolled by the Woodman, who, every one knows,
Wielded the Ax whose steady blows
Cut down the tree of the forest.

This is the family—All are here—
Father, and mother and children dear,
Who live in the House with windows and doors,
With timbers and rafters and roofs and floors,
Which was built by the Carpenter, skillful and strong,
Who planed all the Boards so straight and long,
Cut by the Saws which, with buzzing sound,
Were moved by the Wheel that went whirring round.
Turned by the River whose flowing tide
Carried the Log that was rolled to its side,—
Rolled by the Woodman, who, every one knows,
Wielded the Ax whose steady blows
Cut down the tree of the forest.

EMILIE POULSSON.

THE CLOCK.

To the Teacher:—

At the beginning of the year, when there is danger that the children may be homesick, it is better to talk of something which will take their thoughts away from home and mother, and also away from the strangeness of their kindergarten surroundings. Later, however, the kindergarten room should be consciously observed, and its useful and pretty things rejoiced in. When the children are ready for this, the subject of the clock is to be introduced, since by it the important matter of punctuality can be brought forward, and this should be done as soon as other considerations will allow.

THE TALK.

(Sing one of the clock songs at the end of the morning exercises and so lead directly to the subject.)

Where is the clock? Do you hear it ticking? Let us listen. We must be very quiet or we shall not hear it. What does it say?

All the whole day, while we are singing and playing and working, and all the whole night, while we are sleeping, the clock keeps on saying, "tic-tac, tic-tac."

(Ask the children to look at the clock, and lead them to describe the face, hands, pendulum and case. The mechanism is too complex to be explained to little children, although they will be interested and impressed with a sight of the many little wheels in motion.)

Did you ever see papa or mamma wind the clock? Why must it be wound? Can you show me how the wheels move? How does the pendulum swing? Why do we have clocks?

(The children can give instances of the clock's usefulness.)

The clock tells when it is time for mamma to get up and get breakfast, and for papa to go to his work; and it tells when the children should go to kindergarten, and when they should go home.

All the children who came to kindergarten in good time this morning may stand. Shall I tell you how you can *all* be in time to-morrow? Ask your mamma to please look at the clock and to let you start as soon as the clock points both hands out this way. (Show a quarter before nine by using a card clock-face or old clock, or blackboard picture.) Perhaps some of the big boys and girls will notice for themselves when the clock at home says "time to go to kindergarten."

Where have you seen clocks besides at home and at kindergarten? On churches, railroad stations, etc., etc. Have you seen anything else which shows the time?

Long ago people had no clocks or watches. What do you suppose they did then? They used to tell the time by noticing the sunlight and the shadows. (Describe the sundial and show the picture.)

The sundial was of no use at night, however, nor on stormy and cloudy days when the sun was hidden; so people found other ways of measuring time. (Show an hourglass.) Sometimes water was used instead of sand (in an instrument called the clepsydra) and time was measured by the falling of drops of water.

None of these ways were very convenient, however, and men were constantly trying to make something better for telling the time, but they had to think and study and work and try very hard, over and over again, before they succeeded in making clocks and watches as good and useful and wonderful as these which we have now.

THE SUNDIAL.

TEACHER'S READING.

History of the Clock, - - - - - - - - *Encyclopædia*
Frœbel's Explanation of the Clock or Tic-tac Play,
                              Mother's Songs, Games and Stories
The Clock on the Stairs, - - - - - - - - *Longfellow*
A Petiton to Time, - - - - - - - - *Barry Cornwall*
Time's Cure (Anonymous), - - - *Dana's Household Book of Poetry*
Active and Passive, - - - - - - - *Margaret Gatty*

For the Children.

Frances Keeps her Promise, - - - - - - *Jane Taylor*
Cinderella at the Ball.

STORIES.

What the Clock Told Dolly.

Dolly Dimple sat on a rug by the hall fire, thinking. I doubt whether you have ever seen a great old-fashioned hall like the one where Dolly was sitting, for such halls are not built nowadays. This one was part of a great, rambling house which was more than a hundred years old. Dolly Dimple was born there and Dolly Dimple's mother and grandmother had lived in it a long time. They had left their home across the water and come to this one when Dolly's mother was a tiny child. Dolly was certain there had never been another such house, and this hall was her special delight. It was square, and had a shining oak floor, half covered with furry rugs. The walls were made of the same dark wood, and at the end was the cherry open fireplace where mossy logs roared and crackled all winter long, lighting up the dark corners and telling wonderful stories of the summer-time and of their lives in the forest. Near by was a broad staircase, on the first landing of which stood a clock, and it was about this clock that Dolly Dimple was thinking so deeply that wonderful night.

It was a very tall clock,—taller than Dolly's papa,—and it had a long glass door through which she could see the weights and the pendulum which never moved now. Above this was the round, good-natured face which Dolly was morally certain looked very different at different times; when she was good it smiled sweetly upon her, but when she was cross—and I am sorry to say Dolly was cross sometimes—it looked at her so sorrowfully! It could sympathize, too; for Dolly said that when she was in trouble she had seen the tears streaming down the old clock's face; but since she was looking through a mist of tears herself at such times I should not like to say that this was really true.

But the strangest thing of all about this clock was that it *would* strike. Now maybe all you wise little ones do not think it a very strange thing for a clock to strike; but when I tell you that this clock did so in spite of the fact that its wheels had not moved for many years, that will surely make you wonder!

And then it would strike at the strangest times! No one ever knew when it was going off, and it had been known to strike as many as seventeen! Dolly couldn't understand it at all, and as no one explained it to her, it had puzzled her a great deal. That night she was more mystified than ever; for at daybreak the clock had struck five, and how could the clock have known that it was her fifth birthday?

She lay curled up on the soft rug, thinking about it, until she began to grow drowsy. The crackling of the wood sounded farther and farther away; the shrill chirp of the cricket which lived at the back of the fireplace grew fainter and fainter.

Suddenly a voice—a very cracked voice—broke the silence. "Dolly! Dolly Dimple!" it said.

Dolly jumped up so hastily that the startled cricket sprang backward nearly into the fire. Where had the voice come from? Dolly peeped carefully about the hall until her eyes rested upon the old clock, when she was surprised to see that a new look had crept over its face,—a look which told Dolly that it was the clock that had spoken. And, sure enough! as she was gazing at it, it spoke again.

"Would you like to hear a story, Dolly?" it asked.

Now there was nothing Dolly liked better than a story; and forgetting her surprise, in her eagerness to hear what the clock had to say, she answered quickly: "Yes indeed, clock; can you tell me one?"

"That I can," said the clock. "I'll tell you the story of my life."

Dolly felt sure that now the mystery was to be solved, and curled herself up more comfortably to listen; the busy cricket straightened her cap and folded her hands to show her deep attention; the fire gave out a warmer glow, and the clock began:—

"Perhaps, Dolly Dimple, you will understand better what a wonder I am if I tell you that once upon a time there wasn't a clock upon the face of the earth!"

"Why-ee! What a sto—," began the cricket, and then stopped; but it was quite plain that she did not believe a word of it.

"No clocks!" cried Dolly, "why, how did little girls know when it was school-time, or dinner-time, or—or—anything?"

"They had other ways of telling time," answered the clock; "one of the first things by which they measured it was a stick,— a straight stick!"

"A stick!" exclaimed Dolly.

"A straight stick!" murmured the cricket; "I *knew* that clock was crazy."

"*I* was brought up to think that it was impolite to interrupt," said the clock.

"Of course it is," said Dolly, "we will not breathe another word, will we, cricket?"

"But a stick!" groaned the cricket, shaking her head.

"Yes," said the clock, "try it for yourself! Go out of doors the next sunny morning and plant a little stick in the ground. If it is early, the shadow will be a great deal longer than the stick itself, and will look as if hiding from the sun; as noon draws near, you will find the shadow creeping up and up, until just at noon, the stick seems to swallow it; and then, as the sun moves on toward the west, the shadow peeps out and creeps off on the other side of the stick until night, when shadow and stick are both swallowed in darkness.

"Now don't you see how you could tell time by the stick and its shadow?" And it was this which made somebody think of a sundial."

"A sundial," broke in the cricket, who could not keep still; "What is that?"

"It looks like a doll's table with a little piece of metal standing up in the center; and on the table top is marked the length of the shadow which this piece of metal casts at different hours of the day."

"Was that the only clock they had?" asked Dolly.

"If your pussy had lived in those days they would have used her for a timepiece," said the clock.

The cricket evidently thought this too foolish a story to be noticed at all, and even Dolly looked shocked; but the clock knew what it was talking about and went right on.

"If you look at Kitty's eyes when she first wakes in the morning, you will find that the dark place in the middle of the eye is very big and round; but soon you will notice that it is growing narrow, until by noon it is as fine as a hair; and then it will slowly grow larger again, until, when night comes, it will be as big and round as it was in the morning."

"What a bother it must have been to tell time in these ways!" said Dolly.

"Yes, I think so myself," replied the clock, "and people began to think that they ought to have something better to depend upon. So about five hundred years ago, some one invented a clock,—not a big, handsome one like myself, but a very plain affair that had no pendulum and could not *strike*."

"Poor thing!" sighed Dolly.

"Better not strike at all than strike as some clocks do," observed the cricket rather spitefully.

"But it *was* a *clock*, and considered a very wonderful thing in those days," continued the clock; "and people must have been pretty well satisfied, for they did not add a pendulum for several hundred years."

"Are you very old?" asked Dolly.

"Yes, I am very, very old. It must be over a hundred years since my hands began to move.—Ah! that was a proud day for my maker! Every tiny, shining wheel was as perfect as perfect could be, and my case was a beautiful sight. On the day that I was finished the little clockmaker was the happiest man alive. He examined me in every part with the greatest care, and my perfection delighted him. Then he took a big key, and wound me up, touched my pendulum, and with a 'tick-tack, tick-tack,' I started out on my life-work. The little clockmaker did not long have me to admire, however, for very soon an old lady bought me, and I was carried away across the blue rolling water and placed in this hall. I am worn-out and useless now, but then I was of the greatest importance. Nothing was done without consulting me. Ever and ever so many bright-eyed children have raced up and down the stairs and curled up by the fire just as you are doing. I have loved them all and tried to show them that it was only by keeping our hands busy working for others, and by doing right, that we could be happy and make our friends love us. They may have thought that all I said was 'tick-tack, tick-tack,' but really I have always said as plainly as plainly could be,—'Do right, do right.'"

"Dear old clock!" murmured Dolly; and even the cricket turned her head and wiped away a tear.

"Before I stop," said the clock, "I must speak of one thing that others besides yourselves have noticed;" and the clock glanced at the cricket, who looked as if she wanted to sink through the floor.

"You must know that a great while ago my hands refused to move another minute. It was a sorry day for me, and sometimes my feelings overcome me even now when I think of the past. At such times it is a great relief for me to strike."

"You dear old clock," cried Dolly; "You shall strike as often as you please, and if the cricket ever dares—"

"Dolly! Dolly Dimple!" Harry was calling.

Dolly sat up and rubbed her eyes. "What is the matter?" she asked.

"That's what I'd like to know! Why, the very idea of a little girl with a birthday sleeping as if it were any other day!"

"Sleeping! I haven't slept a wink! Why, the clock has been talking, and the cricket, and,—"

"Very likely! As if I'd believe that when I've knocked over the poker and the shovel and the tongs, and you never so much as winked."

Dolly looked up at the old clock, but never a word did it say. The broad, good-natured face beamed down upon her the same as ever, but she fancied it wore a wise expression that said as plainly as so many words: "Keep quiet; boys are not half so wise as they think they are. Don't mind him, but remember all I have told you, and try to learn something every day from everybody. Be glad that you have clocks to tell you the time and to remind you to keep your hands busy and to 'do right, do right'."

"Dolly! Dolly! Why do you keep staring at that old clock? I declare you are half asleep yet!"

Dolly rubbed her eyes and stared at her laughing brother, and then again at the now silent clock. She was glad that she had been warned to keep quiet, for she did not feel like telling the whole story then; but when she grew up she used to tell little children "What the Clock told Dolly."

MINNIE G. CLARK.

The Discontented Pendulum.

An old clock that had stood for fifty years in a farmer's kitchen without giving its owner any cause of complaint, early one summer's morning, before the family was stirring, suddenly stopped. Upon this, the dial plate (if we may credit the fable) changed countenance with alarm; the hands made a vain effort to continue their course; the wheels remained motionless with surprise; the weights hung speechless; each member felt disposed to lay the blame on the others. At length the dial instituted an inquiry as to the cause of the stagnation, when hands, wheels, weights, with one voice, protested their innocence.

But now a faint tick was heard below from the pendulum, who thus spoke: "I confess myself to be the sole cause of the present stoppage, and I am willing, for the general satisfaction, to assign my reasons. The truth is, that I am tired of ticking." Upon hearing this, the old clock became so enraged that it was on the very point of *striking*.

"Lazy wire!" exclaimed the dial plate, holding up its hands.

"Very good!" replied the pendulum; "it is vastly easy for you, Mistress Dial, who have always, as everybody knows, set yourself up above me—it is vastly easy for you, I say, to accuse other people of laziness! You, who have had nothing to do all the days of your life but to stare people in the face, and to amuse yourself with watching all that goes on in the kitchen! Think, I beseech you, how would you like to be shut up for life in this dark closet, and to wag backwards and forwards year after year, as I do."

"As to that," said the dial, "is there not a window in your house for you to look through?"

"For all that," resumed the pendulum, "it is very dark here, and, although there is a window, I dare not stop, even for an instant, to look out at it. Besides, I am really tired of my way of life; and if you wish, I'll tell you how I took this disgust at my employment. I happened this morning to be calculating how many times I should have to tick in the course of only the next twenty-four hours; perhaps some of you there above can give me the exact sum."

The minute-hand, being quick at figures, replied, "Eighty-six thousand four hundred times."

"Exactly so," replied the pendulum. "Well, I appeal to you all, if the very thought of this was not enough to fatigue one; and when I began to multiply the strokes of one day by those of months and years, really it is no wonder if I felt discouraged at the prospect; so, after a great deal of reasoning and hesitation, thinks I to myself, I'll stop."

The dial could scarcely keep its countenance during this harangue, but, resuming its gravity, thus replied: "Dear Mr. Pendulum, I am really astonished that such a useful, industrious person as yourself should have been overcome by this sudden suggestion. It is true, you have done a good deal of work in your time; so have we all, and are likely to do, which, although it may fatigue us to *think* of, the question is, whether it will fatigue us to *do*. Will you now give about half a dozen strokes to illustrate my argument?"

The pendulum complied, and ticked six times in its usual pace. "Now," resumed the dial, "may I be allowed to inquire if that exertion was at all fatiguing or disagreeable to you?"

"Not in the least," replied the pendulum; "it is not of *six* strokes that I complain, nor of sixty but of *millions*."

"Very good," replied the dial, "but, recollect that, though you may *think* of a million strokes in an instant, you are required to execute but *one*; and that, however often you may hereafter have to swing, a moment will always be given you to swing in."

"Then I hope," resumed the dial plate, "we shall all immediately return to our duty, for the maids will lie in bed if we stand idling thus."

Upon this the weights, who had never been accused of *light* conduct, used all their influence in urging him to proceed; when, as with one consent, the wheels began to turn, the hands began to move, and the pendulum began to swing; while a beam of the rising sun, that streamed through a hole in the kitchen window, shone full upon the dial plate, when it brightened up as if nothing had been the matter. When the farmer came down to breakfast that morning, upon looking at the clock, he declared that his watch had gained half an hour in the night.

JANE TAYLOR.

LEAVES.

AUTUMN.

TO THE TEACHER:—

Bring all of nature that is possible into the kindergarten—colored leaves, autumn flowers, deserted nests, chrysalides, bare twigs, etc. Ask the children to bring, during the week, whatever they can find which shows that autumn has come. To revive the memories of summer and contrast summer and autumn, is the special aim of this talk. Reach back to spring and forward to winter incidentally.

The thought of autumn as the harvest time and the time of preparing for winter should run through all the talks at this season of the year.

THE TALK.

Who can remember the first day we came to kindergarten this year? What can you remember before that? Why did we not have kindergarten then? What do we call that time of year when the weather is so warm? Tell me something about the summer. If the children have been to the city parks or gardens or playgrounds, speak of the beauty and advantages of such places, not forgetting to give credit to the city for providing them. Did any of you go to the seashore? Tell us about it.

Did any of you go into the country? to a farm? What was the farmer doing? Taking care of what he had planted in the spring—cutting the grass, raking and taking in the hay, hoeing corn and potatoes, weeding the garden, etc. Tell me what some of the animals were doing in the summer. Farm horses working, cattle enjoying the pasture, squirrels, birds and insects playing merrily in the woods and fields.

(Contrast all these summer activities with the autumn doings at the farm and in the woods.) Is it summer now? Let us see how many signs we can think of which show that autumn is here.

Once upon a time some little children had been talking about the signs of autumn just as we have, and they asked a friend of theirs to write some autumn verses for them. They told her just what to put into the verses. Suppose I tell you what she wrote. Listen carefully and see whether we had thought of all the signs of autumn which the verses mention. (Read or recite slowly "An Autumn Song.")

TEACHER'S READING.

Change of Seasons ("Sun, Moon and Stars"),	*Agnes Giberne*
November's Wild Flowers, } ("Sharp Eyes"), The Autumn Pipers,	*W. H. Gibson*
The Sleeping Flowers,	*Emily Dickinson*
The Pomegranate Seed,	*Hawthorne*
The Huskers, } Song of Harvest,	*Whittier*
Times go by Turns,	*Robert Southwell*
In Time's Swing,	*Lucy Larcom*
An Indian Summer Reverie,	*Lowell*
Fringed Gentian, } Death of the Flowers,	*Bryant*
On the Grasshopper and Cricket,	*Leigh Hunt*
On the Grasshopper and Cricket,	*Keats*
The Reaper,	*Wordsworth*
Autumn (From "The Seasons"),	*Thomson*

For the Children.

The Maple Leaf and the Violet ("The Story Hour"),	*Nora A. Smith*
The Anxious Leaf, } ("Kindergarten Stories and The Little Harvest Mouse, } Morning Talks"),	*S. E. Wiltse*
Two Bunnies ("Stories for the Kindergarten and Home"),	*M. L. Van Kirk*

STORIES.
The Baby-Buds' Winter Clothes.

The warm summer had gone and autumn had come with its cooler winds, when one day, the hickory tree said to its leaves: "My pretty yellow leaves, you need not take care of the baby-buds any more, as it is time for them to put on their winter clothes. But I think the flower seeds would like to have you help *them* now. Are you willing to go down to the ground in order to help them?"

"Yes," said the leaves, "we would like to help the dear little seeds to be flowers." So they dropped to the ground, and covered it, that the little seeds might not freeze in their winter home in the earth, but might live to make plants and flowers in the spring.

Then the hickory tree said: "Baby-buds, it is time for you to put on your winter clothes, so that you can keep warm all winter and open into leaves in the spring." "We are all ready," said the buds; so the tree gave them their coats. The outside coat of each bud was a gum coat to keep out the wet. "Why, that was a waterproof coat! How funny for the buds to have waterproof coats." Yes, it is strange, but if you learn how to look, you will find out a great many strange things.

After the little side-buds had been given their winter clothes, the tree said: "My little end-buds, you are so much more exposed to the cold than the other buds that you must be dressed more warmly than they are." So the little end-buds put on one coat after another, till you would have thought, to look at them, that they were at least twice as large as the side-buds, and their gum coats had to be a great deal bigger than those of the others.

I saw an end-bud of a hickory tree once that had *twelve* coats on it.

Then all the baby buds said: "Thank you, dear tree, for our winter clothes. Now we can keep warm until spring."

JOSEPHINE JARVIS.

Cobden, Ill.

An Autumn Song.

The song-birds are flying
And southward are hying,
No more their glad carols we hear.
The gardens are lonely,—
Chrysanthemums only
Dare now let their beauty appear.

The insects are hiding,—
The farmer providing
The lambkins a shelter from cold.
And after October
The woods will look sober
Without all their crimson and gold.

The loud winds are calling,
The ripe nuts are falling,
The squirrel now gathers his store.
The bears, homeward creeping,
Will soon all be sleeping
So snugly, till winter is o'er.

Jack Frost will soon cover
The little brooks over;
The snow-clouds are up in the sky
All ready for snowing;
—Dear Autumn is going!
We bid her a loving "good-bye."

EMILIE POULSSON

The Kind Old Oak.

It was almost time for winter to come. The little birds had all gone far away, for they were afraid of the cold. There was no green grass in the fields, and there were no pretty flowers in the gardens. Many of the trees had dropped all their leaves. Cold winter, with its snow and ice, was coming. At the foot of an old oak tree some sweet little violets were still in blossom. "Dear old oak," said they, "winter is coming; we are afraid that we shall die of cold."

"Do not be afraid, little ones," said the oak, "close your yellow eyes in sleep, and trust to me. You have made me glad many a time with your sweetness. Now I will take care that the winter shall do you no harm."

So the violets closed their pretty eyes and went to sleep; they knew that they could trust the kind, old oak. And the great tree softly dropped red leaf after red leaf upon them, until they were all covered over.

The cold winter came, with its snow and ice, but it could not harm the little violets. Safe under the friendly leaves of the old oak, they slept and dreamed happy dreams until the warm rains of spring came and waked them again.

"LITTLE FLOWER FOLKS."
Educational Publishing Co., Boston, Mass.

The Chestnut Boys.

Chestnuts in the burr.

In a warm little bed, in a little green house, Mother Nature had tucked three baby boys safely away for a long sleep.

The house was not like the ones we live in, for it had only one tiny room, with no windows, and the door was fastened so tightly that no one could get in or out.

For many, many bright sunny days the little boys were sleeping, and all this time they were growing a little larger and a little larger, just as you all are growing.

But by and by the days began to grow cooler. The green leaves put on their autumn dresses of red and yellow, and came rustling down from the tree to play with the wind.

Then the babies stirred in their little bed, for the Wind was busy painting brown their green house, and he whistled so loudly at his work that they heard him in their dreams. Close behind the Wind came his friend, Jack Frost, a roguish little fellow. Gently he knocked at the door of the house, and softly he whispered, "Come out, little boys; come out and play with me!"

But Mother Nature only tucked her babies more snugly into bed, and answered: "No, not yet, dear little ones; sleep a little longer!"

Then Jack Frost went away to play with the red and yellow leaves; but soon he came flying back, calling, "Come out for a frolic with me, boys; come out for a frolic!" And again Mother Nature answered: "Not yet! not yet, my children!"

Again came Jack Frost, and knocked *very* loudly at the door: "Come out! come out!" he called And the little brothers cried, "Yes, yes, dear Mother, let us go and play with Jack Frost and the Wind!"

Then the mother smiled, a little sadly, and answered: "Yes, for you have grown to be big boys now, and it is time for you to go!" So she unfastened the door and opened it wide, and out the three hurried. But soon they found that the big world was not at all like their warm, soft little house. The Wind blew and whistled around them, and made them shiver; and Jack Frost was a rough playfellow, though he meant to be kind, and they soon grew weary and called to their mother: "Dear Mother Nature, we are tired; put us to sleep again!"

Then the mother spread over them, where they lay on the ground, a warm covering of "red and yellow and faded brown."

By and by she heard their sleepy voices again: "Kind Mother, we are cold!"

Then Mother Nature sent a soft, white covering of snow, and wrapped them in it so nicely, that they had hardly time to murmur "Thank you, good Mother," before they were fast asleep.

And there they will stay, till the warm sun and the gentle breezes and the soft rain wake them in the sweet springtime.

Can you guess who the little brothers were, in their snug, warm house?

They were the *Chestnut* boys, and the brown burr is their little house.

HELEN LOUISE TOWNE.

"*Kindergarten Magazine.*"

SEEDS.

To the Teacher:—

This talk, contributed by a friend, is based upon "Treasure Boxes" in "Stories Mother Nature Told," by Jane Andrews.

Provide peach, apple and other fruits; beans and peas in their "boxes;" grains and other seeds.

THE TALK.

Begin the talk by allusions to boxes. What are they for? To put things away in. We have boxes in the kindergarten. Sometimes at home we have boxes in which to put away things that we care very much about; treasure boxes they are sometimes called. Now I am going to show you something that has a treasure box. (Bring out a peach.)

Do you think this peach has a treasure box? Yes, if the peach could talk it would tell you that it has worked all summer storing food and drinking in sunshine, not only to make the delicious soft part which you like to eat, but for the life that is in the "stone," as we sometimes call the hard part in the middle.

(Cut away the fruit. Show the deep color, and how the fibers cling to the stone or shell.) This stone is the peach's treasure box. (Ask if anyone knows what is inside the shell. Show how hard the shell is. Let a child try to open it, then crack it and show the seed.) The seed is the peach's treasure.

Do you know of any other treasure boxes? Apples, plums, flower seeds, peas, beans, etc., etc. (Ask the children to bring seeds for the next day, when you will tell them more about such treasure boxes.)

For the Second Day.

Yesterday we talked about the peach's treasure box; to-day we have many others.

(Place fruits on table. Let the children come in groups, or distribute seeds to a few children. Examine the fruits. Question. Notice similarities and differences. Make a careful study of the common seeds that the children will be most likely to bring—peaches, apples, plums, melons, etc.)

At the End of the week.

What have we been talking about this week? Seeds. We have seen how carefully Mother Nature guards her treasure boxes and has them ready for use in the springtime. Is there any one who helps Mother Nature? Yes; the farmer and all the seed gatherers. Mother Nature says to them, "Unless you gather and take care of my seeds you will not have any peach trees or apple trees and no corn or beans or peas or squashes, etc.," and so the farmer saves his seeds,—not all of them, but those that he needs to plant or sell, for Mother Nature is so generous that she provides a great many seeds.

And now for a wee bit of a story. (Tell how a farmer's children helped to gather and save the seeds, and placed them in boxes, bags and envelopes; how the farmer marked them and put them away in a place where they would keep.)

Do you not think we could put some of ours away in bags or envelopes for next spring? Perhaps we can plant some of them and see them grow here.

We will try to make something out of our colored papers to hold the seeds.

L. B. P.

TEACHER'S READING.

Concerning a Few Common Plants, - - - - - - *Goodale*
How Plants Grow, - - - - - - - - - *Gray*
Planting Seeds in the Schoolroom ("Outlines of Lessons
　in Botany"), - - - - - - - - - *Jane H. Newell*
Seed Tramps,
Quickening Seeds and Seedlings, } ("Sharp Eyes"), - - - *Gibson*
Story of Mary and the Seeds ("Kindergarten Magazine,"
　May and June, 1891), - - - - - - - *E. G. Howe*
Song of the Sower, - - - - - - - - - *Bryant*
The Little Brown Seed, - - - - - *Harriet Lothrop*
Little Brown Seed in the Furrow, - - - - - *Ida W. Benham*

For the Children.

Quercus Alba ("Stories Mother Nature Told") - - - *Jane Andrews*

STORIES.

Sweet Peas

Five Peas in a Pod.

There were once five peas in one shell; they were green, and the shell was green, so they believed that the whole world must be green also, which was a very natural conclusion. The shell grew, and the peas grew; they accommodated themselves to their position, and sat all in a row. The sun shone without and warmed the shell, and the rain made it clear and transparent;

it was mild and agreeable in broad daylight, and dark at night; and the peas as they sat there grew bigger and bigger, and more thoughtful as they mused, for they felt there must be something for them to do.

"Are we to sit here for ever?" asked one; "shall we not become hard by sitting so long? It seems to me there must be something outside, and I feel sure of it."

And as weeks passed by the peas became yellow, and the shell became yellow.

"All the world is turning yellow, I suppose," said they—and perhaps they were right.

Suddenly they felt a pull at the shell; it was torn off, and held in human hands, then slipped into the pocket of a jacket in company with other full pods.

"Now we shall soon be opened," said one—just what they all wanted.

"I should like to know which of us will travel farthest," said the smallest of the five; "we shall soon see now."

"What is to happen will happen," said the largest pea.

"Crack," went the shell as it burst, and the five peas rolled out into the bright sunshine. There they lay in a child's hand. A little boy was holding them tightly, and said they were fine peas for his pea-shooter. And immediately he put one in and shot it out.

"Now I am flying out into the wide world," said the pea; "catch me if you can;" and he was gone in a moment.

"I," said the second, "intend to fly straight to the sun; that is a shell that lets itself be seen, and it will suit me exactly;" and away he went.

"We will go to sleep wherever we find ourselves," said the two next, "we shall still be rolling onwards;" and they did certainly fall on the floor and roll about before they got into the pea-shooter; but they were put in for all that. "We shall go farther than the others," said they.

"What is to happen will happen," exclaimed the last, as he was shot out of the pea-shooter; and as he spoke he flew up against an old board under a garret window, and fell into a little crevice, which was almost filled up with moss and soft earth.

"GETTING WELL."

The moss closed itself around him, and there he lay, a captive indeed, but not unnoticed by God.

"What is to happen will happen," said he to himself.

Within the garret lived a poor woman, who went out to clean stoves, chop wood into small pieces, and perform other hard work, for she was strong and industrious. Yet she remained always poor; and at home in the garret lay her only daughter, not quite grown up, and very delicate and weak. For a whole year she had kept her bed. Quietly and patiently she lay all day long, while her mother was away from home at her work.

Spring came, and one morning early the sun shone brightly through the little window and threw his rays over the floor of the room. Just as the mother was going to her work, the sick girl fixed her gaze on the lowest pane of the window. "Mother!" she exclaimed, "what can that little green thing be that peeps in at the window? It is moving in the wind."

The mother stepped to the window and half opened it. "Oh!" she said, "there is actually a little pea which has taken root and is putting on its green leaves. How could it have got into this crack! Well, now, here is a little garden for you to amuse yourself with." So the bed of the sick girl was drawn nearer to the window, that she might see the budding plant; and the mother went out to her work.

"Mother, I believe I shall get well," said the sick child in the evening, "the sun has shone in here so brightly and warmly to-day, and the little pea is thriving so well; I shall get on better, too, and go out into the warm sunshine again."

"God grant it!" said the mother, but she did not believe it would be so. But she propped up with a little stick the green plant which had given her child such pleasant hopes of life, so that it might not be broken by the winds; she tied the piece of string to the window sill and to the upper part of the frame, so that the pea tendrils might twine round it when it shot up. And it did shoot up; indeed it might almost be seen to grow from day to day.

"Really, here is a flower coming," said the old woman one morning, and now at last she began to encourage the hope that her little sick daughter might really recover. She remembered that for some time the child had spoken more cheerfully, and during the last few days had raised herself in bed in the morning to look with sparkling eyes at her little garden which contained only a single pea-plant. A week after, the invalid sat up for the first time a whole hour, feeling quite happy by the open window in the warm sunshine, while outside grew the little plant, and on it a pink pea-blossom in full bloom. The little maiden bent down and gently kissed the delicate leaves. This day was to her like a festival.

"Our Heavenly Father Himself has planted that pea, and made it grow and flourish, to bring joy to you and hope to me, my blessed child," said the happy mother, and she smiled at the flower, as if it had been an angel from God.

And when the young maiden stood at the open garret window, with sparkling eyes and the rosy hue of health on her cheeks, she folded her thin hands over the pea-blossom and thanked God for what He had done.

HANS CHRISTIAN ANDERSEN.

Psyche's Tasks.

There was once a very beautiful earthly maiden named Psyche. Every one liked to see her joyous face, as she roamed over the meadows gathering the field-flowers, or sat weaving them into garlands for her friends. She had many friends and companions, but chief among them all was one who used to come down to visit her from lofty Olympus, the home of the gods. This was the little winged god, Cupid, who loved her dearly.

Now Psyche, charming and loving as she was, was a thoughtless child, and one day, by a foolish prank, gave such offense to Cupid that he spread his rosy wings and flew away. As day after day passed and he did not come again, she mourned and grieved for her companion, but not her grief nor even her repentance could bring him back.

At last, some one, pitying her sorrow, advised her to go to the temple of Venus, and there to beg the assistance of Venus herself, who was the mother of Cupid. Psyche, with hope revived, went straightway to the temple, with its shining pillars and white marble steps, and humbly made her request, but Venus told her that there were hard tasks to be performed before she could win back what she had so foolishly lost. Psyche willingly undertook to perform these, but when she learned what the first one was, her heart sank. Venus led her to a vast granary, where wheat, barley, millet, and all sorts of grain lay about on the floor, mixed together in hopeless confusion. "Before evening," said Venus, "all these different sorts of grain must be separated from each other, and each kind must be piled by itself."

To poor Psyche it did not seem possible to accomplish such a task; nevertheless, she at once set to work; she would at least do all that she could, she thought; so she sifted and sorted, and arranged without stopping till late in the afternoon. Then, as she looked at her orderly little piles and saw how tiny they appeared beside the great heaps of grain that remained to be sorted, she felt saddened and discouraged indeed. She held bravely, however, to her purpose of doing her best, little as it might prove to be, and her busy hands were working even more quickly than before, when—a wonderful thing happened.

Psyche did not notice it at first, but presently raising her eyes from her work, she was astonished to see that her piles of sorted grain had mounted to a surprising height, and that the big unsorted heaps had become very much smaller. From every side had come swarms and crowds of friendly little ants. Each one had set to work, as patiently and as perseveringly as Psyche herself, to help her to accomplish her task before the end of the day. She could see them tugging away at grains larger than themselves, or marching steadily, one behind another, each setting down his burden in the right place and then returning for more. Now she could work with a light heart, and when evening came and the friendly ants had trooped off through their cracks and crannies, the task was accomplished and everything was seen to be, as if by magic, in perfect order. Psyche did not know who had sent the ants to her assistance. She never thought that Cupid himself, though he could not come to her, was helping her in this way.

The other tasks imposed upon Psyche were no less difficult

than the first had been; but though, one by one, Psyche accomplished them all, still she heard nothing of her beloved companion and was beginning to despair of ever seeing him again. Cupid, however, was nearer to her than she thought and the moment came at last when he could go to her.

One day, when Psyche, weary and discouraged, was least expecting him, a light whirring of wings sounded in the air, and in a moment Cupid himself, like a shining vision, stood before her eyes. She could hardly believe that she was not dreaming, even when he told her that her troubles and labors were at last over and that he was to be separated from her no longer. A beautiful pair of butterfly wings was given to Psyche, that she might be able to fly as Cupid did, and together the two went winging their way through the blue air to Olympus, the abode of the gods. There among the gods and goddesses, Cupid and Psyche lived joyfully ever after; never again were they separated from one another.

F. H.

Apple-Seed John.

Poor Johnny was bended well-nigh double
With years of toil, and care, and trouble;
But his large old heart still felt the need
Of doing for others some kindly deed.

"But what can I do?" old Johnny said;
"I who work so hard for daily bread?
It takes heaps of money to do much good,
I am far too poor to do as I would."

The old man sat thinking deeply a while,
Then over his features gleamed a smile,
Then he clapped his hands with a boyish glee,
And said to himself, "There's a way for me!"

He worked, and he worked with might and main,
But no one knew the plan in his brain.
He took ripe apples in pay for chores,
And carefully cut from them all the cores.

He filled a bag full, then wandered away,
And no man saw him for many a day.
With knapsack over his shoulder slung,
He marched along, and whistled or sung.

He seemed to roam with no object in view,
Like one who had nothing on earth to do;
But, journeying thus o'er the prairies wide,
He paused now and then, and his bag untied.

With pointed cane deep holes he would bore,
And in ev'ry hole he placed a core;
Then covered them well, and left them there
In keeping of sunshine, rain and air.

Sometimes for days he waded through grass,
And saw not a living creature pass,
But often, when sinking to sleep in the dark,
He heard the owls hoot and the prairie dogs bark.

Sometimes an Indian of sturdy limb
Came striding along and walked with him;
And he who had food shared with the other,
As if he had met a hungry brother.

When the Indian saw how the bag was filled,
And looked at the holes the white man drilled,
He thought to himself 'twas a silly plan
To be planting seed for some future man.

Sometimes a log cabin came in view,
Where Johnny was sure to find jobs to do,
By which he gained stores of bread and meat,
And welcome rest for his weary feet.

He had full many a story to tell,
And goodly hymns that he sung right well;
He tossed up the babes, and joined the boys
In many a game full of fun and noise.

And he seemed so hearty, in work or play,
Men, women, and boys all urged him to stay;
But he always said, "I have something to do,
And I must go on to carry it through."

The boys, who were sure to follow him round,
Soon found what it was he put in the ground;
And so, as time passed and he traveled on,
Ev'ry one called him "Old Apple-seed John."

Whenever he'd used the whole of his store,
He went into cities and worked for more:
Then he marched back to the wilds again,
And planted seed on hill-side and plain.

In cities, some said the old man was crazy;
While others said he was only lazy;
But he took no notice of gibes and jeers,
He knew he was working for future years.

He knew that trees would soon abound
Where once a tree could not have been found;
That a flick'ring play of light and shade
Would dance and glimmer along the glade;

That blossoming sprays would form fair bowers,
And sprinkle the grass with rosy showers;
And the little seeds his hands had spread
Would become ripe apples when he was dead.

So he kept on traveling far and wide,
Till his old limbs failed him, and he died.
He said at the last, "'Tis a comfort to feel
I've done good in the world, though not a great deal."

Weary travelers, journeying west,
In the shade of his trees find pleasant rest;
And they often start, with glad surprise,
At the rosy fruit that round them lies.

And if they inquire whence came such trees,
Where not a bough once swayed in the breeze,
The answer still comes, as they travel on,
"These trees were planted by Apple-seed John."

LYDIA MARIA CHILI

"St. Nicholas," June, 1880.

THE WIND.

To the Teacher:—

After the morning greetings the central subject of the morning may be introduced in many ways; perhaps by directing the children's observation to the weather, finding what they noticed about it on the way to kindergarten; or, if they have been singing "Come, little leaves," the subject of the wind may be brought uppermost easily and naturally through the song.

The Wind as an Unseen Power.

(The thought in this form is, of course, only for the teacher's mind. No more than the impression is to be given to the children; and this will be done by leading them to recall familiar manifestations of the wind's power.)

THE TALK.

What does the wind do? Plays with the leaves, gets the trees ready for winter, covers the ground with them to help keep the roots and seeds warm, tells the birds that winter is coming, blows the nuts down from the tall trees in the wood, as well as the apples, pears and other fruits from the orchard trees.

(Anecdote of child in an orchard, who sees an apple but is unable to reach it and asks the wind to bring it to her.)

Going back to other than Autumn work,—the wind rocks the birds in the nests, flies kites, drives sailboats, blows the clothes dry, helps the sun dry the ground after rain, and turns the windmills, which are sometimes used instead of water-mills. Can we hear the wind? Can we feel the wind? Can we *see* the wind? Can we see what the wind does?

THE WIND AT WORK.

The Wind as a Sower of Seeds.

(Recall some of the previous talks on seeds. Let the children tell what seeds need to be planted;—corn seeds, or we will have no corn; wheat seeds, or we will have no wheat; flower seeds or no flowers, etc., etc.)

What has the farmer been doing lately? Gathering seeds from farm and garden to plant in the spring. What pretty yellow flower do we find in the grass in the spring? Does the dandelion have seeds? the daisy? the oak tree? Does the farmer go everywhere to gather such seeds? But we always have dandelions and daisies. Then they must have been planted. Who does this? Some one who works and plays, though we never see him. Yes! the wind sows such seeds,—blows them from the plant, carries them along, drops them, blows dust and leaves over them till they are covered and can take root by and by, and come up in the spring when the other seeds do.

What the Winds Bring.

Contrast gentle breezes and wild, boisterous winds. Notice how Mr. Wind sometimes knocks at one window, sometimes at another;—that is, comes from different directions. North Wind coming from the cold countries, tells us to remember "Agoonack," brings ice and snow, is a friend of "Little Jack Frost." South Wind comes from the warm countries, whispers of summer, comes from the same land as the oranges and bananas, brings warmth. East Wind comes from the ocean, brings moisture, fog or rain. "West Wind, Best Wind" brings bright, clear weather.

Weather Vane useful to tell which wind is blowing. Anecdote of child and weather vane. Child was going on a picnic; weather doubtful; but soon the weather vane turned, showing that the wind had changed, promising good weather. Child happy and grateful. Frœbel's play of the Weather Vane.

A favorite verse about the wind is:—

> "Whichever way the wind doth blow
> Some heart is glad to have it so.
> Then blow it east or blow it west,
> The wind that blows, *that* wind is best."

TEACHER'S READING.

The Four Winds, The White Man's Foot, } ("Hiawatha"), ...	*Longfellow*
The Maiden and the Weather Cock, The Windmill, }	*Longfellow*
The Winds, To the Evening Wind, }	*Bryant*
Sweet and Low, - -	*Tennyson*
What the Winds Bring, -	*E. C. Stedman*
The Wind in a Frolic, -	*William Howitt*
Earth and Man, ...	*Guyot*

STORIES.

How West Wind Helped Dandelion.

There was once a Dandelion plant which grew in the grass just outside a garden fence. The leaves of the plant were thick and green, and its flower (held on rather a high stem, for it was a late blossom) was very full and round, and of the brightest yellow.

The Dandelion was usually as happy as a queen—though not because of the golden crown, oh, no! Nor is it the crown which makes the queen happy, if that is what you are thinking! But the Dandelion was happy in the beautiful world and in her loving friends, and happy in her work and her play.

Who were her friends? Oh! the Sunbeams that came sliding down from the great sun and kept little Dandelion warm, and made her green leaves greener and her yellow flower brighter whenever they came ; and the Raindrops who tumbled their little silvery selves down upon her, as if in a great fury sometimes, but only intending a frolic and not really hurting her. They brought her all the water she had to drink and bathe in, and Dandelion missed them very much if they stayed long away. The great Winds were her friends, too. Dandelion was just the least bit afraid of them, to tell the truth, and liked them best when they were gentle and quiet, or when they sent their messengers, the little Breezes, to play with her.

Dandelion had friends of another sort, too; little creatures made of music, motion, and feathers,—(we call them birds).

Insects, too, visited her;—butterflies as yellow as her flower, grasshoppers as green as her leaves, bees going a-marketing for honey and pollen, ants running nimbly along on their six thread-like legs, and many, many others, down to the tiny, moving, black specks which seemed too small to be alive and yet were as full of life as their larger neighbors.

Besides all these friends, Dandelion had some flower friends, the clovers who lived near her on the roadside, and the garden flowers who lived on the other side of the fence. The nearest neighbors among the garden flowers were some morning-glories who had actually climbed over the fence and were as friendly as possible.

Dandelion's play was with any of these different friends. Her work was to grow and make seeds,—as many good seeds as she possibly could.

As the long, bright days passed, Dandelion worked faithfully, in a flower's quiet, unseen way of working; and at last her seeds were formed. Instead of the golden crown of a flower which she had worn, her stalk held up a beautiful ball of silvery gauze. The tiny seeds were in this ball and would be ripe very soon.

One day Dandelion saw two children, Max and Nannie, walking about in the garden in a very business-like way. When they came to the morning-glory vine, she could hear what they were saying.

"Where is the box for the morning-glory seeds, Max?" called the little girl. "I see ever so many ripe ones."

"Here it is," replied Max, who had been looking in the basket which he carried. "We must gather a great many morning-glory seeds, for you know we want to plant them all along the fence next year; and we are going to send some to Cousin Fan, too."

"Yes, and then she will have the same kind of flowers away off there that we have here," said Nannie, as she poked among the leaves and blossoms of the morning-glory vine to find the plump seed vessels. Soon she had gathered all the ripe ones, and she and Max went back up the garden walk and into the house.

The Dandelion plant pondered on what it had heard. Seeds! Why, Dandelion plants had seeds as well as morning-glory vines! Probably Max and Nannie would come for her seeds. They would soon be ready,—in a few days, surely.

The few days passed quickly. Every morning Max and Nannie came out with their basket and little boxes and went to the garden plants, gathering the ripe seeds. But alas! for the hopes of the Dandelion plant! They never looked at her or even thought of her seeds, although they loved dandelions as well as any other children.

Poor Dandelion felt very much slighted. Why did not Max and Nannie want her seeds to plant next year or to send to Cousin Fan? Who would gather her seeds? She had tried so hard and worked so faithfully, and arranged her seeds so beautifully. Was it all for nothing?

Hark! "Cheer-up! Cheer-up!" sang a robin in the orchard; and a little whispering breeze rustled past her, breathing softly; "Wait, oh, wait!"

"Ah! but what will become of my seeds? No one will gather them and they will all be wasted."

The breeze passed on and then came a stronger puff of air.

"West Wind is coming," thought Dandelion, trembling a little; and just then she heard him calling.

"What, ho! there, Dandelion! Are you too warm? I will fan you. Are you too wet? I will help you shake the heavy drops from your leaves and flowers."

"No," said the Dandelion, "my leaves are not laden with water, nor is my heart parched with heat; but my seeds, my precious seeds are all to be wasted. No one will gather them."

"Ho, ho!" laughed West Wind, noisily, but kindly. "And what do you wish to have done with your seeds?"

"I wish they could be planted next year," said Dandelion, "some of them here, and some of them far away,—just as will be done to the seeds of the garden plants."

"Ho, ho!" laughed West Wind again, as noisily and kindly as before. "That is an easy matter to arrange. In fact it *is* arranged. It is one of the things I was to attend to this very morning, if your seeds were ripe."

"And have you brought a little box with you?" asked Dandelion.

"Not I!" replied West Wind. "I manage differently from the children. I sow the seeds as I gather them, and I also cover them. Then they are all ready to wake up and grow in the early spring."

"Oh! thank you, good West Wind," said Dandelion. "What a kind friend you are!"

"It is a part of our work," said West Wind. "My brothers and I have a great deal of seed-sowing to do in all the forests and fields over the whole earth. But I must not talk any longer. Now, ready! One, two, three, whew! Away they go."

Dandelion heard a merry whistle and felt a sudden strong puff against her. At the same instant all her seeds were gone. Where the feathery white ball had been there showed now a little bald knob.

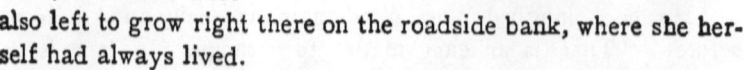

"Why!" said Dandelion rather bewildered, "how quickly that was done!"

She looked about her. Here and there on the grass near her she saw several of her seeds; and then looking farther and yet farther away she could see others whirling and dancing through the air carried along by the friendly seed sower, West Wind.

The little silky plumes which each seed wore, and which had made Dandelion's ball of silvery gauze, made it easy for the wind to take the seeds as far as Dandelion could wish; and some were also left to grow right there on the roadside bank, where she herself had always lived.

Dandelion was very happy. The robin in the orchard sang again his hearty "Cheer-up! Cheer-up!" and a little breeze which followed after West Wind whispered softly as before : "Wait! oh, wait!"

"Yes," said Dandelion; "there was no need of my worrying. But who would have thought that the great West Wind would take care of the seeds of a plain little Dandelion!"

EMILIE POULSSON.

The Dandelion Cycle.

" Pretty little Goldilocks, shining in the sun,
  Pray, what will become of you when the summer's done?"

" Then I'll be old Silverhead; for, as I grow old,
  All my shining hair will be white instead of gold.

" And where rests a silver hair that has blown from me,
  Other little Goldilocks in the Spring you'll see!

" Goldilocks to Silverhead, Silverhead to gold,
  So the change is going on every year, I'm told."

E. P.

Odysseus and the Bag of Winds.

Far-famed Odysseus was on his way across the sea, to his home in rocky Ithaca, when he came to the island of Æolia. Many had been his wanderings, by sea and land, since he had left his own fair dwelling, and most welcome was the sight of this friendly shore. Here lived the great King of the winds—Æolus—who could send gentle zephyrs murmuring over the sea, and could call back the wild tempests when they played too roughly with the waves. Well might Odysseus and his companions rejoice at coming to the wonderful floating island of King Æolus, for here they were kindly treated, after their toils and troubles, and when the time came for them to start once more on their way Æolus stowed in their boat gifts and provisions of all kinds for their voyage.

One of these gifts was very strange in its appearance—a great bulging sack, as large as an ox; in fact it was made of an ox's skin—tied tightly about with a cord of shining silver. This

Æolus placed carefully in the boat, and taking Odysseus aside told him that in this skin he had bound up the blustering winds, so that no storms should disturb the calm of the ocean, and drive the little boat out of her course. If, however, Odysseus should at any time be in need of a powerful blast to carry the boat swiftly away from some dangerous coast, or from some enemy, he was to open the bag with great caution and, letting out only the wind he wished, to close it again quickly, and bind it fast with the silver cord. When Æolus had bidden farewell to Odysseus and his crew, he sent a gentle west wind after him, to bear them prosperously on their way.

Day after day they sailed peacefully over the gleaming ocean, the soft gale bearing them along, while Odysseus managed the sail, and kept watch night and day. On the tenth day Odysseus was lying asleep in the boat, resting from his labors, when the sailors began talking among themselves of the mysterious-looking bag. "It must be full of treasures," said they, "and why should not we have our share of them?"

Speaking thus foolishly, they finally decided to open the bag. They loosed the silver cord, but they need to do no more, for the boisterous winds at once burst forth, and in a twinkling had lashed the quiet waves into foam, and whirled the boat far out of her course. The helmsman could do nothing, since the boat no longer obeyed the rudder, and even Odysseus, awakened by the commotion, was powerless against these roaring, whistling winds that tossed the little boat hither and thither at their will.

At last Odysseus and his men, driven far from their native shores, saw land once again. The foolish sailors were glad enough to pull the boat up on the beach, and in safety once more to built their fire and prepare a comfortable meal.

Many days and years went by before Odysseus at last reached his home. He had many adventures after this, but when he dwelt in peace and quiet at last, in the home from which he had been absent so long, he was always fond of telling the story of the bag of winds given him by King Æolus, and of the great disaster brought upon his sailors and himself by their foolish curiosity.

F. H.

The North Wind at Play.
(*From the German.*)

Once upon a time, in a house under a hill, lived Æolus and his four sons: North Wind, South Wind, East Wind and West Wind.

One day North Wind said to his father: "May I go out to play?"

"Oh, yes!" said his father, "if you don't stay too long."

Then away ran North Wind with a merry shout and song banging the door behind him.

As he ran along the road he saw in the orchard a beautiful tree upon which were green apples.

"Oh! come and play with me," said North Wind. "Come and play with me!"

"Oh, no!" said the tree; "I must stay quite still and help the apples to grow, else they will not be large and round and red in the autumn for the little children. Oh, no, North Wind, I cannot go."

"Puff!" said the North Wind—and down all the apples fell to the ground.

The next thing North Wind saw was a beautiful waving field of corn.

"Oh! come and play with me! Oh! come and play with me!" said North Wind.

"No, no!" said the corn; "I must stand quite still and grow. If you will look under this beautiful green silk you will see some little kernels lying. These must grow big and yellow to be ground into meal to make golden pudding for the children. So you see I cannot go to play."

At this the North Wind sighed—"Ah-ha-a-a!" and the corn lay down on the ground.

Running along, North Wind saw a lily growing under a window.

"Oh, you lovely lily! come and play with me," said North Wind.

"I cannot," said the lily, gently; "I have to stay here because the farmer's little girl is not at all well, and I am her friend, and every morning she comes and smiles down at me and I smile back again. I am sure she would miss me very much if I should go; so I must stay here, dear North Wind."

North Wind touched her very gently,—but she hung her head and never again looked up.

Now the farmer went out to work, and when he saw the corn and the apple tree, he said: "Ah! Mr. North Wind has been here!" But when he went home, his little girl told him about the lily. And the farmer said: "I'll go right up to Mr. Æolus and tell him all about it!"

So away he went; and he said: "Good morning, Mr. Æolus. Your boy, North Wind, has been down my way; and he has blown the apples from the trees, and the corn is lying down on the ground; but, worse than this, he has hurt my little girl's lily!"

"Ah!" said Mr. Æolus, "I am very sorry. I will speak to North Wind when he comes in." And then the farmer went home.

By and by in came North Wind.

"My boy," said Æolus, "the farmer has been here, and he has told me all the harm which you have done." And then the father told North Wind the story of the apples and the corn and the lily.

"Oh, well," said North Wind, "I know I did it; but I didn't mean to. I just meant to have a little fun with the apple tree; but when I said 'Puff-f-f' all the apples fell down! And it was just the same with the corn; it lay down before I knew that I had hurt it. As for the lily, that was the loveliest thing you ever saw, father; I only kissed it when I came away."

"I believe that what you tell me is true, my boy; but if you cannot help being so rough and rude when you play, you must go out only when the farmer has gathered the apples and corn, and when the flowers have been taken safely into the house. When the snow is on the ground, you and Jack Frost may have fine frolics together."

As told by HARRIET RYAN.

THE PIGEONS.

To the Teacher:—

In "Birds of America"· Audubon's wonderful book—may be found detailed descriptions of all the doves and pigeons known. Much of this detailed description does not concern us; but I have gleaned a few facts which may not be too familiar to us all.

The pigeon or dove almost invariably builds a loose, exposed nest, out of which eggs and birds often drop. Many pigeons will build nests in the same tree; doves will not. This seems to be the only difference noted between pigeons and doves.

Some doves are found only in the tropics. The California dove is found from Louisiana to Middle Massachusetts; while the Passenger pigeon lives everywhere in the United States except the southern tip of Florida, and is well known in Newfoundland.

The average speed of the Passenger pigeon is a mile a minute; and it has equally remarkable power of vision, as shown from its sighting food from immense distances.

From fifty to one hundred or more nests are often found in one tree.

Audubon says that the constancy and devotion of the dove to its mate and its young are not excelled by any other creatures; so that we rightly use this beautiful bird as the emblem of love and gentleness.

THE TALK.

(Points of connection between this subject and the preceding ones of "The Winds" and "Seeds" will readily suggest themselves. The farmer has gathered the seeds from the farm and garden, the wind has taken them from the trees and plants in other places. Cold weather is coming; so the birds have, most of them, flown away to warmer countries where they can find food in plenty.)

Have the children seen *any* birds lately,—canaries, sparrows, **pigeons?**

Where do pigeons live? Wild ones in the woods; build very loose nests—(show with hands); tame ones in a pigeon house in the top of the barn; sometimes, on a pole in the farmyard.

The pigeon lays two pure white eggs. Can fly far and fast—a mile a minute.

How does it sleep? Roosts on a branch, if wild; on a stick in pigeon house, if tame. Why does it not fall off? Toes hold it  firmly. Find out how many toes in front; how many behind. Watch the pigeons on the street, or ask father or mother about it. (Play the game of the Pigeon House and talk it over.) When we let the pigeons out of the pigeon house, where do you think they will fly? Where does the song say they will fly? Will they find something to eat? Yes; what the farmer has not gathered, and what the wind has dropped and not covered up—especially seeds of grains.

What do you think they talk to each other about when they go home again? (Try to give the children the idea of sharing experiences.)

What does the pigeon say? "Coo, coo!"

A loud noise? No; always soft and gentle.

Do we love to hear the pigeons? Do we love to hear people speak gently?

Whenever we see the pigeons, or play "The Pigeon House," let us remember how gentle and loving these little birds are.

Verse for Children.

Happy as a robin,
Gentle as a dove—
That's the sort of little child
Every one will love.

THE PIGEON HOUSE.

TEACHER'S READING.

Daddy Darwin's Dove Cote, - - - - - - - *Mrs. Ewing*
Hilda and the Doves (" Marble Faun "), - - - - - *Hawthorne*
The Doves, - - - - - - - - - *Mrs. Browning*
The Belfry Pigeon, - - - - - - - - *N. P. Willis*
The White Pigeon, - - - - - - - *Miss Edgeworth*

For the Children.

Birds and their Nests. From "Kindergarten Gems." - - *A. T. Ketchum*

STORIES.

The Fantail Pigeon.

"I wonder why I am not wise!" said the little white fantail pigeon, sadly. "It seems to me I am not good for anything at all. The hens lay eggs for our mistress's breakfast; the cow gives milk to drink and to be made into butter and cheese; the turkey-cock will be fatted for Christmas, he says, and will be served on a big dish, with a string of sausages all round him; that will be grand! The pigs will be made into pork, but I am good for nothing. The thrush and the blackbird can sing beautifully, and the owl is wiser than all the other birds. I cannot sing and I am not at all wise. Ginger, the cat, catches the rats and mice; Monarch, the dog, guards the house. But I cannot catch rats and mice, and how could a pigeon keep guard?"

Poor little white pigeon! What was she to do? I am sure you must feel sorry for her. It is so very sad to be of no use in the world.

"I will go to the owl," said she. "He is the wisest of all the birds. Perhaps he will teach me how to be of use."

The owl lived in a hollow tree behind the farmyard. All day long he sat in his tree and blinked, for the sunshine hurt his eyes. That was because he was so wise, the other birds said. But when the sun went down and the world grew dark and still the owl came out from his hollow tree and flew about. He had a hooked beak and his eyes were large and round; he looked very solemn and severe, as was proper for the wisest of all the birds.

The white pigeon flew up to the hollow tree and bent her head humbly before the owl. The wise old bird blinked twice, but said nothing, because his words were so precious.

"Pray, sir," said the pigeon, "may I speak to you?"

The owl blinked again, which if it did not mean "yes," at any rate did not mean "no." So the pigeon went on: "Sir, you are very wise and I am very foolish. I am very unhappy because I know nothing and am good for nothing. Pease, sir, will you help me."

The owl said nothing at all for a long time. The little white pigeon sat on a bough and waited. She said to herself: "He is slow, but that is certainly because he is so kind as to think very hard about some way to help me."

So she waited patiently, long past the time when Jeggo gave all the birds in the farmyard their supper.

Then the sun went down, and the owl opened his large, round eyes and looked at the little white pigeon.

"Now," said she, "he is going to speak;" and her heart beat fast with hope and excitement.

"I am wise," said the owl; "you are foolish." Then he waited so long that the little pigeon ventured to put him in mind that he was speaking. "Yes, sir," said she; "what can I do?"

"You must make the best of it," said the owl, and spreading his large, browny-white wings he flew away into the darkness, calling out: "Too-whit, too-whoo."

"He has certainly much wisdom," said the little white pigeon. "But I do not see what is the good of it, if he keeps it all for himself like that. I want to know how to make the best of it." And home she went again feeling sadder than ever.

Next day the little white pigeon was still very miserable, and instead of flying down as usual when her mistress came into the yard, she hid in a corner and hung her head. So the mistress went away, feeling sad and anxious; for she thought one of her pets was lost.

Now the old drake had a very kind heart, and watched over all the animals in the farmyard. He knew that the little white pigeon was unhappy, and made up his mind to find out what was amiss, and set it right if possible. He was a clever old bird, and had seen a deal of the world, for he was nearly three years old.

He sent a message to the pigeon to say he wanted to see her, and she came at once. No one ever thought of disobeying the old drake.

"What is wrong with you, little pigeon?" said he, kindly. "The sun shines; peas and Indian corn are plentiful, and you are not moulting; yet for three days you have done nothing but mope and look miserable. Come, now, and tell me what is the matter."

"I am of no use in the world," said the little pigeon, sadly. "All the other birds and animals are good for something, but I am good for nothing."

"Oh! silly bird," said the old drake. "How can you say you are of no use in the world? Everything that is made is, and must be, of some use in the world. Some are strong and can do much work, like Short, the horse who draws the heavy cart. Some have the gift of teaching others, and that is what they are good for. Some have beautiful voices to listen to, and others beautiful feathers to look at. It is true that the turkey is good to eat and that the hen can lay eggs; it is true that the owl is wise and the blackbird can sing; but which of them all has such a pretty white tail and such nice pink feet as you?"

"I forgot all about my tail," said the little pigeon.

"Just so," said the old drake. "You forgot what you had, in fretting for what you have not. Nay, you even neglected your gift and let your pretty white tail get all dirty and crumpled. So it happened that our mistress went away sad this morning, because her little white bird did not come to greet her. Go away home, little pigeon, and do not be miserable any more. Make the best of what you can do, and never mind the things you cannot do."

Then the little pigeon thanked the old drake for his good advice. She went home and put her feathers tidy, and I need hardly tell you that next day the mistress did not look in vain for her pretty, white pet.

MARY DENDY.

"*Lesson Stories*," Sunday School Association, London.

Pearl and Her Pigeons.

When Pearl was seven years old her Brother Freddie gave her two pretty white pigeons. The little girl was as happy as a queen when she saw her pretty pets. She named one Dot and the other Phil. Pearl loved dearly to play with them, but she did not like to keep them shut up in a cage.

Sometimes she would open the window and say to them: "Fly away, my dearies, and play with other birds! I do not wish to keep you here this beautiful morning." They would flutter their wings joyously, peck her hand, and make a funny little noise which sounded very much like "good-bye, sweet mistress! We will return soon, and tell you all about the sunny world, and what the birds are doing."

When Pearl went out into the garden to pull flowers, or give her dollies a ride the pigeons would come to her and light upon her head; and sometimes they would poke their bills into her mouth for a kiss.

She fed them with crumbs from her hand, and every morning she gave them some fresh, sparkling water to bathe in.

Phil called Dot his little wife, and he often invited her to take a walk with him. When Dot was not busy she went with him. In the beautiful springtime Dot laid two white eggs and sat on them till the wee birds crept out. Dot and Phil were as happy as they could be, and so proud of their little family! Pearl put crumbs enough for all beside the nest, which pleased Mother Dot very much. Then she would sit down beside the cage and watch the mother-pigeon patiently teaching the little ones to eat.

Pearl often heard the mother-bird putting her little family to sleep; and she would say to her darling baby brother: "Listen, dear! I hear the mother-pigeon cooing softly to her little ones."

HELEN A. KELLER.

The Constant Dove.

The white dove sat on the sunny eaves,
And "What will you do when the north wind grieves?"
She said to the busy nut-hatch small,
Tapping above in the gable tall.

He probed each crack with his slender beak,
And much too busy was he to speak;
Spiders, that thought themselves safe and sound,
And moths, and flies, and cocoons, he found.

Oh! but the white dove she was fair!
Bright she shone in the autumn air,
Turning her head from left to right—
Only to watch her was such delight!

"Coo!" she murmured, "poor little thing,
What will you do when the frost shall sting?
Spiders and flies will be hidden or dead,
Snow underneath and snow overhead."

Nut-hatch paused in his busy care;
"And what will you do, O white dove fair?"
"Kind hands feed me with crumbs and grain,
And I wait with patience for spring again."

He laughed so loud that his laugh I heard;
"How can you be such a stupid bird?
What are your wings for, tell me, pray,
But to bear you from tempest and cold away?

"Merrily off to the south I'll fly,
In search of the summer, by and by,
And warmth and beauty I'll find anew;
O white dove fair, will you follow. too?"

But she cooed content on the sunny eaves,
And looked askance at the reddening leaves;
While low I whispered, "O white dove true,
I'll feed you, and love you the winter through!"

CELIA THAXTER.

Houghton, Mifflin & Co.

The Dove and the Ant.

The Ant, compelled by thirst, went to drink in a clear, purling rivulet; but the current, with its circling eddy, snatched her away, and carried her down the stream. A Dove, pitying her distressed condition, cropped a branch from a neighboring tree, and let it fall into the water, by means of which the Ant saved herself, and got ashore. Not long after a fowler, having a design upon the Dove, planted his nets in due order, without the bird's observing what he was about; which the Ant perceiving, just as he was going to put his design in execution, bit him on the heel, and made him give so sudden a start that the Dove took the alarm, and flew away.

ÆSOP.

A True Pigeon Story.

A gentleman had two pairs of pigeons living in dovecotes placed side by side. In each pigeon family there was a father and mother-bird and two little ones. On a certain day the parents in one dovecote went away to get food, and while they were gone one of their little birds fell out of the dovecote and down to the ground. The poor baby bird was not much hurt, strange to say, but it could not get back for it was too young to fly.

Now the parents in the other dovecote were at home when this happened and it seemed as if they said to themselves: "One of our babies might fall out in just that same way. We must do something to make the dovecote safer." And then this wise, careful father and mother went to work. They flew about until they found some small sticks. These they carried to their own dovecote and there in the doorway they built a cunning little fence of sticks! Not so high but that the baby pigeons could look over it, but high enough to keep them from ever falling out of the dovecote as their little neighbor had done. The owner of the pigeons, who had seen the birdling fall and had put it back into its dovecote, watched the birds the whole time as they gathered the sticks and built the little fence across the doorway. This is a true story and it is often told to some children in Boston by a lady who knows the owner of these very pigeons.

M. P.

THE BAKER.

To the Teacher:—

Frœbel believed that "Pat-a-cake" and similar games "arose because people felt that the cultivation of the child's love of activity and his strivings to get the use of his limbs ought to be carried on in such a way as to lift him at once into the complexity of his outside life." Thus, in the "Pat-a-cake" play, instead of the simple relation of need and supply between child and mother—the child needing food and the mother giving it—the child is shown another "link of the great chain of life's inner dependence," in the baker who bakes the bread and the cake which the mother gives to the child.

"Whenever opportunity occurs," says Frœbel, "make this inner dependence of life clear, visible, impressive, tangible and perceptible to your child, even though it be in only a few of the essential links of this great chain, until you come to the last ring that holds all the rest—God's father-love for all."

Of course, in foreign countries, where it is common for the mother to prepare bread and cake, etc., and send it to the baker to have it baked, the relation is closer; but even in this country the baker is near to the child's life. Food being a primary necessity, the baker, the miller and the farmer who are the providers of food, are among the first of the world's workers which the kindergarten brings to the child's notice.

THE TALK.

Some of the children have dear little babies in their homes. What does baby play? Does baby play "Pat-a-cake?" Shall we play it?

(After playing baby's "Pat-a-cake,"—the old Mother Goose rhyme,—teach the children the kindergarten play, "Now my child," etc., which is, after all, only an extension of the same idea and principle.)

THE BAKER.

Recall a little of the talk with the children about the pigeons, and speak especially about the food. The point to be brought out is that the pigeon's food is ready for it, whereas the child's food, our food, must generally be prepared.

The pigeon likes grains of wheat. Do we like *grains* of wheat? Tell some of the things we do like to eat; meat, potatoes, bread, etc., etc. Where does the bread come from? From the baker. Where did the baker get his flour? From the miller. Where did the miller get the wheat to grind? From the farmer. So the story of the bread is quite a long story, isn't it? And tells of a great many workers.

Sometimes the mother makes the bread instead of buying it at the baker's. Have any of the children seen their mothers make bread? Who can tell how she does it, and what she uses?

What kind of an oven does she bake the bread in? Have the children ever been to a baker's shop? What does the baker make? What kind of an oven does he have? A very, very large one; as large as a small room (eight feet by ten feet). He uses something like a big shovel with a long handle when he puts the loaves into the oven or takes them out. The baker also uses a large mixing trough instead of a bread pan; long, smooth table instead of bread board; rolling pins, cooky cutters, baking tins, etc., etc.

The baker must build a fire and heat his oven before the bread can be baked.

(Speak a little upon the usefulness of fire. If advisable, more links of the chain of dependence could be disclosed here, in the wood chopper and the miner whose work prepares the wood and coal for the baking of the bread.)

TEACHER'S READING.

Each and All, - - - - - - - - - *R. W. Emerson*
Daily Bread, (Sermon 1879), - - - - - - *E. E. Hale*
Daily Bread, (Stories), - - - - - - - *E. E. Hale*

For the Children.

Amy Stewart,
The Little Cookie Boy, } ("Kindergarten Stories and Morning
The Baker,   Talks"), - - - - - *S. E. Wiltse*

STORIES.

The Johnny Cake.

Little Sarah, she stood by her grandmother's bed,
" And what shall I get for your breakfast? " she said.
" You shall get me a johnny cake; quickly go make it,
In one minute mix, and in two minutes bake it."

So Sarah, she went to the closet to see
If yet any meal in the barrel might be.
The barrel had long time been empty as wind:
Not a speck of the bright yellow meal could she find-
But grandmother's johnny cake—still she must make it
In one minute mix, and in two minutes bake it.

She ran to the shop, but the shopkeeper said,
" I have none—you must go to the miller, fair maid.
For he has a mill, and he'll put the corn in it,
And grind you some nice yellow meal in a minute;
But run, or the johnny cake, how will you make it,
In one minute mix, and in two minutes bake it?"

Then Sarah, she ran every step of the way,
But the miller said, "No, I have no meal to-day;
Run, quick, to the cornfield, just over the hill,
And if any be there, you may fetch it to mill.
Run, run, or the johnny cake, how will you make it,
In one minute mix, and in two minutes bake it?"

Then Sarah looked round, and she saw what was wanted:
The corn could not grow, for no corn had been planted.
She asked of the farmer to sow her some grain,
But the farmer he laughed till his sides ached again.
" Ho! ho! for the johnny cake—how can you make it,
In one minute mix, and in two minutes bake it? "

The farmer he laughed, and he laughed out aloud—
" And how can I plant till the earth has been plowed?
Run, run to the ploughman, and bring him with speed;
He'll plough up the ground, and I'll fill it with seed."
Away, then, ran Sarah, still hoping to make it,
In one minute mix, and in two minutes bake it.

The ploughman he ploughed, and the grain it was sown,
And the sun shed his rays till the corn was all grown.
It was ground at the mill, and again in her bed
These words to poor Sarah the grandmother said:
" You shall get me a johnny cake, quickly go make it,
In one minute mix, and in two minutes bake it."

ANONYMOUS.

The China Rabbit Family.

Mrs. China Rabbit and her four little rabbits were very much crowded. They lived in a small pasteboard box, and there was scarcely room for their legs and paws. As for their long ears— why, Mrs. China Rabbit and Hoppit actually had to poke theirs through the broken corners of the top!

"Be patient, my children," the mother would say. "This cannot last always; and we ought to be thankful that we have this soft cotton to lie on, at any rate."

It is no wonder that the little China Rabbits grumbled. How would you like to live in a house so small that you had to lie just the way you would fit in best, whether it was comfortable or not?

The shabby pasteboard box filled with the China Rabbits was in a toy shop. Furthermore, the toy shop was near Baby Bun's house. More than that, Baby Bun's mamma went into the toy shop one day. And, best of all, she bought the whole China Rabbit family!

When she reached home she gave them to the cook ; and the cook smilled and nodded, and said: "Oh, yes'm! I'll do it with pleasure for the little boy, bless his heart!" and she immediately went to work to bake a cake.

Mrs. China Rabbit and Hoppit and the other China Rabbits were soon taken out of their crowded house. The cook gave them a good bath, and then she put each in a bed of cake dough, in a tiny tin, and set all the tins in the oven.

When the oven door was shut, and the cook could not hear, Mrs. China Rabbit called out: "Hoppit, my child!"

"Here I am, mother!" said Hoppit. "Is Chubby here?" said Mrs. China Rabbit. "Yes, here I am," said Chubby.

"And Johnny Jumper?" "Yes," Johnny Jumper answered, and so also did Tiny, the baby.

"This is well," said Mrs. China Rabbit. "Are you all comfortable?"

"Oh! it is delightful!" said the children.

As the cakes began to bake, however, Mrs. China Rabbit and the children found it rather warm. They had never felt such heat. They almost wished themselves back in the pasteboard box. "For, at least, the ventilation was good!" gasped Hoppit.

Just as they thought they would die of the heat, the oven door opened with a clang. "They're just done beautiful!" they heard the cook say, and soon all the little cakes were cooling on the pantry shelf, and the China Rabbit family quickly revived.

"Shall we live here always, mother?" asked Chubby.

"I do not know, my dear", said Mrs. China Rabbit; "but let us enjoy it while we may. These are sweet little homes."

"Yes, I've tasted mine," said Johnny Jumper, smacking his lips.

At this all the China Rabbits began to nibble the cake. "No one will grudge us a little lunch, I am sure," the mother said.

Very soon the cook put the cakes on a pretty plate and sent them to the nursery. Baby and his brothers and sisters were having a tea party; and when the children had eaten their bread and butter, they each had one of the "fairy cakes," as Baby's mamma called them.

"Oh! there's something hard in my cake!" said Baby, who

had taken a big bite. "So there is in mine!" "And mine!" "And mine!" shouted the other children.

You know what they had found, don't you?

Yes! Of course it was Mrs. China Rabbit, and Hoppit, and Chubby, and Johnny Jumper, and Tiny! And the China Rabbit family lived happily ever after among the other playthings in the nursery toy closet.

EMILIE POULSSON.

Teddy's Birthday Cake.

Outline for Simple Story.

Teddy's birthday—little friends invited. Mamma's plan of birthday cake, with as many candles on it as Teddy is years old. Eggs, flour, butter, sugar, milk, all ready to mix. Mamma looks at oven, finds stove broken so that oven could not bake the cake nicely. Is puzzled to know what to do; cannot bear to disappoint Teddy; thinks of the baker, mixes cake and takes it to the bakery. Leaves it; baker watches it as it bakes, takes it out with his long shovel. When mamma goes to the bakery for it, she pays and thanks the baker. Enjoyment of the cake. Mamma tells how the kind baker helped her out of her trouble.

E. P.

Nero at the Bakery.

"There!" said the Baker, as he took the last loaf of bread out of the oven, "that's as handsome a batch of bread as ever was baked. I'll take it right upstairs to the store."

Very soon little Sophie came into the bakery and said, "My mother wants a loaf of fresh bread, please."

"Here it is," said the Baker, "just fresh from the oven. It will keep your hands warm all the way home." So saying he wrapped the bread in a brown paper and handed it to the little girl, who then gave him the money for it.

As she door opened to go out, a big dog walked in,—a great shaggy fellow with a basket in his mouth. He was all alone, but he evidently knew just what to do. Sophie stopped to look, for she had never known a dog to go to the store before.

"Why, here is Nero! Good dog! Good Nero!" said the Baker. "Have you come for the bread?"

Nero walked to the Baker and held his head up, as if to offer the basket. In the basket was the money for a loaf of bread. The Baker put the money in the money drawer and then waited to see what the dog would do.

Nero looked at him as if surprised, and then gave a sharp "Bow-wow!"

"Well, it is too bad to tease such a good dog as you are— here's your bread," said the Baker, taking down a loaf. He wrapped it in paper and placed it in the basket and the dog wagged his tail with delight. Then, taking his basket again, he stalked out of the door which Sophie held open and walked up the street. Sophie's home lay in the same direction, so she walked on behind Nero and saw him walk steadily along and then cross the street and go into a house where a lady was watching for him.

"Guess what I saw at the bakery!" said Sophie when she reached home. Her mother and father and the children guessed and guessed. Pies, cakes, cookies, rolls, biscuits, doughnuts, buns, gingerbread, gingerbread men, muffins—yes, Sophie had seen all these, but they were not what she meant. At last when all the things usually seen in a bakery had been guessed, Sophie told about Nero, the clever dog who had bought a loaf of bread.

EMILIE POULSSON.

THANKSGIVING DAY.

To the Teacher:—

This subject has many important sides. It is a harvest feast, a day for giving thanks, a festival of family reunions, a day of interesting historical origin, a purely American holiday and therefore a time for instilling and cultivating patriotic feeling.

Can we compass all these aspects of the subject with the children? Surely not, if we depend on the morning talk and story alone, or if we have not prepared the way. But the farmer and the harvest are already familiar; the children's hearts and voices are attuned to hymns of gratitude and songs of family love; and we have worked toward patriotism by taking loving notice of our beautiful flag, by singing "My Country, 'tis of Thee," cheering the red, white and blue, etc. Therefore the many-sidedness of the subject is not so much an objection as might at first appear, but rather offers a valuable opportunity for recalling and deepening impressions;—each teacher emphasizing particularly that aspect of the subject which is most desirable for her pupils.

The Thanksgiving Day of the Pilgrims, with the Indians sharing their feast, is a beautiful story; but it is so admirably told in "The Story Hour," of which Mrs. Wiggin and Miss Smith are the authors, that I have not attempted to retell it; but have chosen instead the local story*, which may not be quite so well known, although Mr. Hale has told it in his own delightful fashion in his church in Boston on Thanksgiving Day.

THE TALK.

Do you remember that the baker was the worker we talked of last week? What other workers can you name?

What did the farmer do in the autumn? Gathered seeds to

---

* "'The Governor,' says Mather, 'was the Joseph unto whom the whole body of the people repaired when the corn failed them, and he continued relieving of them with his open-handed bounties as long as he had any stock.' When his last batch of bread was in his oven he gave 'the last handful of meal in his barrel to a poor man depressed by the wolf at the door.' At that moment they 'spied a ship arrived at the harbor's mouth laden with provisions for them all.' A day of thanksgiving for this ship's arrival was held on the 22d of February—the first Thanksgiving Day recorded by the Puritans of the Bay colony."

save for next year; yes, and gathered in his harvest. (Children name seeds; and name fruits, and vegetables, etc., harvested for winter.)

How happy and thankful the farmer feels when he thinks of his cellar stored with apples, potatoes, etc., for his family all winter; and of his barns full of hay and oats and corn, etc., for the animals. And because harvest time brings all these things, and is so joyful, people thought it would be the best time to have a special day for giving thanks to God.

Now let us sing the Thanksgiving song, and play that this is Thanksgiving Day and that we are all at grandmother's house.

How glad we are to see her and grandfather and all the uncles and aunts and cousins! We run into the kitchen and peep into the big oven—an old-fashioned one, very much like the one the baker has. Oh! how good everything smells! And there is the big turkey!—isn't he a monster? What else is being prepared for dinner?

(Children always sing with unction:—

> "Hurrah for the fun,
> Is the pudding done?
> Hurrah for the pumpkin pie!"

But we do not want them to think of the good things merely as eatables. A hint of the right way to talk of the dinner is found in the fact that the Thanksgiving feast was formerly intended to show forth some of everything that had been raised on the farm, thus representing the bounteousness of the whole harvest for which the thanks were given.)

Soon we go to church. We sit nicely and do not talk, and we sing as well as we can. (Sing some song expressing thanks. This will be the time to make "the spiritual meaning of the day bright and clear.' Direct the children's thoughts to causes for thankfulness universal and special—and to showing thankfulness by deed as well as by word.

When the regular playtime comes, let it be the afternoon merry-making at grandmother's.)

TEACHER'S READING.

Pilgrims and Puritans, — — — — — — — — *Moore*
Customs and Fashions of Old New England (Chapter IX) *Alice Morse Earle*
Things that Hinder Thankfulness (Sermon), — — *Minot J. Savage*
Love of Country ("Great Thoughts for Little Thinkers"), - *Lucia T. Ames*
The Pilgrim Fathers, — — — — — — — — *Hemans*
"Come, Ye Thankful People, Come," — — — *Hymn*
For an Autumn Festival, — — — — — — — *Whittier*
The Pumpkin, — — — — — — — — — *Whittier*
A Tardy Thanksgiving, — — — — — — *M. E. Wilkins*
Getting Ready for Thanksgiving, — — — *St. Nicholas, 1879*
Peter Crisp's Spectacles ("New Lights on Old Paths"), — — *Charles Foster*

For the Children.

The First Thanksgiving Day ("The Story Hour"), - *Nora A. Smith*
Thanksgiving Story ("Kindergarten Stories and Morning Talks"), — — — — — — — — — *S. E. Wiltse*
Peggy's Thanksgiving Visitor ("Stories for Kindergarten and Home"), — — — — — — — *M. L. Van Kirk*
Chunsey, the Thanksgiving Turkey (A New Year's Bargain), — — — — — — — — — *Susan Coolidge*

STORIES.

A Boston Thanksgiving Story.

Once upon a time Boston, and indeed this whole land, was covered with trees instead of houses; and there were no streets, no stores, no churches, no big buildings of any kind. Yet people lived here—Indians—who loved to live in the woods. There were no carpenters among the Indians, so they did not build real houses, but had tents or wigwams.

By and by some people like us came to this land; but as they came in winter the farmers could not plant anything, the ground being frozen; and so the miller had no wheat to grind into flour, and the baker had no flour to make bread of, and there was very little for the people to eat. They had fish, and clams, and such things, but often had to go hungry. A ship, which they had sent across the great ocean to bring them more provisions, had been gone so long that it seemed as if it must be lost; and the poor, hungry people did not know what they should do.

One day some of the little South Boston boys were at play on a hill near the water, and they saw a ship sailing toward the land. They knew that the ship would bring plenty of food for all the hungry people, so away they ran to tell their fathers and mothers and the neighbors about it. Can't you imagine how glad they were to spread such joyful news? Very soon the ship came to shore and was unloaded. (Let the children tell what the ship probably brought, and get them to imagine how busy the mothers were, cooking and baking for the hungry people; and how glad they all were to have enough to eat again.)

Yes! the people were so glad that they wanted to thank the Heavenly Father; and they said: "Let us have a day for giving thanks." So they had a Thanksgiving Day. They went to church and thanked God for all his goodness, and then had a joyful time at home.

Other people who had come to America had special days for giving thanks; they finally all agreed to keep the same day. And so for a long time we have had the one general Thanksgiving Day over the whole land.

E. P.

How Patty Gave Thanks.

Ah! how snug it was in the barn that cold November night! Farmer Gray shut all the doors as if it were winter weather, and then went away glad to think that the animals were warm and comfortable for the night. No sooner had the sound of his footsteps died away than a Cow raised her head and gave a faint bellow.

"News!" said she, "News! Something beautiful happened to me to-day. It was just before I was turned out into the field this morning. Little Patty came running up to me and began to stroke my forehead. 'You good old cow!' said she; 'I had some milk to drink at breakfast and I know who gave it to me, and so I have come to say thank you. Mother told me this morning that this was "Thank-you" day;' and then the dear child put a delicious apple into my mouth and laughed to hear me crunch it! I am so glad that my milk is good and rich. And she thanked me for butter and cream and for her papa's cheese, too,—the grateful child!"

"You say well, Neighbor Cow; a grateful child she is," said the farm Horse. "I was in the stall just before they harnessed me to take the family to church, and little Patty came to see me, too; and she thanked me for all the rides she had had on my back and in the haycart, and for dragging the plough and for bringing the flour from the mill. Then, bless her heart! she reached up and gave me a big mouthful of sweet-smelling hay. I tell you, I'll trot my prettiest the next time I have her in the

PATTY THANKING OLD BOB.

carriage!'' Bob gave a pleased whinny as he said this, and, as if in response, a noise came from the sheep barn. The sheep barn joined the larger barn, and at the doorway between stood a mild-faced Sheep, who began to speak in her own way.

"So little Patty went to you, too, did she? I can tell you I was surprised when she brought me and the rest of the flock an extra dish of salt this morning. 'This is to say, thank you, good Sheep,' said she. 'We talked about you in the kindergarten and I know that our worsted balls are made of your wool, and my new mittens, and my flannel petticoat, and my winter coat and dress, and Jackie's clothes, and the blankets—and oh, so many things! How funny you would look with them all on your back!' Then she felt of my wool and patted me with her gentle little hand. I do hope that my fleece will be a good heavy one this year, and how I wish that the wool might be used for little Patty!"

"Well, well!" said the Cow, "the child did make it a real 'Thank-you day,' I am sure; for besides thanking me, and you, Bob, and you, Mrs. Fleecy, I heard the Hens saying to-day that she has been showering corn down for them by the double handful and saying 'thank you' for the eggs which they had given her. She told them that she liked the eggs for breakfast, and that her mamma made cake with them, too. I wonder what put it into her head to come and thank us all."

"It was her good little heart that put it into her head," said Bob, wisely; "and I think I know the reason why she came today, for as I was trotting along the road to and from church I heard the family talking a good deal about to-day being Thanksgiving Day. And when Patty's grandpapa asked her if she knew why Thanksgiving Day was kept, she said: 'Oh, yes! It is the day to say "thank you" for everything, and that is why I hurried out to the barn this morning.'"

"And to whom did you say 'thank you' out there?" asked her grandpapa.

"Why, to all of them," answered Patty; "to Bob and Moolly cow, and the sheep and the hens."

"Very good," said Grandpapa, "very good indeed, little Thankful-heart. I am glad you thought of the kind, useful creatures from whom we get so many things for our pleasure and comfort."

As Bob repeated what Patty's grandpapa had said, sober Mrs. Fleecy gave a little caper of delight, and Moolly cow heaved a sigh of deep satisfaction. Kind, grateful words are pleasant to any ears.

It was now bedtime and the animals began to settle themselves for their night's rest. Mrs. Fleecy went back to her woolly companions in the sheep barn; Moolly cow sank down restfully in her stall; and Bob, after stamping and tramping a few times, bent his long legs under him and lay down upon his fresh straw bedding. But before they went to sleep they spoke again of how happy dear little Patty had made them with her thanks and her gifts.

EMILIE POULSSON.

A Morning Thanksgiving.

For this new morning with its light,
For rest and shelter of the night,
For health and food, for love and friends,
For everything his goodness sends,
We thank the Heavenly Father.

M. J. GARLAND

WINTER.

To the Teacher:—

In this talk we consider the seasons, the action of cold (personified as Jack Frost) and preparation for winter.

For further matter on the subject of crystallization, see the story of "Snowflakes."

THE TALK.

What day of the week is to-day? What month is it? Probably few if any of the children will be able to tell. Is it summer? No, summer is past. (Children tell some of the characteristics of summer—hot weather, much sunshine, flowers, grass, birds, bees, butterflies, everything growing.)

Is it autumn? Just the very end of autumn. (Children tell characteristics of autumn—cold weather, falling leaves, birds flying to warmer countries, etc.)

And now winter is coming. (Children tell characteristics of winter—bare trees, birds gone, no flowers, bees and butterflies to be seen out of doors.) And what will come after winter? (Children tell characteristics of spring. Teacher then contrasts the characteristics of summer and winter, and speaks of the shorter days which we have in the latter season.)

Which of the winds will be out to play most of the time now? Did you ever hear the North Wind whistle or blow a bugle? Play that North Wind is in the kindergarten now.

Some one else comes "when the wintry winds begin to bellow." (If this does not bring Jack Frost's name from the children, give more of the words of this song or the other Jack Frost song, or hum the tune.)

What does Jack Frost do? Helps to color leaves, opens the chestnut burrs and other seed vessels so that the wind can sow the seeds; makes pretty white pictures on the windows. When

Jack Frost first comes, in the autumn, he only makes short visits in the night; but in the winter he stays all the time. In the country he puts a thin sparkling carpet over the fields and covers the brooks with a glassy roof. In the city he touches the water on the sidewalks and makes "slides" for the children. I want to tell you another thing Jack Frost does. But will you tell me, first, what hides the sun some days so that we cannot see the sunshine at all? Yes, the clouds. Sometimes when there are gray clouds floating about in the sky, Jack Frost and North Wind fly up there. North Wind goes to the clouds and blows and whistles, and, what do you think! out come the little raindrops that were sleeping in the clouds—all wide awake and ready to go down to the earth, they think. But Jack Frost is watching for them; and as fast as they come out of the cloud, he says: "Don't you want to wear your white dresses this time?" And then he touches them, and each little raindrop is immediately all white and sparkling, and has really become a beautiful snow star or snowflake. So, instead of the rain which might have come down to the earth when North Wind called the sleeping raindrops out of the clouds, we have a beautiful snowstorm, all because Jack Frost was there.

(Speak of the snow as a protective covering for plant life, and of the fun to be had with sleds, snowballs, snow men, etc.)

How did the birds get ready for winter? Most of them by flying away. Have the sparrows and the pigeons gone? They stay with us and we like to have them, and must feed them sometimes, as they cannot find food easily in winter. How did the squirrels get ready for winter? How did the farmer get ready for winter? How do we? Mother makes warm clothes for the children; father works and buys coal to make the house cosy and warm. Children must be careful not to lose the mittens which mother gives them.

The following is a pretty winter motto:—

> "The skies may meet in sadness,
> The blustering winds may blow;
> But if our hearts are cheery
> There's sunshine where we go."

TEACHER'S READING.

Architecture of Snow ("Forms of Water"),	*Tyndall*
The Fairyland of Science,	*Arabella Buckley*
The Story Mother Nature Told,	*Jane Andrews*
Stories in the Snow ("Sharp Eyes"),	*W. H. Gibson*
The Snow Image,	*Hawthorne*
The Snowstorm,	*Emerson*
Snow Bound,	*Whittier*
The Approach of Winter,	*B. W. Procter*
The First Snowfall,	*Lowell*
Winter,	*Tennyson*
Vision of Sir Launfal,	*Lowell*
December,	*C. P. Cranch*
The Snow Shower,	*Bryant*

For the Children

The Frost,	*H. Gould*
A Story for Willie Winkie, } "Kindergarten Stories and Morning	
The Snowflakes, } Talks,"	*Wiltse*
The Ant and the Grasshopper,	*Æsop*
Bright, Sprite and White,	*Holmes's Third Reader*

STORIES.
The Thrifty Squirrels.

In the hollow oak tree on the lawn a squirrel had made his home. He was such a pretty fellow, with his bright eyes and long, bushy tail. He was prudent, too, as well as pretty. That is, he was very careful about little things, and brought up his family to be the same. His family was Mrs. Squirrel and three little squirrels, and they were all of them just as careful and orderly as could be. There was never so much as a nut end or the rind of an acorn wasted in Mr. Squirrel's house, and one of the very first things he and Mrs. Squirrel taught their children was to lay up a store of food to eat in the winter months. They were nice little things, the little squirrels: bright, good-tempered, and obedient. The eldest, whose name was Brownie, was already able to make an acorn pie, or a nut pudding with chestnut sauce, almost as well as her mother.

On this cold winter day about which I have been telling you, Mr. and Mrs. Squirrel, with Brownie, and the little ones, were sitting at tea in the old hollow tree on the lawn. The afternoon was changing into evening, and the light was nearly gone, when there came a tiny tap at the door. It was a very weak little tap, so low that Mrs. Squirrel was not sure that any one had knocked, and listened until it came again. Then Mr. Squirrel got up and opened the door. At first he saw no one. "Who is there?" he asked, in his pleasant, cheerful voice.

"It is I, Neighbor," said some one outside, sadly. "I am nearly famished with hunger and starved with cold. Will you let me come in for a while and warm myself?"

Mr. Squirrel at once opened the door wide and said: "Walk in, walk in. It is a bitter cold night, to be sure. Walk in and let me shut the door; my tail is nearly frozen just with standing here."

Then there came hopping into the house-place a rabbit. Poor Bunny! how miserable he did look! His fur was all dirty and ragged, and his poor little tail hung down behind instead of standing up nice and stiff, as a good rabbit's tail ought to do. His ears dropped, and his whiskers were broken and limp. He had rheumatism in one hind leg, and his eyes, which should have been as bright as Mr. Squirrel's, were dull and dim. Altogether, he looked as shabby and sad as a bunny could; not in the least like a respectable, well-brought-up rabbit.

Mrs. Squirrel threw up both her front paws in dismay. Mr. Squirrel made haste to put poor Bunny into a chair beside the fire, whilst Brownie brought him her own slice of beech-nut bread. Poor Bunny ate it eagerly, and for a little while all the family of squirrels were too much taken up in attending to his wants to ask any questions. When he was warmed and rested, Mrs. Squirrel sent all her little ones to bed, and she and Mr. Squirrel began to try to find out what had brought their poor neighbor into such a sad plight.

"How could I help it?" said he mournfully. "I did not know that it would be so cold, nor that the snow would be so deep that I should not be able to get a bit of winter cabbage to eat. I am sure I am willing to work; I would take any trouble, but it is not a bit of use. Indeed, neighbor Squirrel, I do not know how you have managed." And he looked enviously round the neat, warm little room.

"It was very simple," said Mr. Squirrel, gravely. "We all helped, and we put away some of everything we found. If we found six nuts we put away three in our storeroom, and nuts and acorns were very plentiful this autumn. So, though the winter is so very hard, we shall have plenty, and plenty for a friend, too, Neighbor, so eat as much as you will, and don't spare the loaf."

It was very kind of Mr. Squirrel, but he could not help poor Bunny much. He had been such an idle, wandering fellow that he could not be content to stay with Mr. and Mrs. Squirrel quietly, and help to do the work of the house, so in a few days he wandered away again.

As he shivered in the cold blasts and tried in vain to satisfy his hunger, he often wished that he had been as prudent and thrifty as the Squirrel family. And the Squirrel family, being as kind-hearted as they were prudent, often thought of the poor Rabbit

POOR BUNNY.

with pity, and wondered how he was getting on; but they never heard of him again.

MARY DENDY.

"*Lesson Stories,*" *The Sunday School Association, London.*

Jack Frost and His Work.

"Ho! ho!" said Jack Frost one cold evening near the end of Autumn, "this is just the kind of night I have been waiting for. The clouds have been thick enough to keep back the heat of the sun, and North Wind has been out all day telling people that I should be around to-night. Sometimes I like to surprise people; but I find that I am not always welcome when I make my visits unexpectedly, so this time I have sent word, and I hope that no one will grumble. It is a fine night for work."

So Jack Frost packed his box and started off. By this time the sun and the clouds were gone, and the stars shone clear and bright in the dark sky. The air was keen and cold but very still, for North Wind had gone to sleep at sunset.

As Jack Frost had thought, people were expecting him that night. The farmer had had the young calves brought in from the pasture where they had been all summer. The barn doors were shut early and all the animals were made comfortable for the night. People took in their plants and gathered the autumn flowers from the gardens. "These are the last for this year," they said; "Jack Frost will destroy everything to-night." Mothers went about to the children's beds, putting extra blankets over them, so that the little ones should be snug and warm and cosy. In fact, owing to Jack Frost's kind warning, most people were ready for him by the time he began his work.

In the box which Jack Frost carried he had paint brushes large and small, and a paint box. He had also some sparkling stuff of a silvery white. This was what he used on the window panes. Some coarser stuff of the same kind was for making the ground white. All his tools were not of this kind, however. Jack Frost makes many things beautiful, but he also destroys. It is part of his work to prepare the earth for winter by pinching the late flowers and nipping the grasses and hardening the ground; so, besides the paints and paint brushes which he had in his box, he had sharp nippers and pincers, and hammers, and such things.

When Jack Frost came to the chestnut trees, he said, "Oh! the nuts are ripe! I must open the burrs so that the squirrels and the children can get these nice nuts." So he stayed among the chestnut trees a long time, prying open the prickly burrs. How pretty the brown nuts looked, packed so snugly in their velvet-lined cases!

Jack Frost traveled fast and far, working all the time. How many burrs he opened, how many panes of glass he decorated, I am sure I cannot tell; but I must tell of one sad thing which he had to do.

Little Alan had a garden of his own. His mamma had told him in the afternoon to take up his plants or Jack Frost would destroy them. Alan had put off doing it as he was busy at play when she told him, and he did not think of it again until it was too late.

When Jack Frost came to the little garden, he felt very sorry. "Oh, dear!" said he. "I wish Alan had taken up these plants! I hate to destroy them, but I cannot leave them here in old Winter's way." So out came the nippers and pincers and some black paint, and soon Alan's garden was a sad sight.

The next morning the ground was all white and sparkling, the trees looked very gay with their red and yellow leaves, and the squirrels were very joyful as they gathered the ripe chestnuts But there was a little boy who felt very unhappy indeed as he saw what Jack Frost had done to his garden. "Next time," said Alan to his mamma, as they were talking about his garden that night, "next time, I will take all my plants into the house as soon as you tell me that Jack Frost is coming."

"Then Jack Frost has made my little boy wiser," said his mamma.

EMILIE POULSSON.

THE FLOWER BASKET
OR LOVING AND GIVING.

TO THE TEACHER:—

The fitness of "The Flower Basket" as a subject for this especial time can easily be demonstrated, though not at first evident. Listen to Frœbel's explanation: "It is to lead the child early to notice tenderly and cherish thoughtfully the all-sided bond that, invisible though it is, can be felt, and is inner and mental—that is to say, the bond whereby humanity's life is bound up together; and the life of a child and of the family afford the first opportunity for doing this."

In the "Mutter and Kose Lieder" this play follows the play of "The Bird's Nest" and might be considered its complement; for while "The Bird's Nest" portrays parental love by a most vivid and attractive imagery, "The Flower Basket" offers the child an outlet for his aroused affection—or, rather, shows him the beauty of expressing his reciprocal love.

Neither flowers nor baskets are the real subject of the play therefore, but loving and giving. Hence nothing is more sweetly suitable for our contemplation while we are busy with the little gifts which should one and all be the signs of love.

From the Essay on Gifts, Ralph Waldo Emerson.

"The only gift is a portion of thyself. Therefore the poet brings his poem; the shepherd, his lamb; the farmer, corn; the miner, a gem; the sailor, coral and shells; the painter, his picture; the girl, a handkerchief of her own sewing."

"I fear to breathe any treason against the majesty of love which is the genius and god of gifts and to whom we must not affect to prescribe. Let him give kingdoms or flower-leaves indifferently."

THE TALK.

(Sing "The Flower Basket," using it just now as a finger play, and repeating it as a circle game later, if you wish. If the children do not know the song, the teacher could sing it for them, the children carefully holding their baskets meantime and rising and stepping forward at the last part of the song, as if offering them to papa and mamma. Lead the children to talk of home and parents and brothers and sisters. Let many of them tell what work their fathers do. Show them that this is to provide home, clothes, food, etc., for the family, and that father does it out of love for his family.

Let them tell of the mother's work. Show that this, too, is done for love.) How many of these children love their papas?—their mammas? How many would like to do something for papa and mamma? What can you do? Can you work as papa does, and earn money to buy bread and meat and shoes and clothes, etc., etc.? Can you make clothes and mend, or cook, or wash and iron, as mamma does? No; little children cannot do such things.

But let me see if I can think of something which little children can do. Can you sing some of the kindergarten songs for papa and mamma? Can you tell some of the stories you have heard here? Can you tell them the story we had last week? (Teacher mentions story by name.) Papa and mamma would be so pleased to hear some of the songs and stories. Baby might like to hear the songs, too—and sometimes you might keep the baby happy by singing to it or playing with it while mamma is busy with her work.

(Children tell other things they can do.) All these things will show love. Sometimes we show love by giving presents. Papa and mamma will be so pleased with the presents the children are making. Be sure and put love in the stitches of your sewing; that is, think about papa and mamma while you work, and try to sew your card or weave your mat as nicely as ever you can. That is what "putting love in" means.

> Little gifts are precious
> If a loving heart
> Help the busy fingers
> As they do their part.

TEACHER'S READING.

The Vision of Sir Launfal, - - - - - - - - - *Lowell*
Gifts - - - - - - - - - - - *R. W. Emerson*
The Miraculous Pitcher, - - - - - - - *N. Hawthorne*
Little Tuk, - - - - - - - - - *Hans Chr. Andersen*

For the Children.

Charlotte and the Ten Dwarfs (" Kindergarten Stories and
 Morning Talks"), - - - - - - - *S. E. Wiltse*

STORIES.

Little Servants.

"Oh, what an untidy room! Skip about, little ones, and set it in order."

"I don't like to tidy rooms," said Elsie, with a pucker on her pretty forehead, as she turned the pieces of her dissected map this way and that.

"I think it must be ever so nice to keep plenty of servants," said Ruth.

"Yes, indeed," said Bessie, "just like Mrs. Marshall."

Elsie brought a pout to her lips to keep company with the pucker in her forehead, and looked as doleful as a little girl whose face seemed made rather for smiles than frowns could look.

"Do you think you would be happier with nothing to do?" asked mamma.

"Yes, I'm sure I should," said Elsie.

"And I," said Ruth.

"But," said Bessie, thoughtfully, "I don't know. Mrs. Marshall never looks half so nice and pleasant as mamma, and she says her servants bother her all the time. Do you think they'd bother you, mamma, if you kept them?"

"I dont't know, dear. I never tried keeping more than one,

except these little bits of ones here," pinching Elsie's cheeks and giving Ruth's head a pat; "and as they are not always very willing little servants, perhaps they bother me."

"It's a shame," said Bessie, running to kiss her mother. "I do love to do things for you, mamma. Hurry, girls; let's see how quick we can be!"

And the little maids flew about until the room was in good order.

"But," said Elsie, as mamma settled herself to some sewing, and the three gathered around her for a talk, "I was reading the other day about the little king of Spain—he's only a baby, you know, mamma, and yet he's a king! And he has ever and ever so many servants—all for just himself."

"I once knew some little girls who kept a great many servants."

"Tell us about them, please, mamma. How old were they?"

"Well, about as old as Elsie and Ruth and Bessie."

"How many did they have?"

"You can count up as I go on. There were two bright-looking ones, always dressed alike, in blue, brown, or gray. Their duty was to keep on the watch for what ought to be done."

"Didn't they ever do anything themselves?"

"Not much but that. It seemed to keep them busy if they attended to their duties; but sometimes they were negligent, and then of course the work of all the other servants was thrown into confusion."

"I'm sure it was little enough to do," said Bessie.

"Then there were two more, whose business it was to listen to what their little mistress's mother or teacher told them, and let her know what it was."

"It seems to me," said Ruth, laughing, "they must have been a lazy set, so many to do so little. Any more, mamma?"

"Two more, always dressed in red, who told what the others heard." "It took a long time to get to it, I think," said Bessie.

"When these had settled upon anything to be done," went on mamma, "there were a pair of lovely little fellows, always wearing dark, stout clothing, who carried the little girls to where their work was to be done."

"Oh, oh!" laughed Elsie, "what a queer set you are telling us of, mamma. Were the little girls lame?"

"I hope they did their work well when they got to it, after all that fuss," said Ruth.

"They surely ought to have done so," mamma said, "for they had no less than ten little servants to do it for them."

"Now, mamma, do tell us what you mean," said Elsie.

"I mean," said mamma, "that little Blue Eyes and Brown Eyes and Gray Eyes ought always to be on the lookout for anything to be done for those whom they love."

"Oh, I see! And ears to listen!" cried Bessie, greatly amused at mamma's fancy.

"And dear little lips," said mamma, kissing the pair which chanced to be nearest, "which can not only talk about duties to be done, but can lighten and brighten every duty for themselves and for others by their smiles and merry chatter."

"And feet to walk and run with," said Bessie.

"And fingers. Dear me, just think of all the servants," said Elsie. "I should think they would quarrel once in a while."

"Yes," said Bessie, "supposing the eyes saw something to do, and the ears heard somebody tell about it, and the feet shouldn't want to go to it, and the hands shouldn't want to do it!"

"That would depend on what kind of little mistress they had," said mamma. "If she wanted to do right, she would be sure to keep all her little servants in good order. And they need a good deal of training."

"Yes, I guess they do," said little Ruth, holding up her chubby hands. "They have to learn to put on a thimble, and to tread a needle, and to sew."

"And to sweep, and dust, and to pick up things," said Bessie.

"And to write, and make figures, and play on the piano."

"And there are things they have to learn not to do," said mamma, with a significant smile; "not to meddle with things that don't belong to them; not to idle when they ought to be busy; not to do carelessly or negligently the work which ought to be done well."

"Oh, dear!" said Bessie, with a little sigh, "so many things to do, and so many things not to do."

"Yes, so many," said mamma. "But if the heart which moves all these little servants is a loving, faithful heart, always striving to do faithfully whatever comes in its way, there need be no fear of its not succeeding."

SYDNEY DAYRE.

The Youth's Instructor.

Extracts from the Dream of Little Christel.

Slowly forth from the village church
    The voice of the choristers hushed overhead—
Came little Christel. She paused in the porch,
    Pondering what the preacher had said.

"'*Even the youngest, humblest child
    Something may do to please the Lord*';
Now, what," thought she, and half sadly smiled,
    "Can I, so little and poor, afford?"

"'*Never, never a day should pass,
    Without some kindness kindly shown,*'"
The preacher said. Then down to the grass
    A skylark dropped, like a brown-winged stone.

"Well, a day is before me now;
    Yet what," thought she, "can I do, if I try?
If an angel of God would show me how!
    But silly am I, and the hours they fly."

Then the lark sprang singing up from the sod,
    And the maiden thought, as he rose to the blue,
"He says he will carry my prayer to God;
    But who would have thought the little lark knew!"

Now she entered the village street,
    With book in hand and face demure,
And soon she came, with sober feet,
    To a crying babe at a cottage door.

It wept at a windmill that would not move,
    It puffed with its round red cheeks in vain,
One sail stuck fast in a puzzling groove,
    And baby's breath could not stir it again.

LITTLE CHRISTEL.

So baby beat the sail and cried,
  While no one came from the cottage door:
But little Christel knelt down by its side,
  And set the windmill going once more.

Then babe was pleased, and the little girl
  Was glad when she heard it laugh and crow;
Thinking, "Happy windmill, that has but to whirl,
  To please the pretty young creature so!"

No thought of herself was in her head,
  As she passed out at the end of the street,
And came to a rose-tree tall and red,
  Drooping and faint with the summer heat.

She ran to a brook that was flowing by,
  She made of her two hands a nice round cup,
And washed the roots of the rose-tree high,
  Till it lifted its languid blossoms up.

"O happy brook!" thought little Christel,
  "You have done some good this summer's day,
You have made the flowers look fresh and well!"
  Then she rose and went on her way.

UNKNOWN.

The "Wake-up" Story.

The sun was up and the breeze was blowing, and the five chicks and four geese and three rabbits and two kitties and one little dog were just as noisy and lively as they knew how to be.

They were all watching for Baby Ray to appear at the window, but he was still fast asleep in his little white bed, while mamma was making ready the things he would need when he should wake up.

First, she went along the orchard path as far as the old wooden pump, and said: "Good Pump, will you give me some nice, clear water for the baby's bath?"

And the pump was willing.

  The good old pump by the orchard path
  Gave nice, clear water for the baby's bath.

Then she went a little farther on the path, and stopped at the wood-pile, and said: "Good Chips, the pump has given me nice, clear water for dear little Ray; will you come and warm the water and cook his food?"

And the chips were willing.

    The good old pump by the orchard path
    Gave nice, clear water for the baby's bath.
    And the clean, white chips from the pile of wood
    Were glad to warm it and to cook his food.

So mamma went on till she came to the barn, and then said: "Good Cow, the pump has given me nice, clear water, and the wood-pile has given me clean, white chips for dear little Ray; will you give me warm, rich milk?"

And the cow was willing.

Then she said to the top-knot hen that was scratching in the straw: "Good Biddy, the pump has given me nice, clear water, and the wood-pile has given me clean, white chips, and the cow has given me warm, rich milk for dear little Ray; will you give me a new laid egg?"

And the hen was willing.

    The good old pump by the orchard path
    Gave nice, clear water for the baby's bath.
    The clean, white chips from the pile of wood
    Were glad to warm it and to cook his food.
    The cow gave milk in the milk-pail bright,
    And the top-knot Biddy an egg new and white.

Then mamma went on till she came to the orchard, and said to a Red June apple tree: "Good Tree, the pump has given me nice, clear water, and the wood-pile has given me, clean, white chips, and the cow has given me warm, rich milk, and the hen has given me a new-laid egg for dear little Ray; will you give me a pretty red apple?"

And the tree was willing.

So mamma took the apple and the egg and the milk and the chips and the water to the house, and there was Baby Ray in his nightgown looking out of the window.

And she kissed him and bathed him and dressed him, and while she brushed and curled his soft, brown hair, she told him the "Wake-Up" story that I am telling you:—

> The good old pump by the orchard path
> Gave nice, clear water for the baby's bath.
> The clean, white chips from the pile of wood
> Were glad to warm it and to cook his food.
> The cow gave milk in the milk-pail bright;
> The top-knot Biddy an egg new and white;
> And the tree gave an apple so round and so red,
> For dear little Ray who was just out of bed.
>
> EUDORA BUMSTEAD.

Youth's Companion.

The "Go-Sleep" Story.

"How can I go to bed," said Penny, the flossy dog, "till I say good night to Baby Ray? He gives me part of his bread and milk, and pats me with his little soft hand. It is bedtime now for dogs and babies. I wonder if he is asleep?"

So he trotted along in his silky white nightgown till he found Baby Ray on the porch in mamma's arms.

And she was telling him the same little story that I am telling you:—

> The Doggie that was given him to keep, keep, keep,
> Went to see if Baby Ray was asleep, sleep, sleep.

"How can we go to bed," said Snowdrop and Thistledown, the youngest children of Tabby, the cat, "till we have once more looked at Baby Ray? He lets us play with his blocks and ball, and laughs when we climb on the table. It is bedtime now for kitties and dogs and babies Perhaps we shall find him asleep." And this is what the kitties heard:—

> One doggie that was given him to keep, keep, keep,
> Two cunning little kitty-cats, creep, creep, creep,
> Went to see if Baby Ray was asleep, sleep, sleep.

"How can we go to bed," said the three little Bunnies, "till we have seen Baby Ray?" Then away they went in their white velvet nightgowns as softly as three flakes of snow. And they, too, when they got as far as the porch, heard Ray's mamma telling the same little story:—

> One doggie that was given him to keep, keep, keep,
> Two cunning little kitty-cats, creep, creep, creep,
> Three pretty little bunnies with a leap, leap, leap,
> Went to see if Baby Ray was asleep, sleep, sleep.

"How can we go to bed," said the four white Geese, "till we know that Baby Ray is all right? He loves to watch us sail on the duck pond, and he brings us corn in his little blue apron. It is bedtime now for geese and rabbits and kitties and dogs and babies, and he really ought to be asleep."

So they waddled away in their white feather nightgowns, around by the porch, where they saw Baby Ray, and heard mamma tell the "Go-Sleep" story:—

> One doggie that was given him to keep, keep, keep,
> Two cunning little kitty-cats, creep, creep, creep,
> Three pretty little bunnies, with a leap, leap, leap,
> Four geese from the duck-pond, deep, deep, deep,
> Went to see if Baby Ray was asleep, sleep, sleep,

"How can we go to bed," said the five white Chicks, "till we have seen Baby Ray once more? He scatters crumbs for us and calls us. Now it is bedtime for chicks and geese and rabbits and kitties and dogs and babies, so little Ray must be asleep."

Then they ran and fluttered in their downy white nightgowns till they came to the porch, where little Ray was just closing his eyes, while mamma told the "Go-Sleep" story:—

> One doggie that was given him to keep, keep, keep,
> Two cunning little kitty-cats, creep, creep, creep,
> Three pretty little bunnies, with a leap, leap, leap,
> Four geese from the duck-pond, deep, deep, deep,
> Five downy little chicks, crying, peep, peep, peep,
> All saw that Baby Ray was asleep, sleep, sleep.

EUDORA BUMSTEAD.

Youth's Companion.

CHRISTMAS.

To the Teacher:—

As soon as we begin learning the Christmas carols and making the Christmas presents, we naturally talk much of the approaching happy season and its origin.

The following talk is not meant, therefore, as a first presentation or a full presentation of the sweet old story, but rather as giving a setting for it.

THE TALK.

(Since the children are by this time in the full delight of their Christmas work, gifts and giving are so continually in their thoughts that the talk will probably direct itself into that channel. Try again to make the impression that gifts are to show love; that although we can show our love constantly by doing loving deeds for father and mother and friends, we also like to show love sometimes by giving presents.)

What are some of the times when people give presents? Christmas, of course; and very often on birthdays. (See whether the children have any idea *why* Christmas should be a time for gifts, before you expain it to them.

Speak of Jesus as a gift of love to the world; and, briefly, of how he "went about doing good," "pleased not himself,"— teaching and living a life of goodness and love. That is why Christmas, his birthday, is the "gladdest of birthdays in all the year.")

Let us think about that long-ago Christmas when Jesus was born. It was Winter, but in a warm country;—a country where figs and dates and oranges, and all such things grow. Joseph and Mary had come a long way to this place. Mary riding on a donkey and Joseph riding by her side. People often use donkeys instead of horses in that land. Mary and Joseph went to an inn.

An inn is a place where travelers can stay to rest and get food. We have inns, too, in these days, and sometimes call them hotels.

So many other people had gone to Bethlehem at this time, that all the houses and hotels were crowded, and Joseph and Mary found that there was no room for them except in the stable. That must have been crowded, too; for, besides the cows and oxen, there must have been a good many horses and donkeys there, belonging to the other travelers. What do you think Joseph and Mary did when they went into the stable? I suppose they fed the donkey and tied him near them for the night, and then made their own beds ready. These beds were only piles of fresh, clean straw, but were soft and comfortable. What could be a cosier cradle for any wee baby than the manger where the Christ Child was laid?

(Describe manger if the children do not already understand about it.)

What do you suppose the donkey or the cows would have thought if they had gone to the manger to eat some of the hay and had seen the dear little new baby lying there? I do not oelieve they would have hurt him, do you?

Try and make a picture in your minds of the stable with the shining star above it; the cattle all about; the manger with the baby in its little nest of hay; Joseph and Mary standing near; and then the shepherds, with their long crooks, going in.

Afterwards, other visitors came,—the wise men who had traveled so far. (Let the children tell of the shepherds' vision and of the wise men and the wondrous star; not only in their own words but by repeating the lines of some of their carols. Nothing vivifies a song or carol more than having the familiar words thus used by the children.)

TEACHER'S READING.

Ben Hur,	*Wallace*
Life of Christ,	*Farrar*
A Christmas Carol,	*Dickens*
A Christmas Hymn,	*Alfred Domett*
Hymn of the Nativity,	*Milton*
End of the Play,	*Thackeray*
Under the Holly-bough,	*Mackay*
Christmas-tide,	*Scott*
The Sketch Book,	*Irving*

For the Children.

Daily Bread,	*Mrs. Gatty*
What the Hollies Did ("Stories for Kindergarten and Home")	*M. L. Van Kirk*
The Night Before Christmas,	*C. C. Moore*
The Fir Tree	*Hans Chr. Andersen*
The Story of Christmas ("The Story Hour"),	*Nora A. Smith*
Old Christmas,	*Mary Howitt*

STORIES.

Christmas in the Barn.

Only two more days and Christmas would be here! It had been snowing hard, and Johnny was standing at the window, looking at the soft, white snow which covered the ground half a foot deep. Presently he heard the noise of wheels coming up the road, and a wagon turned in at the gate and came past the window. Johnny was very curious to know what the wagon could be bringing. He pressed his little nose close to the cold window pane, and, to his great surprise, saw two large Christmas trees. Johnny wondered why there were *two* trees, and turned quickly to run and tell Mamma all about it; but then remembered that Mamma was not at home. She had gone to the city to buy some Christmas presents and would not return until quite late. Johnny began to feel that his toes and fingers had grown quite cold from standing at the window so long; so he drew his own little chair up to the cheerful grate fire and sat there quietly thinking. Pussy, who had been curled up like a little bundle of wool in the very warmest corner, jumped up, and, going to Johnny, rubbed her head against his knee to attract his attention. He patted her gently and began to talk to her about what was in his thoughts.

He had been puzzling over the *two* trees which had come, and at last had made up his mind about them. "I know now, Pussy," said he, "why there are two trees. This morning when I kissed Papa goodbye at the gate he said he was going to buy one for me, and Mamma, who was busy in the house, did not hear him say so; and I am sure she must have bought the other. But what shall we do with two Christmas trees?"

Pussy jumped into his lap and purred and purred. A plan suddenly flashed into Johnny's mind. "Would you like to have one, Pussy?" Pussy purred more loudly and it seemed almost as though she had said yes.

"Oh! I will, I will! if Mamma will let me. I'll have a Christmas tree out in the barn for you, Pussy, and for all the pets; and then you'll all be as happy as I shall be with my tree in the parlor."

By this time it had grown quite late. There was a ring at the door bell; and quick as a flash Johnny ran with a happy, smiling face to meet Papa and Mamma and gave them each a loving kiss. During the evening he told them all that he had done that day and also about the two big trees which the man had brought. It was just as Johnny had thought. Papa and Mamma had each bought one, and as it was so near Christmas they thought they would not send either of them back. Johnny was very glad of this, and told them of the happy plan he had made and asked if he might have the extra tree. Papa and Mamma smiled a little as Johnny explained his plan, but they said he might have the tree, and Johnny went to bed feeling very happy.

That night his papa fastened the tree into a block of wood so that it would stand firmly and then set it in the middle of the barn floor. The next day when Johnny had finished his lessons he went to the kitchen, and asked Annie, the cook, if she would save the bones and potato parings and all other leavings from the day's meals and give them to him the following morning. He also begged her to give him several cupfuls of salt and corn meal, which she did, putting them in paper bags for him. Then she gave him the dishes he asked for,—a few chipped ones not good enough to be used at table—and an old wooden bowl. Annie wanted to know what Johnny intended to do with all these things, but he only said: "Wait until to-morrow, then you shall see." He gathered up all the things which the cook had given him and carried them to the barn, placing them on a shelf in one corner, where he was sure no one would touch them and where they would be all ready for him to use the next morning.

Christmas morning came, and, as soon as he could, Johnny hurried out to the barn, where stood the Christmas tree which he was going to trim for all his pets. The first thing he did was to get a paper bag of oats; this he tied to one of the branches of the tree, for Brownie, the mare. Then he made up several bundles of hay and tied these on the other side of the tree, not quite so high up, where White Face, the cow, could reach them; and on the lowest branches some more hay for Spotty, the calf.

Next Johnny hurried to the kitchen to get the things Annie had promised to save for him. She had plenty to give. With his arms and hands full he went back to the barn. He found three "lovely" bones with plenty of meat on them; these he tied together to another branch of the tree, for Rover, his big black dog. Under the tree he placed the big wooden bowl, and filled it well with potato parings, rice and meat, left from yesterday's dinner; this was the "full and tempting trough" for Piggywig. Near this he placed a bowl of milk for Pussy, on one plate the salt for the pet lamb, and on another the corn meal for the dear little chickens. On the top of the tree he tied a basket of nuts; these were for his pet squirrel; and I had almost forgotten to tell you of the bunch of carrots tied very low down where soft white Bunny could reach them.

When all was done, Johnny stood off a little way to look at this wonderful Christmas tree. Clapping his hands with delight, he ran to call Papa and Mamma and Annie, and they laughed aloud when they saw what he had done. It was the funniest

Christmas tree they had ever seen. They were sure the pets would like the presents Johnny had chosen.

Then there was a busy time in the barn. Papa and Mamma and Annie helped about bringing in the animals, and before long Brownie, White Face, Spotty, Rover, Piggywig, Pussy, Lambkin, the chickens, the squirrel and Bunny the rabbit, had been led each to his own Christmas breakfast on and under the tree. What a funny sight it was to see them all standing around looking happy and contented, eating and drinking with such an appetite!

While watching them Johnny had another thought, and he ran quickly to the house and brought out the new trumpet which Papa had given him for Christmas. By this time the animals had all finished their breakfast, and Johnny gave a little toot on his trumpet as a signal that the tree festival was over. Brownie went, neighing and prancing, to her stall; White Face walked demurely off with a bellow, which Spotty, the calf, running at her heels, tried to imitate; the little lamb skipped bleating away; Piggywig walked off with a grunt; Pussy jumped on the fence with a mew; the squirrel still sat up in the tree cracking her nuts; Bunny hopped to her snug little quarters; while Rover, barking loudly, chased the chickens back to their coop. Such a hubbub of noises! Mamma said it sounded as if they were trying to say: "Merry Christmas to you, Johnny! Merry Christmas to all."

FRANCES ARNSTEIN.

Santa Claus and the Mouse.

One Christmas eve, when Santa Claus
   Came to a certain house,
To fill the children's stockings there,
   He found a little mouse.

"A merry Christmas, little friend,"
   Said Santa, good and kind.
"The same to you, sir," said the mouse;
   "I thought you wouldn't mind

SANTA CLAUS AND THE MOUSE.

"If I should stay awake to-night
   And watch you for a while."
"You're very welcome, little mouse,"
   Said Santa, with a smile.

And then he filled the stockings up
   Before the mouse could wink—
From toe to top, from top to toe,
   There wasn't left a chink.

"Now, they won't hold another thing,"
   Said Santa Claus, with pride.
A twinkle came in mouse's eyes,
   But humbly he replied:

'It's not polite to contradict—
   Your pardon I implore—
But in the fullest stocking there
   I could put one thing more."

"Oh, ho!" laughed Santa, "silly mouse!
   Don't I know how to pack?
By filling stockings all these years,
   I should have learned the knack."

And then he took the stocking down
   From where it hung so high,
And said: "Now put in one thing more;
   I give you leave to try."

The mousie chuckled to himself,
   And then he softly stole
Right to the stocking's crowded toe
   And gnawed a little hole!

"Now, if you please, good Santa Claus,
   I've put in one thing more;
For you will own that little hole
   Was not in there before."

How Santa Claus did laugh and laugh!
   And then he gaily spoke:
Well! you shall have a Christmas cheese
   For that nice little joke."

If you don't think this story true,
   Why! I can show to you
The *very stocking* with the hole
   The little mouse gnawed through.

EMILIE POULSSON.

St. Nicholas.

The Birds' Christmas.
Founded on Fact.

"Chickadee-dee-dee-dee! Chickadee-dee-dee-dee! Chicka—"
"Cheerup, cheerup chee-chee! Cheerup, cheerup chee-chee!"
"Ter-ra-lee, ter-ra-lee, ter-ra-lee!"
"Rap-atap-atap-atap!" went the woodpecker; "Mrs. Chickadee may speak first."
"Friends," began Mrs. Chickadee, "why do you suppose I called you together?"
"Because it's the day before Christmas," twittered Snow Bunting. "And you're going to give a Christmas party," chirped the Robin. "And you want us all to come!" said Downy Woodpecker. "Hurrah! Three cheers for Mrs. Chickadee!"
"Hush!" said Mrs. Chickadee, "And I'll tell you all about it. To-morrow *is* Christmas day, but I don't want to give a party."
"Chee, chee, chee!" cried Robin Rusty-breast; "chee, chee, chee!"
"Just listen to my little plan," said Mrs. Chickadee, "for, indeed, I want you all to help. How many remember Thistle Goldfinch—the happy little fellow who floated over the meadows through the summer and fall?"
"Cheerup chee-chee, cheerup chee-chee, I do," sang the Robin; "how he loved to sway on thistle-tops!" "Yes," said Downy Woodpecker, "and didn't he sing? All about blue skies, and sunshine and happy days, with his 'Swee-e-et-sweet-sweet-sweet-a-twitter-witter-witter-witter-wee-twea!'"
"Ter-ra-lee, ter-ra-lee," said Snow Bunting. "We've all heard of Thistle Goldfinch, but what can he have to do with your Christmas party? He's away down South now, and wouldn't care if you gave a dozen parties."
"Oh, but he isn't; he's right in these very woods!"
"Why, you don't mean—"
"Indeed I do mean it, every single word. Yesterday I was flitting about among the trees, pecking at a dead branch here, and a bit of moss there, and before I knew it I found myself

away over at the other side of the woods! 'Chickadee-dee-dee, chickadee-dee-dee!' I sang, as I turned my bill toward home. Just then I heard the saddest little voice pipe out: * 'Dear-ie me! dear-ie me!' and there on the sunny side of a branch perched a lonesome bit of yellowish down. I went up to see what it was, and found dear little Thistle Goldfinch! He was very glad to see me, and soon told his short story. Through the summer Papa and Mamma Goldfinch and all the brothers and sisters had a fine time, singing together, fluttering over thistle-tops, or floating through the balmy air. But when 'little Jack Frost walked through the trees,' Papa Goldfinch said: 'It is high time we went south!' All were ready but Thistle; he wanted to stay through the winter, and begged so hard that Papa Goldfinch soberly said: 'Try it, my son, but *do* find a warm place to stay in at night.' Then off they flew, and Thistle was alone. For a while he was happy. The sun shone warm through the middle of the day, and there were fields and meadows full of seeds. You all remember how sweetly he sang for us then. But by and by the cold North Wind came whistling through the trees, and chilly Thistle woke up one gray morning to find the air full of whirling snowflakes. He didn't mind the light snows, for golden-rod and some high grasses were too tall to be easily covered, and he got seeds from them. But now that the heavy snows have come, the poor little fellow is almost starved, and if he doesn't have a warm place to sleep in these cold nights, he'll surely die!"

Mrs. Chickadee paused a minute. The birds were so still one could hear the pine trees whisper. Then she went on: "I comforted the poor little fellow as best I could, and showed him where to find a few seeds; then I flew home, for it was bedtime. I tucked my head under my wing to keep it warm, and thought, and thought, and thought; and here's my plan:—

"We Chickadees have a nice warm home here in the spruce trees, with their thick, heavy boughs to shut out the snow and cold. There is plenty of room, so Thistle could sleep here all winter. We would let him perch on a branch, when we Chickadees would nestle around him until he was as warm as in the lovely summer time. These cones are so full of seeds that we

---
* Sung to "do, sol, mi."

could spare him a good many; and I think that you Robins might let him come over to your pines some day and share your seeds. Downy Woodpecker must keep his eyes open as he hammers the trees, and if he spies a supply of seeds he will let us know at once. Snow Bunting is only a visitor, so I don't expect him to help, but I wanted him to hear my plan with the rest of you. Now you *will* try, won't you, *every one?*"

"Cheerup, cheerup, ter-ra-lee! indeed we'll try; let's begin right away! Don't wait until to-morrow; who'll go and find Thistle?"

"I will," chirped Robin Rusty-breast, and off he flew to the place which Mrs. Chickadee had told of, at the other side of the wood. There, sure enough, he found Thistle Goldfinch sighing:
* "Dear-ie me! dear-ie me! The winter is so cold and I'm here all alone!" "Cheerup, chee-chee!" piped the Robin:—

> "Cheerup, cheerup, I'm here!
> I'm here and I mean to stay.
> What if the winter is drear—
> Cheerup, cheerup anyway!"

"But the snow is so deep," said Thistle, and the Robin replied:—

> "Soon the snows 'll be over and gone,
> Run and rippled away;
> What's the use of looking forlorn?
> Cheerup, cheerup, I say!"

Then he told Thistle all their plans, and wasn't Thistle surprised? Why, he just couldn't believe a word of it till they reached Mrs. Chickadee's and she said it was all true. They fed him and warmed him, then settled themselves for a good night's rest.

Christmas morning they were chirping gaily, and Thistle was trying to remember the happy song he sang in the summer time, when there came a whirr of wings as Snow Bunting flew down.

---
* Sung to "do, sol, mi."

"Ter-ra-lee, ter-ra-lee, ter-ra-lee," said he; "can you fly a little way?"

"Oh, yes," replied Thistle. I *think* I could fly a *long* way."

"Come on, then," said Snow Bunting. "Every one who wants a Christmas dinner, follow me!" That was every word he would say, so what could they do but follow?

Soon they came to the edge of the wood, and then to a farmhouse. Snow Bunting flew straight up to the piazza, and there stood a dear little girl in a warm hood and cloak, with a pail of bird-seed on her arm, and a dish of bread crumbs in her hand. As they flew down, she said:—

"And here are some more birdies who have come for a Chrismas dinner. Of course you shall have some, you dear little things!" and she laughed merrily to see them dive for the crumbs.

After they had finished eating, Elsie (that was the little girl's name) said: "Now, little birds, it is going to be a cold winter, you would better come here every day to get your dinner. I'll always be glad to see you."

"Cheerup chee-chee, cheerup chee chee! thank you, thank you," cried the Robins.

"Ter-ra-lee, ter-ra-lee, ter-ra-lee! thank you, thank you!" twittered Snow Bunting.

"Chick-a-dee-dee-dee-dee, chick-a-dee-dee-dee-dee, chick-a-dee-dee-dee-dee-dee! how kind you are!" sang the Chickadees.

And Thistle Goldfinch? Yes, he remembered his summer song, for he sang as they flew away:—

" Swee-e-et - sweet - sweet - sweet-a-twitter-witter - witter-witter-wee-twea!"

F. E. Mann.

NOTES. 1. I have invariably found that after children become well versed in color, they are unwilling to call our American Robin, "Robin *Red* breast," but prefer either "Orange breast" or "Rusty breast."

F. E. M.

2. The Robin's song is from "Bird Talks," by Mrs. A. D. T. Whitney.

3. The fact upon which this story is based,—that is, of the other birds adopting and warming the solitary Thistle Goldfinch,—was observed near

Northampton, Mass., where robins and other migratory birds sometimes spend the winter in the thick pine woods. This should be explained to the children, since it is exceptional.

PICCOLA.

Poor sweet Piccola! Did you hear
What happened to Piccola, children dear?
'Tis seldom fortune such favor grants
As fell to this little maid of France.

'T was Christmas time, and her parents poor
Could hardly drive the wolf from the door,
Striving with poverty's patient pain,
Only to live until summer again.

No gifts for Piccola! sad were they
When dawned the morning of Christmas day;
Their little darling no joy might stir,
Saint Nicholas nothing would bring to her.

But Piccola did not doubt at all,
That something beautiful must befall
Every child upon Christmas day;
And so she slept till the dawn was gray.

And full of faith when at last she woke,
She stole to her shoe as the morning broke;
Such sounds of gladness filled the air
'T was plain Saint Nicholas had been there.

In rushed Piccola sweet, half wild;
Never was seen such a joyful child.
"See what the good saint brought!" she cried,
And mother and father must peep inside.

Now such a story who ever heard?
There was a little shivering bird,
A sparrow that in at the window flew
Had crept into Piccola's wooden shoe!

"How good poor Piccola must have been!"
She cried, as happy as any queen;
While the starving sparrow, she fed and warmed,
She danced with rapture, she was so charmed.

Children, this story I tell to you
Of Piccola sweet and her bird, is true;
In the far-off land of France, they say,
Still do they live to this very day.

CELIA THAXTER.

Houghton, Mifflin & Co.

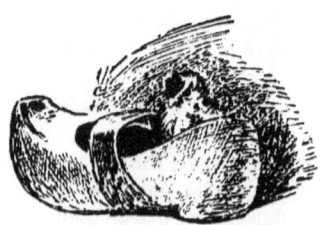

THE NEW YEAR.

To the Teacher:—

Speak of the last time the children and teachers met together. The ten days of vacation have already made this seem long ago to the children; for, as Campbell says:—

" A day to childhood seems a year,
And years like passing ages."

Encourage reminiscences of the Christmas festival. Unless such experiences are recalled again and again they will have no lasting effect upon the child; while the habit of reviewing past delights furnishes the mind with a store of happy memories and tends to develop a permanent joyousness of spirit.

THE TALK.

(Speak of the "new day;" the verse "Good morning to the glad new day" would be appropriate; then of Monday as the beginning of a new week.)

When we were in kindergarten before it was December; now it is January, a new month. So now we have a new day of a new week in a new month. And more than that! This is the beginning of a New Year!

Did any of the children know when it was New Year's Day? That was the very first day of this New Year. Can any one tell the name of the old year? We called it 1900. That means that on Christmas it was 1900 years since Jesus was born. But now another year is beginning, and we call this new year 1901.

A new day comes often, does it not? But it will be many, many days before this new year is ended and another begins.

Let us think about the Old Year and talk about the pleasant things we can remember; Christmas, Thanksgiving, the day we came back to kindergarten, birthdays, etc., etc.

And now this New Year 1901 will bring us just such happy times again. It will bring us a new Spring and a new Summer and a new Autumn and a new Winter. (Remind the children of some of the beauties and pleasures of each season as it is mentioned.) The New Year brings us a great many new days—days to work and play in, and to grow in. Do you know that there are three ways for us to grow? There are—three ways:—to grow big, to grow wise, to grow good. You know what it is to grow big, and to grow good; do you know what it is to grow wise? It is to learn all we can about everything in this beautiful world, and to understand things better, and to know more and more. It is very well to grow big, and better yet to grow wise, but best of all to grow good.

This New Year will give us a great many chances to grow in all these three ways. How many things we have spoken of that the New Year will bring us! No wonder we are glad to have it come! And just as we say "good morning" to each other every day, so we say "Happy New Year" to our friends at the beginning of the New Year.

TEACHER'S READING.

The Death of the Old Year,	- Tennyson
Ring Out, Wild Bells ("In Memoriam"),	- Tennyson
Midnight Mass of the Dying Year,	Longfellow
Pippa Passes,	R. Browning
Next Year,	Nora Perry
The Two Roads,	Jean Paul Richter
* A New Year's Bargain,	- Susan Coolidge
* The Twelve Months,	- Labonlaye

For the Children.

Irene and the Yesterdays,	"St. Nicholas," 1873
The New Year's Cake,	-"St. Nicholas," January, 1893

* Something suitable for re-telling could perhaps be gleaned from these stories.

STORIES.

An All-the-Year-Round Story.

If you had only been in the right place at the right time and had looked in the right direction, you might have seen all this yourself; but since not one of you was anywhere near the Palace of the Future when its great doors swung slowly open, you did not see the people—one, two, three, four, five, six, seven, eight, nine, ten, eleven, twelve of them—as they came out. But they did come, nevertheless, and looked about them in a puzzled way as if they did not know what to do or where to go.

Before they had much time to wonder, however, an old man stepped forward and greeted them heartily.

"Glad to see you, friends! Glad to see you. I knew you would come if I sent for you. One, two, three, four, five, six, seven, eight, nine, ten, eleven, twelve. That's right, you are all here. And now I suppose you would like to know why I sent for you, wouldn't you?"

The twelve friends said they would indeed.

"Look, then," said Father Time, for that was the old man's name, and he opened his big cloak which he had been holding close about him.

The twelve crowded near to see, and what they saw was well worth looking at, for it was a dear, sweet, tiny baby, laughing and cooing and stretching up its pretty hands to be taken.

"There!" said Father Time, "that's my youngest child and his name is 1901. I do not want him to be all alone during his visit upon the earth, and besides there are so many things to be sent with him that he could not possibly carry them all."

"Oh! I'll go with him!" "And I!" "And I!" shouted the twelve in chorus.

"Softly, softly," said Father Time. "You cannot all go at once, but you shall each have your turn. You shall each carry something for little 1901. My storehouse is right here and we can plan now what you shall each take, so as to have no confusion later. Come, January, you must be the first."

"Then I will carry this banner," said January; and he brought a beautiful silken flag from the storehouse. On it was "Happy New Year" in flashing golden letters. January had also a large pack upon his back. This was full of snow, with which he intended to make coasts for the children.

"February!" called Father Time, and a little fellow stepped forward from the group and ran into the storehouse. Presently he came out with a package of valentines in one hand and George Washington's picture in the other. "You have chosen well," said Father Time; "valentines for fun, and George Washington's picture to remind people of that good man."

"March!" "March where?" said February. "March!" said Father Time, a trifle sternly. "Oh! excuse me," said February, skipping off to talk with January.

March was rather a wild looking fellow, and very noisy and blustering; but he showed that he had a good heart and liked to make people happy, for when he came out of the storehouse, behold! he had chosen kites for the children to fly, a big bunch of silvery pussy willows, and a few—a very few—flowers, just one or two daffodils and crocuses and some spears of green grass. "But see," said he, "and listen! This is my greatest treasure and what will be best loved," and there was a warbling bluebird perched upon his hand.

"April!" called Father Time. April danced forth from the waiting group, curtsied to Father Time, and ran to the storehouse. She brought out a lapful of violets, a flock of robins, and a picture of Friedrich Froebel. "Right, right!" said Father Time, nodding approvingly; "that picture belongs to you, and Friedrich Froebel is another good man whom the children should learn about and love. And now, May, my dear, run in and choose your burden." Another pretty maiden answered this call; and a beautiful sight she was, especially after she had been in the storehouse. She was laden with apple blossoms and wreaths, and carried a long pole; and she walked to the sound of music, for velvety bees hummed about her and birds of many kinds filled the air with their warbling.

"Music and dancing and flowers!" said May. "The children shall have a merry time when I am with them."

"Have you forgotten the soldiers?" asked Father Time.

"Oh! no," said May, a tender look upon her bright face. "The most and best of my flowers are for Memorial Day."

May took her place with those who had gone before, and Father Time called June, saying: "Hasten all you can, dear June, for there are still many to follow you."

So June made no delay in choosing, but chose well, nevertheless, for she brought roses—roses in such profusion that one could scarcely see her lovely face peeping out from among the flowery branches. "Strawberries, too, good Father Time," said June; I couldn't resist taking the strawberries, too."

Father Time smiled fondly. People always smile upon June, for every one loves her.

"July!" called Father Time.

Into the storehouse and out again in a thrice bounded a lively boy. "The minute I saw these I knew they were what I wanted," said he, showing Father Time a package of fireworks and waving an American flag.

"Hurrah!" cried Father Time, "that's right! But have you also the book of American history?" "Here it is," said July; "these things were fastened to it, so I brought them all along together."

"Right again," said Father Time. "Flags and fireworks wouldn't be of much account without that. Now, August, see what you would like from the storehouse."

August returned with golden sheaves bound upon his back, and carrying a great flower-decked basket.

"In the basket I have put as much fruit as I can possibly carry," said August; "and yet there is so much left that whoever takes the rest will have a rich load."

"That shall be you, September," said Father Time. "Nothing would suit you better, I am sure, with your warm heart and your strong arms."

September accordingly loaded himself with beautiful fruits—apples, pears, peaches, grapes—not a whit less delicious than those which August had brought.

October was next called. He was a gay, breezy fellow. "Ha,

ha!" he laughed. "Who will be welcomed more than I, with these ripe nuts and these beautiful colored leaves!"

"My faith!" said Father Time. "I fear my storehouse has no more treasures, each one of you has taken so much. Go and look, November."

November came forward rather sadly, but looked cheerful enough after his return from the storehouse. He fairly staggered under the weight of the golden pumpkins and the big fat turkeys which he carried. "What do you say to these?" said he, triumphantly. "But the best thing is in my pocket—a paper which tells that Thanksgiving day belongs to me."

"True enough," assented Father Time. "And now, December," said he, turning to the last waiting figure, "you, I know, will find no warbling birds nor budding flowers; yet are you, above all others, a joy bearer."

December disappeared in the storehouse; but soon stepped out transfigured. No warbling birds had she, indeed, but lacked not for music; for snatches of gladdest carols burst from her lips from time to time. No fresh flowers bloomed for her in beauty and fragrance, but holly berries gleamed brightly among glossy green leaves and a delicious odor came from the little fir tree which she carried over her shoulder. Looking up, one could see a large star which shed its silvery rays upon her.

But the wondrous light that shone all about was not from star or moon or sun, but from a picture in her hand upon which she fixed her gaze. The picture was of a baby lying in a manger.

Father Time's eyes softened as he looked upon it, and his voice was full of love as he said: "Ah! the best of days and the best of gifts is yours, December. Fitting it is that you should be the last and that the love and joy which you bear should be left to the earth as the last memory of 1901. For so it shall be; 1901 shall stay no longer than to your last day. And now, friends all," said Father Time, "will you kindly form in a procession so that each may know certainly when his turn will come?"

The twelve laden friends did as Father time requested and filed slowly past him. He called their names as they went by, that there should be no mistake: (January, February, March, etc.) All were in their right places.

FATHER TIME'S PROCESSION.

"The hour draws near," said Father Time. "Hark!" it is striking! Here, January, take the little New Year in your arms. Farewell!" And lo! at the instant that the clock finished striking the midnight hour, January and 1901 appeared upon the earth.

And all the other friends laden with their beautiful gifts went back into the Palace of the Future and are only awaiting their turn to come and bless the earth with their bounty.

EMILIE POULSSON.

The Fairy's New Year Gift.

Two little boys were at play one day when a fairy suddenly appeared to them and said: "I have been sent to give you a New Year present."

She handed to each child a package, and, at the same instant, was gone.

Carl and Philip opened the packages and found the same thing in each—a beautiful book with white pages, as pure, white, and beautiful as the snow when it first falls.

After a long time, the fairy came again to the boys. "I have brought you each a new book," she said, "and will take back the others to Father Time, who sent them to you."

"May I not keep mine a little longer?" said Philip; "I have hardly thought about it lately. I'd like to paint something on the last page that lies open."

"No," said the fairy, "I must take it just as it is."

"I wish I could look through mine just once!" said Carl. "I have only seen one page at a time; for when a leaf turns over, it sticks fast, and I never can open the book at more than one place."

"You shall look over your book," said the fairy, "and Philip his." And she lit for each of them a little silver lamp, by the light of which they saw the pages as she turned them.

The boys looked in wonder. Could it be that this was the same fair book she had given them a year ago? Where were the pure white pages, as pure, white and beautiful as the snow when it first falls? Here was a page with ugly black blots and scratches upon it; while the very next page had a lovely little picture. Some pages were decorated with gold and silver and gorgeous colors, others with beautiful flowers, and others still with a rainbow of softest, most delicate brightness. Yet even on the most beautiful of the pages there were those ugly blots and scratches.

Carl and Philip looked up at the fairy at last.

"Who did this?" they asked. "Every page was white and fair as we opened to it; yet now there is not a single blank space in the whole book!"

"Shall I explain some of the pictures to you?" said the fairy, smiling at the two little boys. "See, Philip, the spray of roses blossomed on this page when you let the baby have your playthings; and this pretty bird which looks so cunning and as if it were singing with all its might, would never have been on this page if you had not tried to be kind and pleasant the other day instead of quarreling."

"But what makes this blot?" asked Philip.

"That," said the fairy sadly, "that came when you told an untruth one day; and this when you did not mind mamma. All these blots and scratches, that look so ugly both on your book and on Carl's, were made when you were naughty in any way and did not obey your mamma or papa or your teacher. Each pretty thing in your books came on the page when you were good, and each blot when you were naughty."

"Oh! if we could only have the books again!" said Carl and Philip.

"That cannot be," said the fairy. "See! they are marked '1900' and they must now go back into Father Time's bookcase; but I have brought you each a new one. Perhaps you can make these more beautiful than the others."

So saying, she vanished, and the boys were left alone; but each held in his hand a new book open at the first page.

And on the back of this book was "1901." It was the book of the New Year.

EMILIE POULSSON.

THE CAT.

TO THE TEACHER:—

The choice of the cat as the first animal to be studied in the kindergarten scarcely needs justification, since the cat is the most universally familiar of all animals to the children, and therefore one by which we can lead to the notice of others. Being so familiar, most of the items of description should be obtained from the children, the teacher only supplementing their observations.

A live cat is so easily obtainable that one ought certainly to be present when the talk is given.

The other members of the cat family being so far outside the experience of most of the kindergarten children, and there being so much to talk about in this one individual member, I omitted mentioning them, although I should prefer to call attention to them if the children are ready for it; showing them that the lion, the tiger, the leopard, lynx, etc., have the same characteristics which Pussy manifests, that they are light, stealthy, silent of foot, quick of ear and eye, swift to attack,—"carnivorous, beautiful and often terrible."

THE TALK.

(In the New Year's talk the subject of growth was touched upon and might therefore be used as the point of connection between last week's talk and this one.)

We spoke of the New Year bringing us chances to grow. Can the children tell other things that grow besides little boys and girls? (They will probably think first of plants, since their attention has been called to them so often and the fact of a plant's growth is so evident; but a little suggestive questioning will bring animals to mind.)

Which children have pussy cats at home? Who has a big cat? Was it always a big cat? No, it has grown from a wee, baby kitten. What can you tell about the cats you have at home or have seen anywhere? (Question the children separately, appeal to the quiet ones sometimes, as well as receiving what the talkative ones offer.

Pussy has four legs, a long tail,—what kind of a coat? Fur coat of different colors, made of hairs growing very, very close together. How smooth it is when you stroke it! As you pass your hand along her back you can feel something hard, can you not? That is Pussy's backbone. When you look at Pussy's head, what do you see? Eyes, ears, nose, mouth, whiskers.

Can Pussy see well? How does she find the mice in the dark night? (Call attention to the little round, black spots in people's eyes. The children might observe it in each other's eyes.) The little black spot is a window which lets the light in so that we can see. In Pussy's eye the window is of a different shape. (In addition to letting the children observe the cat's eyes, have two pictures drawn on the blackboard representing the cat's eye in daylight and in darkness.) When Pussy is in the dark, the window in her eye stretches out into so much larger a window that she gets light enough to see by, where we could scarcely see at all.

How many ears has Pussy? Are they like our ears? No, they stand up above her head and have pointed tips. Where are Pussy's whiskers? They are feelers to help her in the dark. What has pussy in her cunning little red mouth? Sharp teeth and a tongue. Her tongue is a wonderful thing. Pussy can make it like a spoon when she wants to lap the milk with it. Did you ever notice how she will take up every drop of milk in the saucer? But Pussy's tongue is something else besides a spoon. Haven't you seen her wash herself and make her fur coat all smooth? What does she do it with? This same little red tongue. If you feel of it, you will find it very rough. That is because it is covered with tiny hooks, so small you cannot see them. But there are a great many of them and when Pussy draws her tongue over her fur, these little hooks comb the fur nicely down and make it all clean and smooth. What she cannot reach with her tongue, she does with her paws, first wetting the stiff hairs on the end of them.

Pussy has four feet, you told me. Does she make much noise

when she walks? No, she can go along very, very quietly because she has little cushions on her feet. By and by we will play "Kitty White" and see who can walk as quietly as a real Pussy does.

If you tease Pussy and hurt her, what will she do? Yes, she will scratch you, for she does not like to be hurt.

What does she scratch with? Sharp claws. A little girl who was playing with a cat once said, "Oh! Pussy has pins in her feet."

Cat's paw.
Under side

Showing claws.

Of course it was Pussy's claws that the little girl felt. But if you are always gentle and kind when you play with Pussy she will not scratch you. She will pull her claws in and hide them so that you would never know she had any claws at all.

Did you ever see a mother cat with her little kittens? How she loves them and watches them and teaches them, doesn't she? Before they can walk, the baby kittens get milk from the mother; but they soon learn to drink milk from a saucer. The mother cat washes and combs the fur of her baby kittens, too, with her rough little tongue.

(Speak of the usefulness of the cat in frightening away from our houses the rats and mice which would otherwise be so troublesome. Also speak of the cat's love of home, and affectionate disposition.)

THE CAT.

TEACHER'S READING.

Natural History,	J. G. Wood
Winners in Life's Race (Chap. IX),	Arabella Buckley
An Object of Love,	Mary E. Wilkins
Agrippina,	Agnes Repplier
The Kitten at Play	Wordsworth
The Retired Cat (A Story),	Cowper
The Glove,	R. Browning

For the Children.

Pussy's Class,	Mary Mapes Dodge
Purring when you're pleased,	Mrs. Gatty
Dick Whittington and his Cat,	Old Story
Mrs. Chinchilla ("The Story Hour")	Kate D. Wiggin
Belling the Cat,	Æsop

STORIES.

My Jet.—A True Cat Story

I am afraid Jet was a *little* cross at times; yes, I am sure he was, and I—one of his most intimate friends—ought to know.

It was when I was a little girl, that we had this cat called Jet, a great, shining, black creature. I loved Jet, oh! very much indeed! and I think he liked me a little; but he was never so fond of me as he was of my mother. I liked to hold Jet in my lap, and to smooth his soft fur, but he would soon tire of me and jump down. I never tried to hold him after he was tired, for he had a very bad habit of growling and showing his teeth.

Jet was not at all fond of company either, which troubled me greatly, because I was always pleased to have visitors come to the house. He would run away and hide, and if I tried to coax him out of his hiding place he would growl and put up his back and say: "Scx! scx!"

And if another cat came into our yard—oh! you should have

seen Jet then! He did not wait to put up his back, but, taking one look at the stranger, darted away in full chase after him. All the cats of the neighborhood soon learned that they must never do more than run across our back fence, and the more swiftly they could run across, the better for them.

But, by and by, all this changed. I never understood just how the acquaintance began, but a poor, forlorn old cat, with one ear gone and a part of his tail missing, came to live with Jet. Yes! Jet, who had never allowed another cat within fifty feet of our house, took this friendless stranger under his care, let him share his bread and milk, and even permitted him to sleep in the soft bed which had been made especially for Jet's own use in a box under the back porch. Little by little Jet's nature changed, until he became so gentle that he would lie sleepily on the door-mat and only wink when other cats wished to cross the yard.

I used to think that as the tramp cat and Jet lay together after dinner in the sunshine, old Tramper would chat between naps with his younger friend. He would tell Jet how glad he ought to be that he had always had such a good home, and that he ought to be getting wiser as he grew older; and that wise people do not like to growl and to be cross and quarrelsome. They are cheerful and happy, and like to see others have good times.

I felt sure that Tramper, as I called him, used to talk in this way to Jet, although I never could catch him saying anything; whenever I came near they would both doze or pretend to be fast asleep, or, at any rate, not talk so that I could understand. However that may be, I do know that Jet was better as an old cat than ever he was as a kitten; and that his growing better dated from the time when he was kind to poor, friendless Tramper.

M. V. GILLIN.

A Kitten Rhyme.

See my Kitty,—
Little Dot;—
Very pretty,
Is she not?
Soft and silky

Is her fur;
If you stroke it
   She will purr.
Dot won't hurt you
   With her claws;
Keeps them hidden
   In her paws.
She's all white but
   One wee spot,
That is why her
   Name is Dot.
Often when my
   Grandma knits,
Close beside her
   Kitty sits,
Watching, watching
   Grandma's ball,
Wishing she would
   Let it fall.
When it *does* drop,
   Oh! the fun!
You should see how
   Dot can run!
Dot has never
   Caught a rat;
She's too little
   Yet for that;
She is only
   Good at play
But she'll catch the
   Rats *some* day.

       EMILIE POULSSON.

Spotty's Family.

Once we had a beautiful cat with blue eyes and a coat of soft fur which was entirely white, except for a black tip on the tail and a black spot over each eye. We called her Spotty, and she was a great pet in the household.

When my brother played on the violin in the evening, Spotty, who was always in the parlor at that time, would try to catch the shadow of his bow on the door. Why she could not catch it puzzled her greatly; but, of course, she never did.

At meal-times she was allowed to sit in my brother's lap, but she never lifted her head above the table, even when he was eating fish, of which, you know, cats are very fond.

Spotty had four kittens. One was white, one black, one gray, and one looked just like Spotty. She kept them on a carpet bed under the front doorstep. When Spotty chose this place, she thought it would be very safe and comfortable for her babies, but it did not prove so. One day, before the kittens were old enough to open their eyes, there came a cold rainstorm. Down poured the water through a crack between the doorstep and the house, and poor Spotty found that her babies were getting wet. I suppose she said to herself: "Mew! Mew! What shall I do? It is not good for such little babies to be wet. Let me see— Whitie, I'll put you into this little corner where the rain does not come. Blackie, I'll wrap you in the carpet. Graylie, I can cover you with my body. But what shall I do with my poor little Spotty. I know you are uncomfortable, dear child, but what can I do? Ah! I know! I will call the master; he will take care of my babies!"

I suppose that is what Spotty said to herself; at any rate, as we sat in the parlor we heard a loud mewing. My brother ran out and found Spotty and her family just as I have described them to you, under the doorstep in the wet. He took up the kittens and carried them into the house. Spotty followed, purring loudly and rubbing against his legs, which was her way of saying: "Thank you, master, for saving my babies."

Although poor Spotty's fur was wet through, she paid no attention to herself, but stood and watched while he rubbed the kittens dry, wrapped them up in warm flannel, and laid them by the stove. Then she went to the stove also, and began to lick her fur. Before long, the heat of the fire and the use of her tongue had dried her coat nicely, so that she could lie down beside her babies. They nestled up to her as if they were very glad to have their mother again.

After the storm was over, my brother made another bed for them in a place where the rain could not come, and Spotty had no more trouble in bringing up her family.

JOSEPHINE JARVIS.

Cobden, Ill.

THE HORSE.

To the Teacher:—

A Shetland Pony

We cannot, of course, make anything like an exhaustive study of any subject which we take up. Agassiz's whole lifetime and all his intellectual power were inadequate to the one creature—the fish—to which he devoted them; and the Greek professor who had been absorbed in the study of Greek grammar all his life regretted on his death-bed that he had not confined himself closely to one of the Greek particles!

Hopeless indeed would be our task if the only result aimed at were the actual knowledge which the children could formulate after our talks. But we can hope to increase their interest in the wonders that surround them and to train them to observant habits of mind. So, although we must take all manner of pains to have our knowledge accurate and thorough, in order that whatever impression is made upon the children shall be correct, we must ever remember that our object is to lead to observation, not to formulation.

THE TALK.

(Begin the talk with a few review questions on the cat, so that some of the salient points will be fresh in the children's minds. These points would be that the cat has a backbone, gives milk to its little ones, has four feet, ears that stand up, eyes that can see in the dark and skin covered with hair, and is affectionate and useful.

Having thus established a basis for comparison of the two animals, let some child go to the window and tell what animal he sees. If a dog is spoken of, notice the same points, though not dwelling at length upon this animal.

A horse will doubtless soon be spied from the window. Let

the description be given by different children, each child contributing an item.

As the items are given, lead to comparison, noticing both likenesses and differences.) The horse has four feet. Is that like the cat? like the dog? like a man? like a bird?

When Pussy walks, does she make much noise? Suppose one of those horses out in the street should come into the kindergarten and walk about, could we hear him? What makes the difference? Yes; the horse is so big and heavy, that is one reason; and another reason is that he has iron shoes on his feet instead of just little soft cushions. Those little cushions grow on Pussy's feet; do the iron shoes grow on the horse's feet? Who makes the horse's shoes? If the horse had no shoes on, could he step as softly as Pussy? No; because he is heavier, and because his hoofs are hard and would make a noise. What are his hoofs? (Probably none of the children have seen a horse's foot without a shoe on. If a picture can be obtained, show it while making the explanation.)

Look at the ends of your fingers. What do you see there? Yes, finger-nails. And what does Pussy have on her feet besides the cushions? Yes, sharp claws. Now the horse's hoof is something like our finger-nails and Pussy's claws, only very much larger and thicker and harder and stronger. So, if the horse should walk into the kindergarten, even without his iron shoes on, we could hear him because of his hard hoofs.

What is the shape of the horse's face? Where are the horse's eyes? He can see in front, at the side, and far back at the side; and can see in faintest twilight also, though his eyes are not like Pussy's. Instead of feeling about with whiskers, the horse feels with his lips—can pick up even shortest grass by their help.

What is the horse's tail made of? Is it of any use? Where is his mane? Is that of any use? What does the horse eat? Fresh green grass, hay, oats, bran, etc. Where do they come from? Yes, they grow. Who plants the oats? Who cuts the grass? Does the horse do anything for the farmer? What other work can horses do? Watch the horses in the street and see what you can find out to tell us about them—what color they are, what kind of work they are doing, how they are fastened to the carts and wagons which they draw; perhaps your mamma or papa will tell you a story about a horse.

(Draw the children's attention to the intelligence of the horse by telling how the wild horses go in troops, little colts and weaker ones in the center, and big, strong horses on the outside, the biggest and strongest of all being the leader. Tell how obedient all are to the leader, and how much safer and happier they are because of that obedience.

As regards kind and unkind treatment of horses, something should be said, but our efforts should mainly be directed toward establishing such sympathetic feeling as will effectually dictate kind treatment.

The discomfort of check-reins and blinders, the unwarrantable mutilation of the dock-tail and the cruelty of whipping should be discountenanced, of course; but better than much inveighing against these things, especially with little children, is the relating of stories suggestive of kind deeds.

For instance, tell of a child who prevented an accident by picking up a big piece of paper which was blowing about the streets and frightening the horses; or tell of the little girl who lived on a hilly street and was sorry for the poor horses who slipped so in going up and down, and how she used to go out and sprinkle ashes on the slippery places.)

TEACHER'S READING.

Winners in Life's Race (Chap. X),	*Arabella Buckley*
The Trouble Grandpa Nature had with the Horse,	*Wide Awake, Oct., 1891*
In the Country of the Horses ("Gulliver's Travels"),	*Dean Swift*
Description of Horse,	*Job, xxxix: 19*
The Chimera,	*Hawthorne*
Pegasus in Pound,	*Longfellow*
Pegasus in Harness,	*Schiller*
Muleykeh (Dramatic Idylls. 2nd Series),	*R. Browning*
"How they brought the Good News from Ghent to Aix,"	*R. Browning*
East and West,	*Rudyard Kipling*
John Gilpin,	*Cowper*
Paul Revere,	*Longfellow*
Sheridan's Ride,	*T. Buchanan Read*

For the Children.

Black Beauty,	*Anna Sewell*
Kicking,	*Mrs. Gatty*
The Bell of Atri,	*Longfellow*
At the Back of the North Wind,	*George MacDonald*

STORIES.

A Wise Old Horse.

I will tell you a true story of this horse.* He was the horse of a Mr. Lane; and Mr. Lane, on going home one day, turned the horse into a field to graze.

A few days before this, the horse had been shod, but had been "pinched," as the blacksmiths call it, in the shoeing of one foot; that is, the shoe was so tight as to hurt the foot.

The next morning, after Mr. Lane had turned the horse into the field to graze, he missed him. "What can have become of old Sol?" asked he. The name of the horse was Solomon. He was so named because he was wise.

---

*The animal belonged to the late Mr. J. Lane, of Frescombe, Gloucestershire, England, and the anecdote on which the story is founded is told by the Rev. Thomas Jackson.

When Mr. Lane asked where old Sol was, Tim, the stable-boy, said, "I think some thief must have got him; for I cannot find Sol in the field or in the cow-yard."

"What makes you think that a thief has got him?" said Mr. Lane.

"Well, sir," said Tim, "the gate of the field has been lifted off the hinges, and left on the ground."

"That is no proof that a thief took the horse," said Mr. Lane. "I think that old Sol must have done that himself." I will tell you how we can find out. We will look at the gate; and, if there is a mark of Sol's teeth on it, we shall know he has let himself out."

So they went to the gate, and there, on the top rail, was the mark of a horse's teeth.

"Now, why should old Sol want to get out of this nice field, so full of grass and clover?" thought Mr. Lane.

"Perhaps," said Tim, "the blacksmith can tell us about him."

"I will drive over to the blacksmith's shop, and see," said Mr. Lane.

So Mr. Lane drove over to the blacksmith's shop, which was a mile and a half off, and said to Mr. Clay, the blacksmith, "Have you seen anything of old Sol?"

"Why, to be sure!" said Mr. Clay. "Old Sol came here to-day, and told me I had made a bad job of it in putting the shoe on his right fore-foot."

"What do you mean, Mr. Clay?" said Mr. Lane. "A horse cannot talk."

"Oh, true! he did not say it in words; but he said it by acts as plainly as I can say it. He came to the forge where I stood; and then held up his foot, and looked at me, as if he would like to say, if he could, 'Mr. Clay, you are getting careless in your old age. Look at that shoe. See how it pinches my foot. Is that the way to shoe a decent old horse like me? Now, are not you ashamed of yourself? Ease that shoe at once. Take it off, and put it on in a better way.'"

"Can it be that old Sol said all that by his look?" asked Mr. Lane, laughing.

"All that, and more," said Mr. Clay. "He stood still as a

GOING TO THE BLACKSMITH'S.

post while I took off the shoe. And then I put it on so it might not hurt him. And, when I had done it, he gave a merry neigh, as if to say, 'Thank you, Mr. Clay,' and off he ran. And now, if you will go back to the field, you will find him there eating his breakfast."

So Mr. Lane laughed, and bade Mr. Clay good-morning; and back to the field he drove. And there he found Tim putting up the gate; and there in the field was old Sol eating grass, and as happy as could be.

Was not Sol a wise old horse?

EMILY CARTER.

The Nursery.

Pegasus.

In the land of Lycia, with its fertile grain fields and gardens, there once came a terrible great creature which ruined the crops and laid everything waste before it. The king of the country was in great trouble and knew not what to do. It happened that a young man seeking adventures had just come to the court, and the king bade him make ready to fight the monster. The young man—whose name was Bellerophon—was eager to succeed, but he knew that this was a dangerous undertaking.

One night, as he lay pondering how he should accomplish this great deed and bring safety to the people, he fell asleep and dreamed that Minerva (Athene) the Wise Goddess, came to him and put a golden bridle in his hand. When he arose in the morning, his foot touched something on the floor. He looked down, and there lay the golden bridle of his dream. Minerva, he thought, must have given it to him, and must have meant to show him that she would lend him aid; but what he was to do with a bridle he did not know. He still held it in his hand as he crossed the grass to the spring. The water was bubbling from its source just as usual, but what was the wonderful creature drinking there? Bellerophon stopped, filled with astonishment and delight, and stood gazing at its beauty. It was a horse of snowy whiteness, with great, dazzling white wings; one dainty hoof was in the water and his long mane fell forward as he stooped to drink. The moment he caught sight of Bellerophon he threw up his head with a startled look and seemed on the point of dashing away or of rising into the air on his broad wings.

As Bellerophon took a step forward—the horse eyeing the golden harness in his hand—he hardly dared think he could bridle such a beautiful wild creature. Yet it seemed to him that this must be what Minerva meant him to do. When he made the attempt the horse trembled a little, but did not resist, and even allowed him to vault upon his back. As Bellerophon sat securely in his place and the horse pranced and curvetted over the grass, the two were certainly a fine pair to look upon. Still more so when the horse suddenly spread his wings and the two were seen sailing through the air as easily as an eagle soars over the fields and hills.

Now Bellerophon felt that, with the aid of this wonderful horse, he might hope to conquer the monster. The next day he set out with Pegasus—that was the horse's name—and they did conquer it, so that all the land was free again.

When they came back to the spring where the horse had first appeared, Bellerophon led him to the water and stood watching as Pegasus drank of the cool stream. Bellerophon knew that he must free the horse now, and let him return to his favorite abiding place high upon the mountains. There among the snowy peaks Pegasus loved to dwell, though he came down now and then to some flowery meadow to crop the young grass or to drink of the clear waters of the springs. Bellerophon grieved to lose him, and Pegasus, too, seemed sorry that they must part. After Bellerophon had taken off his bridle the horse whinnied and thrust his nose into Bellerophon's hand, as if to tell him he would come back again. Then with a bound and a rustling of wings the wonderful creature was gone.

Pegasus did come back afterwards to help in other brave deeds, and Bellerophon and the swift-winged horse were always fast friends.

F. H.

The Horse That Fed His Friend.

L. H. sends this true story about a horse :—

There were two horses, one of them blind, belonging to a country doctor out West, who for eighteen years drove them on his rounds of visiting, generally harnessing them together.

One evening, the doctor took out his blind horse alone, and drove him until late. On his return he put the horse into a stall next to that of his mate, there being a tight board partition between them from floor to ceiling. Then he threw some ears of corn into the manger and went in-doors.

By and by, the doctor was startled by curious sounds from the stable, and he took a lantern and went to see what was the matter. As he drew near, he heard the two mates calling and answering each other in cheerful tones; and, when he looked into the stable, there was the blind horse pushing ears of corn to his friend through a big knot-hole in the partition! The two old chums were having a brotherly chat, and enjoying it all the more because they were going halves in something good to eat.

St. Nicholas.

June, 1880.

THE COW.

To the Teacher:—

In taking the cow for our subject, it seems advisable to lay *most* stress upon its products, since they are more familiar to city children than the animal itself. But this has been so admirably, indeed so perfectly, done already in the series of object lessons on the cow in Miss Wiltse's book " Kindergarten Stories and Morning Talks," that a different line is taken here, recurring to the idea presented in " The Baker "—that is, that even our commonest necessities are procured for us by the self-sacrifice and labor of many people.

THE TALK.

(A little guessing play is usually much relished by children, and is also rather quickening to their wits ; so it may well have place occasionally in kindergarten.

Give a few easy objects first, like the piano, the plants, the flag, etc., to get the children started in guessing the object from a brief description; then let them guess the cat and the horse in the same manner.)

And now, says the teacher, I am thinking of another animal. It has a backbone, it has four legs, it gives milk to the little ones. It is like the cat and the horse both, in all those things, isn't it?

It is a large animal, it has hoofs, and it eats grass. Is that like the cat? No. Like the horse? Yes. But it has two horns. Is that like the horse?

It lives in the barn and the farmer takes good care of it, for it is a good, kind creature and very useful.

(Do not prolong the guessing beyond the point of lively interest, nor allow random guesses. If the children do not know by this time that it is the cow you are describing, tell what the animal says or show a picture. The talk should not be given without a good picture or pictures, since the cow is certainly not familiar to all the children.

As the picture is shown, let the children give what descriptive items they can from it. The teacher will probably need to explain and supplement, noting the difference between the cow's noof and the horse's hoof, etc.)

When the cow bites off the grass or hay, she does not really eat it at first, but packs it away in a paunch or bag which she has inside her big body. (This paunch holds from fifteen to eighteen gallons.)

When this big bag is full, the cow lies down; and the grass or hay, or whatever she has eaten, comes up into her mouth, one little ball of it at a time, and then she chews it and really eats it. Sheep, camels and deer also chew the cud.

Who knows what the cow can give us for our breakfast? Yes, indeed! All the nice milk we drink comes from the cow. Perhaps some of you only thought of the milkman bringing the milk, but he has got to get it from the farmer; and who do you suppose gave it to the farmer but the good old cow!

Many people have been working already this morning so that we could have milk for our breakfasts, to drink or to put in tea or coffee.

Somebody had to get up early to milk the cows and get the cans of milk ready for the milkman; and the milkman had to start out early, too, no matter how cold or stormy it was; and the horse had to leave his nice, cosy stable and draw the wagon loaded with the heavy cans of milk all the way to the train or to town for us; and then the mother had to get the breakfast ready.

Which of you children had milk to drink this morning? Let us count how many there are to whom we must say "Thank you" for it.

MILKING.

TEACHER'S READING.

Winners in Life's Race (Chap. X),	*Arabella Buckley*
Our Rural Divinities ("Birds and Poets"),	*John Burroughs*
Rudder Grange,	*Frank R. Stockton*
Europa and the White Bull, } Cadmus and the Stray Cow, } ("The Dragon's Teeth"),	*Hawthorne*
The Drovers, } Among the Hills, }	*Whittier*
High Tide on the Coast of Lincolnshire,	*Jean Ingelow*
Milking,	*Celia Thaxter*
The Milkmaid,	*Henry Austin Dobson*
The Cowboy's Song,	*A. M. Wells*
Farmyard Song,	*J. T. Trowbridge*

For the Children.

Thank you, pretty Cow,	*Jane Taylor*
Stories about the Cow ("Kindergarten Stories and Morning Talks"),	*S. E. Wiltse*

STORIES.

The Story the Milk Told Me.

Did you have a drink of good, sweet milk this morning? Yes! Well, so did I, and let me tell you the story it told me as it stood, white and creamy, in the tall glass.

You see, just as I was lifting it to my lips, it looked so foaming and fresh, that I said, "Good milk, do tell me where you came from before the milkman brought you to me?"

The milk bubbled up a little, then settled down quietly and said, "Yes, I will tell you about it. Before the milkman brought me to you I stood in a bottle with ever so many other bottles, in a dark, cool ice box in the milkman's shop, where we shivered and grew very cold." "Then that is what makes you so cold now, is it?" said I. "Yes," bubbled the milk. "Well, before I lived in the milkman's shop, I was swimming around with ever so much other milk in a very large milk-can, out in the country, waiting to be bottled and carried to the city"—"Oh!" I interrupted, "I didn't know you came from the country. Do you grow on trees or in the ground?" The milk laughed so hard and shook so, that it almost spilled itself over on the tablecloth, and I was afraid it would break the glass. As soon as it could speak again, it said: "Dear me! Didn't you know that before I was put into the milk-can, I came right from the old "bossy cow," who stands in the meadow by the river, chewing her cud? But before that, and before I was white, creamy milk as you see me now, I grew tall and green on the river bank. No wonder you look astonished. Yes, I was grass for the good old cow to eat." "And before you were milk you were grass! How funny! And before that?" "That is too long a story," rippled the milk; "and too difficult for me to tell and for you to understand."

"But where do you go after I drink you?" I asked. "Oh! after you drink me," answered the milk, "I change into rich, red blood, to make your body grow strong and healthy."

"Dear, good milk," said I, as I once more lifted the glass to my lips, "then I won't say good-bye to you, before I drink you but I will thank our Heavenly Father for making you, and thank the good old cow for giving you, and the kind milkman for ringing you to me."

Then I drank the cool, sweet milk, but I remembered its story to tell to you.

GERTRUDE H. NOYES.

The Cow That Lost Her Tail.

There was once a Cow who had the misfortune to lose her tail. History does not tell us the exact manner in which this unhappy event took place. Perhaps some enemy struck the foul blow which deprived the poor animal of this useful ornament. Perhaps some tail disease made amputation necessary. Perhaps the mowers struck the tail off accidentally with their scythes. Perhaps —but there are so many "perhapses" in the world that I will not try to guess any more, but will tell you what I really *do* know about the matter, which was told me by the fillet of veal we had for dinner the other day, which belonged to a Calf who was own son to the very Cow to whom the affair happened. Wise old George Herbert, who, in his day, wrote pretty poetry and invented curious proverbs, had one saying, the truth of which our Cow certainly proved. Said he, in his wisdom; "The Cow never knoweth the value of her tail till she loseth it;" and this was the case with our poor friend. In former days she had thought but little of her tail, and, indeed, had sometimes spoken of it as rather an inconvenience, getting between her legs in an awkward manner, and being of little use at best. But the blessings we think least of in our hours of idle prosperity are really often those the loss of which would be the most serious misfortune which could happen to us. And thus, when the Cow found that her tail was actually gone, she began to miss it greatly, and to regret its loss uncommonly.

In the hot summer days, when the cattle collected around the trees to stand under the welcome shade, the flies came buzzing about as usual, annoying the poor creatures as much as they could. Swish, swish, went the tails of the other cows, brushing off the tiresome insects, and fanning their own poor sides at the same time. But our Cow was a helpless victim to the tormentors, who settled upon her by hundreds at a time, and drove her nearly wild. Then when the animals were tired of standing still, and scampered across the field down to the pond at a fast gallop, with their tails stretched out at full length, our poor Cow galloped too, but she cut the most ridiculous figure without a tail, and felt very small among the well-tailed cows around her. In the pond, too, it was no better; the flies were more troublesome than ever there, and she was obliged to walk in much deeper than she liked, because she could not brush them away for want of a tail.

What made it most trying of all was the scorn and ridicule of the other cows, who would never leave off laughing at her misfortune. Nay, the very calves would not let her alone, and old Jessie, the Donkey, was almost the only one who had a kind word for her; for she herself had been so jeered at and insulted through life that she had learned to have some feeling for other people when they were in the like case.

At first the Cow tried to endure their laughter quietly, and put the matter off with a joke, saying that, "at least no one could now accuse her of being a tale-bearer." But this was foolish, you know, particularly as the words are not spelt the same, which the other cows knew perfectly well, and only "chaffed" her all the more, until her life really became a burden to her.

Under these painful circumstances, she at last determined to seek the assistance of a venerable Farrier who lived near, and who had great experience in all the diseases and afflictions with which mortal cows are surrounded. He was as kind-hearted as he was skillful, and, on the promise of a pint of milk daily for a week, expressed his readiness to provide the Cow with a new tail. The promise was willingly given, and the bargain struck. Before the week was out, a tail, carefully made of thick-plaited straw, was cleverly fastened to the Cow's back, painted the color of a proper tail, and warranted by the Farrier to act in every way like the lost ornament.

Proud and happy at her cure, the Cow returned to her companions, and swished her tail about as merrily as any of them for a couple of days. The other animals, whatever they might have thought, said but little, and were in truth glad enough that a cure had been found which might be required by any one of them at a future time.

Not long, however, did this state of things last. A shower of rain washed off some of the paint, and, as she was lashing her sides near to a thick hedge, her tail caught in a bramble, which tore out several straws when she moved on. After this, every thing she caught in, or touched, damaged the tail more and more —the straw became unplaited, some fell out each time she lashed her sides, and in a very short time she was as tail-less and miserable as ever.

Again she sought the Farrier, and laid her case before him, complaining with a melancholy "moo," that his cure had proved ineffectual. The worthy man expressed his deep regret, but, in consideration of her grief, agreed to furnish another tail at the same price as before. This time it was one which no bramble could tear, for it was made of clay, thoroughly beaten up and hardened, and then twisted into the form of a tail. It was carefully fastened on by the Farrier, painted again as the straw tail had been, and appeared likely to answer in every respect.

The Cow returned again to her friends with joy, and, although she found her new instrument rather awkward at first, was in great hopes that it would be of much service to her. For several days all went well, and she recovered her health and spirits, which had begun to suffer. But one afternoon, while the cattle were out in the meadows, a storm came on, which raged for several hours. The rain came down in torrents, and there was no shelter to be had. Alas for our Cow! The paint of her tail gradually dropped off in large drops, and little by little the hard clay softened with the wet. When she lashed her sides, a long clay mark was left behind, just as if some one had struck her with a muddy whip, and she felt her tail slipping from her, and becoming lighter and smaller at every lash. By the next morning she presented a lamentable appearance, and it was impossible for her to make any use of the stunted and injured bit of tail which was left.

She betook herself at once to her friend the Farrier, who did his best to comfort her, and, after some thought over the matter, agreed to supply her with a third tail, for the gift of a pint of milk every day for a fortnight. This was to be a more expensive tail, and required more care in making, and greater strength in the fastenings. So you will think, when I tell you that it was made of iron, and in fact was very like a pump-handle. It was duly painted and put on, and once more our Cow appeared among her friends with a respectable appendage.

But a new and cruel difficulty now appeared. The weight of the new tail was so great as to cause the Cow serious inconvenience. She did not feel it at first, but, as days wore on, it seemed to drag her backward by its weight, and made it necessary for her to rest frequently and for some time. Then, when she lashed her sides, it struck her such a blow as nearly to break her ribs, and in a short time she found she really had no strength left to lash her sides at all. Day by day she grew weaker and weaker, until at last it was evident that her constitution would break down under the suffering which she had imposed upon herself by the purchase of this iron tail. She therefore went to the Farrier, who was much shocked at her appearance, but at once carefully removed the tail and gave her some strengthening medicine. He then told her that it was plain that a light tail was the only thing for her case, and that, although straw had failed, he thought a hay tail might answer the purpose. He therefore twisted a tail of hay with great care, secured it as firmly as he could, and sent her off without asking for payment.

The change was indeed delightful; she swished the flies away as easily as possible—ran with her tail stretched out as well as the best of them, and speedily recovered her health and spirits. But at the end of a week her dream of happiness suddenly ended in an unexpected manner. She was standing lazily under a tree, close to the wire fence by the road, dreaming of the past and speculating on the future in a sleepy manner, when, a fly having settled on her back, she attempted as usual to brush it off with her tail. Some slight resistance appeared to be offered, as if some one was holding her by the tail, and when it yielded, to her horror the tail fell far short of the fly, and in fact only just touched her side at all. Turning round in the most indignant surprise, she beheld a half-starved Tinkers's Horse, who had been browsing by the roadside, and, seeing what he supposed to be a tempting wisp of hay hanging to a cow within his reach, had quietly put his head over the wire fence and eaten off more than half her tail before she found it out. She moo'd loudly with rage, but could do nothing, and had, moreover, the mortification of seeing the wayfaring beast enjoying his last mouthful with the keenest relish.

Driven to despair by this new misfortune, the poor Cow now applied once more to her friend the Farrier, assuring him that she would do anything in the world to obtain real and lasting relief from her affliction, for she felt that if she could not be re-tailed, she should meet her end before long in tail-less despair.

The man replied that he certainly thought hers a peculiarly hard case, and that luck seemed against her altogether. He thought, however, that if she could go to the expense of a pint of milk daily for a month, he could afford her a remedy with which she would not be disappointed.

The poor Cow eagerly consented to his demand, and he then produced an india-rubber tail, of great strength and beauty. It was at once light enough to enable her to brush off the flies without the least difficulty, pliant enough to be easily moved to and fro at pleasure, and strong enough to resist the assaults of brambles, while it afforded no temptation to the hay-loving horse, and was superior to the effects of the most drenching rain that ever descended upon the earth.

When fairly in possession of this splendid tail, the delight of our old friend knew no bounds. There was no tail like it in the field. She could now run, fling out her tail, and swish her sides to her heart's content. She could brush away flies with the best of them, and apparently there lay before her a long life of uninterrupted happiness. Alas! how sad it is that the bright and beautiful fades so soon from off this earth! The happiest moments of our lives are always the shortest; and the sun of our prosperity only seems to shine for a moment, that we may feel the contrast more bitterly when the clouds of sorrow darken and shut it from our sight. Man's joy is brief; and cows are no better off than men. One short month our Cow wagged her tail in blissful security, and then came a return of trouble.

On one memorable evening, after a day passed in the usual routine of a cow's life, she was duly milked and driven into her happy lodge, where she lay down peacefully to sleep. She dreamed of grassy meadows along the river's side, where the cowslips seemed to flourish and to kiss the streamlet's tide; and she fancied she was wandering about the flowery mead, and stopping here and there upon the clover-grass to feed. She thought of happy days gone by, and joys she used to feel; of calves that she had loved and lost—all long since turned to veal. And she wished that cows did not to men less valuable seem, for calves that they present to them, than for their milk and cream. She slept, I say, so peacefully and dreamt of former joys, and all around were hushed to rest—she never heard a noise; but on she slept, and seemed to feel her milk would never fail, as long as she her treasure kept—that india-rubber tail!

That was the kind of dream our Cow had, full of pleasant things and no thought of coming evil. But towards morning she woke with a start, and looked sharply round, as she heard a pattering of little feet hurrying away over the straw on which she lay.

Milkpails and dairymaids! What on earth was this? More sorrow, more trouble, more misfortune. The thievish, wicked and ravenous rats had been at her tail. They had been sharp enough to discover that it was not real flesh, and, this being the case, that they could freely nibble it without being detected by its sleeping owner. And it must be confessed that the rascals had made the best of their opportunity. It was so gnawed, nibbled, torn, and eaten, that a mere apology for a tail was all that remained. No more peace—no more comfort—no more repose and happiness for the wretched Cow. She bellowed with anguish, rendered worse by the appearance of a venerable Rat, who sat upon the manger hard by, licking his lips, with greedy remembrance of his last bite.

"Oh, you vile robber!" exclaimed the poor Cow; "what have I ever done to *you* that you should treat me thus? Cowardly thieves that you all are, I wish the rat-catchers had the whole lot of ye!"

"Madam," returned the Rat, gravely, "your observations are scarcely polite; but I can make every allowance for your wounded feelings. But let this event teach you to avoid shams. If people *will* wear things which are not their own, sooner or later they are sure to be found out; and whether it be the case of a young lady's back hair or a cow's tail, of course it is not pleasant for deceivers that their deceit should be exposed; this exposure, however, is part of an honest Rat's duty, and I confess I am rejoiced to have been able to assist in detecting an impostor."

So saying, the Rat retired to his own place, leaving the untailed Cow to moo out her grief alone. What could she do now? Where could she go? Her confidence in the Farrier was really shaken, for had he not re-tailed her five times, and each time failed to produce an article that would really last? Straw, clay, iron, hay, and now india rubber, all had come to nought! Was it of any use to try once more, or should she leave off in despair, and make the best of a bad job? In her doubt and difficulty she bethought herself of kind Jessie, the Donkey, and sought her advice.

"Mother Cow," said Jessie, somewhat flattered at the confidence in her judgment which was shown by her neighbor in consulting her, "I am a meek and humble animal, and fear to give advice which may not be agreeable. At the same time, if you value my poor opinion, which is based upon my own experience of the world, it is very much at your service. I, too, have not been without my trials in life. I have constantly been called an ass to my face, and that, too, possibly not without reason. I have been told that I am stupid, when I feel that I am only somewhat less quick than might be in understanding matters of a subtle nature. I have been called idle and lazy when I am really only constitutionally slow; and I have not unfrequently been termed an obstinate brute when I was really only showing that patient resolution which true wisdom dictated. Along with all this abuse, I have had quite my full share of kicks and blows, and may fairly say that my life has had more of the rough than of the smooth in it. I have always found it best to endure patiently and quietly the trials which come upon me, and time has wrought its own cure. My skin is now so tough that I feel but little of the blows given me, and the abuse falls upon my accustomed ears without producing the smallest effect upon my tranquil spirit. Why should not the same line of conduct prove of advantage in *your* case? I think you have perhaps taken some unnecessary trouble, and flurried yourself a good deal too much. Learn to put up with that which cannot be avoided, and you will be a happier Cow, as I am sure that my misfortunes and hardships have made me a more contented Donkey."

The Cow listened with attention to Jessie's remarks, and then told her of the words which had fallen from the Rat, and asked her whether she thought there was anything in them; because, if shams were really as wrong as he had represented, she had certainly not done well in applying to the Farrièr for false tails, and accepting them at his hands.

"Upon that point," replied the Donkey. "I am hardly capable of giving an opinion. Undoubtedly it is better to be always honest and straightforward, and not to pretend to have that which you do not really possess. But you cannot say that a man is wrong to wear a cork leg if he has lost his own limb; and although ladies' hair is a matter quite out of *my* line of business, I don't see any great harm in their using any device to make themselves look as nice as possible. The case of a Cow and her tail is very different. A useful article is lost, and you try to replace it by one as nearly like it as you can get. There is no sham in the matter of which any decent Cow need be ashamed, and the Rat's remarks only sprang from his own evil nature and nasty disposition."

Somewhat reassured by the words of her friend, the Cow thanked her with a grateful bellow, and, after pondering for some time over what she had said, determined to go to the Farrier once more; not to ask for any more tails, but to have the stump of her old tail so treated that she might suffer as little future inconvenience as possible.

She found the good man as kind as usual, and he expressed both surprise and sorrow at the result of his last experiment. He was quite ready to suggest that other tails should be tried, and produced an article manufactured of rope, which he said would be by no means a disagreeable substitute for the lost appendage. But the Cow steadily refused. The words of the Donkey had made a great impression upon her, and she was resolved to endure with patience the affliction with which she had been visited.

Now, in this particular, my children, you will do well to follow the example of our friend the Cow. It is true that Providence has not adorned you with tails, and you are therefore secure from the particular misfortune which befell this worthy animal. But aches and pains are things to which children—and grown-up people, too—are unhappily subject; and when you have these, or any more serious illness, to bear, the great thing is to determine to be patient and gentle, and endure the pain bravely and quietly; by which means, not only does it really become more easy to bear, but your conduct makes those with whom you live love you better, and become more anxious to do all they can to help and comfort you. So it was with our Cow. When she returned to the field with her stump of a tail properly dressed, and made no further pretence of concealing her misfortune, the scorn and laughter of the other animals soon gave way to pity. This pity grew into admiration as they beheld the meek spirit with which the Cow submitted to her affliction, the patience which she displayed under the attacks of the flies, and the ready kindness with which she assisted any other animal to whom her services could be of value.

In fact, she became celebrated among all the animals as one to whom anyone might apply for advice, with the certainty that it would be cheerfully and wisely given. This calm disposition of mind and contented spirit were not without their effect upon her bodily condition. Her milk became so plentiful and so rich that she was soon confessed to be the most valuable Cow upon the whole farm, and the dairymaid could never say enough in her favor, while her owner declared that he would never part with her while she lived.

But her chief reward was yet to come. Standing one day by the wire fence, near the very spot where her hay-tail had been so unceremoniously taken from her, she heard a noise of approaching hoofs upon the road, and up trotted the same half-starved Horse who had inflicted the injury upon her. Accosting her with his politest neigh, he told her that he had heard of her good deeds and kindly disposition from many animals, and had often regretted the ill deed towards her of which he had been guilty.

"I do not know, madam," he continued, "how far I may be able to make any atonement for my crime, but in the course of my rambles, I have met a venerable Giraffe, attached to a traveling circus, who having long studied the subject of tails, told me that he was possessed of an ointment which had performed some most remarkable cures in cases which had been previously deemed hopeless. After much earnest solicitation, I obtained from him a pot of this priceless medicine, which I respectfully offer for your acceptance."

The Cow was much touched by this act of kindness and generosity on the part of the Tinker's Horse, and, though she had but little faith in the ointment, and felt it but too probable that the Giraffe might turn out to be one of those quack doctors who only deceive people and injure their constitutions by the pretended remedies which they sell, yet she could do no less than accept the gift so freely offered, and promised the good Horse that she would certainly try it.

The some evening, therefore, she got Jessie, the Donkey, to rub a little of the ointment upon her stump, and repeated the operation three times a week, according to the directions on the ointment pot.

Extraordinary to relate, at the end of the first week a change really appeared in the stump. Hair came upon it, and Jessie said she could almost fancy that it was a trifle longer. A fortnight passed, and doubt changed to certainty. Yes! the Cow's tail was undoubtedly growing!

In her delight, the honest creature was for hurrying off to show the Farrier, but gave up the idea at the advice of the Donkey, who reminded her that, as a regular doctor, he was quite certain to be jealous of the Giraffe as a mere quack, and that mischief might possibly follow. Besides, she was going on well, and had better let well alone.

Accordingly, our Cow staid quietly at home, and continued to use the ointment until the pot was empty. It had, however, lasted her for two months, at the end of which time her tail had grown to more than half its original length; and, having got a start, I am glad to say that it persevered in growing, until, in another couple of months' time, she had as good and serviceable a tail as any of her neighbors!

Her past sorrows were now all forgotten. Kind words and congratulations were poured in upon her from every quarter. Her master wondered at the change for the better in her appearance, and the dairymaid was delighted at the good fortune which had befallen her favorite Cow. She herself was most thankful for the blessing which she now enjoyed, and always felt that it was owing to the patience with which she had borne her troubles, and the kindness which she had shown to all around her—which is a thing that, as in this very case, alway brings its own reward.

So she lived on, a happy, prosperous, and contented Cow all the days of her life. And what do you think the Farrier said when he came to hear of it? Why, he declared that the Giraffe's ointment was all nonsense—it was his own dressing of the stump once which had wrought the cure, and that those quacks were always trying to claim credit for cures which the regular doctors had really made. But if the Farrier knew he could make the Cow's tail grow all right again, why did he bother her at first with all those false tails?

E. H. KNATCHBULL-HUGESSEN.

Puss-Cat-Mew Stories for my Children Harper Brothers.

Lord Cornwallis's Knee-Buckles.

Have you ever heard about the Revolutionary War? It was fought between the British and the Americans more than a hundred years ago. I will tell you a true story of a little girl who lived at the time.

Her name was Anne Randolph, and she lived on a farm not far from Philadelphia. Her father and her two brothers had joined the American army. So Anne and her mother were left alone to take care of the farm.

Two years before this time Anne's father had given her a beautiful calf, as a pet. The two had become great friends. The young cow knew her little mistress, and always came to be stroked when Anne went into the field.

At one time during the war the English army was in Philadelphia.

One day the soldiers came to the farm of Mr. Randolph, and seized Anne's pet cow. They tied a rope to her horns and drove her away. Anne begged for her pet, and was in great grief, but her words had no effect.

It did not take long for Anne to think what she could do. She ran to the stable and saddled her pony, and then rode at full speed to see Lord Cornwallis, the general of the English army. It was a brave thing for a little girl only twelve years of age to do.

A soldier with his gun was marching back and forth in front of the place where the general was.

"What do you want?" he asked Anne, as she galloped up.

"I wish to see Lord Cornwallis," she said.

"What is your business with him?" said the soldier.

"I must see him; let me pass," replied the girl.

The soldier let her pass, thinking, no doubt, she had very important news to tell.

Lord Cornwallis and some of his friends were at dinner when little Anne rushed into the room.

"What do you want, my child?" said the general.

"I want my cow, sir. Your soldiers have taken her away, and I have come to get her. Oh! please, sir, you must let me have her."

"And who are you, my little girl?" said the general, kindly.

"I am Anne Randolph, and I live three miles from here with my mother. Have you seen my cow, sir?" "Oh, sir," she continued, "I raised my cow myself. She has always been mine. She can't belong to you. I must have her. I would never steal your cow, sir," she said, proudly.

The general rose. "Come here, my child. I promise you that your cow shall be safe in your barn to-morrow; and here, take these," he said, unfastening a pair of silver knee-buckles. "Keep them to remember me by, and if the soldiers trouble your cow again, come to me at once."

The general kept his promise, and the next morning Anne's cow was once more safely housed in her own snug stable.

The buckles were kept, and are kept to this very day. One of Anne's grandchildren has them.

—*Holmes' New Third Reader.*
University Publishing Co., New York.

THE DOG.

To the Teacher:—

The preceding talks upon animals have indicated sufficiently a way of dealing with such subjects. Therefore, instead of a talk upon "The Dog," this composition, written by Helen Keller, is offered as containing the material from which the teacher can take what is suitable for her children.

Most people will have read of this wonderful little girl, who, though blind and deaf and formerly dumb, has acquired such a command of language and such a fund of information, and who has such a lovely character.

The stories and this composition are exactly as Helen wrote them, save for the omission of a few sentences. Everything of hers which has been used in this book was written by Helen when she was about ten years old and had been under instruction about three and a half years.   E. P.

THE TALK.
The Dog.

Come here, Lioness, I have many strange things to tell you about yourself. You may not believe it all, but it is true, and you must be still, like a good dog, and listen to what I have to say.

Of course you know that you belong to the animal kingdom. You never could have thought you were a plant or a mineral, and everything else in the world belongs to the animal kingdom. You have a backbone, and that is why you are called a vertebrate; and when you have some cunning little puppies, you will feed them with milk, as other mammals do, and that is why the wise men put you in the class Mammalia. Then, Lioness, you know perfectly well that you like raw meat better than anything else; and animals that eat raw meat are canivorous.

How many feet have you? Can't you count four? See, here are your two fore paws, and there are your two hind legs; and animals which have four feet are quadrupeds.

Your legs are not as slender as Guy's, but they are very muscular. You are covered with pretty, soft, brown hair. It is straight, but generally dogs wear curled coats. Your chest is broad and deep, so that you can take a good breath when you wish to run swiftly. Your head is pointed, but not nearly so much so as Spoke's. Your mouth is filled with powerful teeth, similar in shape to the cat's teeth. You must not pull away your head so, for it is true. You are like Pussy in many things. Your tongue is soft, and you use it to lap up liquids. You never perspire through your skin as other animals do. When your body is heated, the moisture passes off from your tongue. That is why you always run with your tongue hanging out of your mouth. The under parts of your feet are padded, like the cat's. There are five toes on your fore feet, and five on your hind feet. The two middle ones are longest and equal. The fifth toes of your hind feet never touch the ground. Each toe has a strong, blunt claw, which is not retractile. Hence you cannot walk as noiselessly as Kitty. Your claws are better fitted for digging and holding.

Your sense of sight, hearing and smell are very perfect, but your sense of taste is not well developed. If you are hungry, you will eat things which are not good at all. You can live a long time without food or drink. You have relations in all countries. Wherever there is a man, the dog is his best friend. You love people much better than the place where you live; but I am afraid, dear, you dislike cats. You turn round many times before you lie down. Can you tell me why? You prick up your ears, and bark at the least noise; and I am sure there never was such a brave and faithful dog as you are, my own Lioness.

HELEN KELLER.

TEACHER'S READING.

Origin of Species,	*Darwin*
Natural History,	*J. G. Wood*
Rab and his Friends,	*John Brown, M. D.*
A Dog of Flanders,	*Ouida*
To Flush, my Dog,	*Mrs. Browning*
Lewellyn and his Dog,	*R. Southey*
Scragg's Mission,	*C. E. Bowen*
Tray,	*R. Browning*
Song, "Old Dog Tray,"	
Elegy on a Mad Dog,	*Goldsmith*
Dog Stories,	"*St. Nicholas,*" November, 1886, March, 1887
Famous Pets, ("Wide Awake," December, 1886),	*Eleanor Lewis*
The Dog and the Water Lily, }	
On a Spaniel called Beau, }	*Cowper*
Beau's Reply, }	

For the Children.

Brave Bobby, - - - - - - - *Monroe's Third Reader.*

STORIES.

How Frisk Came Home.

One of my friends had more dogs than she knew what to do with; so she thought, "I will give one of my dogs to my aunt in Troy, for I think she will like to have such a nice black-and-white dog as Frisk."

So Frisk went to his new home, twenty miles off.

But Frisk did not like his new home so well as his old one. In his old home he was a great pet; but in his new home, no one cared much for Frisk; and they put a chain on his neck, and tied him up in the yard.

So Frisk sat in the yard, and tried to get rid of his chain. But this he could not do. Then he was quite sad; and he thought, "Oh! if I could but get back to my old home—if I could but get back to my old friends once more!"

But Frisk did not know the way back to his old home; for, when they sent him to his new home, they had put him in a bag, and they had tied up the top of the bag, so that Frisk might not see the way they took him. So Frisk was sad because he was tied by a chain, and because he did not know the way back to his old home.

But it is said, "Where there is a will, there is a way;" and so Frisk found it, as you shall learn.

One day, when the man took Frisk out in the road for a run, Frisk thought to himself, "This man does not like me much, for he will chain me up if I let him take me back to my new home. So I will take a run all by myself, and not with the man."

And then Frisk ran under a bush, and sat there till the man was far off; and when the man turned round and did not see Frisk at his heels, the man called out, "Frisk! Frisk! Here, sir, here! Good dog! Here, Frisk! Frisk! Frisk!"

"No; I will not come; I will stay here and hide," thought Frisk. "You may call me *good dog*, but I will not come. I try to be a good dog, and yet you chain me up."

Then the man thought he should find Frisk at home; but, when the man got home, no Frisk was to be seen. The night came, and still no Frisk was to be seen.

"I think Frisk must be dead," said the man.

"But was Frisk dead?"

Wait, and you shall hear. A whole week went by, and nothing was seen or heard of poor Frisk.

But one day when my friend, with whom Frisk had first lived, went out with her children, Mary and Edgar, to walk, they saw, a short way from the house, a poor, thin, black and white dog by the roadside.

He was quite lame, for his feet had been cut with sharp stones, and his hair was red with blood.

Then all at once Edgar cried out: "O, mother! look! look! See if that is not our own poor Frisk come back to his old home!"

"So it is our own poor Frisk," said my friend. "But how

could he have found his way back twenty miles, all the way from Troy to this place? For he was tied up in a bag when we sent him off. Poor Frisk! How thin and ill you look!"

Then Edgar went up to Frisk, and the poor dog did not well know what to do, so glad was he to see the little boy. And my friend went up, and Mary went up, and they all patted Frisk on the head.

Then they took Frisk home, and gave him nice milk and good meat, for he had not had food for days. He was glad to be fed, but he was still more glad to be in his old home, and to see my friend and her children once more.

—*Nursery Stories.*

Cleverness of a Sheep Dog.

Some years ago, there was a terrific snowstorm in Scotland. The snow lay in great drifts many feet deep.

The farmers were very anxious about their sheep, for there were hundreds of them unsheltered on the hills at the time. In one farm, no fewer than three hundred were missing, and the farmer with his men and a faithful sheep dog, named Rough, started to search for them.

When they reached the fields, nothing was to be seen but great masses and drifts of snow, several feet thick, under which the poor sheep were buried. The men tried to penetrate the snow in order to get at the missing animals; but their labor was almost in vain, for it was only by the merest chance that they came across a sheep.

The snow was still falling fast when Rough came to the rescue. He understood what was to be done, and, running quickly over the snow, with short, sharp barks, he dug with his paws little holes in various places.

The men went to work beneath these marks, and under each they found a sheep! Thus they worked hard all night, Rough showing where the sheep were buried and the men digging them out, and most of the sheep were saved.

FIVE DOGS.

The farmer was very thankful to his clever dog and told his friends that had it not been for Rough he would have lost every one of his sheep that night. As it was, they had suffered but little, and, with careful attention, soon recovered.

—*Little Folks.*

Cassell & Co.

The Dog and the Kitten.

A schoolmaster had a small dog which became much attached to a kitten. They were in the habit of associating together before the kitchen fire, sometimes sleeping and sometimes playing. One day they were enjoying a comfortable nap, when the kettle boiled over and scalded the dog, who ran away howling piteously. He had not gone very far, however, before he recollected his companion; he returned immediately, took up the kitten in his mouth, and carried it to a place of safety.

—*Selected.*

A True Story of a Dog.

The following anecdote, which is perfectly well known in the town in which the circumstances occurred, places the intelligence, kind feeling, and noble disposition of the dog in a strong light, and is quite equal to what has been recorded of the elephant under nearly similar circumstances. A grocer in Worcester, England, had a powerful Newfoundland dog, which was reposing on the step of his door, when a sort of brewer's sledge was going rapidly down the hill leading to the bridge. Just as the sledge was passing the house, a little boy in crossing the street fell down in the way of the sledge, and would have been killed, had not the dog seen the danger, and, rushing forward, seized the child in his mouth just in time to save his life, and deposited him on the footway uninjured.

—*Selected.*

THE COBBLER.

To the Teacher:

"Carlyle used to rhapsodize about the importance of realizing the wonder that surrounds our daily life, and he himself, if he were going to portray an object, inveterately sought a point of view from which he could contemplate it in a kind of surprise."

This is a wise course for us to pursue when we feel ourselves in danger of regarding anything as commonplace or uninteresting; though it seems to me that kindergartners or any others who live close to child life catch flashes of the "wonderlight" that invests all things for these new denizens of our familiar world, and thus often discover beauty and marvel unnoticed before.

Beauty and marvel are high words to apply to so common a thing as a shoe, but study its whole history for your children's sake and then *with* your children, and you will not reject marvel, at least.

The process which converts the animal skin into leather is long and varied. I have only copied one little note referring to the tanning proper; that is, the long soaking in a solution of oak bark and water, made stronger from day to day.

"The change in the nature of the skin is brought about by the action of the *tannin* of the oak bark on the gelatine of the skin, and so causing all traces of the animal substance to disappear. In proportion as this change is thoroughly or only partially effected, is the quality of the leather."

THE TALK.

(In an old reading book there was a story of a little boy whose clothes suddenly began talking to him and relating in turn their several histories.

His jacket announced that it had once been white wool on a sheep's back; the brass buttons told of dark mines and hot furnace fires, and his boots added their tale of wonder.

Some such story as this would make an interesting beginning

to the talk upon the shoemaker. For use throughout the talk have a shoe, some bits of leather,—sole leather and the thinner kinds for the uppers,—as well as a picture of the cow.)

Don't you think it would be very funny if your clothes should begin to talk to you? What did the little boy's jacket say? If Leo's jacket spoke would it say it came from the sheep's back, too? And Amy's dress? Yes. But Mary's apron would tell a different story. That feels smooth when we touch it, but Leo's jacket and Amy's dress have a rough, woolly feeling like the worsted balls and the worsted we sew with, so we know that they are made from the wool the sheep gave us.

How would you like to have this shoe tell you its story? Let us listen!

No, it does not say a word, so I shall have to speak for it.

First I will show you a picture of an old friend, a good, useful animal.

What does the cow give us? (Children name such products as they became familiar with through the lesson on the cow.

Teacher then shows them the sole of the shoe and the piece of sole leather.) Does this leather look like the skin of the cow? No; the hair had to be all taken off and the skin had to be cleaned; then it had to be soaked—sometimes a month, sometimes a whole year—and then dried before it was like this. Still, it *is* a piece of the cow's skin, so we must thank the cow for the good thick leather for the soles of our boots.

But if Rosie's shoe or Tommy's shoe were talking, it would say: "I am not all made of the thick cow-skin." And we can see how much thinner the upper part is than the sole, can we not? (Let the children compare the thinner pieces of leather with their own shoes.) Men have boots of cowhide, but it is very thick and stiff. This thinner leather is better for ours, and what do you suppose it is made of? Some of calfskin, some of goatskin; and this very soft, thin leather, of the skin of a kid or young goat. So we must thank these animals, as well as the cow, for the leather out of which our boots and shoes are made, must we not?

Do you think there is anyone else to thank? Some one had to make the leather into shoes; who was that?

(Recite the words of "The Cobbler," explaining the use of the awl, the last, the waxed ends, pegs, lapstone, hammer, etc. Have the children recall the other workers they have learned of or noticed.)
Suppose no one worked, what would happen?

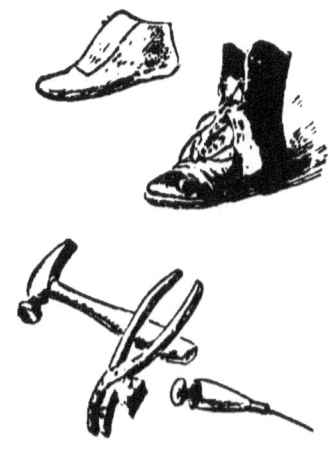

TEACHER'S READING.

Sir Gibbie,	*George MacDonald*
Only an Incident ("The New England Magazine," December, 1891),	*Herbert D. Ward*
The Goloshes of Fortune, The Red Shoes,	*Hans Christian Andersen*
Blessed be Drudgery,	*W. C. Gannett*
Hannah Binding Shoes,	*Lucy Larcom*
Baby's Shoes,	*W. C. Bennett*
The Shoemakers, Cobbler Keezar's Vision,	*Whittier*
Urania. A Rhymed Lesson,	*O. W. Holmes*
Much Coin, Much Care,	*Mrs. Jameson*

For the Children.

Rosemond and the Purple Jar,	*Edgeworth*
The Elves and the Shoemaker,	*Folk Story*
Gutta Percha Willie,	*George MacDonald*
Leather ("Kindergarten Stories and Morning Talks"),	*S. E. Wiltse*

STORIES.
Goody Two Shoes.

A queer name for a little girl, to be sure, but it was no wonder that people called her "Goody Two Shoes," as you shall soon hear.

Her real name was Margery, and her brother's name was Tommy; and the two poor little things had no kind father to work and earn money to buy food and clothes for them, and no mother "good and dear" to take care of them. So they wandered about, always together, hand in hand, poor and ragged and lonely, and often tired and hungry.

The people in the village used to give them something to eat, and the children often found berries in the woods and along the roadside. Every night, when the sun set and it began to grow dark, Tommy and Margery would walk up to some farmhouse and say to the farmer or his wife: "If you please, may we sleep in your barn to-night?"

"Yes, indeed, and very welcome," the farmer would say; and then the two children would run to the barn and make themselves a cosy, warm nest in the hay and be as happy as two little birds.

But there are so many kind people in the world that children are not long left to wander about without a home, as Tommy and Margery had been doing; and it happened that a kind gentleman who saw them trotting about together one day felt very sorry for them.

He saw Margery's fat little feet all scratched with walking barefoot over stones and stubble. "I can cure that," he said to himself; and he took the children to the cobbler's and said: "Good Mr. Cobbler, here is work for you. Will you do it?"

"That I will, and gladly," answered the cobbler. So he measured Margery's foot, that he might know just how large to make the shoes, and set to work immediately.

He cut two pieces of leather from a large, thick piece which he had, and shaped them for the soles. And he cut the uppers

THE COBBLER.

from the thin leather; and busy enough he was then, boring holes with his "nice little awl," and "puttting his waxed ends through and through" as he stitched away, sewing the leather together for Margery's shoes. But while the cobbler was working away, the kind gentleman who had told him to make the shoes had been making some more kind plans.

"Tommy," said he, "I will take you with me when I go back to my ship, and you shall learn to be a sailor;" and good Mrs. Smith said: "Surely, then, little Margery shall live with me."

So it was settled; the only sad thing being that Tommy and Margery had to be separated. They cried and kissed each other many times when the day came for Tommy to go away. After he had gone, little Margery went one day and looked in at the cobbler's window.

There he sat with a big flat stone on his lap and a hammer in his hand, and what was he doing but rap-tap-tapping away, putting the pegs into Margery's shoes and fastening the uppers and soles together! You may be sure it was not long after that before the shoes were finished: and a good thing it was, too, for they say that poor little Margery was so very lonely without her brother, that she might have cried herself sick but for the new shoes that were brought home to her.

Dear me! if you could but have seen how pleased she was! She had had to go barefoot a long time, you must remember, and her little feet had often been cold and scratched and hurt. Besides, the new shoes were so shiny and black, and creaked a little when Margery walked. Yes, indeed, it was delightful altogether.

Margery showed them to Mrs. Smith as soon as ever the cobbler had put them on for her.

"Two shoes, ma'am! Two snoes!" said the happy little creature over and over again. I suppose she could scarcely remember having had two shoes before, because she had been barefoot so long; and before that she had gone about with only one shoe on for a long time! The other shoe had been lost when she and Tommy first began their wanderings.

At any rate, little Margery seemed overjoyed at having two new shoes at once, and ran about first to one friend in the village and then to another, always putting her feet out and saying: "Two shoes! See, two shoes!"

Everybody was glad to see the little girl so joyful, and they used to smile at one another in a happy way and say: "Have you seen little Two Shoes?" or, "There goes Goody Two Shoes, bless her heart!" till finally people scarcely ever remembered to call her Margery.

So now I have told you, as I said I would, how a little girl came to have such a queer name as "Goody Two Shoes," and, if you like, you shall hear more about her another time, for she was a little dear and no mistake, and did many things well worth your hearing about.

Retold by EMILIE POULSSON.

Seeing Shoes Made.

Now and then I take the children of my kindergarten to see the actual doing of work which we represent in our play.

One day we went to see shoes made. There were several people working in a large room and each one was doing something different. One man was cutting out the soles of shoes; another the uppers, as they call the leather which covers the upper part of the foot. As soon as these were cut they were put into water to soak, so as to soften the leather.

Another man was fastening an inner sole to a last, or wooden foot, by means of pegs which he was driving in with his shoemaker's hammer. This hammer has one end "like our roller" (the cylinder of the second gift), as the children said, "only the edge is rounded."

"Why do you have a rounded edge to your hammer?" asked Jack of the man.

"If it were not rounded it might damage the leather, and even make holes in it when I hammer hard," said the man.

"You *pound* with the roller end of the hammer," said Nellie, "but what do you do with the *flat* end?"

"Look and see," said the man.

"Oh! you rub the leather with that, don't you? Why?"

"To make it softer. If we did not soften the leather it would hurt people's feet."

"What do you do next?" asked Mary.

"That is all *I* do; but if you will go over there (pointing to another part of the room) you will see what is done next."

So we all went where the man had pointed, and saw another man stretching the uppers over a last and trimming them until they fitted exactly When this was done he handed the uppers to a girl who sewed them together with a sewing machine. Then they were lined, and the stiffening was put into the heel. Then a man stretched the uppers over a last again, and fastened them to the inner sole which had been nailed upon it; after which the outer sole was laid on. The next thing that was done amused the children greatly. The man filled his mouth with wooden pegs! Then, picking up his hammer, he seized a peg from his mouth, placed it quickly where the sole joined the upper, and drove it swiftly in with his hammer; took another peg and drove that in in the same way; then another and another, as fast as he could make his hands go.

"We should have to play 'cobbler' a long time before we could make our fingers fly like that!" said one of the children.

Then we went to examine the sewing machines by which the shoes were bound, and also the grummet machine which puts in the grummets, (those rings through which the shoestrings are laced). The children thought the grummet machine looked somewhat like the machinery of the oil mill in Froebel's "Mother Play Book."

Some of the shoes made at this factory were buttoned instead of laced. The buttonholes are made in that extra piece which folds over on one side, then the piece is stitched on, and the buttons sewed in place.

There were several other things done before the shoes were ready for sale, but they cannot all be talked of now. When we went back to the kindergarten we had a fine time playing "Cobbler," which, at the children's request, was followed by the "Grummet Machine Play," which we originated for the occasion.

JOSEPHINE JARVIS.

Cobden, Ill.

* The Cobbler and the Children.

A great many years ago a cobbler lived in a large city on the other side of the ocean. He was very fond of children, and was sorry for those poor little children who had no "play-place" but the street, and no one to take care of them all day. The fathers were at work, and as they were so very poor, the mothers too, had to be away all day washing, or cleaning house, or doing other work; so they could not do much for their children. This cobbler thought that if he could persuade the children to come to his shop, they would have a better time and would at least learn more than they could by playing in the street. He began with one child. One day when a little boy, whom we will call Johnnie, came to his shop with a pair of boots that needed patching, the cobbler said: "Johnnie, suppose you come in to-morrow and see me mend these boots. Then you will be ready to take them home when they are done."

"Yes, I will," said Johnnie.

He came quite early the next day, but the cobbler was in his shop still earlier and had put some leather to soak in water so as to make it softer than it would otherwise be. He meant to make the patch of this leather. When Johnnie came the cobbler took the leather and pounded it with the cylinder end of the hammer, and rubbed it with the flat end till it was soft enough to use.

"Was the cylinder end of his hammer like our kindergarten cylinder?"

Yes, but the edge was not sharp like the edge of yours; it was rounded so as not to cut the leather. Then the cobbler put the boot on a last, (that is a solid wooden shoe or boot, you know), and cut a paper pattern of the piece he wanted to put over the hole in the boot. Then he cut out the leather by the pattern and sewed it on the boot, with—what do you suppose?

"Needle and thread?"

You are partly right. He used strong, black linen thread, but instead of a needle he used hog's bristles. He raveled one end of the thread, put a strong bristle in among the loose ends and then with shoemaker's wax like this (showing a piece) he

---

* John Pounds, who lived in Portsmouth, England. 1766-1839.

fastened the threads and the bristle together. He made holes in the patch and in the boot, just as far apart as he wished for the length of his stitches, and sewed the patch on with his bristle and thread. Long before he had finished his work, which Johnnie watched with great interest, another boy had looked into the shop, and seeing Johnnie there, had come in; then another child came, and another, until there were as many as a dozen children looking on at the cobbler's work. These children had such a good time that they came back again and again, and brought others with them, till the shop was full every day. After a while the cobbler began to teach them to read and to spell. He taught them to count, too. They counted his pieces of leather and his awls and pegs and other things. Some of the boys learned to mend shoes themselves, so that when they grew up they could be cobblers and earn their own living in that way. The children learned other things from the good man; and so, because this poor cobbler loved children so much, and did what he could for them, many who might otherwise have had no teaching at all, grew up to be good and useful men and women.

JOSEPHINE JARVIS.

Cobden, Ill.

ST. VALENTINE'S DAY.

To the Teacher:—

Though a less important red-letter day than the others which we celebrate in the kindergarten, there is good reason for taking notice of Valentine's Day. We can show the children how to put a loving, friendly message into the gay missives so attractive to children's eyes; and how to have all the pleasure of the pretty old custom without the use of the coarse and hideous " comic " valentine.

The disputes concerning the origin of the day's observance need not trouble us. The story of the good old St. Valentine, who was so distinguished for love and charity, is as probable as any, and is the most suitable for children.

STORIES.

Philip's Valentines.

In the month of January, in the year of eighty-eight,
Little Master Philip Urbis had been so unfortunate
As to have the mumps and measles both, besides the whooping cough,
So away to get the country air his mother packed him off.
'T was in vain his little brothers both declared it was too bad,
That already more than one boy's share of fun had Philip had;
They had only had the mumps, and so it surely wasn't fair
That with Philip's other extras he should have the country air.
But their mother took no heed of any hints or discontent,
And, in spite of all their grumbling, to the country Philip went.

In the month of February, in the year of eighty-eight,
Little Philip for the fourteenth day could scarcely bear to wait;
For he dearly loved the valentines that came upon that day,
With their wonders of lace paper and their pictures gilt and gay.
He had saved his pocket money, and the whole he hoped to spend

In valentines for those at home, each schoolmate and each friend.
And his Auntie said, " Yes, Philip, we'll have *great* fun, you and I,
When we drive to Danvers Center, all the valentines to buy."
And she secretly expected to get some for Philip then,
But we know what oft befalls the best-laid plans of mice and men.

On the tenth of February, in the year of eighty-eight,
There set in a dismal snowstorm that seemed most unfortunate;
For in such a blinding, drifting way the snow kept coming down,
As to make it quite impossible for Phil to go to town.
The eleventh, twelfth and thirteenth, and the longed-for fourteenth came
And still the country roads were blocked with snowdrifts just the same.
And not a single valentine had Phil to send away,
And not a one could he expect upon this stormy day.
So it seemed that snowy morning as if not a ray of joy
Could be coaxed to shine upon the disappointed little boy.
But his Auntie put her wits to work to *somehow* celebrate
On this fourteenth day of February, eighteen eighty-eight.

Now, as Philip rose at seven, Auntie had to rise at six,
So that Philip should not catch her at her little secret tricks;
But that hour sped so swiftly that her work was scarcely done,
When there came a shout from Philip's room: "O Auntie dear, what fun
I was just about disgusted when I saw the snow and sleet,
But I've found a little letter pinned right here upon my sheet.
It's directed to me, Auntie, so it surely must be mine,
And, although it's only ' pen and ink,' it's like a valentine."

" Philip my darling, Philip my dear,
 Valentine's Day is surely here;
 And yet I hope you will not repine,
 Although you don't get any valentine;
 For, Philip my darling, Philip my dear,
 I love you every day of the year."

Just as Philip finished reading and was getting out of bed,
A letter flew in at the door and hit him on the head.
And his Auntie heard him laughing as he picked it up and read, —

" The snow may fall, the sun may shine,
 Still I'm your loving valentine;
 But do not waste your time in guessing
 Who I may be, but go on dressing;
 For in this wild and wintry storm
 My love alone can't keep you warm."

" Well," said Auntie from the stairway, "hope you'll take that good advice!
" O, yes! " answered Philip gaily, " I'll be ready in a trice,"

PHILIP'S FIRST VALENTINE.

And he soon was at the table, bright and happy as could be,
Where the oatmeal porridge waited, steaming most invitingly.
"I've two valentines already—do you s'pose I'll get some more?"
And his napkin then unfolding, something dropped upon the floor.
"Yes! it *is!* it *is* another, though a very little one;
Now I'll read it to you, Auntie; don't you think they're jolly fun?"

"Porridge hot,
Porridge cold;
My love for you
Cannot be told."

So read Philip from his valentine, and then his porridge ate,
And Auntie served the breakfast soon and passed to Phil his plate
But no sooner did he take it than he shrieked out with delight,
For beneath his baked potato was a little paper, white.
And he knew it was a valentine, it looked so like the rest,
So he quickly tore it open and then read the rhyme with zest:—

"When Philip does his breakfast eat,
Of baked potato and minced meat,
Oh! may his heart to me incline,
For I'm his loving valentine."

Little Philip's expectations now were raised up very high,
And his eyes were roving everywhere a valentine to spy;
Even looking in the milk pitcher and in the sugar bowl;
And breaking open carefully his nice hot breakfast roll.
But there was no use in looking, for he found no tell-tale signs
Of the whereabouts of any more of those queer valentines;
Till a little after breakfast, Auntie said: "Now, Philip dear,
We must not forget your medicine, so bring the bottle here."
Now of course Philip hated dosing, so he started with a frown,
But it quickly changed to laughter as he took the bottle down;
For upon the cork was fastened something which he knew must be
Another of those valentines which he so liked to see.
And upon it neatly written, this the legend that it bore,
And though Phil had liked the others, he liked this one even more:

"Oh! take the 'iron, beef and wine,'
But sweeten well this dose of thine
With loving thoughts of
VALENTINE."

That he took his spoonful smilingly I scarcely need to say;
Then to look at the thermometer outside he rushed away;
And in half a second Auntie heard him give another gleeful shout.
For behold! from the thermometer a valentine peeped out!

"A funny place indeed for one," both Phil and Auntie said;
Then opening the frosty note, this bit of rhyme they read:—

> "Thermometers may go to zero,
> But I will bear it like a hero,
> If little Phil will not decline
> To take me for his valentine."

Now the storm had ceased, and though it was not yet a pleasant day,
Auntie said that Phil might bundle up and go out doors to play.
So he put his little valentines all carefully aside,
Reading all the verses once again with fresh delight and pride.
Disappointment was forgotten and he seemed to have no thought
Of the gorgeous fancy valentines the "fourteenth" should have brought.
"Arctics will be better, Philip, than your rubber boots, I know,
For this storm of sleet has made a good firm crust upon the snow."
"All right, Auntie; come here, arctics! Oh! where is the buttonhook?
I declare! Another valentine! It's well I chanced to look
In my arctics, though I didn't think a valentine was there.
But I guess the safest way will be to look sharp everywhere."

> "Time flies, and with him bears away
> Our winter sports and frolics gay;
> But all may go, I will not repine,
> If Phil will be my valentine."

Phil put this one with the others and got ready then to go
With his fur cap and big ulster, looking like an Esquimau.
Then he asked his Auntie if he might the old umbrella take,
"For if the crust will bear, you see, I may an ice-boat make,
Like the one I had the other day—oh! *how* my sled did go!
Just like lightning on the pond, and so I want to try the snow."
Now a twinkle came in Auntie's eyes as Philip asked her this,
But she put a sober face on as she gave the boy a kiss,
Telling him the old umbrella must be somewhere in the hall,
And that he might take it *if* he wouldn't get a dreadful fall.
So away went Philip with the big umbrella and his sled,
And to watch him as he started, to the window Auntie sped.
When Philip opened the umbrella, out fell something on the snow,
And in spite of walls and distance, Auntie faintly heard his "*Oh!*"
And he soon rushed in the house again with this new valentine,
Reading it as though he thought it was particularly fine:—

> "I know a little fellow,
> Who takes a big umbrella,
> And he holds it for a sail
> Right before the wintry gale;

Andit takes him straight ahead
As he sits upon his sled,
And he skims across the ice
In a twinkling—in a trice!
Now who is it, do you say,
Who behaves in such a way?
'T is the boy who reads each line
Of this wondrous valentine!"

"Auntie do you think the valentines will come like this all day?"
Phil inquired, but his Auntie said she really could not say.
"Well, if you find any, Auntie, you will surely let me know."
Then away again went Philip to his ice-boat and the snow,
And his Auntie, seated at her desk, took up her pen to write,
Resigned to grinding out more rhymes—they gave Phil such delight;
When suddenly, to her surprise, there broke upon her ear
A merry, ringing, jingling sound that told a sleigh was near.
She had scarcely reached the window to look out of it before
The sound had ceased, and lo! the sleigh was at the very door.
And the jolly, red-faced butcher called out in his friendly way:
"Well, I guess you didn't calculate I'd get around to-day;
And I've had a mighty job of it a-ploughing through the snow,
For puttin' fust tracks in the road makes progress mighty slow.
'But business must be 'tended to and folks must eat,' says I;
And then I brought your mail up, too, as I was comin' by.
Most of them is for that youngster, and if I can read the signs,
I should say the little fellow has a lot of valentines."
Auntie thanked the butcher heartily, and glad indeed was she
So many fancy envelopes, addressed to Phil, to see.
Then when she had chosen what she wished from out the butcher's sleigh,
And the jolly butcher once again had started on his way,
Auntie put away her writing, feeling very glad indeed
That of home-made valentines there now should be no further need.
As for Phil, it disappointed him a little bit to find
That these other valentines were all the "ordinary" kind.
And although he liked their splendor, still 'twas with a fonder pride
That he showed the little home-made ones that looked so plain beside.
And a few weeks later when he went back home quite strong and well,
And his little brothers asked him of his country life to tell,
Oftener than other doings, he would all the fun relate,
Of that fourteenth day of February, eighteen eighty-eight.

EMILIE POULSSON.

WASHINGTON'S BIRTHDAY.

To the Teacher:—

A Flag of 1779.

So many ways of beginning this talk offer themselves that it is difficult to choose into which link of the past we shall clasp this new one. Shall we look back to Thanksgiving Day and its bit of history? Shall we review the New Year Story and let February's gift of George Washington's picture be the starting point? Or, shall we link our great man and his work with the humble workers we have spoken of heretofore! Approach it as we will, let us try through the week's talks, stories, lessons and plays, to draw a clear picture of Wasnington's impressive character. Let us tell those stories of his childhood, youth and manhood which will enable the children to see for themselves some of his strong and noble traits, instead of their merely memorizing the fact that George Washington was a good man for our asseverations. The impression upon their minds and hearts will thus be deeper and truer.

One of my little pupils gave a very appreciative estimate of Washington in answer to her little sister's question as to whether Washington was a king. " No," said Anna, thoughtfully, " he was not a king. He was a president; but I think he was a king in his heart."

THE TALK.

A holiday is coming soon. You know Thanksgiving Day was a holiday, and Christmas Day, and New Year's Day; and now in February we shall have Washington's Birthday.

The schools and a great many of the shops will be closed ; the fathers will not go to their work that day ; flags will be out, and guns will be fired, and bells rung, morning, noon and night.

Not only in your city or town but everywhere in our land, Washington's birthday will be a holiday.

(Let the children name all the places they can think of to help them get as much of an idea of the widespread observance of the day as is compatible with their scant geographical knowledge.)

Who can find George Washington's picture? Who can tell anything about him? We will talk about him to-day, so that when his birthday comes, and you hear the guns and the bells, and see the pretty flags flying, you will know what it is all about.

(Teacher tell stories :—
1. George and his hatchet, exemplifying truth.
2. Wishing to be a sailor, showing his unselfish love for his mother.
3. The young surveyor, showing faithfulness in work—at lessons and in surveying; (writing books, account books, etc., still to be seen.) Speak of the difficulties of surveying—penetrating into the forests alone, sleeping on the ground, walking many, many miles, etc.,—so that the children may see what bravery, strength and endurance were demanded.
4. Washington and the corporal. The rebuke to the arrogant little corporal may not be appreciated, but Washington's ready helpfulness certainly will.)

What kind of a *little* boy was George Washington? A boy who told the truth. What kind of a *big* boy? Loving and obedient; he gave up what he wanted to do to please his mother. What kind of a man? A hard worker, ready to help, strong, brave, wise and true.

(Questioning the children will help them deduce the qualities dislayed in the stories.)

It was long ago that George Washington lived, and the people in this land were having a good deal of trouble. The king— who ruled this country, too, then, although he lived over the sea—was very unkind and unfair to the American people, and made them very unhappy.

"What shall we do?" said they. "We must find some way to stop all this. We want somebody to manage our soldiers and not let the king treat us so unfairly. Where shall we find the right kind of a man?"

"Here he is! Here he is!" said those who knew Washington.

And surely he was just the right kind of a man, because he was strong and brave and wise and true.

So Washington was chosen to be the Commander-in-chief of the army, and everyone called him General Washington.

After a while, when the people were free from the king, they decided to have a President.

Do you know whom they would be likely to choose? Yes, indeed—George Washington. How glad his mother must have been to see her son so useful and so honored!

Who is the president now?

But George Washington was the *first* president.

People called him "The Father of his Country." Do you see why that is a good name for him?

TEACHER'S READING.

Washington and his Country,   • • • • • •   *Irving and Fiske*
Rules of Conduct, Diary, etc. (Riverside Literature Series, No. 24.)
Life of Washington ("St. Nicholas"), • • • • • *H. Scudder*
Birthday of Washington, - • • • • • • *Rufus Choate*
Apostrophe to Washington, • • • • • • • *D. Webster*
Ode to Washington, - • • • • • • • • *Lowell*
Ode on Washington's Birthday, • • • • • *O. W. Holmes*
The Spy, • • • • • • • • *J. Fenimore Coope*
The Virginians, • • • • • • • • *Thackeray*

For the Children.

Little George Washington, } in "The Story Hour," • *Nora A. Smith*
Great George Washington,

THE BLACKSMITH.

To the Teacher.

In the explanation of the play, "The Charcoal Burner's Hut,"—(*Mutter und Kose-Lieder*),—Froebel declared his aim to be to teach the child to respect the hand; first, the child's own hand in its power of representation, and second, to "also respect and honor not only a man who, by his hand, gives us some bread and satisfies our body's need for food and other things, but a man who is active by the work of his hands in any business, however lowly, whereby he not only keeps off injury and danger from individuals as well as from the whole community, but even directly furthers the good of mankind."

This intent—the intent to inculcate respect for the hand and its work—underlies all the trade songs and games, and can be as well carried out through the Blacksmith as through the Charcoal Burner. We need not always cling to the particular trades which Froebel chose, provided we do not lose the kernel of truth which is enveloped by them.

Before talking upon the Blacksmith, I pray you go and visit a blacksmith's shop, if possible, in order to have your own impression fresh and vivid.

THE TALK.

(After singing "The Cobbler Song," tell the children there is another man who makes shoes besides the cobbler.) The shoemaker that I am thinking of makes shoes without any leather. He uses a hammer and nails, but no waxed ends or pegs.

How many shoes does your mamma buy from the shoemaker when she gets new shoes for you? Two shoes—a pair. This other shoemaker has to make four shoes, or two pairs, for each customer that comes to him. Can you guess what sort of customers these are? They must have four feet, mustn't they?

And who is the horse's shoemaker? Have any of the children been to a blacksmith's shop, or looked in at the door? I wish you could all look in! What would you see? (Describe shop and tools, etc.) Did you ever notice the blacksmith's apron? It is made of leather and is often cut up through the middle so that he can take the horse's front foot between the two parts. Sometimes it is fringed at the bottom.

The blacksmith takes one of the new shoes, tries it on the horse, and finds out just where it is not of the right shape or of the right size. Then he takes the shoe in his tongs and holds it in the fire, and with his other hand he works the bellows. Do you know what the bellows are for? They are to blow more air under the fire, so as to make the fire very, very hot. Sometimes the blacksmith covers the shoe with the fire Does the shoe burn? No. Why not? Because it is made of iron. It was hard and black and cold when he put it into the fire; but when he takes it out it is very different. The fire has made it hot and soft and red; oh! so red and glowing! It looks like a horseshoe made of fire as he lays it on the anvil. How quickly he works now! And how the sparks fly and the anvil rings as he hammers the red-hot shoe, shaping it to fit the foot of the waiting horse. Do you know why he must work so quickly? If the iron cools it will be hard again. If we should hammer on this hard, black, cold horseshoe that we have, could we change its shape?

When the blacksmith has finished the shoe, he dips it into a barrel of cold water. Why? The next thing is to nail the shoe on the horse's foot. It seems as if this would hurt the horse very much, but the hard hoof has no feeling in it, and if the blacksmith puts the nails in the right place he will not hurt the horse at all. If the blacksmith does not know how to put the shoe on, or is not careful, he may hammer the nails through the horse's hoof so as to hit the bone; and that would make the poor horse lame. So the blacksmith, as well as the cobbler and the carpenter and the cooper, needs to be a good, careful worker.

(Speak of the difference between summer and winter horseshoes—the necessity of calks on the latter to keep the horses from slipping.)

THE BLACKSMITH.

Riddle.

"What shoemaker makes shoes without leather,
With all the four elements put together?
Fire and water, earth and air,
Every customer has two pair."

TEACHER'S READING.

Life of Elihu Burritt, "The Learned Blacksmith."
Industrial Biography, - - - - - - - - - *S. Smiles*
Tubal Cain, - - - - - - - - - - *C. Mackay*
The Song of the Forge ("Watson's Independent Fifth Reader.")
The Village Blacksmith, - - - - - - - *Longfellow*
The Ballad of the Blacksmith's Sons ("St. Nicholas,"
    December, 1887), - - - - - *Mary E. Wilkins*
Wayland Smith ("Kenilworth"), - - - - - - *Scott*
Thor's Hammer (Norse Studies), - - - - - - *H. W. Mabie*

For the Children.

Who Slit the Blacksmith's Apron? ("Wide Awake,"
    November, 1888), - - - - - *Prof. Otis T. Mason*
Gutta Percha Willie, - - - - - - *George MacDonald*

STORIES.
Nahum Prince.

This is the story of Nahum Prince, and the tears are in my eyes now as I think of him. He must have lived a hundred or more years ago, and he died, I do not know when. He was lame. Something had mashed his foot so that he could hardly walk.

It was at the time of the fighting with Burgoyne, and General Lincoln was at the front, and was ordering out every man from the New Hampshire grants and Western New Hampshire. And all the regular companies of troops had been marched out. Then there came the final call for all who could go, and all the old men and boys volunteered; and there was not a boy over thirteen years of age in the village that didn't go, except Nahum Prince. When they were getting ready to go he stood up, as well as he could, with an old Queen Anne's arm on his shoulder. And the captain came along and saw him, and said:—

"Nahum, *you* here!"

"Yes, I am here," said Nahum.

Then the captain said: "Go home, Nahum; you know you don't belong here; you cannot walk a mile."

So he called to the doctor, and the doctor said: "Nahum, it's no use; you must go home."

Then they all marched off without him. Rub-a-dub-dub, rub-a-dub-dub, went the drums; and every man and boy of them went off and left poor Nahum Prince alone. He had a good home, but he was very homesick all that night, and didn't sleep much; and the next morning he said: "I shall die before night if I stay here all alone, the only boy in town; I must do something." It was coming autumn. It was not late, but he knew he must do something; so he went down and split old Widow Corliss's wood for her, for he could split wood though he could not march. He had not been splitting wood for more than an hour when four men on horseback came down the road and stopped. He could see them stand and talk. They all went off, and then one came back again and beckoned to Nahum; and when he came up, the man on horseback said:—

"Where are all the men gone?"

"They have all gone off to join the army," answered Nahum.

"And isn't there any blacksmith in the town?"

"No, there isn't a man or a boy in the town except me, and I wouldn't be here only I am so lame I cannot walk."

"Do you mean to tell me that there is nobody here who can set a shoe?"

"Why, I can set a shoe," said Nahum.

"Then it is lucky you are left behind. Light up the forge, and set the shoe."

And now comes the most interesting part of the story. Nahum lighted up the fire, blew the coals hot, and set the shoe on the horse; and the horse and the rider went away, after the man had thanked Nahum; and Nahum finished splitting the widow's wood. And when the next week the boys came home, and told how Colonel Seth Warner came up on his horse just in time, leading the First Regiment, and took the prisoners and won the day, Nahum didn't say anything, but he knew that Colonel Warner never would have been on that horse if he hadn't set that shoe. And it was Nahum Prince and Seth Warner that won the splendid victory which ended the Battle of Bennington.

EDWARD EVERETT HALE.

Vulcan, The Mighty Smith.

High above the fleecy clouds in the sky, the gods and goddesses used to live. A wide road stretched across the heavens—you may see it now on a clear night—and on each side of it stood the great palaces of the gods. Most beautiful of all, with its great portico and smooth pillars, was the palace of Vulcan (Hephæstos). It was built of shining bronze, which flashed and gleamed in the sunlight so that it could be seen for miles around. Vulcan had built the palace for himself, for he was a wise and cunning workman with metals.

Many were the wonderful things he made with his great anvil and hammer—suits of armor, shields and spears, silver cups, golden necklaces—all wonderful to behold. Once he made two dogs out of gold and silver, and so lifelike were they that they were set to guard the palace of a king! Perhaps Vulcan had learned to work so well at his forge because he could not go about as easily as the other gods. He had a crooked foot which made him limp as he walked, but no one remembered that who saw his broad shoulders bending over his forge, or his mighty arm raised to bring down the hammer ringing on the anvil.

One day as Vulcan was working away at his bellows—very warm and very grimy from his toil—there came to him the beautiful goddess Thetis. The wife of Vulcan went out to meet her, led her in, and placed her upon a silver-studded seat. Then she called Vulcan to come since Thetis had need of him. Now Thetis had a brave and noble son—a great warrior, named Achilles—and she knew that he was soon to risk his life in battle. She had been greatly troubled on account of this, and also because she knew that Achilles had lost the armor he usually wore in the fight. As she was considering what could be done, she remembered having heard of wonderful armor, so strong that no man could pierce it —armor fit for a king—which only Vulcan could make. Achilles was not a king, but he was one of the bravest of men. Would Vulcan perhaps make such a suit of armor for him? Thetis hardly dared ask this of the mighty smith of the gods. At last, however, she had come to his palace, and now sat waiting to hear what answer he would give to her request.

Vulcan, at the call of his wife, turned the bellows from the fire, and put away his tools in a silver chest. Then he washed the black dust from his face and hands, and, taking his staff, went limping into the palace. He saw that Thetis was in trouble, and, sitting down beside her, he asked what it was. When Thetis had told him, Vulcan bade her be of good courage, and said he would at once set to work to fashion the armor. He limped quickly back to his workshop, took his tools from the silver chest, turned the bellows toward the forge and threw strong bronze and gold and silver to heat in the fire. The bellows blew a mighty blast, and the flame leapt up like a living thing. When all was ready he took the pieces of hot metal from the fire with his tongs, and, laying them upon the anvil, shaped and hammered them with cunning hands, until at last there lay before him a finished piece of armor—a breast-plate brighter than the flame itself. He made, too, a hemlet, massive and with a crest of gold, and other pieces to protect the warrior; but the most beautiful thing was a great shining shield, and truly this was marvelous to behold. Its shining surface was graven with so many pictures that when you had seen all of them it was as if you had looked through a whole picture-book! And so lifelike had Vulcan made everything appear, that the men seemed to walk about,—the sheep seemed to be cropping the grass, and the boys and girls with wreaths round their heads seemed to dance upon the meadow and to laugh as they ran races with each other.

When all was done Vulcan took the whole, and laid it before the mother of Achilles. As the pieces clanged against each other, Thetis looked at them full of joy. Then Vulcan, taking up the shield said : "This is strong to protect the warrior who can use it, and I have made it to be beautiful also in the eyes of men. For as I wrought I remembered those days long ago when I was a child, lame and miserable, and kind Thetis gave me shelter, care and love Therefore have I right gladly made strong the work, and wrought upon it pictures to delight the eye."

Vulcan made many famous things, but this was the best of them' all. Long afterwards men loved to talk of the marvelous shield of Achilles which Vulcan had wrought to such beauty, his hand strengthened with skill by the exceeding gratitude of his heart.

F. H.

THE MINER.

To the Teacher:—

This seems a rather remote subject for many of our children; but let us try whether their imagination will not enable them to receive a picture of the miner and his surroundings.

That the children may realize how many things the miner's work brings to them, the teacher should have as many as possible of the common objects which are made wholly or in part of substances obtained by the miner's toil— horse shoes, nails, scissors, weaving needles, silver and copper money, spoons, jewelry, etc.

Also ask the children to notice things at home which were once hidden away in the earth and for which the miner has worked.

THE TALK.

Do you remember the shoemaker who makes shoes without leather? What *does* the blacksmith make shoes of? Iron.

What is this made of? (Hold up a nail or other object made of iron.) How do you know it is made of iron? (Through this question gather descriptive items from the children. Iron is cold, black, heavy, strong; also soft and red when heated, and can be hammered into shape. Demonstrate the ringing sound which iron gives when dropped or struck.)

Find things in the room which are made of iron. Name iron things which you have seen in the street; iron things at home. (Let the children include steel things, since steel is one of the three forms of iron— *i. e.*, cast iron, wrought iron and steel.)

Which of the carpenter's tools are made of iron?—the blacksmith's?—the cooper's?—the cobbler's?

Could we have carriages, wagons, locomotives, steamboats, etc, without iron? Is iron very useful, then? Do you think men would take much trouble to get it?

Yes; they have to work very hard, for iron is found in rocks, often deep down in the earth.

Men who work at getting iron or gold or silver or coal out of the earth are called miners. When a miner goes to his work in the morning he does not go to a big shop as many workmen do. His workshop is a mine, inside of a mountain. Sometimes he goes in at the side of the mountain, and walks or rides down a sloping path till he gets into the mine. Sometimes he goes to an opening in the ground called a shaft. Then he gets into a big basket or cage. Down, down, down it goes; so far down that the opening at the top is only a little spot of light. At last he reaches the bottom and is in the mine.

Here the ground has been dug away, and the rock cut away, so that there are paths in all directions, and sometimes even big rooms.

But how dark it is! As black as night! How can the miner find his way? How can he see to work? He cannot carry a lamp in his hand, because he needs both hands to work with; so he has a little lamp fastened in the front of his cap. Isn't that a good plan?

He walks along one of the paths, the lamp in his hat throwing its light a little ahead. When he gets to his place of work he takes his sharp pick and strikes at the rock, breaking off piece after piece of it.

In this rock are bits and streaks of iron or gold or silver; or, if it is a coal mine, the pieces are solid coal instead of rock.

All day the miner works in that strange, dark place, away under ground—no sunshine, no light but the little twinkling lights of the lamps that the other miners carry. At night he gets into the big iron basket again, and goes up, up, up, as if in an elevator, to the top of the shaft again, and steps out upon the ground and into the fresh air once more.

How much he must enjoy his Sundays and holidays, when he can see the sunshine, and the sky, and all such beautiful things, instead of being in the black darkness of the mine!

THE MINER.

TEACHER'S READING.

The History of a Piece of Coal ("Fairyland of Science"),   *Arabella Buckley*
Haworth's, ...   *Frances Hodgson Burnett*
That Lass o' Lowrie's, ...   *Frances Hodgson Burnett*
The Led Horse Claim, ...   *Mary Hallock Foote*
Bret Harte's Stories.
Charles Egbert Craddock's Stories.
Industrial Biography, ...   *Samuel Smiles*
The Pine-Tree Shillings,   . .   *Hawthorne*

For the Children.

The Blind Brother, ...   *Homer Greene*
The Golden Opportunity, ...   *Jean Ingelow*
The Pomegranate Seeds, ...   *N. Hawthorne*
The Golden Bread, ...   *Laboulaye*
The Golden Touch, ...   *N. Hawthorne*
The Tinsmith ("Kindergarten Stories and Morning Talks"),   *S. E. Wiltse*

STORIES.

Suggestions.

The day after the talk upon "The Miner," I gave to the children of my kindergarten a story of a little boy who visited a mine with his father, in that way describing the mine through

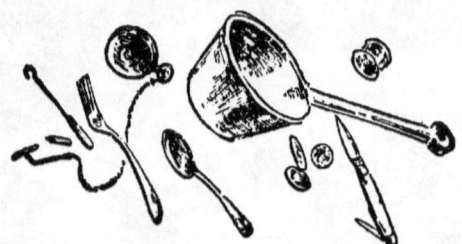

his experiences. In the review of the week I drew from the children their own experiences for a day, beginning with breakfast, which required fire made of *coal*, and stove made of *iron;*

the articles used at table, forks and spoons, made of *silver;* the dishes washed in dishpans, made of *tin;* things eaten, seasoned with *salt;* and all bought with money—*gold* and *silver.*

All these things came from *mines* and were dug by *miners.*

We sang songs about other busy men—carpenter, shoemaker, baker, blacksmith; and told what things they used which came from mines.

A KINDERGARTNER.

The Golden Touch.

Listen to the famous story
  Of King Midas, who of old
Gifted was with wondrous magic,
  Turning all he touched to gold.
Everything he laid his hands on
  Underwent the same bright change,
Till familiar things about him
  Had a golden glitter strange.

Bedsteads, tables, chairs and curtains.
  Silken fabric, common wood,
By his passing touch converted
  Each a golden marvel stood!
Ev'n the trees within the garden
  Spread out shining boughs afar—
And a merry dancing sunbeam
  Stiffened to a golden bar!

Much King Midas gloated over
  All the dazzling splendor wrought;
Well he loved the untold riches
  That his touch of magic brought:
But his exultation ended
  And his pleasure turned to pain.
For the trouble that it caused him
  Far out-weighed the golden gain.

Tempting viands filled the table
  And the poor king's hunger pressed,
But they turned to metal mouthfuls
  Far too solid to digest.

So it was with all about him,
  Making Midas almost wild—
But his fury changed to heartacne,
  When a touch transformed his child.

Well he loved his little daughter—
  Wondrous fair and good was she;
And King Midas on her ringlets
  Laid his hand caressingly,
Thoughtless of the fatal magic,
  But its power was still the same;
For a lifeless, golden statue
  Instantly the child became.

Starving, childless, yet more wretched
  Grew King Midas hour by hour,
Till he loathed the shining treasure,
  And the gift of baneful power.
All these glittering possessions
  Gladly, freely, would he give,
If without this curse—though beggars·—
  He and his dear child might live.

So the gift was taken from him
  And the mischief it had wrought
Quickly righted; and King Midas
  Did not miss the lesson taught,
But lived happy ever after,
  Cured of all his greed for gold
And to wond'ring children's children
  Often this strange story told.

EMILIE POULSSON.

Coal.

* * * * Mother and Father and their friends have gone to see a huge furnace. The furnace is to make iron. The iron ore is found in the ground; but it cannot be used until it has been brought to the furnace and melted, and all the dirt taken out, and just the pure iron left. Then it is all ready to be manufactured into engines, stoves, kettles and many other things.

Coal is found in the ground, too. Many years ago, before people came to life on the earth, great trees and tall grasses and huge ferns and all the beautiful flowers covered the ground. When the leaves and the trees fell, the water and the soil covered them; and then more trees grew and fell also, and were buried under water and soil. After they had all been pressed together for many thousands of years the wood grew very hard, like rock, and then it was ready for people to burn. Can you see leaves and ferns and bark on the coal? Men go down into the ground and dig out the coal, and steam cars take it to the large cities, where it is sold to people to burn, to make them warm and happy when it is cold out of doors.

HELEN KELLER.

WATER, I.

To the Teacher:—

One kindergartner told me of the enthusiastic interest her children took in this subject. She let them work out all the suggestions of the talk. They got snow from out of doors, melted it before the fire, boiled the water and condensed the steam on a slate held over the teakettle spout.

THE TALK.

Uses of Water.

(Let the children first tell the obvious and well-known uses of water; *i. e.*, as a drink for *all*—animals and plants—and as a cleansing agent. Speak of the beauty and healthfulness of clean skin, clean clothes, etc.)

Forms of Water.

What does Jack Frost do to water? Freezes it—turns it into ice. Can it be changed to water again? How? If you melt snow, what does it become? What is snow made of, then? Where does the snow come from? (See talk on "Winter" for

formation of snow.) Jack Frost makes snow out of the raindrops away up in the sky, and makes ice wherever he finds water on the earth.

What does he decorate our windows with sometimes? Frost.

Do you know what the frost is made of? It is made of water, too, for the window is wet when the frost melts, as you may have seen for yourselves.

Do ice and snow and frost all look alike? Do they look like water? Jack Frost is quite like a fairy, isn't he, changing water into all these different and beautiful forms?

Will ice and snow and frost melt if they are kept in the cold? What will melt them? Here is a funny little verse for you:—

> "Simple Simon made a snowball
> And brought it in to roast;
> He put it by the kitchen fire
> And soon the ball was lost."

What had happened to Simple Simon's snowball? The heat of the fire had melted it. What melts the snow out of doors on a warm, sunny day? The heat of the sun. Jack Frost could change water into frost or snow or ice, but he could not change them into water again. Heat is the fairy to do that kind of work. And heat can make some wonderful fairy changes with water itself, too. Have you ever noticed steam coming out of the teakettle spout? If you have, you have seen what the fairy Heat has done to some of the water in the teakettle. Water usually goes in drops like this: (Dip the hand in water to show the drops which cling to the hand; also shake some off on the floor or table.) But when the fairy Heat takes hold of the water drops in the teakettle they are changed into this fine, thin steam which floats out of the teakettle spout.

You would think steam to be very gentle, seeing it float off in those thin little clouds, but it is really so strong that we sometimes call it a giant, and wise men have found out how to make it do a great deal of work. They shut this giant "Steam" up, leaving him only a little place through which to escape, and then they put the machinery right where he will push against one little part of it when he rushes out, and thus set all the machinery in motion. That is the way giant Steam is made to turn the wheels of the steamboats and locomotives and mills, and to do all kinds of work.

But we must not forget that it is the fairy Heat who changes water into steam, for the same kind of fairy work is going on out of doors, too. Wherever the warm little sunbeams find water, the fairy Heat will work away at some of it, changing it and making it so fine and thin that we often cannot see it at all as it floats up through the air.

In the sky, however, it sometimes gathers together into one mass, and then we call it a cloud; and the cloud lies there in the sky until North Wind or East Wind comes that way. And then what happens? Why, the fairy Heat has to let go, and the cloud of water dust changes into drops of water; and the drops of water are so heavy that they immediately fall down to the earth again. And when that happens, the little kindergarten children sing some of their pretty songs about the rain.

TEACHER'S READING.

Forms of Water, - - - - - - - - - *Tyndall*
Fairyland of Science (Chaps. I, IV, V), - - - *Arabella Buckley*
Hymn before Sunrise in the Vale of Chamouni, - - - - *Coleridge*
Clear and Cool, - - - - - - - - *Charles Kingsley*
Ode on Introduction of Cochituate Water into Boston, - - - *Lowell*
The Old Oaken Bucket, - - - - - - *Samuel Woodworth*
The Steamboat, - - - - - - - - - *O. W. Holmes*
The Song of Steam, - - - - - - - - *G. W. Cutter*
Robin's Rain Song, - - - - - "*St. Nicholas*," *April, 1887*

For the Children.

Tom, the Water Baby ("Kindergarten Stories and Morning Talks"), - - - - - - - - - *S. E. Wiltse*
The Crow and the Pitcher ("Kindergarten Stories and Morning Talks"), - - - - - - - *S. E. Wiltse*

STORIES.

To Whom Shall We Give Thanks.

A little boy had sought the pump
   From whence the sparkling water burst,
And drank with eager joy the draught
   That kindly quenched his raging thirst.
Then gracefully he touched his cap,
   " I thank you, Mr. Pump," he said,
" For this nice drink you've given me."
   (This little boy had been well-bred.)

Then said the Pump: " My little man,
   You're welcome to what I have done·
But I am not the one to thank,
   I only help the water run."
" Oh! then," the little fellow said,
   (Polite he always meant to be),
" Cold Water, please accept my thanks,
   You have been very kind to me."

" Ah! " said Cold Water, " don't thank me!
   For up the hillside lives a spring
That sends me forth with generous hand
   To gladden every living thing."
" I'll thank the spring, then," said the boy,
   And gracefully he bowed his head.
" Oh! don't thank me, my little man,"
   The spring with silvery accent said.

" Oh! don't thank me, for what am I
   Without the dews and summer rain?
Without their aid I ne'er could quench
   Your thirst, my little boy, again."
" Oh, well, then," said the little boy,
   " I'll gladly thank the rain and dew."
" Pray don't thank us! Without the sun
   We could not fill one cup for you."

" Then, Mr. Sun, ten thousand thanks
   For all that you have done for me."
" Stop," said the Sun with blushing face,
   " My little fellow, don't thank me.

'Twas from the ocean's mighty stores
  I drew the draught I gave to thee."
" O Ocean, thanks," then said the boy.
  It echoed back: " No thanks to me!"

" Not unto me, but unto him
  Who formed the depths in which I lie,
Go give thy thanks, my little boy,—
  To him who will thy wants supply."
The boy took off his cap and said
  In tones so gentle and subdued,
" O God, I thank thee for thy gift.
  Thou art the Giver of all good."

UNKNOWN.

Snowflakes.

(With suggestions for a stick lesson.)

Once upon a time, a little Raindrop thought it had played long enough up in the clouds, and said it would go down to the earth and see what good it could do. So it started.

While it was falling it had to pass through a cloud that was very cold, and this funny little Raindrop, instead of shrinking together as we do when we are cold, stretched out and stretched out till it was not round any more, but was long and thin and hard like a needle: and that is just what it was—a little ice needle.

As it went on falling, it met another just like itself.

The second one said: "Little Ice Needle, where are you going?"

"Down to the earth to see what good I can do."

"I'll go, too;" so the second ice needle joined the first (put the two sticks together at angle of sixty degrees), and they fell together.

Pretty soon they met a third, and it said: "Little Ice Needles. where are you going?"

"Down to the earth to see what good we can do."

"Then I'll go, too." So it joined the others and they fell together. (Add a third stick at the same angle, and so on till a

Some of the Forms of Water.
Ice, rain, clouds, etc.

six-pointed snow-star is made.) Then they met another and another and another, who all joined them. Then there were six little ice needles falling together, and they had a new name — "Snowflake."

Little Snowflake met others who asked it where it was going.

"Down to the ground to see what good I can do."

"We'll go, too. But where shall we go?"

"I know," said one of the little ice needles. "Last summer, when I was warm and round, I saw a place where a poor little sick boy had planted some seeds which a kind lady gave him, and I think it would be so nice to fall on that place and keep it warm, so that the seeds in the ground may not freeze, and the little boy may have some flowers next summer."

"Oh! so we will," said they all, and they fell faster and faster, that they might get there sooner. Other snowflakes saw them and went too, and the ground was covered more and more thickly with snow till there was enough to keep the seeds from freezing all winter.

When the weather began to be warmer, the snow turned into water and ran down into the earth, and the seeds drank it and swelled and swelled until, by and by, little leaves came out above ground, from each seed. Then other leaves grew, and, when summer came, little Frank had his flowers again, and all because one little raindrop wanted to do some good in the world.

JOSEPHINE JARVIS.

Cobden, Ill.

The Immortal Fountain.

In ancient times two little princesses lived in Scotland, one of whom was extremely beautiful, and the other dwarfish, dark-colored and deformed. The sisters did not live happily together.

Marion hated Rose because she was handsome and everybody praised her. She scowled when anybody told her how pretty her little sister Rose was. No wonder all the family and all the neighbors disliked Marion, and no wonder her face grew uglier and uglier every day.

One summer noon, when all was still save the faint twittering of the birds and lazy hum of the insects, Marion entered a deep grotto. She sat down on a bank of moss; the air around her was as fragrant as if it came from a bed of violets; and with the sound of far-off music dying on her ear, she fell into a gentle slumber

When she awoke, a figure of real loveliness stood before her, and thus she sang:—

> The Fairy Queen
> Hath rarely seen
> Creature of earthly mould
> Within her door,
> On pearly floor,
> Inlaid with shining gold.
> Mortal, all thou seest is fair;
> Quick thy purposes declare.

As she concluded, the song was taken up and thrice repeated by a multitude of soft voices in the distance. It seemed as if birds and insects joined in the chorus. All these delightful sounds soon died away and the Queen of the Fairies stood patiently awaiting Marion's answer. Courtesying low, and with a trembling voice, the little maiden said:—

"Will it please your Majesty to make me as handsome as my sister Rose?"

"I will grant your request," said she, "if you will promise to fulfill all the conditions I propose."

Marion eagerly promised that she would.

"Go home, now," said the Queen:—"for one week speak no ungentle word to your sister; at the end of that time, come again to the grotto."

The end of the week arrived, and Marion had faithfully kept her promise. Again she went to the grotto.

"Mortal, hast thou fulfilled thy promise?" asked the Queen.

"I have," said Marion.

"Then follow me."

Marion did as she was directed, and away they went over beds of violets and mignonette. The birds warbled above their heads, butterflies cooled the air, and the gurgling of many fountains came with a refreshing sound. Presently they came to the hill, on the top of which was the Immortal Fountain. Its foot was surrounded by a band of fairies clothed in green gossamer.

The Queen waved her wand over them, and immediately they stretched their thin wings and flew away. The hill was steep, and far, far up they went; and the air became more fragrant and more distinctly they heard the sound of waters falling in music. At length they were stopped by a band of fairies clothed in blue, with their silver wands crossed.

"Here," said the Queen, "our journey must end. You can go no farther until you have fulfilled the orders I shall give you. Go home now; for one month do by your sister, in all respects, as you would wish her to do by you, were you Rose and she Marion."

Marion promised and departed. She found the task harder than the first had been. When Rose asked for any of her playthings, she found it difficult to give them gently and affectionately, instead of pushing them along.

When Rose talked to her, she wanted to go away in silence; and when a mirror was found in her sister's room, broken in a thousand pieces, she felt sorely tempted to conceal that she did the mischief. But she was so anxious to be made beautiful, that she did as she would be done by. All the household remarked how Marion had changed. "I love her dearly," said Rose, "she is so good and amiable."

"So do I," said a dozen voices.

Marion blushed deeply, and her eyes sparkled with pleasure. "How pleasant it is to be loved!" thought she.

At the end of the month she went to the grotto again. The fairies in blue lowered their silver wands and flew away. They traveled on; the path grew steeper and steeper; but the fragance of the atmosphere was redoubled, and more distinctly came the sound of the waters falling in music. Their course was stayed by a troop in rainbow robes, and silver wands tipped with gold.

"Here we must pause," said the Queen; "this boundary you cannot yet pass."

"Why not?" asked the impatient Marion.

"Because they must be very pure who pass the rainbow fairies," replied the Queen. "They must be pure in thought as well as in action. Return home; for three months never indulge in an envious or wicked thought. You shall then have a sight of the Immortal Fountain."

Marion was sad at heart, for she knew how many envious thoughts and wrong wishes she had suffered to gain power over her.

When she again visited the Palace of Beauty, the Queen smiled and then led her away to the Immortal Fountain. The silver specks on the wings of the rainbow fairies shone bright as she approached them, and they lowered their wands, and sang as they flew away :—

> Mortal, pass on,
> Till the goal is won,—
> For such, I ween,
> Is the will of the Queen,—
> Pass on! Pass on!

And now every footstep was on flowers, it yielded beneath their feet. The delicious fragrance could almost be felt, and loud, clear and liquid came the sound of the waters as they fell in music. And now the cascade is seen leaping and sparkling over crystal rocks, and deep and silent below the foam is the Immortal Fountain. Its amber-colored waves flow over a golden bed ; and as the fairies bathe in it, the diamonds on their hair glance like sunbeams on the waters.

"Oh, let me bathe in the fountain!" cried Marion, clasping her hands in delight.

"Not yet," said the Queen. "Go home ; for another year drive away all evil feelings, not for the sake of bathing in this Fountain, but because goodness is lovely and desirable for its own sake."

This was the hardest task of all. For she had been willing to be good, not because it was right to be good, but she wished to be beautiful. Three times she sought the grotto, and three times she left it in tears. The fourth time she prevailed. The purple fairies that guarded the brink of the fountain lowered their wands, singing :—

> Thou hast scaled the mountain,
> Go, bathe in the Fountain;
> Rise, fair to the sight
> As an angel of light;
> Go, bathe in the Fountain.

Marion was about to plunge in, but the Queen touched her, saying, "Look in the mirror of waters. Art thou not already as beautiful as heart could wish?"

Marion looked at herself, and saw that her eyes sparkled with a new lustre, that a bright color shone through her cheeks, and dimples played sweetly about her mouth.

"I have not touched the Immortal Fountain," said she, turning in surprise to the Queen.

"True," replied the Queen," but its waters have been within your soul. Know that a pure heart and a clear conscience are the only immortal fountains of beauty."

Ever after the sisters lived happily together. It was the remark of every one, "How handsome Marion had grown! The ugly scowl has gone from her face, and the light of her eye is so mild and pleasant, and her mouth looks so smiling and good natured that, to my taste, I declare, she is as handsome as Rose."

L. Maria Child.

WATER, II.

To the Teacher:—

(Review briefly the effects of cold and heat upon water, especially the lifting up of vapor and the formation of clouds and rain.)

THE TALK.

When the rain falls, what becomes of it? The little drops soak into the ground and the thirsty roots drink with delight all that they need. But they do not use it all. The rest of the water runs along in the ground till by and by it finds a chance to bubble out somewhere. I wonder whether it is as glad to get out of the dark earth and into the air and sunshine again as the miner is? It sparkles as if it were!

The first chance it gets to run down hill, away it skips, and soon finds another dancing, sparkling little stream like itself and perhaps another and another. "We are so little, each alone," they say: "let us all go together."

So the tiny streams of water weave themselves into one, and people say: "What a pretty brook!" (Sing the Froebel song of "The Brook" and talk of the bridge. It might be well to see whether the children have kept the sequence thus far: Rain, spring, streamlet, brook.)

The pretty brook flows along—dancing, leaping, sparkling, laughing and even singing. I have heard it sing many a time! Let us play we are sitting by the side of this little singing brook and watching its visitors. (Try to have the children *see* the little birds splashing in the brook and sipping its waters, the flowers and grasses leaning over its brink, the silvery fishes flashing through its ripples, the child sailing his toy boat in the safe shallowness of one of its pools, the solemn frog plunging clumsily out of sight if it hears us, the cows and the big horse walking into the brook to get a refreshing drink. The children's imagination might be quickened by letting them personate the birds, cows, horses, etc., which come to the brook to drink.) The little brook gives freely to all and ripples joyously along. Whenever it finds another brook it calls out, "Are you going my way? We are so small, each alone—let us go together;" and so, just as the tiny streamlets wove themselves together to make the brook, the brooks flow together into one and make a river. (Rain, spring, streamlets, brooks, river. Help the children to picture now a river with its increased size and force; the rocky places over which it leaps; the life in and about it, the large boats, the logs floating down from the forest, the bridges and the mills grinding corn, sawing wood, etc., which its flowing water works.)

The river is a great worker! All along its way it finds something to do. Sometimes, indeed, the river spreads itself out into a pond or lake and lies there more quietly, but soon it rushes on again and at last it reaches the ocean—the great meeting place of all the waters.

Have any of you been to the seashore and seen the ocean? Have you ever watched its little curling waves creeping up to the shore and then running back into the big sea as fast as they could? Or the great, high waves, rolling grandly up only to hurry back again in the same way? The water of the river is now part of the ocean and races up to the shore and back again when its turn comes. (Rain, spring, stream, brook, river, ocean.)

What a long journey the water has taken! But it is going to travel farther yet; for the bright, hot sun sends his heat fairies down, and as soon as they have made some of the water from the top of the waves fine enough and light enough, up it goes to the sky again and is made into clouds. And then what does it do but turn into drops of rain just as before, and start on the same long journey again!

WATER AT WORK.

TEACHER'S READING.

Forms of Water,	*Tyndall*
Fairyland of Science,	*Buckley*
"The Bridge,"	*Froebel's Explanation*
Undine,	*De la Motte Fouque*
The Fountain,	*Lowell*
The Brook,	*Tennyson*
The Marshes of Glynn,	*Lanier*
Mad River, } Songo River, }	*Longfellow*
Song of the Chattahoochee,	*Lanier*
To Seneca Lake,	*J. G. Percival*
How the Water comes down at Lodore,	*Southey*
The Sea,	*Barry Cornwall*
Childe Harold's Pilgrimage (Canto IV, 178),	*Byron*
The Coral Grove,	*J. G. Percival*
The Merman,	*Tennyson*
The Mermaid,	*Tennyson*
The Forsaken Merman,	*Matthew Arnold*
The Tides,	*W. C. Bryant*
Break, break, break, } A Farewell, }	*Tennyson*

For the Children.

Aqua ("The Story Hour"), - - - - - - *Kate D. Wiggin*

STORIES.

Stony and Rocky.

Once upon a time there was a great family of limestones, all piled up on the bank of a river. They had been so close together that one could not be told from another. They had finished the work they had to do together. The time had now come for them to separate and do another kind of work.

Away up on top, Stony and Rocky, two lively boys of this family, could look down into the river. There they saw some of their brothers and sisters who long ago had left their home, and whose sharp corners and edges had been worn away by the water, which rolled them over and over, rubbing them against each other until all the rough edges were gone, and they were smooth and round. These little pebbles kept calling to Stony and Rocky up on the cliffs, to come down. They wanted to go very much, but they could not break off from their old home without some help. As they sat up there wishing very much to go into the river below, Jack Frost went rushing by on the wings of the wind. Rocky called to this jolly little fellow and asked if he could not help them. Jack said, "Of course I can; what help do you need?" "Oh!" said Stony, "we are fastened here so tight that we can't get away. Can't you set us free? Our brothers and sisters are having a good time down in the water, and we want to go there." "All right," said Jack, "you shall go, and I will help you." So he set to work, and marked off with his ice pencil a cold, white line. "The sunshine will soon be along," he said, "and will help you, too." Then away he flew. Sure enough, the sunshine did come, and set to work to thaw out Jack Frost's ice lines, and make the rocks warm. The wind blew on them, and the tiny raindrops came to help, too. All worked very hard together, and the rocks felt themselves loosening from their old homes. At last, one night, Jack Frost brought his ice chisel and gave them a hard knock, and they kept getting looser and looser, until—plunge!!!—they went headlong into the water.

Oh, dear, how frightened they were! The water was so cold and dark, and rushed around them so rapidly, that they were shaken up and trembled with fear. How they wished they had never left their quiet home to come down here in this busy rush.

In a little while they had the courage to look up, and there they saw the tiny twinklers up in the sky, looking down at them as they had always done, and the moon sending them light and smiling upon them as she had done ever since they could remember. Their little pebble brothers and sisters comforted them, and they were soon better contented.

The next day, Stony and Rocky began to run and play in the water, like the pebbles. They had rather a hard time of it at first, because they never had been with such busy people before, and they had such sharp corners that they were always getting badly hurt.

They soon grew to love the soft, singing water, and to like the busy life, even with the sharp knocks — much better than the old life on the cliffs.

After a long, long time, more years than any of us have lived, Rocky and Stony were worn down into round, smooth pebbles, and others from their old home were falling down into the water.

Their work here, in the water, had made them ready for another kind of work. One day, a man came down to the river with a wheelbarrow and gathered it full of pebbles out of the river. The pebbles wondered what work they had to do now.

The man carried them away off into the great city, and made with them some beautiful walks in a large park where a great many little children come to play, as soon as the spring comes every year. They love to play with the pebbles, and the pebbles like to take care of their tiny feet and keep them out of the mud.

This is the last home that Stony and Rocky ever had and they lived there ever after.

ANNIE E. ALLEN.

The Kindergarten Magazine.

The Little Hero of Haarlem.

At an early period in the history of Holland, a boy, who is the hero of the following narrative, was born in Haarlem, a town remarkable for its variety of fortune in war, but happily still more so for its manufactures and inventions in peace. His father was a *sluicer*—that is, one whose employment it was to open and shut the sluices, or large oak gates, which, placed at certain regular distances, close the entrances of the canals, and secure Holland from the danger to which it seems exposed—of finding itself under water, rather than above it.

When water is wanted, the sluicer raises the sluices more or less, as required, and closes them again carefully at night; otherwise the water would flow into the canals, overflow them, and inundate the whole country. Even the little children in Holland are fully aware of the importance of a punctual discharge of the sluicer's duties.

The boy was about eight years old when, one day, he asked

permission to take some cakes to a poor blind man, who lived at the other side of the dike. His father gave him leave, but charged him not to say too late. The child promised, and set off on his little journey. The blind man thankfully partook of his young friend's cakes, and the boy, mindful of his father's orders, did not wait, as usual, to hear one of the old man's stories, but as soon as he had seen him eat one muffin, took leave of him to return home.

As he went along by the canals, then quite full, for it was in October and the autumn rains had swelled the waters, the boy now stopped to pull the little blue flowers which his mother loved so well, now, in childish gayety, hummed some merry song.

The road gradually became more solitary, and soon neither the joyous shout of the villager, returning to his cottage home, nor the rough voice of the carter, grumbling at his lazy horses was any longer to be heard. The little fellow now perceived that the blue of the flowers in his hand was scarcely distinguishable from the green of the surrounding herbage, and he looked up in some dismay. The night was falling; not, however, a dark winter night, but one of those beautiful, clear, moonlight nights, in which every object is perceptible, though not as distinctly as by day.

The child thought of his father, of his injunction, and was preparing to quit the ravine in which he was almost buried, and to regain the beach, when suddenly a slight noise, like the trickling of water upon pebbles, attracted his attention. He was near one of the large sluices, and he now carefully examined it, and soon discovered a hole in the wood, through which the water was flowing.

With the instant perception which every child in Holland would have had, the boy saw that the water must soon enlarge the hole, through which it was now only dropping, and that utter and general ruin would be the consequence of the inundation of the country that must follow.

To see, to throw away the flowers, to climb from stone to stone till he reached the hole, and put his finger into it, was the work of a moment, and, to his delight, he found that he had succeeded in stopping the flow of the water.

This was all very well for a little while, and the child thought only of the success of his device. But the night was closing in, and with the night came the cold. The little boy looked around in vain. No one came. He shouted—he called loudly—no one answered.

He resolved to stay there all night, but, alas, the cold was becoming every moment more biting, and the poor finger fixed in the hole began to feel benumbed, and the numbness soon extended to the hand, and thence throughout the whole arm. The pain became still greater, still harder to bear, but still the boy moved not.

Tears rolled down his cheeks as he thought of his father, of his mother, of his little bed where he might now be sleeping so soundly, but still the little fellow stirred not, for he knew that did he remove the small, slender finger which he had opposed to the escape of the water, not only would he himself be drowned, but his father, his brothers, his neighbors—nay, the whole village.

We know not what faltering of purpose, what momentary failures of courage there might have been during that long and terrible night; but certain it is that at daybreak he was found in the same painful position by a clergyman returning from an attendance on a death bed, who, as he advanced, thought he heard groans, and bending over the dike, discovered a child seated on a stone, writhing from pain, and with pale face and tearful eyes.

"In the name of wonder, boy," he exclaimed, "what are you doing there?"

"I am hindering the water from running out," was the answer, in perfect simplicity, of the child who, during that whole night, had been evincing such heroic fortitude and undaunted courage.

The Muse of history, too often blind to true glory, has handed down to posterity many a warrior, the destroyer of thousands of his fellow men—she has left us in ignorance of this real little hero of Haarlem.

Sharpe's Magazine.

Do What You Can.

There was once a farmer who had a large field of corn; he ploughed it and planted the corn, and harrowed and weeded it with great care, and on his field he depended for the chief support of his family. But after he had worked hard, he saw the corn begin to wither and droop for rain, and he began to have fears for his crop. He felt very sad, and went over every day to look at his corn, and see if there was any hope of rain.

One day as he stood looking at the sky, and almost in despair, two little raindrops up in the clouds over his head saw him, and one said to the other:

"Look at that farmer; I feel sorry for him, he has taken so much pains with his field of corn, and now it is drying up; I wish I could do him some good."

"Yes," said the other, "but you are only a little raindrop; what can you do? You can't even wet one hillock."

"Well," said the first, "to be sure I can't do much, but I can cheer the farmer a little at any rate, and I am resolved to do my best; I'll try. I'll go to the field to show my good will, if I can do no more; and so here I go."

The first raindrop had no sooner started for the field than the second one said:

"Well, if you are going, I believe I will go, too; here I come." And down went the raindrops—one came pat on the farmer's nose, and one fell on a stalk of corn. "Dear me," said the farmer, putting his finger to his nose, "what's that? A raindrop! where did that come from? I do believe we shall have a shower."

By this time a great many raindrops had come together to hear what their companions were talking about, and when they saw them going to cheer the farmer and water the corn, one said: "If you are going on such a good errand, I'll go, too," and down he came. "And I," said another, "and I," and so on, till a whole shower came, and the corn was watered, and it grew and ripened—all because the first little raindrop determined to *do what it could.*

—Selected.

Neptune.

Far down under the green water, where the sea-sand lies smooth and white, and fishes dart about like flashes of silver among the seaweeds, there lived the old ocean god, Neptune (Poseidon). "Father Neptune," people used to call him. There he had his palace, and there he kept the wild sea horses which he had trained and taught to draw his chariot over the water.

One morning, as Neptune came from his palace, he was surprised to find everything in great disorder. The water, usually still and clear as crystal, with the green light shining through it, was dim and disturbed; it beat against the walls of the palace and was full of bits of broken shell and of seaweeds torn from their stems. As Neptune stood looking about him, the big, good-natured dolphins came rolling uneasily about his feet, as if to ask what could be the matter. The dolphins were wise creatures, and were often sent about as messengers by Neptune. So he chose one now to go and find out the cause of all this confusion. The dolphin soon came back, saying that a terrible storm was raging above; that the winds were rolling great waves to the shore and tossing the spray high in the air; that he had seen ships, too, driven upon the rocks by these wild winds, or on dangerous shoals and shallows.

Neptune straightway harnessed his horses, mounted the chariot, and with firm rein guided his steeds upward to the scene of the storm. Calm and majestic the ocean god sat in his chariot, holding his trident like a magic wand, and the rough waters smoothed themselves out before him as he went. His son Triton swam alongside, a twisted seashell in his hand, on which he sometimes blew a bugle call. The dolpins, too, followed, swimming hither and thither and tumbling over each other in their eagerness to help. At last they reached the top of the water. No sooner did Neptune's calm head rise above the surface than, like magic, the tossing waves were still and the sea became smooth as glass; the winds subsided, and all was peaceful as a summer's day.

Neptune called the winds to him, and reproving them severely for their rough play, sent them home again to King Æolus. Then he looked for the unfortunate ships that were in danger. Those that were on the rocks Triton pried off, Neptune helping with his trident, and those that had been driven among the shallows they led back to deep water. At last all was in order— and it was a grand sight to see calm old Father Neptune in his chariot, gliding over the sea he had made quiet again, while the dolphins played about him, their smooth backs glistening in the sun.

F. H.

The Brook and the Water Wheel.

The water wheel in a gristmill went round and round, by day and by night, without stopping. Said the brook one day, as it passed over the wheel:

"Are you not tired of being always at work, and of doing the same thing to-day that you did yesterday? When I have done my work in making you turn, I glide on and take my pleasure in flowing through the fields and woods."

"But my pleasure," replied the wheel, "is in continuing to work and go round and round grinding up the corn."

"Yesterday," continued the brook, "as I flowed through the meadow, I heard some people who were wandering there say how beautiful I was, and what sweet music I made as I rippled over the stones."

"And no doubt they said what was true," replied the wheel, "but it could never be said of me. How would I look rolling through the meadow? I would not be admired by others, nor would I enjoy it myself."

"You are to be admired for your humility," said the brook, "in being contented with so dismal a place."

"Not at all," replied the wheel, "for when this place was given me, I was given also a liking for it."

"But do you not long for the sunlight and the breeze and a sight of the birds and the flowers?"

"No more than you do for this dim chamber under the mill.

Here I was made to dwell, and here I am satisfied to be. I greet you tumbling in from the mountain side over my head, and bid you adieu as you flow out joyously under my feet; but I do not long to follow you. The summer's heat does not parch me here, nor the winter's frost stop me from turning. Even in this dim twilight I revolve and listen to the sound of the grinding. I delight to hear the farmer drive his team to the mill door loaded with grain, and afterward haul it away when I have made it into flour for his wife and children to eat. I am content to stay here and labor—not by constraint nor for duty's sake alone, but because the place accords with my nature and therefore it is my choice.

CHARLES FOSTER.

From " New Lights on Old Paths," Chas. Foster Pub. Co., Phila., Pa.

FISHES.

To the Teacher:—

Unless you have been a dweller in the country, a student of nature, a haunter of rivers and brooksides, a lover of watery scenes, or have learned your incompetency as a judge from some such person, fishes will seem a most prosaic and unattractive division of the animal creation. But if you will kindly lay down your prejudice and contemplate the subject earnestly (through books for lack of better opportunity), you will find your prejudice a mistaken one, and it will be replaced by admiration and delight. Read from science the wonderful history and structure of the fishes, their weapons and devices, their infinite variety of form, color, size, motion, and then let the poets enhance the wondrous revelation.

Sticklebacks, goldfishes or minnows can be kept in the kindergarten, but are often short-lived because of being overfed or kept too warm.

THE TALK.

Do you remember the brook we talked about, and the busy river, and the wonderful great ocean? Do you remember what creatures lived in all these waters?

(The children's knowledge being the true starting point, elicit what they already know about fishes. Many who have not seen them in their native element will have seen them in the fish markets.)

Have you noticed what big mouths fishes have, and what round eyes? Their ears do not show, but they can hear for all that. Their noses, although sharp enough for smelling, especially when something good to eat floats along in the water, are of no use to them for breathing, as ours are. But the fishes do not mind that, for, since they live in the water, they need a different way of breathing from animals who live in the air. So they have gills, with little thin, hard covers which open and shut, on each side of the head.

A fish gulps water into his mouth continually and sends it out through his gills. Before he sends the water out through his gills he gets all the air out of it. This is his way of breathing.

The skin of the fish, instead of being covered with hair like that of the cat and the cow and the horse, is covered with little hard, shiny bits, called scales. These are often of beautiful colors. I believe you could find fishes to match all the pretty balls we have in kindergarten!

What shape is the fish's body usually? Long and narrow, that he may go through the water easily. Do you remember that the cat, the horse and the cow all had backbones, and all had four legs—two pairs, that is? People have backbones, and have two legs and two arms—which make two pairs, also.

The fish has a backbone. (Show by a picture previously drawn upon the blackboard.) Has he any legs? Any arms? No; but he has fins—two leg-fins and two arm-fins. (If not possible to show these facts by a real fish, make a clay model of good size—five or six inches long—from which the children can get the idea of the position of the fins.)

Fishes often have single fins on one place or another, but these single fins only grow out from the skin and are not part of the body in the same way that the leg-fins and arm-fins are.

The tail is a single fin. Do you see the angle in the tail? What kind of an angle is it?

Do you know what the fish uses his fins for? To balance himself with, and as a help in swimming. His tail is very strong. He pushes himself along in the water with it, and also uses it to steer himself in whatever direction he wishes to go, while his arm-fins and leg-fins keep him from falling over.

What do you suppose the fishes do all day and every day in the water? Swim? Yes, they swim and play and chase each other about; they dive away down, sinking deep into the cold, dark water, and then rising up to the top, where it is warm and bright with sunshine.

In the deep, deep parts of the ocean it is dark, just as it is deep down in the earth where the miner works. The sunlight cannot reach so far through the water, but if we were down there we should see lights gleaming through the darkness, for the fishes that live so far down have a strange kind of light flashing from their bodies, and so can see their way. Doesn't that make you think of the miners and the little lamps which they wear so that they can see their way deep down in the earth, where the sunlight cannot reach?

But we need not go to the farthest depths of the great ocean to find wonderful and beautiful fishes. Even the brooks have pretty little fellows in them that look as if they were made of silver or gold.

It is difficult to tell whether the bright colors or the curious shapes or the graceful motions of the fishes are most interesting, but when you hear how the father fishes sometimes build nests and take care of the eggs, and feed and protect the baby fishes and the mother, you will think that is the strangest and best of all the many facts which the wise men have learned.

TEACHER'S READING.

Froebel's Explanation of "The Fish in the Brook."
Winners in Life's Race (Chaps. I, II, III), - - - *Arabella Buckley*
The Origin of Species, - - - - - - - - *Darwin*
The Song of Life, - - - - - - - *Margaret Morley*
The Compleat Angler, - - - - - - - *Izaak Walton*
Speckled Trout, }
Locusts and Wild Honey, } - - - - - *John Burroughs*
Paradise Lost (Book VII, Line 387), - - - - - *Milton*
The Fish, the Man, and the Spirit, - - - - - *Leigh Hunt*
Hiawatha's Fishing, - - - - - - - *Longfellow*

For the Children.

Birds and Fishes, ("Kindergarten Stories and Morning
   Talks"), - - - - - - - - - *S. E. Wiltse*
Water Babies (The Salmon), - - - - - *Charles Kingsley*

STORIES.
The Minnow's Adventure.

Oh! such a beautiful lake! The water was so clear and pure that it had not only its own beauty, but could take the beauty of whatever was near it. Pictured by the lake, the slender, white-robed birches and the graceful willows that grew on the bank were as beautiful as in their reality; and so were the blue of the sky, the gold of the sunshine and the silvery light of the moon.

The lake was very, very deep. In some places near the shore, however, it was shallow, and rippled over the sand with only depth enough to float a leaf.

Out in the deep parts of the lake lived the black bass and the pickerel and other large fishes; but the tiny minnows, and their friends liked better the shallows, where the water was gilded and warmed by the sunshine. The fishes knew that there was an upper world, for many of them used to jump up a little way out of the water in their play, but they never stayed long, and did not like what little they knew of this upper world. To them it seemed too bright and hot and dry.

The older and more experienced fishes told strange tales to each other of wonderful creatures which, from time to time, had been known to come into the water. After swimming about in a more or less clumsy manner, these creatures always disappeared entirely; but back they would come, again and again, yes—the very same beings! The splashing and shaking of the water which most of them made was something astonishing, and the fishes were usually too much frightened by it to get more than hasty glimpses; but as each fish told the others whatever it had been, they knew that there were many different kinds of creatures among these visitors, and that it must be that they came from the dry upper world. I cannot tell you what the fishes tell them, but I know that wild ducks and frogs and dogs and boys loved to plunge into the clear, cool water of the lake, and dive and swim and float and be as much like fishes as they could. "Poor things!" said the fishes. "What a pity that they cannot stay always in the beautiful water world! Then they might learn to swim properly."

The minnows knew very little of all these things, however, though they, too, sometimes jumped out above the water; but one of their number had a strange adventure not long ago, during which he learned a great deal.

He was darting about in the sparkling water, chasing his playmates and having a merry frolic with them, when he suddenly found himself swimming round and round alone, and in a very small place. It surely was not the lake, nor yet the little river down which he had come some time ago. The minnow knew only these two places—the river and the lake. He had never been anywhere else, and had never heard of any world beside the water world, or of any living creatures larger than the black bass. You see he was very little and very young, scarcely more than a baby fish.

As he swam round and round in the tin dipper—for it was a tin dipper in which he had been caught—he wondered what part of the lake was this, and why he could not swim farther, and where his friends were.

While he was wondering, a black shadow covered the water and the minnow thought that night was coming on; but it was only the shadow of a little boy's head, as Philip, the owner of the tin dipper, looked in to see what he had caught.

"Oh! it's a shiner!" said he. "I never thought I could catch a shiner, they are so lively. I've often tried before, but they always got away. Isn't he pretty?"

"Oh! let me see, do, Philip!" said another eager voice, and another little head bent over the dipper.

"Oh! Oh! Oh! What a darling little fish! And how fast he goes! What round eyes he has and what a big mouth! O Philip, let's take him home and have him for a pet!"

"All right," said Philip; "we can put him in the goldfish globe."

The two children scrambled up the bank and ran into the house. They carried the dipper to their mamma and showed her the treasure they had in it.

"Where is the goldfish globe, mamma? May we have it? Isn't he a dear little thing? See how he shines!"

Mamma was almost as much interested as the children. She lifted the glass globe down from the high shelf where it stood, and helped to fill it with fresh, cold water.

"Now, dearies," she said, "I think we can probably keep this little fellow happy and well for a little while, and you can take care of him and watch him. But we must soon let him go back to his friends in the lake, for I am sure he will like that better than to stay here, no matter what we may do for him."

Philip and his sister were less disappointed at this than you might think; for they had often had pets in this way before, and had learned to enjoy it.

"Let's make it as much like the lake as we can," said Philip. "Don't you know it was all sandy there where I caught him? We can put some sand in the bottom of the globe."

"There were stones there, too," said Nannie, eagerly. "I will bring those two pretty stones I found yesterday."

In a little while the globe was ready and the water in the dipper was poured gently into it, the minnow scarcely knowing when change was made.

When he first noticed the white sand at the bottom of the
water, he darted down and nestled in it, thinking for a moment
that he was back in the lake ; but he soon found that he was still
in a small place and alone. When he tried to swim straight
ahead, he always came against the glass side of the globe ; and
this puzzled him very much, for it was as clear as water and yet
so hard. He knew he had never seen anything like that in the
lake. I suppose an older fish would have thought it was ice.
When the minnow found that he could not swim a long way in
this place, and that it certainly was not the lake, he began to
explore very carefully, and soon decided that it was, at any rate,
a very pleasant place.

The sand and the pretty stones at the bottom seemed very
homelike, and the minnow soon found that he could play very
much as he used to in the lake, although, of course, he missed
his companions.

The stones had been placed a little way apart, and it was
great fun to swim between them and around them part of the
time. He could play "sink and rise," too, and that is one of
the favorite plays among fishes. He was so glad that the water
in the globe was deep enough for that game. Altogether the
minnow decided that he could be very comfortable in this new
home, although it was not to be compared with the lake, and
although he could never be quite happy without any companions.

While he was swimming about and his little fish brain (for fishes
have brains) was full of these thoughts, Philip and Nannie were
watching him with great delight. They enjoyed seeing his graceful motions as he darted back and forth between the stones or
swam around near the side of the globe, sometimes stretching and
straightening himself out, but usually curving his wavy little body
one way and another.

The children wondered whether he was ever perfectly still ; for
they saw that even when he floated, as he did occasionally near
the top of the water, he moved either his tail or his fins slightly
and lazily.

Mamma was kept busy answering their questions and they were
very much interested in all she told them. They could see the
minnow gulp in water with his big mouth, and open and shut his

gill covers as he sent the water out again, and their mamma explained that he did not send the water out through his gills until after he had used the air from it, and that this was the fish's way of breathing.

"I think 'shiners' is a good name for these minnows," said Philip.

"Yes," said Nannie, "but this one ought to have a special name. What shall we call him, Mamma?"

Mamma suggested several names: Silversides, Flash, Speckle, Twistabout, Ripple and Dart;—and the children finally decided on "Ripple Silversides." "He ought to have two," said Nannie, "just as we have."

All that day the children hovered about the globe, finding more and more to admire in their active little pet, and wondering more and more at his shining scales, his delicate, gauzy fins, his round, staring eyes, and funny mouth.

The next morning, the children's first thought was for Ripple Silversides. They found him as lively as ever, and flashing brightly in the sunlight which streamed in at the window.

Philip caught him at last by dipping a little cup into the globe, but he had to try a great many times. Nannie had the dipper ready filled with fresh water, and Ripple was soon transferred.

The next thing was to take him to the lake, and Philip and Nannie ran down the bank with almost as much eagerness as when they had scrambled up the day before; for they had been thinking what fun Ripple would have in telling his friends where he had been and what he had seen, so they were in a hurry to put him back into his old home. They went to the very place where they had found him, put the dipper down under the water and saw him an instant as he swam over the dipper's edge and out into the lake.

"Now he is gone!" said Philip. "Oh, see! There is a whole crowd of them! Now I cannot tell which one is Ripple!"

Nannie looked rather wistfully at the swift flashes gleaming farther and farther away in the water. "I suppose Ripple is delighted to be back there again," she said. "Of course it is more fun than it would be for him to live alone in a glass globe in the house."

In the meantime, Ripple Silversides was enjoying to the utmost the freedom of swimming in a big place, and the fun of being again one of a throng. The excitement of the other minnows at his return and at what he told them was very great; and for a long time Ripple Silverside's adventure was one of the favorite stories of the water-world!

EMILIE POULSSON.

Mr. Stickleback.

A certain little fish was swimming about in the river one day, wondering what he should do with himself. He was usually a happy fellow, quite satisfied to pass his time as the other young fishes did; but now he was getting older and began to feel as if he wanted to do more than simply find his own food and amuse himself.

True, there was plenty of fun to be had. Perhaps you think that children are the only ones who enjoy playing "tag" and "hide-and-seek," and running races; but, if so, you must change your mind about that, for the fishes know all these games and many more, and have merry times down in the water.

But "Fun is not fun if you have too much of it," thought this little fish; (oh, but he was a wise one!) "I wonder what else I can find to do! He swam idly toward the bank of the river, and wandered among the plants that grew there. Suddenly he caught sight of something fastened to one of the plants.

"Oh! how beautiful! how convenient!" thought Mr. Stickleback as he swam nearer and looked more closely at the newly discovered object.

"No dinner here for you, sir!" gasped an excited voice; and our little friend found himself nose to nose with another fish very much like himself, and who seemed all ready to be angry with him.

"Dinner! I've just had my dinner, and a good one, too; I shan't be hungry for some time yet," said Mr. Stickleback. "I was merely admiring this pretty nest here. No harm in that, is there, friend?" he added peaceably.

The other fish grew quiet as Mr. Stickleback said this, and

answered, a little apologetically: "I thought you might be after eggs; and though I have no eggs as yet, I want to discourage all prowlers. Of course, while I have a spine in my body I will defend my nest and my eggs."

"Why, that is just the way I should feel, I know it is. I do not blame you one bit," said Mr. Stickleback. "And, speaking of spines, aren't mine something like yours? and isn't your family named Cottoida?"

"Yes, indeed," said the other pushing himself a little nearer with his right fin; but I am usually called Stickleback,—Purple Stickleback, on account of my color, you see."

"And I am Stickleback, too,—Scarlet Stickleback, on account of *my* color; and we are of the very same family. How delightful! Let's have a race!" and off they started with one vigorous whisk of their tails which sent them swiftly down the stream.

They never knew how pretty they looked; but as they flashed along, one in deep beautiful purple, the other in "glowing scarlet trimmed with white and green," their color gleamed out with wonderful brightness. They soon swam back to the group of plants, for Purple Stickleback would not go far from his nest; and Mr. Stickleback said: "*Now* I know what to do. I am going to make a nest like yours."

"Very well," said the other. "There's plenty of room here, and I do not think there is a better place along the whole bank."

Mr. Scarlet Stickleback was already too much interested to care to talk or play any more. He peered about among the plants looking for strong stems to which to fasten his nest, and soon decided.

"I can make it firm here," he said to himself, "even if the river rushes as wildly as it did after the last storm." Then Mr. Stickleback went to work indeed. He bit off pieces of leaf and carried them to the plant stems which he had chosen, fastening each bit with some glue which he found he had with him. Back and forth he went, patiently biting, carrying, gluing the tiny bits of leaf, until at last he had pieced together a leafy floor large enough for the bottom of his house.

Then he stopped to rejoice over his work and to consider what to do next. "It seems to be rather thin and light," he said, as

MR. STICKLEBACK AND HIS NEST.

he watched it swaying up and down in the water, although fastened by its edges to the plant stems. "I know how I can make it steady;" and quick as thought Mr. Stickleback folded his fins close to his body and darted down through the water to the sandy bottom of the river. His plan was to take sand up to his nest and so make the floor of it heavy and steady. Perhaps you are wondering how he was going to carry the sand, he, a little fish, with no hands, nor claws, nor feet; but he wasted no time in wondering. He would not ask any better way than his way, which was to fill his mouth with sand. Rising to the clump of plants, he very carefully emptied the sand from his mouth on the green floor, and then dived again. This he did several times, until he had sprinkled the whole floor with sand and made it so heavy that it no longer bobbed up and down in the water, but kept its place undisturbed, even when he tested it as he did by lashing his tail about furiously and making a great commotion in the water.

"So far, so good," he said to himself: "and now I must make the walls. This *is* going to be a beautiful nest!" Then followed more biting of leaves, and carrying, and gluing the bits together. Slow work it was, with no tools, remember! no hands, or feet, or claws. But little by little the green sides were built up higher around the edge of the platform, and finally a roof was made in the same way—of leaf bits glued together. As he built he constantly rubbed against the inside walls of the house, and a sort of sticky stuff which oozed out of his body was rubbed off; and, what do you think? this hardened into a sort of varnish, so that the inside of his house was as smooth and nice as could be!

Mr. Stickleback's nest was not like a bird's nest, all open on the top. It was more in the shape of a barrel, and about as large as a man's fist; and he made two round doorways in it. When he had finished these, he swam through and through the nest with great delight, rejoicing in the smooth walls, the strong floor, and the doorways *just* large enough for him to swim through easily. When he was perfectly satisfied that there was nothing more he could do to make the nest prettier or better, he swam swiftly away.

It was some time before he came back; but when he did come, he was not alone. He brought Mrs. Stickleback with him; and you can imagine how happy he was to show her the nest he had built, and how pleased she must have been.

By and by when the nest was full of eggs, Mr. Stickleback was so busy he scarcely knew what to do. He was so anxious about those eggs! and with good reason, too, for some of the hungry fishes would have been glad to eat them if they could have found a chance. But Mr. Stickleback was too watchful for them. The way he swam about that nest—first to one door and then to the other, to see that the eggs were safe—was something wonderful to see.

He was very particular about leaving both doorways open, although it made more for him to guard, of course; but the wise little fellow knew that the eggs needed the fresh, cool water of the river to flow over them in order to hatch them, so he was more than willing to watch both doors. Besides protecting the eggs, Mr. Stickleback had to turn them over sometimes, taking those which were underneath and putting them on the top so that the water should flow over them all.

This busy time lasted for several weeks* and then—then Mr. Stickleback became busier than ever; for all the tiny eggs over which he had been watching hatched into little fishes, hundreds and hundreds of baby Sticklebacks, his own little ones!

Back door, front door, back door, front door—more like a fierce little soldier than ever was Mr. Stickleback as he went his rounds now, defending his babies as he had defended his eggs from the hungry fishes. And how they grew, those babies! It seemed to Papa Stickleback as if they were scarcely hatched before they began to get out of the nest. "In, in! stay in, my dears!" he would say as he looked at them through the front door; but in the meantime, one or two would slip out of the back door and swim away. They were too little to know any better and Papa Stickleback could only chase after them as fast as his fins could carry him and take them back to the nest, one at a time. How did he carry the children? Why, just as he had carried the sand when building his nest. In his mouth! By the time he had caught the little runaways, or swimaways, and had poked them into the nest again, one or two others would have gone out of the front door; and he would have to swim after them and catch them

---

* Some authorities say two. or three some say six weeks.

and carry them back in his mouth. Yes, indeed, it was a time of great anxiety.

When the poor father was very much worried, his gay colors would grow dull and pale, but they would brighten again when all went well with his family; while if an enemy came near the nest, the red and green of Mr. Stickleback's uniform became more brilliant as he bravely fought to protect his little ones. So brave was this tiny little father, in fact, that he would rush out and drive away fishes a great deal bigger than himself if he thought they were coming to trouble his family.

Fish babies grow fast, however, as I said before, and the happy day soon came when Papa Stickleback had all his children out of the nest and away from the plants, and was teaching them the games which he used to play when he was young.

In the midst of the fun they were joined by Mr. Purple Stickleback and his children. "Hurrah for a race between us,—you and your children on one side, and I and my children on the other," said he. So the two companies started off, and it was a sight to see!—their gauzy fins waving, their bodies shining, and their colors—the deep, beautiful purple and the "glowing scarlet trimmed with white and green"—making the water glow with splendor as they flashed through it. You would almost have thought that a rainbow had fallen into the stream!

How the race ended I do not know; but I do know that by this time some of those Stickleback children must have grown up and made nests of their own, and they probably were just as busy and as happy and as faithful in taking care of their children as their little father had been; for it is said that all the Stickleback fathers are of just that kind!

EMILIE POULSSON.

TREES.

To the Teacher:—

(For ourselves, in our study of trees, we might take a first word from Emerson, who says in his essay on Nature: "It seems as if the day was not wholly profane in which we have given heed to some natural object."

Have ready some twigs with leaf-buds on them. By keeping these in the house a few days in water and where they get the sunshine, and by having besides a few twigs freshly gathered on the day of the talk, you can have leaf-buds in different stages of opening. Have also pieces of wood, some with bark and some without, and a transverse slice which will show the rings of growth.

Maple sugar—enough for each child to have a taste—and pieces of india rubber should be provided also, but kept in reserve till the subject of sap is reached.

Begin the talk by letting the children examine twigs, leaf-buds, bark, etc., and tell that they come from the tree.)

THE TALK.

How do trees look in winter? Is it winter now? No, it is spring—early spring. In early spring how do the trees look? What have we found on the tree twigs this morning? How will the trees look in summer? How will they get all the pretty, green leaves they have in summer? From the leaf-buds, of course. The leaves—tiny, tiny ones, but a great many—are packed tightly away in all the buds on all the twigs, and when the spring rains have watered them and the spring sunshine has warmed them, the leaf-buds will open wider and wider each day, and finally spread out these little new leaves to the air and sun and showers.

The tall, thick part of the tree is called the trunk. (Show rings of growth and explain them; explain also that by counting these rings the age of the tree may be approximately determined.) Do you know any other parts of the tree? (Branches, boughs, roots, etc.)

Was the tree from which I broke this twig *always a big tree?* No, it has been growing for many years. Long ago it was a tiny tree, and before that it was only a seed. This seed sent little roots down into the ground and pushed a little stem up through the ground, and so it became a tiny tree. It drank the water which the rain brought, and it breathed the fresh air which the winds brought, and rejoiced and grew green and strong in the warm sunshine, and grew larger and larger every year; and so it became a tall, thick tree, with many branches. (Speak of the roots, reaching out on all sides in the ground, as the branches do in the air, and of the firm support this gives the tree. How does the tree drink water? Through the little spongy mouths at the tip ends of the roots. The water soaks through the roots to the stem or trunk, up through the trunk into the branches, and from the branches into the twigs and stems, and then into every leaf. The water which the roots drink is not just the same as when it fell from the clouds in rain, because it has soaked through the ground and now has in it just what the trees need. As it passes up into the tree it is called sap (crude sap). After it has flowed out to the leaves the (elaborated) sap flows back all through the tree again, and it helps the tree to grow; just as what we eat and drink helps our bodies to grow.

A tree or plant cannot live and grow without sap. When you break a flower from a plant and find the stem wet and juicy, it is because sap was flowing through the stem. At the time when the bluebird and the robin first come back, the sap starts, and flows up and down in the tree most busily, as if to hurry and make its thousands of leaves grow to hide the nests of the birds.

People found out that they could make something very delicious out of the sap of a certain kind of maple tree. It is called the *sugar-maple* tree. Does n't that make you think of something? (Sugar-maple, maple sugar!) Surely maple sugar is made of the sap of the sugar-maple tree! The farmer away off in the country cut a hole in the tree just deep enough to reach the sap as it flowed down, put a little wooden pipe into the hole, and hung a pail on the pipe. The sap flowed through the tree trunk, but when it came to the hole it ran out into the pipe. The farmer put the sap which he gathered from all his sugar maples into a big boiler and boiled it till the water went off in steam and left just the thick sugar. Should you like to see some? Should you like to *taste* some? You shall, at lunch time. The farmer does not take all of the sap. There is plenty left for the sugar-maple tree to use for its growing.

There are other trees whose sap is useful for different purposes; but we will only speak of one other now—the india-rubber tree (the caoutchouc)—which grows in the hot countries. (Let the children name articles made from the sap of this tree.

Speak of the beauty of trees, the grateful shade afforded by their foliage, the fruits, the vari-colored leaves of autumn, and then again of the usefulness of the sap to the tree and to us; and, lastly, of wood and its manifold uses.)

TEACHER'S READING.

Trees, - - - - - - - - - - George B. Emerson
Trees of North Eastern America, - - - - - - - Newhall
Succession of Forest Trees, - - - - - - - - Thoreau
Trees. How to tell some of them in Winter ("The Kindergarten," January, 1891), - - - - - - - E. G. Howe
North American Trees, - - - - - - - Charles Sargent
A Taste of Maine Birch, - - - - - - John Burroughs
Hiawatha's Canoe, - - - - - - - - Longfellow
Forest Hymn, - - - - - - - - - - Bryant
Planting of the Apple Tree, - - - - - - - Bryant
The Birch Tree,
The Oak,
The Beggar,   - - - - - - - - - - Lowell
Rhoecus,
The Dryads, - - - - - - - - - - Leigh Hunt
The Plucky Prince, - - - - - - "St. Nicholas," 1883
The Wood Giant, - - - - - - - - - Whittier
The Palm Tree, - - - - - - - - - Whittier
The Talking Oak, - - - - - - - - - Tennyson
O Woodman Spare that Tree! - - - - - George P. Morris

For the Children.

The Miraculous Pitcher, - - - - - - - N. Hawthorne
The Little Tree that Wanted Other Leaves.
A Story for the Staffs and Rings ("Kindergarten Stories and Morning Talks"), - - - - - - - - S. E. Wiltse

---

STORIES.

The Four Apple Trees.

Many years ago there was a man who wanted to have a beautiful orchard. So he sent for some young trees, knowing that he should not have to wait so long for his orchard if he planted trees which had already had a good start in growing.

Unfortunately, however, the trees arrived just at a time when the man was obliged to leave home for several days. He was afraid the trees would not live unless they were planted very soon, and yet he could not stay to attend to them. Just then a man came along who wanted work.

"Do you know how to set out trees?" asked the owner.

"Yes, indeed," said the other man.

"Then you may stay and set out these young apple trees. I am going to have an orchard, and I have marked the places for the trees, with stones."

By and by the owner of the trees came back and went to look at his orchard. He had been gone four days.

"How is this!" said he; "only four trees set out?"

"That is all I had time for," answered the other man. "I dug great holes, so that the roots might be spread out to the farthest tip; I hauled rich earth from the woods, so that the trees might have the best of food; I set the trees straight and filled the holes with care. This took all the time, but these four trees are well planted."

"That is too slow a way for me," said the owner. "I can plant the whole orchard in one day."

So he went to work and planted the other trees in his own way. He did not dig the holes large enough or deep enough, and so, many of the little root-mouths were broken off when he set the trees into the holes. He did not take pains to get soft, rich earth to fill the holes, and so the trees could not have as good food as they needed.

The poor little trees lived for a while, but they were never very strong, never bore very good apples, and at last were cut down. All that was left of the orchard were the four trees which had been planted with such faithfulness and care.

These four trees are now older than an old man, and have been bearing delicious great apples for many, many years.

As Dr. E. E. Hale says, when he tells the story, these four apple trees stand as a memorial of what it is to do a thing well.

The Story of Echo.

Among the trees of the forest, and where the cool streams run, beautiful wood-nymphs used to have their homes. They loved to play in the flickering sunlight and under the dancing leaves, and people sometimes caught sight of the gleam of their white feet as they dipped them in the rushing waters of the brook.

There was one gay nymph named Echo, whose chief amusement was to play tricks upon, and to tease her companions. "Daphne! Oh, come here!—quick—just see!" she would sometimes call, and when Daphne came running to the spot, eager to see what there was to be seen, Echo would have vanished as completely as if she had never been there—until presently a stifled laughed showed her hiding place.

Echo was, too, a great chatterer; she never listened long to any one else, but was sure to talk a great deal herself. One day she came upon a shepherd sitting on a rock, and, watching his sheep as they cropped the grass below, she noticed that some of the sheep were beginning to stray from the flock, and, thinking this a fine chance for a bit of fun, she at once began to laugh and talk with the shepherd, to keep him from thinking of his charge. Presently not one of the flock was left in sight, and then, with a laugh at the dismayed face of the shepherd, Echo, too, ran away and left him.

At first the other nymphs used to laugh at her nonsense, and enjoyed the fun as much as Echo herself did; but as she was continually playing her tricks upon everybody in season and out of season, and as the tricks, like that she played on the shepherd, were often unkind ones, her companions gradually came to leave her out of their sports and plays, and after a time, as she did not mend her ways, avoided her altogether. One day it happened that Juno (Hera), the queen of the gods, came to the forest, and Echo troubled her so much with her foolish chattering that, finally, Juno declared a just punishment upon the teasing nymph. "Since Echo talks and jokes only to weary every one," Juno said, "she shall no longer be able to speak unless some one first speaks to her. She shall have power to answer, but never to begin a conversation."

Echo, ashamed and sorry, went away into the deep woods, where ever after she dwelt alone. She was seldom seen by men, but a traveler, once, coming out of the wood, told how he had lost his way at nightfall, and had called loudly, hoping some one might hear and come to his aid; he seemed to have a faint answer, he said, but as he could not tell whence it came, he called again, saying "Come here!" "Here," the voice answered. "Where are you?" he called. "Where are you?" replied the voice. Finally, out of patience, "Away with you!" he shouted. "Away with you," came back with an angry sound. After that he heard no more, nor, although he searched the wood, was he able to find a trace of any one.

Echo's voice is still heard sometimes in lonely places—but only when some one calls to her;—if the call is a laughing one, she laughs back; if it is sad, she answers mournfully, but, merry or sad, she never shows herself.

F. H.

The Tree.

The Tree's early leaf-buds were bursting their brown;
"Shall I take them away?" said the Frost, sweeping down.
   " No, let them alone
   Till the blossoms have grown,"
Prayed the Tree, while it trembled from rootlet to crown.

The Tree bore its blossoms, and all the birds sung;
"Shall I take them away?" said the Wind, as it swung.
   " No, let them alone
   Till the berries have grown,"
Said the Tree, while its leaflets, quivering, hung.

The Tree bore its fruit in the midsummer glow;
Said the girl, " May I gather thy sweet berries now?"
   " Yes, all thou canst see;
   Take them; all are for thee,"
Said the Tree, while it bent its laden boughs low.

BJORSTERNE BJORNSEN.

The Maple Tree's Surprise.

When David Wylie went to live in the country he did not know which way to turn, there was so much to see and so much to hear.

He coasted on the snow, and skated on the ice, and watched the winter birds, and helped to feed the horses and cows and hens and chickens. Just back of the house was a grove of great maple trees, where he liked to play when the snow was not too deep. In the midst of this grove was a small log house. David often asked his Papa what this house was for, and Papa always replied: "Wait until spring, and you shall see; these big maple trees have a surprise in store for you!"

One morning in early spring, when the sun shone very warm, and the snow was beginning to melt, Papa said: "David, after breakfast you will find me at the log house;" then he hurried away. David soon finished his breakfast and started off in great haste, but stopped short at the first maple tree, for there hung a bright, shining, tin pail! He wondered how it came there, and started to take it down, when he saw that it was hanging on a spout, which was driven into the tree-trunk. From the spout was trickling something which looked like water as it "drip, dripped" into the pail below. As he looked about, he saw that every tree in the grove had one, two or even three pails hung on spouts! This must be the surprise, but what was it for?

Off he went to the log house; and there he found that his father had built a fire, and over the fire was swinging a great iron kettle. "Papa," said he, "why is the water running out of the trees? What is the kettle for? Why have you built the fire?" "Well," replied Papa, "I am very busy, but here comes Mamma, who can tell you all about it, while you watch the rest of us work."

Then Mamma told him how the maple trees had been sleeping and resting all winter, and how the warm sunshine and soft spring rains had wakened them, and set the sweet sap running from the roots way up to the highest branches. "But the trees do not need all of the sap," said Mamma, "so Papa has driven these spouts in, that he may catch some of the sap as it hurries through the tree-trunk. And what you thought was water was this juice or sap of the tree trickling into the pails." Just then up came two or three men with buckets full of sap which they had gathered from the tin pails; they poured it into the kettle, but Papa first gave Mamma and David some to drink. It tasted like water with a little sugar in it, and David did n't care for it at all.

They then watched the sap in the kettle as it boiled and bubbled away; and every little while Papa skimmed it with a big

GATHERING SAP.

spoon, till by and by it was clear. David said, "It smells like maple syrup!" and Papa replied, "That's just what it is!" He next poured it into big pans and little pans, and middle-sized pans, and it looked thick and brown and sweet, and David knew that when it was cool and hard it would be maple sugar!

Then Mamma said: "There are ever so many kinds of maple trees, but only this kind gives us sugar. Now what do you suppose we call it?" David thought its name must be sugar-maple, and sure enough it was! And now he wonders if there are any other children whom the sugar-maple is waiting to surprise.

F. E. MANN.

Pussy Willow.

Pussy Willow wakened
   From her Winter nap
For the frolic Spring Breeze
   On her door *would* tap.

"It is chilly weather
   Though the sun feels good;
I will wrap up warmly;
   Wear my furry hood."

Mistress Pussy Willow
   Opened wide her door;
Never had the sunshine
   Seemed so bright before.

Never had the brooklet
   Seemed so full of cheer;
"Good morning, Pussy Willow,
   Welcome to you, dear!"

Never guest was quainter;—
   Pussy came to town
In a hood of silver gray
   And a coat of brown.

Happy little children
   Cried with laugh and shout,
"Spring is coming, coming,
   Pussy Willow's out!"

KATE L. BROWN.

The American Teacher.

SPRING.

To the Teacher:—

(The prevalent custom of ta'*k*ing about the " glad new day " and it* name each morning, often noting also the current month and year, affords an easy opportunity for questioning the children upon the whole round of the seasons, thus leading to a talk upon Spring.)

THE TALK.

Jack Frost and North Wind will soon be gone altogether and Winter with them. How has the earth looked during the Winter? The ground brown and hard, or covered with snow and ice, trees leafless, no grass, no flowers, few birds. But Spring is coming. What will the spring-time bring? Grass, leaves on the trees, pussy willows, flowers, birds, etc., etc. Will the flowers come while the ground is frozen and the air so cold? What will thaw the ground and warm the air? Have we not had sunshine all Winter? Yes, but we shall have more sunshine now.

Do you remember how dark it was in the Winter mornings? Sometimes we needed lamplight or gaslight at breakfast. Perhaps you remember, too, how dark the Winter afternoons were! Towards Spring we have sunshine earlier in the mornings and later in the afternoons, so that the days are longer and brighter and warmer.

What will the warm Spring sunshine do? Can sunshine alone get the earth ready and make the flowers grow? What will the rain do? Which wind brings the rain? What other winds are about in Spring? What is the name of the wind which comes from the warm lands? Where have the birds been all Winter? Which birds are the first to come back to us in the Spring? What will they be busy about soon? Did you know that birds sometimes like to weave bits of string or worsted in with the grasses and straws of which they make their nests? (If the kindergarten is in a likely neighborhood for nest-building, let the children place some bits of string or thread where the birds will find them.

Which flowers come first? Tell the colors of each.

Are we glad that spring is coming?

(Speak of the gladness the season brings to all; to the cattle who rejoice in going to the fields once more; to the birds who are so happy in their nest-building; to the animals and insects who have been curled up in hiding somewhere, waiting for warm weather; even to the fishes who leap joyously in the waters, no longer icebound.

We must not forget to sing the song of the farmer and talk a little about his spring work, of gathering sap, and plowing and planting.)

TEACHER'S READING.

A Year of Miracle,	*W. C. Gannett*
Spring ("Sharp Eyes"),	*W. H. Gibson*
April ("Birds and Poets"),	*John Burroughs*
The Bluebird, } ("Wake Robin"), The Return of the Birds, }	*John Burroughs*
Prologue to Canterbury Tales, } The Flower and the Leaf, }	*Chaucer*
Grass,	*Emily Dickinson*
The Voice of the Grass,	*Sarah Roberts*
Spring ("In Memoriam"),	*Tennyson*
Suthin' in the Pastoral Line, } To the Dandelion, }	*Lowell*
Nature and the Poets,	*Keats*
Early Spring,	*Wordsworth*
Home Thoughts from Abroad,	*R. Browning*
Spring has Come,	*O. W. Holmes*
Daffy-down-dilly,	*Warner*
The Daffodils,	*Wordsworth*
The Daffodils,	*Herrick*
The Secrets of the Spring, } March Winds, }	*Nora Perry*
March,	*Celia Thaxter*

For the Children.

My Friend in Green,	*Holmes' Third Reader*

STORIES.

Spring and Her Helpers.

One day in March old Winter received a message from Father Time, saying that Spring was ready to take charge of the land and that Winter might go away for his long vacation, as soon as he liked.

Winter immediately pulled out his pocket calendar. "Surely, surely," said he, "I must be off in a day or two. I suppose every one will be glad," he continued, a little mournfully; "they are alway in a hurry for me to go!"

"But they are glad to see you come again," whistled North Wind. "Don't you remember how joyful the children were over the first snow and ice? And how glad the plants were to have a chance to rest? And how sleepy some of the animals were getting? They would miss you dreadfully if you didn't take your turn—even more than they know, perhaps."

"Very true, friend," said old Winter, brightening. "Spring and Summer and Autumn could not do their work if I neglected mine. So I'll go as soon as Spring appears, and rest and be ready to come back in December."

A few days after this Winter started on his journey, and Spring became the ruler of the land. Scarcely any one realized the change at the time, for many of Winter's belongings were left lying about, and Spring could not do her work all at once. Nor could she do it without help, for her work was nothing more nor less than to make the earth beautiful, and Winter had certainly left it looking very bare and dreary. But I assure you Spring knew whom to ask for help. First she went to the Sun. "Good Sun," said she, "pray, send me more and more of your light and heat every day, if you will; for the earth is hard and bare and cold."

The great Sun said not a word, but smiled brighly from his home of golden fire, for great companies of his messengers, the sunbeams, had already trooped down to the earth with permission to go earlier each morning and stay later each night, that they might help Spring to make the earth beautiful.

But Spring knew that she and the sunbeams could not do it all. So she spoke to King Æolus. "Good Æolus," said she, "North Wind has served Winter well, but he cannot do my kind of work. I pray you keep him at home now and let me have his three brothers—the gentle South Wind to be with me most of the time, and East Wind and West Wind to help when I need them.'

King Æolus had been expecting this request, for Spring made it every year; and there was already a great bustle in his rocky caverns as the three brothers began to bestir themselves. South

Wind sent a little breeze as a messenger to Spring, to say that they would be ready whenever she called them, and would gladly help her to make the earth beautiful.

Then began a busy time indeed for Spring and her helpers.

The sunbeams worked with never a sound. They shone here and they shone there. They melted the ice and snow, and coaxed vapor from the surface of the water and carried it up to the blue sky, where it floated in downy white clouds. They warmed the earth and gilded the waters and made the sky bluer than ever.

The Winds worked, too, each in his own way. When Spring saw that rain was needed, she called East Wind, and he immediately emptied the clouds of all that the sunbeams had saved. "People make a great mistake when they think that the sunbeams and I have nothing to do with each other," said he; "for if the sunbeams didn't bring up the vapor for me, and if I didn't empty the clouds for them, how would the earth have rain, I wonder? To be sure, I always carry some with me, but I should not have enough without that which is stored away in the clouds."

East Wind hovered about, seeming to be everywhere at once in his big gray cloak, while the raindrops were hurrying down to the earth. They ran here and they rolled there. They softened the ground, they gave water to all the thirsty roots, helped the trees and other plants to make their sap, washed the dust off of everything and filled up the little brooks. The raindrops also unfastened the coats of the seeds that were in the ground, and loosened the covers of the pussy willows and the furry hoods which the ferns had worn all winter; and, with their tapping and drumming, they really awakened the grasses and some of the flowers, but the sleepy things only stirred a little, saying drowsily: "Spring does not want us to get up yet; it is too cold and too early."

Spring herself shivered a little whenever East Wind was around, but he and the raindrops were so useful that she bore the cold and dampness very willingly. "Thanks, little Raindrops, and to you, too, East Wind," said she. "You have done your work well. And now the sunbeams must take their turn again. South Wind, too, will find something to do, I dare say." South Wind was ready at the first mention of his name. He had come by way of the sunny lands where the birds live in the winter, and had brought a few back with him—two or three bluebirds and robins.

"You dear things," said Spring, caressingly. "I can work so much better now that you have come. Your singing cheers me on. Fly abroad now, and let the people hear your glad songs and catch a glimpse of you now and then."

Spring gazed fondly after them. "Robin is such a cheery fellow," said she; "and Bluebird is so bonny in his sky-tinted feathers. No other birds are quite as dear to me, and I am sure they carry joy wherever they go."

"The joy they give is because they sing of you," whispered South Wind.

While Spring welcomed the birds, South Wind had not been idle. His first work was to roll up the big gray cloak which East Wind was trailing after him.

"Take that with you, please, brother," said he; "I have no use for it, and, in fact, it is rather in my way." After that he and the sunbeams worked together, warming and drying the air and the ground, and coaxing all the growing things to make haste.

The South Wind whistled sweet, merry little tunes, while the sunbeams touched the seeds and the half-awake leaves and flowers, and they started up, one after another, fresher and prettier than ever "from their long, long wintry nap."

But Spring's work was not yet finished. She called for West Wind. He knew just what to do, and he did it well. He blew here and he blew there. He swept the hillsides and meadows, and took away the old leaves which had been such useful blankets for the plants all winter. Then he and the sunbeams, for they always work with him, went into the farthest corner of the woods and dried the soaked mosses and tree trunks, and greeted the bears, woodchucks and squirrels who were running about to stretch themselves after keeping still all winter. West Wind whistled a louder and jollier tune than South Wind had. The sunbeams shone their brightest; the smooth waters flashed splendor; the rushing streams murmured music; fishes darted about under the clear ripples; frogs sang their gurgling song; insects sported joyously in the air, and birds warbled to each other everywhere.

Spring looked and listened, and looked again over the land which Winter had left so bare and silent and dreary. Soft, green grass covered the ground and blossoms beautified the orchards, while on every tree tiny leaf-banners fluttered and rustled. All her pretty flowers—and who has prettier flowers than Spring?—stood in their places—daffodils, crocuses, tulips, dandelions, violets—none was missing.

Spring gazed with joy. Her work was done, for the world was radiant with beauty.

EMILIE POULSSON.

The Meeting of the Winds.

The North and the South Winds met one day in a field beside a river. The North Wind had brought some snow the night before, but the South Wind blew soon after, and melted nearly all of it. Only a few white patches were left, here and there, along the sunny banks of the stream.

As soons as the winds came near each other, the South Wind said: "Good morning, brother; I am glad to meet you, though your cold breath quite chills me."

"But I am not glad to meet you," answered the North Wind. "Why did you melt my snow so quickly? Could you not let it lie for one day?"

"The time has come for the grass and flowers, you know, brother, and I must be at work," said the gentle South Wind.

"There was no need of such haste," said the burly North Wind. "When friends meet, they should be polite."

"I have to call up the daisies and waken the roses," said the South Wind, "and make all the fields green by the first of May; I have no time to lose. Look at yonder meadow, how brown it is; and at these trees, how bare! Scarcely a fly is buzzing in the sunshine, and not a tortoise has yet crept out of his hole in the ground."

"I do not care for your daisies and your tortoises," muttered the North Wind; "you want to hurry me off, but I will not go so soon."

"Have you not had the whole winter to yourself?" asked the South Wind—"freezing the brooks, driving away all my birds and butterflies, and covering the fields and roads and bushes and barns with snow? If I chanced to come then to pay you a little visit some bright morning, how quickly you drove me away again! Never might I stay till the sun went down."

"The winter is my time," said the North Wind; "it belongs to me, and you had no right to come then."

"And the spring is my time," said the South Wind; "you know the law is that I must have the fields now."

"You think a great deal of yourself," said the North Wind, angrily, "but I am stronger than you. I can fly farther and see things you never see. Where do you think I came from this morning?"

"Tell me; I cannot guess," whispered the South Wind.

"I came all the way from the icy pole, where the sea is frozen over, and the land is covered with snow that never melts. The white bear lives there; I saw one but a few hours ago, watching for fish by a hole that he had broken through the ice."

"But you never saw my home or the strange sights that are there," said the South Wind. "I come from the far-off torrid zone, where the snow never falls, and the frost never kills the buds and flowers. There the panther lives. I passed by one last night in the forest, lying out on the branch of a great tree watching for his prey, that he might spring down on it as it passed beneath."

"But I see the Esquimaux," answered the North Wind, "in their strange skin dresses, living in houses of snow. They fight the fierce walrus on the ice, and spear the fur-covered seal from their little boats that dance on the waves. I watch the Northern Lights, so red and beautiful, shooting up like bright flames in the sky, and the night is almost as bright as the day. Then the Esquimau harnesses his dogs and the Laplander his reindeer, and they travel swiftly over the frozen plain. Yesterday I blew with all my might until I loosened a field of ice and sent it out to sea. A white bear was on it, and he sailed on his ice-boat across the sea to Iceland. As I passed the steep, high rocks on the shores of Greenland, I saw the eider ducks brooding there. Each one had lined her nest with soft down plucked from her own breast. Then I frightened them with my hoarse voice, and thousands of them—yes, hundreds of thousands—rose up in the air like a cloud."

"But let me ask you," murmured the South Wind, "did you ever hear among your icebergs and frozen waters, the song of the oriole and mocking bird that I hear every day in the woods where I live? You look at your Esquimaux in their snow houses, but I peep in at the hut of the Indian that stands under the forest shades, or I blow against the sail of his canoe and waft it up some quiet river, where the trees grow thick on each side and meet overhead. The red flamingo wades out into the water, and the monkeys and parrots chatter among the high branches. I see the boa constrictor coiled among the roots on the shore and watch the alligator floating down the stream. My home is among the orange trees and in the fields where the sugar cane grows. There I lie still and sleep, or wake to go forth on my journeys over the earth, not to freeze up the ground and make barren and bare, but to cover it with green, and bring out the buds and flowers in every bush and tree."

While the Winds were talking in this way, the River, which had been listening to them, said: "Why do you thus boast and provoke each other? Why not speak gently and kindly of the wonderful things you have seen? You would not change homes, would you?"

"No, indeed," each one replied; "I love my own the best."

"Then," said the River, "what good can come of disputing when both are satisfied? As for me, I love you both. I am glad for the North Wind to blow cold, and cover me with ice in the winter, so that the merry skaters can come and glide swiftly over my smooth surface. And I love the South Wind to breathe softly in the spring, and make my banks smooth again, and waken the frogs along my shore, and bring the fisherman in his boat, and the boys to swim. Let us all be friends, then, and love each other, and be satisfied with what our good Creator has given us, and be happy in pleasing him."

Then the North Wind said: "I am willing to be friends again. It is true that the Spring is your time, gentle South Wind. I will not stay to nip your opening flowers, but will fly away to my cold home."

And the South Wind said: "Forgive me if I was rude, brother. When November shall come once more, I will leave the fields and woods to you. Take this sprig of evergreen to remember me by, and may it not fade until we meet again. Farewell."

CHARLES FOSTER.

"*New Lights on Old Paths,*" Chas. Foster Pub. Co., Phila., Pa.

The Little Worm That Was Glad to Be Alive.

Once there was a little worm about as long as the nail of my thumb, and no larger round than a big darning needle. This little worm lived in a little house that he had made for himself in the ground, just big enough to hold him when he rolled himself up like a little ball with his head sticking out. There were no windows nor doors in his house, except one on top which was his door to go in at and his window to look out of. When he had made this house he was tired, and crawled into it and curled himself up and went to sleep and slept all night.

In the morning the sun rose and spread his beams all over the world, and one of the bright sunbeams shone into the window of the little worm's house and touched his eyes * and waked him, and he popped up his head and looked out and saw that it was very pleasant in the garden, and he thought to go out to walk.

---

* The following quotations are for the help of the teacher who wishes to make Miss Peabody's exquisite story truer to nature:

"As these animals have no eyes, we must suppose that the light passes through their skins, and in some manner excites their cerebral ganglia."

"Worms are poorly provided with sense organs, for they cannot be said to see, although they can just distinguish between light and darkness; they are completely deaf, and have only a feeble power of smell; the sense of touch alone is well developed."

CHARLES DARWIN.

From "The Formation of Vegetable Mould through the Action of Worms."

THE BOY RAN ON THE OTHER SIDE OF THE PATH.

He squirmed himself up out of his hole, and, because he had no feet, he crept along the garden path. The warm beams of the sun put their arms all around his cold little body and made it as warm as could be, and the sunbeams went into his little mites of eyes and filled him all full of light, and the songs of the birds went into his little mites of ears and filled him all up with music, and the sweet smell of hundreds of flowers went up that little mite of a nose and filled him up with their perfumes. And so the little worm went creeping along, as glad as he could be that he was alive.

Now in the house that stood in that garden lived a little boy about four years old; and when the morning came, the sunbeams had gone into the window of his nursery and waked him, and he was washed and dressed, and had his breakfast of bread and milk, and then his mamma took him to the door that led down the steps to the piazza into the garden, and told him he might go down the path and have a good run to make himself warm. So down he ran.

Now, if that little boy should put his strong foot on that dear little worm, it would break him all to pieces; but that little boy would not do such a cruel thing for the world! He saw the little worm creeping along, so glad to be alive, and he ran on the other side of the path; and the little worm nibbled a blade of grass and drank a little dew for his breakfast, and then he felt tired, and went creeping back, full of good food, to the little hole that was his home, and curled himself up like a little ball and went to sleep.

ELIZABETH P. PEABODY.

In " Lectures to Kindergartners," D. C. Heath & Co.

A Surprise.

Mr. Chipmunk was playing among the trees one lovely autumn day, when he came across such a pile of delicious looking acorns!

"What a feast!" he cried. "I'll cover these acorns and keep them until spring, for I have nuts enough in my storeroom for my winter's use; when they are gone I'll come for these."

The little acorns heard him talking to himself, and laughed softly: "Ha, ha, Mr. Chipmunk! Spring is a long way off, and you cannot be so sure of finding your acorns then. Mother Oak Tree has told us that if we go to bed like good children, and lie very still, something beautiful and wonderful will happen to us when the warm spring days come."

The little acorns lay very quiet where Mr. Chipmunk had put them. Soon they could hear the cold winds blowing, but the brilliant leaves, falling, made a beautiful warm coverlet for them.

Then Jack Frost came, and the snow fell softly on their bed like white wool. The wind singing through the trees, lulled them to sleep, and they had a long, long nap.

When they awoke it was warm and sunny.

"It must be nearly time for us to throw off these heavy blankets and stretch up where we can see the sky, for I can feel the sun's warm rays," said one. "And I can move!" cried another. "Oh!" exclaimed a third, "I have burst by brown shell, and now I am reaching up!"

Soon the little roots had grown down deep into the earth, and the tiny green shoots had pushed their way through the darkness to a bright, glorious world—a world very different from the cold, dark earth they had known before!

There were beautiful flowers and green grasses all around them and tiny new leaves on the trees, and birds singing on the branches, and the acorn shoots hardly knew Mother Oak Tree, she was so gay in her new spring gown of green.

The little shoots were very happy, for they knew that they were to grow taller and more beautiful each year, like their grand and stately mother who stood near by.

Mr. Chipmunk came running along one day soon after this, looking for his acorns. When he reached the place where the baby oaks grew he looked in amazement, for he was sure that they stood in the very spot where he had hidden his nuts.

"Well," he said, after thinking a long, long time, "perhaps some hungry little chipmunk found my acorns and carried them home. But who can have put all these green things here, I wonder?"

SUE CLARKE KIMBALL.

FRIEDRICH FROEBEL.

To the Teacher:—

The most appealing and expressive image of Froebel which has been preserved for us is that of the tall old man, with long gray hair parted in the middle, his old-fashioned attire adding to the plainness of his aspect, leading a troop of village children up on the hill to play—he himself being a very child in simplicity and freedom as he joined in the game, while yet a seer in discernment of its meaning and a priest in ardent devotion to his purpose and principles.

But we have other interesting portraiture of the founder of the kindergarten, delineated by his contemporaries; and if we turn our gaze toward these images of Froebel from time to time, we shall find ourselves doing his work in fuller sympathy and with quickened comprehension. The lonely, unhappy little child, perplexed at the discords in the lives about him, is a sad picture. But how noble the lesson so plainly taught when we read how the remembrance of the ungratified longing of his own early life bore the fruit of plans for the amelioration of such ills in the lives of other children.

So, too, his glimpse of the harmony and beauty of nature, disclosed by an elder brother, was remembered for the benefit of childhood, and his system, based upon natural laws, keeps the child in close and loving communion with nature. Froebel was extremely fond of flowers, even to the day of his death, when he asked for them toward the very last. He had before said to some of his friends: "Take care of my flowers, and spare my weeds—I have learned much from them." The sunset was a favorite sight and almost every evening he resorted to a hilltop to gaze at the trailing splendor of the departing light. Indeed, Froebel was keenly sensitive to all beauty, whether in nature or art. It is related that although he was usually quite obscure in the presentation of his theories of education, yet that when speaking to the Grand Duke of Weimar upon them he succeeded in stating them with great clearness, and attributed this success to the beautiful architecture of the dining hall with its marble pillars and vaulted roof. "I felt as if I were in a temple," he said, afterwards.

This sensitiveness was not confined to beautiful sights alone. Froebel perceived with extreme keenness and enjoyment the distinctive fragrance of wines, food and plants. A man whose senses were less delicate might perhaps have omitted from his scheme of education the special cultivation of the senses. not realizing the value and pleasure derived from such cultivation.

"THE SUNSET WAS A FAVORITE SIGHT."

Thus whatever he had or lacked tended toward the perfecting of his educational plans and was made to serve the good of others.

His love of children always aroused a corresponding love on their part. They would run to meet him in the village streets, clinging to him and following him about. "I see in every child the possibility of a perfect man," he said to the Baroness Von Bulow. What a rebuke to the hopelessness which sometimes attacks us concerning some small reprobate !

Froebel's estimation of the requirements of a teacher were very high, and he felt himself so far below his own standard that he returned to the University at Gottingen for more study, having saved a little money; and again, after the close of the war, in which he served, we find him in the mineralogical museum at Berlin, resuming his studies that he may be better fitted for teaching. He craved classical and scientific knowledge; and history, anthropology, theoretical pedagogy and ethics attracted him no less strongly. He labored indefatigably to repair any defects in his own education. His humility was beautiful, making him ready to confess ignorance and to learn from everything and everybody—even from his normal pupils or kindergarten children—concerning some new application of his idea, although the idea itself he guarded as a sacred trust.

To a man of Froebel's gentle nature and peaceful habits the soldier's life could not have been attractive; nevertheless patriotism led him to respond to a call for soldiers, although there were various reasons why he need not have served. He felt it his duty the more strongly in his capacity as teacher, for as he says: "It was hardly possible for me to conceive how any young man, capable of bearing arms, could think of becoming an educator of children whose country he would not defend with his blood or his life. It was impossible for me to imagine how a young man who should not be ashamed then to hang back like a coward, could later, without shame, and without incurring the scorn and derision of his pupils, stir them to any great thing, to any action requiring effort or self-sacrifice."

During this soldier life a friendship of the most fervent and enduring kind was formed with two of his comrades, one of whom afterwards continued Froebel's work. This friend, Middendorff, relates an interesting anecdote of this time: "Once when their Jager corps was lying in a ditch behind a hedge, and under fire of the enemy, whose balls were passing over them, Froebel turned to Middendorff, who was lying behind him, and asked him whether he knew how many seconds faster musket bullets moved than the balls from the flint locks. While he was in immediate danger of his life, Froebel had the coolness to solve this mathematical problem." The secret of this intrepidity was probably in Froebel's conception of death, which he defined as "an enlargement of life."

Another anecdote which Middendorff tells shows Froebel's simple and generous impulsiveness. " Froebel came home one day much heated by a walk in the neighborhood, and wished to change his clothes. When his wife opened the wardrobe she exclaimed with alarm: 'The closet is almost empty! Thieves have been here.' Froebel answered, laughing: 'I am the thief.' And then he told her that the inhabitants of a neighboring village which had been destroyed by fire had been there that morning and asked for assistance, and as he had no money, he felt obliged to give them some of his effects."

One cannot wonder that such a man did not achieve financial success in life. He was surely akin to our own Agassiz, who had " no time to make money," and who preserved under all circumstances the integrity of his life-purpose—"the ennobling of humanity."

THE TALK.

(Call attention to the things which make the kindergarten room attractive—the windows where the merry sunshine enters, the plants, birds or fishes, if any, the flag, the children's work, which is often an effective decoration and one much appreciated by them, and to the pictures.)

To-day we will talk about Froebel, for his birthday is coming in a few days, and all the little kindergarten children should know about him.

Do you remember how the bells were rung and the guns fired and the flags were put out on Washington's birthday? Froebel's birthday will not be kept in that way, but we will have a happy time in kindergarten, because it was Froebel who thought about the kindergarten and planned it all.

Washington lived in what country? In America—the country we live in and sing about when we sing " My country, 'tis of thee." Froebel lived in Germany, a land away over the sea, so he was a German. He loved little children, and wanted them to grow strong and wise and good, and so he thought of having kindergartens where they could work and play and learn and be happy.

What do you like to do in kindergarten? (Draw out as many expressions as you can from the children, and tell them that Froebel planned all these pleasant things.)

Would you like to hear some stories about him?

When Friedrich Froebel was a little boy he was very lonely

His brothers were away from home, so there were no children to play with him; and, worse than that, he had no mother to love him and take care of him. He had a father, but his father was a very busy man, and did not have time to play with his little boy or to talk to him very much. Do you not think poor little Friedrich must have been very lonely?

He used to look out of the window, and see the men at work on a church which was near his home, and as he watched them he wanted to build something, too; but he had no blocks, so he tried to build with the chairs and footstools and such things which were in the room. But poor little Friedrich! He was so little that the chairs were heavy and clumsy for him, and, besides they fell over as often as he tried to put them on top of each other. He could not build nicely with them at all.

By and by, when he was grown up, he remembered this and planned nice, smooth blocks for little children, so that they could build churches, or gates, or towers, or pigeon houses, or anything they liked.

When Friedrich was ten years old he went to live with his uncle, who loved him dearly. Here he went to school and had a great many playmates, so he was not unhappy and lonely as he had been before.

After this he had to go to work. He wanted to be a farmer because he liked to be out of doors and plant things and watch their growing; but he learned to be a surveyor, too, and was also a soldier for a while.

At one time the soldiers had to march a long way in the hot sun and grew so tired that they threw everything they could out of their knapsacks to make them less heavy to carry. Froebel was tired, too, but as he walked along he noticed many beautiful and interesting things, as he always did when out of doors. When he saw curious stones or pretty mosses or flowers or leaves, he picked them up and put them in his knapsack. The stones were heavy, of course, but Froebel wanted to study them as well as the mosses and flowers. When the soldiers reached their resting place Froebel took out all his treasures and showed them to the other men, and they all enjoyed hearing his wonderful stories about the plants and rocks.

After he had been a soldier, Froebel became a teacher; and then it was that he planned the kindergarten. Shall you not like to talk about him and sing a birthday song about him? And will you try to remember that it was Friedrich Froebel who planned the kindergarten for us because he loved little children and wanted them to be busy and happy, and to grow in three ways, as we have said—to grow strong, to grow wise, to grow good!

TEACHER'S READING.

Life of Froebel, - - - - - - - - *Alex. Hanschmann*
Reminiscences of Froebel, - - - - *Baroness von Marenholz-Bulow*
The Kindergarten and the School (by Four Workers).
Friedrich Froebel, - - - - - - - - - *Kriege*
Froebel and the Kindergarten System, - - - - *Joseph Payne*
Froebel and Education by Self-Activity, - - - - - *H. C. Bowen*
Life of Froebel in "Paradise of Childhood," - - - *Henry W. Blake*

Song For Froebel's Birthday.

Let us sing to-day with gladness
 Of a friend to childhood dear,
One who thought and labored for us
 And whose name we honor here.

Lovingly he planned for children
 Happy work and merry play;
Let us, then, be glad and grateful
 As we think of him to-day.

EMILIE POULSSON

The Kindergarten Magazine.

BIRDS.

To the Teacher:—

(Let the children tell the signs of Spring as spoken of in the Spring talk and story, and when they mention the return of the birds let them tell the names of the first comers and then of any other birds which they know.

The special bird to be studied will be the one which can be obtained. Where a live canary is not already the happy possession of the kindergarten, one can easily be borrowed. If not, a stuffed bird will do, and pictures are always useful.

Place the bird where all the children can see it, and as they describe this special creature lead them to compare it with those previously observed. For instance, when the bird's feathers are mentioned, question concerning the covering of four-footed creatures and fishes. Recall the gorgeous colors of many fishes in connection with the brilliant plumage of the birds, and so on through all the most noteworthy points of appearance, and of activity as well.)

THE TALK.

Birdie can fly, hop, sing, build nest, lay eggs; has two legs and two wings. Has it a backbone? Yes. Name all the animals you know which have backbones; those which have four feet; four fins; two feet and two hands; two feet and two wings. (Such grouping will lead to the observation that all backbone animals have two pairs of limbs.)

Look at birdie's legs. Do you see that they are covered with scales? How many toes has this birdie? Where does he sleep? Where do most birds sleep? The young birds in the nest, the older birds perched on the trees, holding firmly to the twig with their four toes.

Do you remember how the fish guided himself through the water? Birdie, too, uses his tail to guide him through the air, but his wings also help.

How daintily neat birds keep themselves! Many of them like to bathe in the clear, cold water of the brooks or ponds. After a splash they shake their wings and fluff out their feathers, and then set to work to make them all smooth again. This the birds do with their bills and a little oil. You could never guess where they get the oil. Each bird carries a little with him in a gland or tiny bag by his tail.

What does birdie eat? Grains and other seeds, worms, caterpillars and many kinds of insects. Are birds useful? (Tell briefly the story of the "Birds of Killingworth.")

What kind of homes do birds have? Who makes the nests? Isn't it wonderful that they can make such dear little nests when they have only their bills and feet to use for hands and tools? (Show a bird's nest, and tell how the father and mother bird work together—the father often collecting the materials for the mother to weave into a nest. Sing the nest-building songs—"The swallow is a mason," etc.—and the finger play of "Fly, little birds, fly east and west." Speak of the beautiful music which adds so much to the joyousness of the world; and lastly, tell of the love and devotion of the parent birds, and the helplessness of the nestlings, that the children may behold their own family life through this beautiful imagery.)

TEACHER'S READING.

Winners in Life's Race (Chaps. VI, VII),	Arabella Buckley
Birds of America,	Audubon
Key to North American Birds,	Elliot Cones
Land and Game Birds,	Minot
Birds and Poets,	John Burroughs
Song of Life,	Margaret Morley
Birds through an Opera Glass,	Florence Merriam
April Birds ("Sharp Eyes"),	W. H. Gibson
My Aviary,	O. W. Holmes
Birds of Killingworth,	Longfellow
The Skylark,	Shelley
The Nightingale,	Keats
To a Skylark,	Wordsworth
Robert of Lincoln,	Bryant
The Singing Lesson,	Jean Ingelow
Sing on, Blithe Bird,	William Motherwell
The Eagle,	Tennyson
Elizabeth's Concert, ("St. Nicholas," June, 1887),	Robina S. Smith
The Lover and Birds,	William Allingham
The Robin, The Bluebird, The Humming Bird,	Emily Dickinson
Under the Lighthouse, The Emperor's Crown,	Celia Thaxter

For the Children.

The Nightingale,	Andersen
Dick and Topsy ("Stories for Kindergarten and Home.")	A. T. Ketchum
Singer's Lesson ("Kindergarten Gems.")	
Story of Birds and Fishes ("Kindergarten Stories and Morning Talks"),	S. E. Wiltse

STORIES.
Jack and Jenny Sparrow.

A sparrow that lived with many others in a public park offended his neighbors by getting up too early in the morning and beginning to chirp before they were willing to be waked. They called a meeting of all the flock, and after considering the matter told him that he and his mate must look for another home.

This he refused to do, saying that he had as good a right to stay where he was as they had.

"These trees do not belong to you," he said, "and you don't pay rent for the bird-boxes we live in. They were put up by the people who own the park, because they love to see us building our nests and flying about here.

"Besides this," he continued, "I have done nothing with which you ought to find fault, for I never wake till the break of day, and do not begin to chirp for several minutes after that, when all industrious sparrows should be ready for breakfast. This very morning I heard a cock crow before I opened my bill, and what sparrow would not be ashamed to be lazier that the chickens?"

When the other birds heard this speech they did not try to answer it—for, indeed, it was every word true and they could say nothing against it—but they attacked the sparrow and his mate and drove them from the park

As winter was just coming on, they knew not where to go or what to do. For the first few nights they roosted on the roof of a stable; but this was a forlorn, lonely place, and, as they had no perch to clasp with their little feet, the wind almost blew them away. Besides this, the man who kept the stable was so saving of his corn, and swept the yard so clean, that they could hardly pick up as much as would make a good meal in a whole day.

From the roof of the stable they moved under the eaves of a carpenter shop, and thought they were nicely fixed, until one dark night a cat stole softly along the roof to the spot where they were sleeping, and, suddenly putting out her paw, almost caught them both in her sharp claws!

As it was, she caught poor Jenny's tail and pulled out every feather of it, which did the cat no good, but was a great loss to Jenny, for she could hardly guide herself in flying, and looked very odd beside.

After this they led a sad, wandering life for the rest of the winter, always sleeping in fear on clotheslines and fences, and picking up a bare living—mostly from frozen slop buckets and around kitchen doors.

But toward spring better fortune came to them, for a little girl, looking out of the dining-room window one morning, spied them hopping about the pavement below, and threw them some crumbs. Her joy was great when she saw them quickly eat what she had thrown and then seem to look up for more. She ran back to the table and brought them as much as they wanted.

The next day they came again, and after this, every day, almost as soon as it was light, they might be seen waiting for their breakfast from the hands of their little friend.

But think of their surprise one April morning, when the sun was shining brightly and the buds were just beginning to swell on the rosebushes, to see the carpenter come in at the garden gate carrying a new bird-box fastened to the top of a high pole, which he at once began to set up in the middle of the grassplot, digging a deep hole to set it in, so that it would stand firm in spite of wind and weather.

Their kind little friend ran out from the house and almost danced for joy around the pole while it was being planted. And her father and mother, and brothers and sisters, sharing in her delight, all left the breakfast table to watch the carpenter at his work.

That very day the happy pair—little Jack and Jenny—went into their new home, and before night were picking up dried grass and twigs with which to begin building their nest.

CHARLES FOSTER.

From " New Lights on Old Paths," Chas. Foster Pub. Co., Phila., Pa.

THE SPARROWS' HOME.

Little Yellow-Wing.

"The brook! the brook! let us go to the brook!" cried Willie and his cousins, George and Eddy, as they looked from a window after a storm, and saw the overflowed banks of a small stream.

Thick shoes and a cloak were brought for Lizzie; and she walked by her father's side, while the boys ran shouting and jumping before them.

They found the brook changed indeed by the rain. A few days before they had built a dam across it, which made a pretty waterfall; but now it was all swept away, and the brook was no longer a narrow stream, but had spread out wide, and ran furiously over the stones.

While the boys were running after chips of wood which they threw into the water for boats, the father, who stood with Lizzie under a tree, saw something move near his feet, and picked up a poor, half-drowned bird. Lizzie called her brother and cousins, and they all looked sorrowfully at the bird, and said, "Poor fellow! poor fellow!" and begged to take him to the house, for he shook with cold, and seemed to be dying. He was laid in Lizzie's hand; she gently covered him and carried him home to her mother. The little creature was dried and warmed; and his feathers, which, when wet, did not hide his body, spread out and covered him with a thick plumage.

"Is it really the same bird?" asked Lizzie. "Oh, I am so glad papa found him!"

"See," said Eddy, "the bright yellow on his brown wings! Let us name him Yellow-wing."

Crumbs of bread were offered to him, but he would not eat, and cried. "Peep, peep," long after he was laid in a warm basket.

"The next morning Yellow-wing looked quite lively, and no longer cried, "Peep, peep," but cheerfully sang, "Chirp, chirp." "He is a yellow bird," said George; "and when he is older, he will be as pretty as a canary."

Willie looked at his mother, and his eyes seemed to say, "May I keep him?"

She answered: "No, my son, it would be cruel to take him from the green trees and fields; for

> "'How pleasant the life of a bird must be,
> Living in love in a leafy tree!'"

"I know," said Willie, "that I should not like to be shut up in a cage; but what shall we do with him?"

"He cannot fly, poor fellow," said Lizzie; "we must keep him until he can fly."

Eddy told of a nest in the barn, and said that Yellow-wing might be squeezed in among those young ones.

"But," said George, "the nest in the barn belongs to a swallow, who will not like to have a yellow bird among her little ones."

At last it was agreed to take him back to the brook, and try to find the nest from which he fell. The children soon started on their errand of love and kindness, more happy in taking a poor bird to his father and mother than if they had been allowed to keep him in a cage. They carried him to the tree under which he was found, and stood him on a fence near it. Yellow-wing cried, "Peep, peep," and "Peep, peep," was heard from the tree.

> "'Come up, come up,' they seemed to say,
> 'Where the topmost twigs to the breezes play!'"

But he could not fly up, and Willie said: "The old birds will not come down while we are so near." So the children went to a pile of stones, and sat there quite still.

"See, see his mother!" whispered Lizzie, as a larger bird flew from the tree and alighted close to Yellow-wing. Soon the old bird flew off a little, and the young one spread his wings and followed her; a little further went the mother bird, and Yellow-wing flew after her; and thus, by flying a short distance at a time, he soon learned to fly well enough to reach a low branch of a tree, than a higher one, and at last both birds were hid among the leaves. And Lizzie said: "Hark! I hear the 'Chirp, chirp,' of dear little Yellow-wing. He is so glad to get back into the warm nest!"

—Selected.

Child and Bird.

" Birdie, Birdie, will you pet?
 Summer is far and far away yet.
 I've a silken quilt and a feather bed,
 And a pillow of satin for your head."

" I'd rather sleep in the ivy wall,
 No rain comes through, though I hear it fall;
 The sun peeps gay at dawn of day,
 And I sing and wing away, away."

" O Birdie, Birdie, will you pet?
 Here are diamonds, amber and jet!
 I'll make a necklace, fair and fine,
 To please this pretty bird of mine. "

" Oh! Thanks for diamonds and thanks for jet
 But there is something costlier yet:
 A feather necklace, round and round,
 That I wouldn't sell for a thousand pound. "

" O Birdie, Birdie, *won't* you pet?
 I'll give you a dish of silver fret,
 A golden cup and an ivy seat,
 And carpets soft beneath your feet."

 Can running water be drunk from gold?
 Can a silver dish the forest hold?
 A rocking twig is the finest chair,
 And the softest paths lie through the air.
 Good-bye, good-bye, to my lady fair! "

WILLIAM ALLINGHAM.

The Sandpipers.

Children, did you ever see a sandpiper? "No." (Show a picture of one.) "What long legs it has for such a little bird!" Yes. Why do you suppose he has such long legs? "To wade with?" Yes. Mr. Sandpiper lives by the side of a great piece of salt water called an ocean. The land that is close to the water is called a beach. It is sometimes rocky, but where Mr. Sandpiper lives it is sandy. He is not very sociable, for he and his wife and the babies live where there are no other families of Sandpipers very near him. Mrs. Sandpiper makes her nest near the beach.

One day the whole family were on the beach, running up and down, and the father and mother were scratching in the loose sand and getting worms for the baby Sandpipers and for themselves to eat. Every time one of the little Sandpipers called, the father or mother put a worm into its open mouth. But the babies wanted so much food that, after a while, their mamma thought they had better learn to catch worms for themselves; so she called them and showed them how to scratch up the sand, and how to catch the worms when they were in sight. The Sandpiper family were having a very good time eating and playing, when suddenly they saw some men coming. Each of these men carried a gun.

Then Mamma Sandpiper was frightened and ran to her nest, and the baby Sandpipers hid under her wings. But Papa Sandpiper was afraid that the men would find them, and what do you suppose he did? He made believe that he was hurt, and, with his wings drooping, ran along before the men to make them follow him; but he would not let them get near enough to fire at him. So he led them along, farther and farther from his family, till he thought the men were far enough away; then he hid from them, and after a while, when he was sure they could not see him, he went back as fast as he could to the other birdies who were very glad to see him safe and well, and thanked him for saving them. What do you suppose they said? "Peep, peep." Yes, that is just what they did say. Then they all went back to the beach, but they did not see the men again.

JOSEPHINE JARVIS.

Cobden, I'.

BIRDS' NESTS.

To the Teacher:—

In preparation for this talk the teacher should get several nests—as many as possible—in order to show the ingenuity and skill of the little builders and the variety of materials used.

Sing a bird song to introduce the subject of nests, or lead to it from the finger play of "The Family," speaking of the child's home and then of other homes.

THE TALK.

When do the birds build their nests? They usually seem anxious to have a home as soon as possible after they come back in the spring. What is the first thing they do about it? Choose a place. Ah! yes; and if you had a chance to watch them you would find they thought that a very important piece of work.

Why do they choose so carefully, do you think? Where do they build their nests? Not only in trees, but sometimes in low bushes, sometimes on the ground, sometimes in the barn, or even in a  chimney or stone wall or a sand bank. The place which one bird likes would not suit another bird at all; for instance, the robin often chooses the apple trees while the Baltimore oriole seeks the tallest elm, and the little ground sparrow feels safest on the ground. (The children will not know much of nests being built in other places than trees, but should be shown the advantage of different sites.)

Now let us look at these nests. Look sharply and see what the birds have woven together—strings, leaves, hay, straw, sticks, mud, moss, bark, feathers, hair, wool, etc., etc.

Does it seem possible that a home could be made of such bits and scraps? Do you think we could make anything out of them

Baltimore Orioles and Nest

that would be strong enough to hold a mother bird and her eggs, and, by and by, the young birds? (If practicable let the children gather materials and attempt making a nest, and they will be the more impressed with the wondrous skill of the bird.)

How do the birds get all these things for building their nests? They have to find them. Can they carry much at one time? Just think how many times they must fly back and forth before they can have enough. Perhaps you can put some strings and threads out of doors where the birds can see them easily and get them. Shouldn't you like to give something towards building a bird's nest?

What tools does a bird use? Only her beak and her feet; and yet she can weave, or sew, or plaster, or bore holes, or dig, just as she finds the best and safest way for making her nest.

"Of all the weavers that I know the oriole is the best." Her nest is like a deep pocket and so closely woven that the rain cannot get through the sides at all. She must have long pieces for her weaving, so she tears strips from the tough stems of plants and finds long hairs from the horse's tail.

The best sewer is the tailor bird, who does not come to our land, however. She takes long leaves and actually sews them together with real stitches. How interesting it must be to see the little creature making the holes and putting the thread through with her sharp bill!

The swallow plasters her nest under the eaves with mud, so we call her a mason. Robin, too, likes mud and is wise enough to mix straws with the mud so that it shall not crumble away.

The woodpecker is the most like a carpenter, for he works with wood instead of these soft things. He hammers at a tree with his sharp, strong bill till he makes a round, smooth hole large enough to pass through, and then he and Mrs. Woodpecker take turns working till they have hollowed out a nice nest. They carry out their chips as they work, too.

The chimney swallow makes a kind of glue with which she glues the sticks together and fastens them to the side of the chimney.

All these are perching birds, which are the best nest-builders, because they have the strong yet delicate feet and bills, which make the best tools. The ground birds make loose, simple nests, most of them digging their nests in the sand.

The smallest and prettiest nest is made by the smallest and prettiest bird in the world—the humming bird. With softest cotton or wool on the inside, and pretty bits of moss and bark on the outside, and put together with a filmy spider's web, it is really beautiful. And it shows how wise and careful the humming bird is, too, for the moss and bark make the nest so like the tree on which it is placed that it is seldom found.

Birds do not always build new nests. Some of them find their own old one where they lived the year before, and use that, mending it if necessary; others take nests which another kind of bird has built; but the most of them make a new nest for each brood of little ones, as if they wanted to be sure to have as strong and safe and nice a home for their other children as they had had for their first nestlings.

TEACHER'S READING.

Homes without Hands,	*J. G. Wood*
Preface (" Merry Songs and Games "),	*Susan E. Blow*
Birds' Nests (" Wake Robin "),	*John Burroughs*
The Tragedies of the Nests ("Signs and Seasons "),	*John Burroughs*
Sharp Eyes (" Locusts and Wild Honey "),	*John Burroughs*
Bird Nest Materials (" Sharp Eyes "),	*W. H. Gibson*
The White Heron,	*Sarah O. Jewett*
An Order for a Picture,	*Alice Cary*
Choosing a Building Spot,	*Emily Braddock*

For the Children.

The Bramble Bush and the Lambs }
A Queer Place for a Bird's Home } (" Kindergarten Stories
   and Morning Talks "),   *S. E. Wiltse*

STORIES.

The Scarecrow.

The farmer looked at his cherry tree,
   With thick buds clustered on every bough;
"I wish I could cheat the robins," said he;
   "If somebody only would show me how!"

"I'll make a terrible scarecrow grim,
   With threatening arms and with bristling head,
And up in the tree I'll fasten him
   To frighten them half to death," he said.

He fashioned a scarecrow tattered and torn—
   Oh! 'twas a horrible thing to see!
And very early, one summer morn,
   He set it up in his cherry tree.

The blossoms were white as the light sea-foam,
   The beautiful tree was a lovely sight,
But the scarecrow stood there so much at home
   All the birds flew screaming away in fright.

The robins, who watched him every day,
   Heads held aslant, keen eyes so bright!
Surveying the monster, began to say,
   "Why should this monster our prospects blight?

"He never moves round for the roughest weather,
   He's a harmless, comical, tough old fellow;
Let's all go into the tree together,
   For he won't budge till the fruit is mellow!"

So up they flew; and the sauciest pair
   Mid the shady branches peered and perked,
Selected a spot with the utmost care,
   And all day merrily sang and worked.

And where do you think they built their nest?
   In the scarecrow's pocket, if you please.
That, half concealed on his ragged breast,
   Made a charming covert of safety and ease!

By the time the cherries were ruby-red,
   A thriving family, hungry and brisk,
The whole day long on the ripe fruit fed;
   'Twas so convenient! They ran no risk!

Until the children were ready to fly,
   All undisturbed they lived in the tree;
For nobody thought to look at the Guy
   For a robin's flourishing family!

CELIA THAXTER.

The Nest of Many Colors.

Mr. and Mrs. Oriole arrived from the South one bright day in May. They had had a pleasant journey, but were glad to find themselves once more at the old summer home—the great elm tree which stood on the top of the hill and swung its branches over the farmhouse in which Ned and Kitty lived You would never have thought that those two birds had been traveling hundreds of miles, if you had seen the way they darted about, Mr. Oriole's yellow feathers showing like flashes of sunshine as he flew swiftly past.

The two birds were very happy to be back, and had so many things to do that they had no desire to sit still, not they! Mr. Oriole wanted to see the Robins and Bluebirds and all the other friends who had arrived, and to get the spring news. He also wanted to see the Pigeons and hear how the winter had gone with them. But Mrs. Oriole was anxious to get to nest-building at once.

"My dear mate," said she, "you know how much material it takes to make a nest and how much work it is to weave it. Do help me first to collect some things for weaving. There will be plenty of time for visiting later."

"But if we go to the barn where the pigeons are perhaps I can get you some of those long hairs which are so good for weaving," suggested Mr. Oriole.

"Oh! then we'll go, by all means," said Mrs. Oriole; and away they went.

Now while the orioles had been chatting together, Ned and Kittie had been watching them with great delight. Ned could not remember seeing the orioles last year; but Kitty, who was older, felt that she had known them a long while, for she had watched them build their nest several times.

This year the children had a great plan. Kitty had thought of it one day when she was crocheting, and she had saved some pieces of bright worsted which she had at first thought of throwing away.

"The orioles will soon be back," she had said; "I may as well keep these worsteds. What a gay spot they will make in a nest!" After this she had saved other pieces, and now had a bright bunch of red and orange and yellow and green and blue and purple; and she and Ned had planned that the oriole nest this year should be the most gorgeous that was ever woven.

When Mr. and Mrs. Oriole returned from their visit to the barn they were in high glee, for they had each found one of the long hairs from the farm-horses' tails, and this was a great good fortune! Kitty and Ned slipped away from the bushes near the elm tree just in time. They had spread some bright red worsted out in plain sight, and now stood in the doorway watching.

Mr. Oriole was flying ahead of her mate, and, reaching the tree first, alighted on the tip of a long, slender branch high up in the tree. This was the spot which they had decided upon for their nest.

No sooner had they perched on the branch with the horsehairs trailing from their bills, than they spied the red worsted on the bushes below. You cannot think how delighted they were.

"We can get to work very soon if we have such good fortune as this," chirped Mrs. Oriole. "Now let us go and find one of those plants * which have such good stalks to tear strips from."

Mr. Oriole agreed, and the two flew away again. They found

---

* "For fibrous materials she broke, hackled, and gathered the flax of the *asclepias* and *hibiscus* stalks, tearing off long strings and flying with them to the scene of her labors."

NUTTALL.

"A peculiar flax-like substance seems to be always sought after and always found."

BURROUGHS.

"Vincent Barnard of Pennsylvania says that a friend of his, on observing the bird (an oriole) beginning to build, hung out near the prospective nest skeins the plant they wanted and tugged away with their beaks and their claws till they each had a good long strip. They flew back to the elm tree again, and behold! upon the same bush where the red worsted had so mysteriously appeared, were now some orange and yellow strands, as gay as the orange and lemons which they had seen in the land where they had spent the winter.

"Quick! Quick!" called Mrs. Oriole in great excitement. "Let us get that, too! I must begin to work immediately."

And begin she did, while Mr. Oriole fluttered about,—sometimes helping, sometimes looking on, and often bursting into joyous song.

Ned and Kitty watched—oh! so quietly—as long as they could see, and wished that the leaves did not hide the little weaver. Every day after this Ned and Kitty put more worsteds out on the bushes—green, and then blue, and then purple—until all their colors were used. The birds always spied the worsted very soon, and twittered and warbled joyfully over it. Day after day they worked busily and happily; and the strips torn from the plants, the long wisps of hay, the gay worsteds and the horsehair were woven together and soon took shape as a nest.

It was wonderful how cleverly the little birds managed and how patiently they worked. The long strips caught and tangled on the twigs of the tree sometimes, and sometimes the wind carried off a whisp of hay just when Mrs. Oriole was going to weave it; but the two weavers chirped and twittered gaily all the while, notwithstanding.

At last, within a week, the happy day came when the nest was finished, and Mr. and Mrs. Oriole had a rollicking jubilee of song over its completion. No wonder they were happy! How safe their little home was! No eggs could fall out of such a deep nest as this. No rain could get through its thin but closely woven sides to chill the·eggs or the baby birds who would by and by come from the eggs. And what could be more delightful for the little ones than the swaying, rocking motion which even the gen-

---

of many-colored zephyr yarn, which the eager artist readily appropriated. He managed it so that the birds used nearly equal quantities of various high, bright colors. The nest was made unusually deep and capacious, and it may be questioned if such a thing of beauty was ever before woven by the cunning of a bird."

From John Burroughs' "Wake Robin."

tlest breeze gave to this high swinging home? Thus far it was just like the nest of many other orioles, for, as we often sing:—

"Of all the weavers that I know
The oriole is the best.
High in the branches of the tree
He hangs his cosy nest."

But the worsteds which Kitty and Ned had supplied made brilliant spots and bands of color such as had never been seen before in the nest of a bird.

"See! See! See!" caroled Mr. Oriole as he flew round and round the nest in ecstasy. "It is as gay as a flower garden! It must be those wonderful strings which we found on the bushes below which make it so beautiful."

"Flower garden, do you say?" sang Mrs. Oriole. "There are colors more dear and beautiful to me than the bright flower colors. That soft green reminds me of the leaves which rustle about our home and shade it and hide it. But this little spot right here, my dear, is what I most rejoice to see; not because it is like yellow flowers or sunshine, though it is like both; but because it is the color of your own golden, bright feathers. I remember well when I wove that string into the nest."

Then the two birds joined in the oriole song of "Home, Sweet Home," which is of a different tune from the one we people sing, but which has the same meaning, I am sure.

While the orioles were rejoicing thus over their beautiful home, Ned and Kitty, with their papa and mamma, were looking up at the completed nest. They were filled with wonder and delight.

"Who would ever think that such a beautiful and perfect thing as that was made without hands and without tools?" said Papa.

"I am so glad I saved the worsted!" said Kitty. "I mean to put some out every spring."

EMILIE POULSSON.

The Sparrow's Nest.

Nay, only look what I have found!
A sparrow's nest upon the ground;
A sparrow's nest, as you may see,
Blown out of yonder old elm tree.

And what a medley thing it is!
I never saw a nest like this,—
So neatly wove with decent care.
Of silvery moss and shining hair.

But put together, odds and ends,
Picked up from enemies and friends:
See, bits of thread, and bits of rag,
Just like a little rubbish bag!

See, hair of dog and fur of cat,
And rovings of a worsted mat,
And shreds of silks, and many a feather
Compacted cunningly together.

Well! here has hoarding been and living,
And not a little good contriving,
Before a home of peace and ease
Was fashioned out of things like these!

Think, had these odds and ends been brought
To some wise man renowned for thought,
Some man, of men the very gem,
Pray, what could he have done with them?

If we had said: "Here, sir, we bring
You many a worthless little thing,
Just bits and scraps, so very small
That they have scarcely size at all;

And out of these, you must contrive
A dwelling large enough for five;
Neat, warm, and snug; with comfort stored;
Where five small things may lodge and board.'

How would the man of learning vast
Have been astonished and aghast,
And vowed that such a thing had been
Ne'er heard of, thought of, much less seen.

Ah! man of learning you are wrong;
Instinct is, more than wisdom, strong;
And He who made the sparrow, taught
This skill beyond your reach of thought.

And here in this uncostly nest,
These little creatures have been blest;
Nor have kings known in palaces,
Half their contentedness in this—
Poor, simple dwelling as it is!

MARY HOWITT.

THE BUTTERFLY.

To the Teacher:—

A good time to catch the early spring butterfly is, paradoxically, the previous autumn, when it is in its chrysalis state; or, better still, when it is in its caterpillar childhood.* This requires forethought and some little trouble; but, to use an expression of the Welsh peasant, "The trouble's a pleasure, mem." For, however familiar the fact of the metamorphosis of insects may be, to watch a caterpillar through its changes is to be present at one of nature's miracles more wonderful than any transformation scene of fairy land.

The teacher should not defraud herself of this delight, and should bring it to the children; for it is perfectly feasible to have the whole cycle of changes accomplished in kindergarten.

In the following talk it is assumed that the teacher has a butterfly and the chrysalis from which it emerged, and the talk should surely *not* be given without such specimens.

By obtaining the specimen in its caterpillar or chrysalis state cruelty is avoided, and the considerate treatment during the short captivity and the prompt freeing of the insect when strong enough to fly away can be a lesson in mercy.

The butterfly could be in a glass jar, with mosquito netting over the top, for a short time while the children observe it, after which they will enjoy giving it its liberty. Flowers, with a drop of sugar syrup added to their own nectar, or sweetened water sprinkled on the plants in the window, may tempt it to eat when it is flying about the room.

The perfected insect—the butterfly—is brought to the children first, rather than the caterpillar or chrysalis, because of its beauty, because it is more common than the caterpillar at this time (mid-April), and because it corresponds with the other spring symbols of renewed life. But the observation of the caterpillar should follow soon and should be extended over the whole caterpillar stage of the insect's existence, including the dormant period, and coming again to the butterfly which lays the eggs from which the caterpillar grows.

Caterpillars will be placidly comfortable and happy in boxes or glass jars covered with netting, if supplied daily with enough fresh leaves of a kind to suit their taste.

---

* From the latest autumn brood of the Vanessa Antiopa, etc. found on willows, poplars and elms.

THE TALK.

What season of the year is this? What signs of spring have you noticed? Even in the city we can see some, but out in the country we should see many more. I have brought one of the beautiful signs of spring to show you to-day. It can fly like a bird and is as pretty as a flower, but it is neither flower nor bird. Here it is. What is it?

(Direct the observation by questioning so that the children will notice the color, the number of wings—two on each side or four in all—the slender legs—three on each side or six in all—the  large eyes which can see in all directions, the two antennæ or feelers, the three divisions of the body. Call attention to the rings of the abdomen, since they will be noticed again in the caterpillar, and to the neck, which is the distinguishing mark of insects, the name being derived from *in* and *secto*, to cut. That wings and legs are both joined to the thorax or middle part of the insect, is also important to notice.) What does the butterfly eat? Honey from the flowers. Do you know where the flowers keep their honey (nectar, to speak more exactly)? Deep down in the bottom part of the flower. The butterfly could not get his mouth away in there, but he has a wonderful tongue—a long tube or pipe—long enough to reach the honey in the deepest flowers. When the butterfly is not sipping honey his long tongue is curled up out of the way and out of sight.

What does the butterfly like to do? Fly about in the hot sunshine, moving its pretty wings up and down, alighting now on this flower and now on that. Is it noisy? No, it makes no sound, but flies about very lightly and silently. We must remember this when we play that we are butterflies.

Did we see any butterflies in the winter? Do you know where they were then? It is a wonderful story. Many of them were in little cases like this (showing chrysalis). You would not think a butterfly, with his four large wings, was ever in such a little place, would you? But the first part of the story is more wonderful still; for, although a butterfly came out of this case (or chrysalis), a *caterpillar* made it!

How many children have seen caterpillars? How do they look? Have they wings? What do they eat? Do they look like butterflies? (Show caterpillar and compare with the butterfly, bringing out differences chiefly.)

Yet, although they are so different, a butterfly always grows from a caterpillar. The caterpillar crawls about, eating almost all the time, and grows very fast. In fact it grows so fast that it gets too large for its skin, and the skin splits open down the back and drops off, and there is a new, bright, looser skin underneath. After the caterpillar has outgrown its skin three or four times and had as many new dresses, it stops eating, fastens itself up somewhere and shakes itself out of its skin once more. This time there is no new caterpillar skin ready, for the caterpillar has begun to change to a butterfly and will not need it. So, instead, this covering forms all over its body and the creature stays safely shut up in its chrysalis, until its wings have grown and it has become a perfect butterfly. As soon as this has happened it makes a little opening in the chrysalis, puts out its head and looks about, and at last crawls out. You would not think the butterfly very pretty as it stands on the outside of the empty case; for its colors are dull, and its dripping wings cling to its wet sides, making it look very limp and forlorn. But after it has stretched its legs, and stroked and spread and dried its wings, the beautiful colors grow more and more brilliant; and when the butterfly floats off in the sunshine it is so beautiful that we almost think it is a flower on wings.

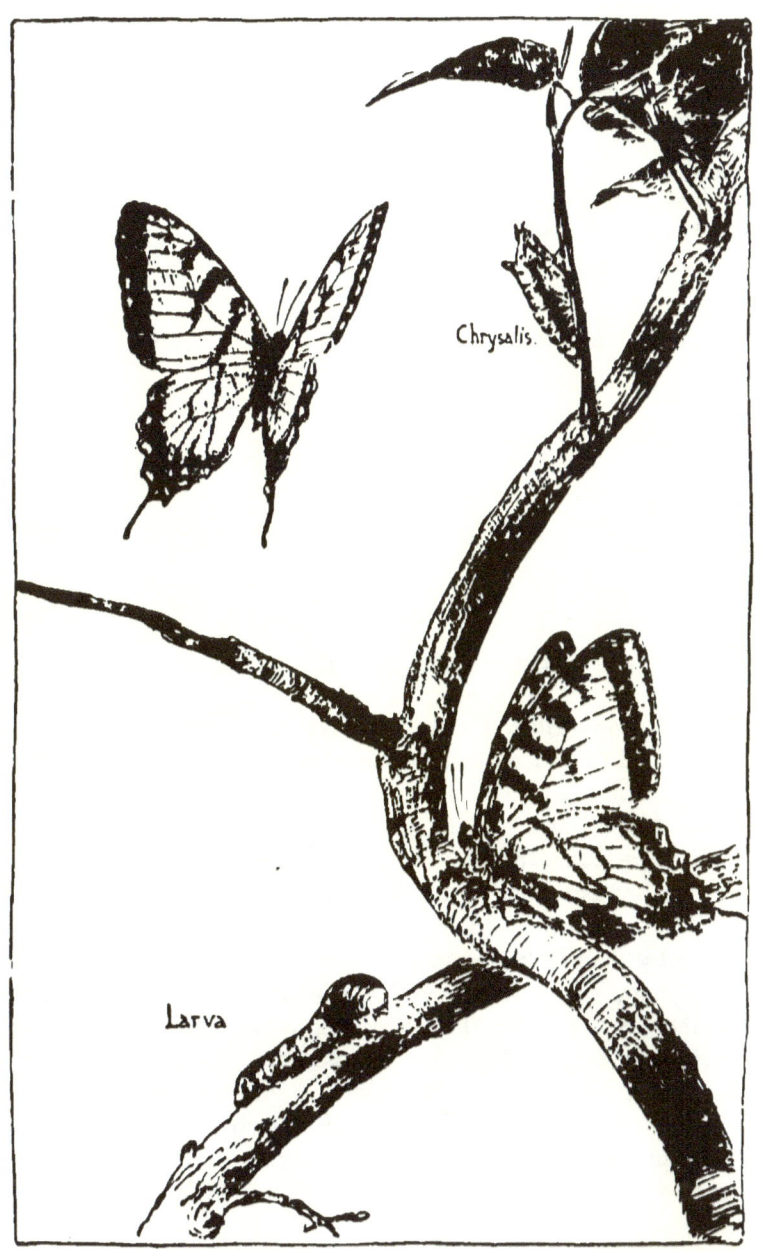

PAPILIO TURNUS.

TEACHER'S READING.

The Thaw Butterflies ("Sharp Eyes,") - - - - - *W. H. Gibson*
Life and her Children (Chap. XI), - - - - *Arabella Buckley*
Insects Injurious to Vegetation, - - - - - - *Harris*
Butterflies of New England, - - - - - - *C. J. Maynard*
Butterflies of North America, - - - - - *C. J. Maynard*
The Butterflies of Eastern United States and Canada, - *Samuel H. Scudder*
Insect Lives; or Born in Prison, - - - - - *J. P. Ballard*
Worms or Caterpillars, etc. ("Kindergarten Magazine,"
   October, 1891), - - - - - - - - *E. G. Howe*
Paradise Lost (Book VII), - - - - - - *Milton*
The Nomades, - - - - - - - - *Lowell*
To a Butterfly, - - - - - - - - *Wordsworth*
The Butterfly's Day, - - - - - - *Emily Dickinson*

For the Children.

An Object of Terror, } ("Little Folks in Feathers and Fur"), *O. T. Miller*
Scale Winged,

Some Common Butterflies.

The first butterflies of the spring are those which have hibernated in their winged state—Vanessa Antiopa, Comma, Semicolon, and Atlanta. They are sometimes tempted out by warm days in March, and in April are quite common.

Here are some hints from Wm. H. Gibson, that sharp-eyed observer and charming chronicler:—

"The butterflies are now frequenting the tender foliage of the willows by the brook, and in a few weeks the first brood of their black, spiny caterpillars will literally weigh down the slender branches as they strip the leaves and leave their cast-off skins fringing the twigs. Hundreds of the caterpillars may be gathered in a few moments, and the walls of your collecting box will soon be hung closely with chrysalids, nearly all of which will have been transformed into butterflies within a period of a fortnight. There are two, or, I am led to think, even three of these caterpillar broods during the year, the butterflies from the last in autumn, surviving the winter." * * * * * * * *

"Any one of these angle-wing butterflies (Vanessa Antiopa, Comma, Semicolon and Atlanta), may be kept in domestication through the winter months, becoming very tame and familiar, and forming a pretty feature of the conservatory, or even the window garden."

On any of the parsley family of plants will be found a black-banded, gold-spotted, green caterpillar, with malodorous yellow horns. Its chrysalis is gray; the butterfly, black swallow-tail—Papilio Asterias.

On any of the milkweed family will be found a black-and—yellow-banded caterpillar. Its chrysalis is emerald green, studded with golden points; the butterfly, orange-red wings, veined with black—Danais Archippus.

On spice or sassafras bushes, a strange looking caterpillar, with horns like the Asterias caterpillar, feeds. It wears first a green skin with blue spots, and afterwards (just before the chrysalis stage) a skin of a rich yellow color. Its chrysalis is of pale wood color; the butterfly, the blue swallow-tail—Papilio Troilus.

STORIES.

A Lesson of Faith.

"If a man die, shall he live *again?* All the days of my appointed time will I wait, till my change come."—JOB xiv: 14.

"Let me hire you as a nurse for my poor children," said a Butterfly to a quiet Caterpillar, who was strolling along a cabbage leaf in her odd, lumbering way. "See these little eggs,' continued the Butterfly; "I don't know how long it will be before they come to life, and I feel very sick and poorly, and if I should die, who will take care of my baby butterflies when I am gone? Will *you*, kind, mild, green Caterpillar! But you must mind what you give them to eat, Caterpillar!—they cannot, of course, live on *your* rough food. You must give them early dew, and honey from the flowers; and you must let them fly about only a little way at first; for, of course, one can't expect them to use their wings properly all at once. Dear me! it is a sad pity you cannot fly yourself. But I have no time to look for another nurse now, so you will do your best, I hope. Dear! dear! I cannot think what made me come and lay my eggs on a cabbage leaf! What a place for young Butterflies to be born upon! Still you will be kind, will you not, to the poor little ones? Here, take this gold-dust from my wings as a reward. Oh, how dizzy I am! Caterpillar, you will remember about the food"—

And with these words the Butterfly drooped her wings and died; and the green Caterpillar, who had not had the opportunity of even saying yes or no to the request, was left standing alone by the side of the Butterfly's eggs.

"A pretty nurse she has chosen, indeed, poor lady!" exclaimed she, "and a pretty business I have in hand! Why, her senses must have left her, or she never would have asked a poor, crawling creature like me to bring up her dainty little ones! Much they'll mind me, truly, when they feel the gay wings on their backs, and can fly away out of my sight whenever they choose! Ah! how silly some people are, in spite of their painted clothes and the gold-dust on their wings!"

However, the poor Butterfly was dead, and there lay the eggs on the cabbage leaf; and the green Caterpillar had a kind heart, so she resolved to do her best. But she got no sleep that night, she was so very anxious. She made her back quite ache with walking all night round her young charges, for fear any harm should happen to them; and in the morning, says she to herself: "Two heads are better than one. I will consult some wise animal upon the matter, and get advice. How should a poor, crawling creature like me know what to do without asking my betters?"

But still there was a difficulty—whom should the Caterpillar consult? There was the shaggy Dog who sometimes came into the garden. But he was so rough!—he would most likely whisk all the eggs off the cabbage leaf with one brush of his tail, if she called him near to talk to her, and then she should never forgive herself. There was the Tom Cat, to be sure, who would sometimes sit at the foot of the apple tree, basking himself and warming his fur in the sunshine; but he was so selfish and indifferent!—there was no hope of his giving himself the trouble to think about Butterflies' eggs. "I wonder which is the wisest of all the animals I know," sighed the Caterpillar in great distress; and then she thought, and thought, till at last she thought of the Lark; and she fancied that because he went up so high, and nobody knew where he went to, he must be very clever and know a great deal; for to go up very high (which *she* could never do) was the Caterpillar's idea of perfect glory.

Now in the neighboring cornfield there lived a Lark, and the Caterpillar sent a message to him, to beg him to come and talk to her; and when he came she told him all her difficulties, and asked him what she was to do to feed and rear the little creatures so different from herself.

"Perhaps you will be able to inquire and hear something about it next time you go up high," observed the Caterpillar, timidly.

The Lark said, "Perhaps he should;" but he did not satisfy her curiosity any further. Soon afterwards, however, he went singing upward into the bright blue sky. By degrees his voice died away in the distance, till the green Caterpillar could not hear a sound. It is nothing to say she could not see him; for, poor thing! she never could see far at any time, and had a difficulty in looking upwards at all, even when she reared herself up most carefully, which she did now; but it was of no use, so she dropped upon her legs again, and resumed her walk round the Butterfly's eggs, nibbling a bit of the cabbage leaf now and then as she moved along.

"What a time the Lark has been gone!" she cried at last "I wonder where he is just now! I would give all my legs to know! He must have flown up higher than usual this time, I do think. How I should like to know where it is that he goes to and what he hears in that curious blue sky! He always sings in going up and coming down, but he never lets any secret out. He is very, very close!"

And the green Caterpillar took another turn round the Butterfly's eggs.

At last the Lark's voice began to be heard again. The Caterpillar almost jumped for joy, and it was not long before she saw her friend descend with hushed note to the cabbage bed.

"News, news, glorious news, friend Caterpillar!" sang the Lark; "but the worst of it is, you won't believe me."

"I believe everything I am told," observed the Caterpillar, hastily.

"Well, then, first of all, I will tell you what these little creatures are to eat," and the Lark nodded his beak towards the eggs. "What do you think it is to be? Guess!"

"Dew, and honey out of flowers, I am afraid," sighed the Caterpillar.

"No such thing, old lady! Something simpler than that. Something that *you* can get at quite easily."

"I can get at nothing quite easily but cabbage leaves," murmured the Caterpillar, in distress.

"Excellent! my good friend," cried the Lark, exultingly; "you have found it out. You are to feed them with cabbage leaves."

"*Never!*" cried the Caterpillar, indignantly. "It was their dying mother's last request that I should do no such thing."

"Their dying mother knew nothing about the matter," persisted the Lark; "but why do you ask me, and then disbelieve what I say? You have neither faith nor trust."

"Oh! I believe everything I am told," said the Caterpillar.

"Nay, but you do not," replied the Lark; "you won't believe me even about the food, and yet that is but a beginning of what I have to tell you. Why, Caterpillar, what do you think those little eggs will turn out to be?"

"Butterflies to be sure," said the Caterpillar.

"*Caterpillars!*" sang the Lark; "and you'll find it out in time;" and the Lark flew away, for he did not want to stay and contest the point with his friend.

"I thought the Lark had been wise and kind," observed the mild, green Caterpillar, once more beginning to walk round the eggs, "but I find that he is foolish and saucy instead. Perhaps he went up *too* high this time. Ah, it's a pity when people who soar so high are silly and rude nevertheless! Dear! I still wonder whom he sees and what he does up yonder."

"I would tell you if you would believe me," sang the Lark, descending once more.

"I believe everything I am told," reiterated the Caterpillar, with as grave a face as if it were a fact.

"Then I'll tell you something else," cried the Lark; "for the best of my news remains behind: *You will one day be a Butterfly yourself.*"

"Wretched bird!" exclaimed the Caterpillar, "you jest with my inferiority. Now you are cruel as well as foolish. Go away! I will ask your advice no more."

"I told you you would not believe me," cried the Lark, nettled in his turn.

"I believe everything that I am told," persisted the Caterpillar; "that is"—and she hesitated—"everything that is *reasonable* to believe. But to tell me that Butterflies' eggs are Caterpillars, and that Caterpillars leave off crawling and get wings, and become Butterflies!—Lark! you are too wise to believe such nonsense yourself, for you know it is impossible!"

"I know no such thing," said the Lark, warmly. "Whether I hover over the cornfields of earth, or go up into the depths of the sky, I see so many wonderful things, I know no reason why there should not be more. O Caterpillar; it is because you crawl, because you never get beyond your cabbage leaf, that you call *any* thing *impossible.*"

"Nonsense!" shouted the Caterpillar. "I know what's possible, and what's not possible, according to my experience and capacity, as well as you do. Look at my long, green body and these endless legs, and then talk to me about having wings and a painted feathery coat. Fool!"—

"And fool you! you would-be-wise Caterpillar!" cried the indignant Lark. "Fool, to attempt to reason about what you cannot understand! Do you not hear how my song swells with rejoicing as I soar upwards to the mysterious wonder-world above? O Caterpillar; what comes to you from thence, receive, as *I* do, upon trust."

"That is what you call"—

"*Faith,*" interrupted the Lark.

"How am I to learn faith?" asked the Caterpillar.

At that moment she felt something at her side. She looked round—eight or ten little green Caterpillars were moving about, and had already made a show of a hole in the cabbage leaf. They had broken from the Butterfly's eggs!

Shame and amazement filled our green friend's heart, but joy soon followed; for, as the first wonder was possible, the second might be so, too. "Teach me your lesson, Lark!" she would say; and the Lark sang to her of the wonders of the earth below and of the heaven above. And the Caterpillar talked all the rest of her life to her relations of the time when she should be a Butterfly.

But none of them believed her. She nevertheless had learned the Lark's lesson of faith, and when she was going into her chrysalis grave, she said, "I shall be a Butterfly some day!"

But her relations thought her head was wandering, and they said, "Poor thing!"

And when she was a Butterfly, and was going to die again, she said: "I have known many wonders—I have faith—I can trust even now for what shall come next.

MARGARET GATTY.

Parables from Nature.

THE CATERPILLAR.

To the Teacher:—

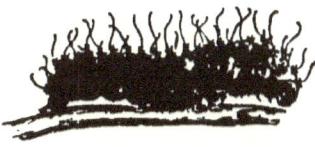

Whoever has once had the pleasure of bringing the beautiful marvel of the caterpillar's metamorphosis to a child's notice will scarcely need any other incentive than the delight of that experience to lead her to repeat it as often as possible. Perhaps there are some people who only know the wonder by hearsay, and accept it indifferently among other zoological facts. Let me tell you, friends, the world has a new delight to offer you. Do not forego it any longer. Get a box, fill it half full of earth and fasten a piece of netting over the top.

When you see a caterpillar on plant or tree, capture him and place him in this box, taking care also to break off some leaves of that particular plant or tree for him to eat. Keep the caterpillar supplied with food, and then watch and wait, and you will surely be repaid for your trouble.

The caterpillar which feeds on the milkweed is a very obliging creature. I remember how a dozen of them hung themselves under my window at the farmhouse; and some were even so kind as to split their old coats and drop them off while we watched them. And when the marvelous chrysalis appeared!—vivid green with tiny spots of bright gold!—and when my first little butterfly crawled out, cripping and bedraggled looking, to be sure, but soon as gay a creature as ever spread wings!—ah! there are few pleasures like the pleasure of that experience. This change of outward form, while the inner life continues uninterruptedly, is one of nature's most beautiful symbolisms, and every child should be in possession of it.

While the teacher and children are watching the miracle, the work and play in the kindergarten will, of course, illustrate the same idea.

A good series in clay is first a leaf with tiny eggs upon it; then the caterpillar; then the chrysalis (or cocoon if your caterpillar makes one); the butterfly or moth is rather difficult, but is an interesting and valuable lesson. Model the parts separately.

In the butterfly game, the change which is now made from "a little worm is on the ground" to "a caterpillar's on the ground" is a welcome one as being nearer the truth. A worm lives and dies a worm. It does not turn into a butterfly.

Neither does the chrysalis break up into numerous butterflies, as one could but infer from seeing the game as played in some kindergartens. "But," says one of these kindergartners, "it is so pretty, and gives so many children something to do in the game." "And then," says another, "we must not be too literal. Children are natural poets. We must give them poetic interpretations."

Are the kindergarten games, then, merely pretty spectacles or merely outlets for the effervescence of childhood? The teacher who finds nothing more in the games, and the one who thoughtlessly allows the playing of the games to degenerate into these, has missed a vital point in Froebel's theory.

The kindergarten surely provides ample scope for the development of the child's imagination. There will be no danger of hampering it, however careful we are as to the accuracy of all the impressions we give in the plays and songs. And, if any impressions last, be sure that the false ones, given in our strivings against being too literal, will last as long as any of the others.

To return to the part of the butterfly game which is under discussion. In some kindergartens the game is made a true representation as well as a charming play.

After the butterfly has emerged, the winds whistle and blow the empty chrysalis about and break it into pieces. As the one butterfly from the chrysalis flits here and there seeking honey, it discovers other butterflies (children previously chosen) hiding among the flowers.

Many other ways might be suggested, but whatever may be the way in which this or any representative game is played, let it be one which is essentially true and according to nature.

As to the untrue *finale* being more "poetic," is that really the case? Ready to my hand I find a quotation from an essay "On Poetic Interpretation of Nature," by Prof. J. C. Shairp:—

"*Every new province of knowledge which science conquers, poetry may in turn enter into and possess.* * * * * And here we see how finely science and poetry may interact and minister to each other."

Wordsworth also affirms that "*the remotest discoveries of the chemist, the botanist and the mineralogist*" (if familiarized to men) are "*as proper objects of the poet's art as any upon which it can be employed.*"

Shall we not, then, trust the word of critic and poet regarding these relations, and avoid putting science and poetry in opposition, when they may so beautifully agree?

E. P.

The Kindergarten Magazine.

THE TALK.

We are going to have some pets in the kindergarten. When we keep pets we must be very careful to make them comfortable and happy.

What pets have you at home? What do they need? Food and shelter for comfort; love, shown by kindness and petting, for happiness.

The little pets which we shall have here will need food and air. The kindest thing we can do for them is to give them plenty of fresh leaves of just the kind they like; they do not seem to care for anything else.

What shape is the caterpillar's body? What is it covered with? What colors do you see on it? How does it move? How many legs at the front part of its body? At the back part? Those at the front part are its real feet; the short, thick ones at the back are only folds of the skin to help the caterpillar to cling to leaves and stems, and to support his body as he crawls.

Somebody with very sharp eyes may come and look at the side of the caterpillar and tell me what he sees. Little spots? Yes, spots which are not merely pretty but which are very necessary, for they are the caterpillar's breathing holes. How do *we* breathe? (An opportunity comes here for a hygienic hint concerning breathing through the nostrils, so carefully lined with protecting hairs, instead of through the mouth.)

How do fishes breathe? (Let the children have a picture of a fish and point out the gills. Ask again how the caterpillar breathes. Notice its small eyes and compare with the large and brilliant eye of the butterfly. The observation of the caterpillar should be carried on from day to day. If you do not succeed in being present when the skin is being cast, you will at least find the old skin in a little bunch somewhere in the box or jar; that is, unless your caterpillar belongs to the kind which eats its old clothes everytime it comes out in new ones! The rewards of constant watching are well worth the trouble.)

There are some things about caterpillars that our eyes are not sharp enough to see; but the wise men have used glasses and found out many wonders. They tell us that some caterpillars have a spinning tube in the lower lip and two bags in the body out of which they get a silky stuff. This silky stuff comes out through the spinning tube and stiffens to a thread as soon as the air touches it.

When this kind of caterpillar has eaten and grown all it can and is ready to make its chrysalis, it winds this fine, filmy thread all around itself till it is entirely shut in by a silken wall with no windows or doors, no opening anywhere.

(Show cocoon.) Inside this snug cocoon the caterpillar makes its chrysalis. Should you think there was anything alive in the cocoon? Is it not a safe resting place for the caterpillar? And is it not wonderful that the little creature could make it?

Other caterpillars make other kinds of cocoons. Some will wrap themselves about with leaves, fastening them with the silky threads. Some of the hairy caterpillars pull the hairs out of their own bodies and weave them together. And some make comfortable and safe cocoons out of bits of wood, held together by the same home-made silk

The caterpillars which make these curious homes for themselves do not change into butterflies, but into moths, which are very much like butterflies in some ways and different in others.

TEACHER'S READING.

The same as under " The Butterfly."
Larvæ, - - - - - - - - - - - *A. D. T. Whitney*

For the Children

The Green House with Gold Nails (" Kindergarten Stories
  and Morning Talks "), - - - - - - - *S. E. Wiltse*
A Funny Little Log House (" Little Folks in Feather and
  Fur "), - - - - - - - - - *O. T. Miller*

STORIES.

"Such a Beauty."

" Chip-chip-chee-ee-e,
What shall our breakfast be-ee? "

sang a mother bird, her bright eyes glancing here, there, everywhere.

" O mother! mother! See-ee!
Here upon the tree-ee-e,"

sang one of the young birds, peeping through the leafy branches and imitating his mother's tones as well as he could.

The mother hopped nearer to the eager young bird and looked down. There she spied a plump, big caterpillar of a handsome pale green color and ornamented with bright little knobs of red, yellow and blue.

" Chip-chip-chee-ee,
None of that for me-ee,"

sang the mother bird in a most excited manner. And then she called her young birds to look at the caterpillar. She earnestly told them to notice well every mark upon it, for it was not at all good to eat, and they must never touch it. Not only was this kind of caterpillar disagreeable to the taste, but she had heard that it was poisonous.

"Now tell me just how it looks," said the anxious mother, "so that I may be sure that you know and will never try to catch this kind."

So the young birds described the caterpillar, peering down so as to tell exactly how it looked. They said that it was like new leaves, or the lettuce in the garden; that it had some spots like tiny cherries, and some like the bluest of blueberries. "It is very strange that this caterpillar should not be good to eat," said one of the young birds, "when it looks like so many things which are *very* good."

"See, mother, there are yellow seeds on its back, too!" chirped the other little bird.

"They look like seeds, I know," said the mother; "but of course they are not. All these gay colors and knobs will help you to remember the kind of caterpillar you are not to eat. I am glad it is such a beauty." Satisfied that her birdlings now knew the pretty caterpillar as an unsafe kind of food, she spread her wings and flew away, singing:—

> "Chip-chip-chee-ee e!
> Off to the apple tree-ee-e.
> Fruit shall our breakfast be.
> Away, away with me."

And the little ones followed, trying to keep up with her, and doing well, considering how short a time they had been out of their nest and on their wings, so to speak.

What about the caterpillar all this time? Oh! it had been placidly eating as usual, not at all disturbed by the bird-talk going on above. Very well contented that its gay coat should be such a good protection, it wriggled itself along farther and began to nibble a fresh leaf.

A few days later the caterpillar, whose appetite had failed, begun to feel very strangely.

"I feel as if I should like to hide and sleep," it thought. "I must be ill—I am so"—

"O you beauty!" said a voice. "You look as if you had tiny red and yellow and blue beads sewed on your back. I wonder whether Aunt Helen will not tell me a story about you. Crawl along here and get on this stick—that's right—I won't hurt you."

The caterpillar clung to the stick, and the little boy started to get down from the tree into which he had climbed "just for fun." But getting down was not as easy as climbing up had been, and the little boy had to leave the caterpillar on the tree after all.

"I'll ask Aunt Helen to come," he said to himself. "Then I can climb and get the caterpillar and reach it down to her." So saying he ran off to the house.

"Yes," said the caterpillar, on finding itself alone again

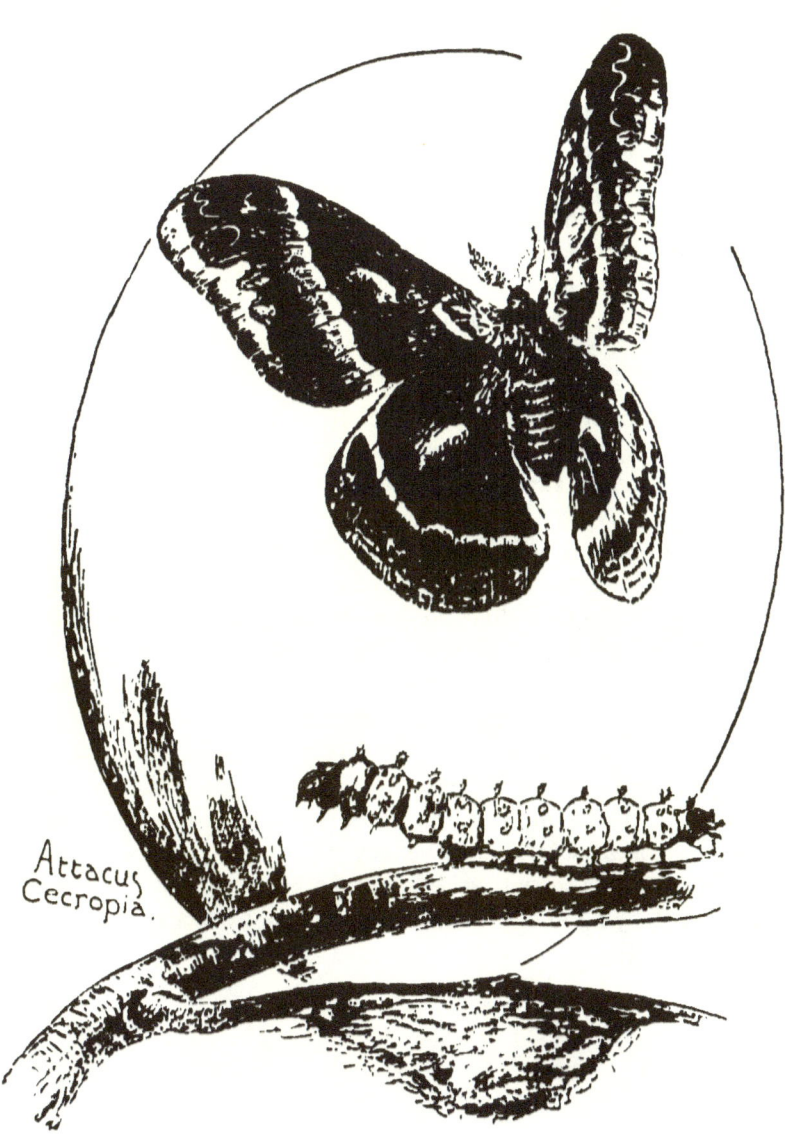

"I think I *had* better hide." And it did. It crawled off a little way from where the boy had left it, and began to spin immediately.

By the time the little boy had reached the house and had found Aunt Helen, and she had finished some work which she could not leave, and they had both reached the tree at the end of the garden, the caterpillar had wound a mesh of silk about itself and could no longer be seen. The little boy was greatly puzzled as he looked in vain for the green caterpillar.

"It was such a big fellow, auntie—as big as your thumb. I thought it would be too clumsy to get far away. I wish I *could* find it. I never saw such a pretty caterpillar—such a perfect beauty!"

"I know where it is," said Aunt Helen. "I see a cocoon up there, and I am sure your caterpillar must be in it. Just break that twig off gently—that one which has something fastened to it—and reach it down to me. This is part of the story," she added, with a smile, as she saw how puzzled the little boy was.

"Oh! is it?" he exclaimed, hastening to break off the twig and to hand it to her. In a twinkling he was down from the tree, all eagerness for the explanation. So they sat in the swing and Aunt Helen told him the whole story then and there; and several months later, the little boy ran to his auntie, saying: "The story has come true! There's a beautiful moth, oh! such a beauty! flying about in my room, and the cocoon is empty."

E. P.

THE FARMER.

To the Teacher:—

This talk treats more especially of the farmer's spring work of preparation, since we reviewed, during the harvest season, the farmer's summer work and dwelt upon its results

For city children, have as many pictures of farm life as possible. A box in the window planted with corn and beans will be a miniature field and the children will feel themselves farmers in the care of it.

Watching the growth of seeds planted by themselves will be a delightful experience to the children.

Besides the seeds planted in earth, some should be grown without earth, that the roots may be observed. Let a piece of cotton batting float on some water in a tumbler, and lay two or three beans on the cotton. Replenish the water when necessary. Beans are very satisfactory because of their size and familiarity. Peas are also good, and corn will give an example of the contrasting endogenous plants.

In the explanation of the "Grass-Mowing" play, Froebel says: "Early and and whenever it is at all possible, we ought to make the chain of conditions and relations visible which must be gone through and fulfilled before it is possible to say simply, ' Go away and get this or that person to give you bread or something else.'" Therefore it is not enough that we help the children, (through games, songs, stories and talks,) to enter into the farmer's life and work; we must try to make visible the chain of conditions and relations by which all life is bound together. This thought also underlies the talks on " The Baker " and " The Cow."

THE TALK.

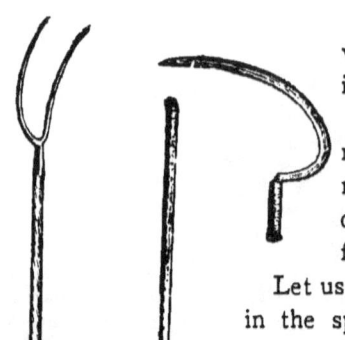

I am thinking of a worker—one who works out of doors instead of in a shop.

Can you guess what worker I mean? It is the farmer. Do you remember any one we have talked of lately who wished to be a farmer? (Froebel).

Let us play we are all visiting at a farm in the springtime. What shall we hear early in the morning? The cocks crowing, the pigeons cooing, other birds singing, the cattle lowing, being so eager to get out to pasture—all the farmyard noises.

What shall we see? The big barn and farmyard where the animals live, the pigeon house on its tall pole, the orchard where the trees are standing in even rows, the gardens for flowers and vegetables, great fields stretching away, and woods in the distance. (Some of the children who have been to the country will be ready to contribute to this description. Contrast with city sights and sounds.)

What places in the city look a little like the country? The Common, Public Garden, etc., (whatever parks the children are familiar with), because of the trees and grass and space.

The people at the farm are up very early; for the cattle and poultry must be fed and the cows milked, and the farmer wishes to get out to his fields very soon. He has so much to do.

In the spring he must plough his fields—this breaks the soil which has been getting hard and packed together all winter—

then he must harrow them "to make the ground more soft and loose."

(Describe plough and harrow, and speak of the usefulness of the horse to the farmer.)

When the ground is ready the farmer must sow his seed. What kinds of seeds do you think he will sow? Grass seed, barley and wheat, oats, buckwheat, etc. Some kinds he sowed last autumn, and they have been waiting all winter for the spring warmth and the spring rains before they sprouted and sent out their green blades.

How will these crops be useful? What else will the farmer probably plant? Corn, beans, potatoes, etc., and sometimes trees. What do all seeds need to make them grow? Earth, sunshine, rain.

Besides the plowing and the planting and the raking, the farmer has other spring work to do. He must cut off the dead and useless branches of the trees in the orchard and of the vines where the grapes grow. Very early in the spring he gathers sap from some of the trees. Who can tell what kind of trees, and what he makes of the sap?

What tools does the farmer use? Plough, harrow, spade, hoe, rake, pitchfork, etc. Tell some other things he needs in his work. Ladders to enable him to reach the high branches of the trees, baskets and barrels for his eggs and fruit and vegetables, milk pails and milk cans, churn, etc., etc. (Many of these can be made in clay and other kindergarten materials.)

Tell all the things we use which come from the farm. Do we not use some of these things every day? Let us not forget how much we have for which we must thank the good farmer.

TEACHER'S READING.

Nature,	Emerson
My Summer in a Garden,	C. D. Warner
Hiawatha's Fasting, } Blessing the Cornfields, }	Longfellow
The Barefoot Boy,	Whittier
Farmyard Song,	J. T. Trowbridge
Up at a Villa, Down in a City,	R. Browning
The Rescue of an Old Place,	Mary C. Robbins
Rosanna,	Miss Edgeworth

For the Children.

Queen Hildegarde,	Laura Richards
The Farmyard, (" Kindergarten Stories and Morning Talks "),	S. E. Wiltse
The Farmer and his Sons,	Æsop

STORIES.

A Barnyard Talk.

(From the Norwegian.)

"Cock-a-doodle-doo!" crowed the Cock early in the morning. "I am the cleverest of all on the farm. Every morning I wake the people up so that the children can get to school at the right time, and not have to stay in for being late. That is the reason the children like me so much. They feed me with corn and bread every day."

"Cluck, cluck!" said the Hen. "You ought not to be so conceited, little father. You never give the children anything to eat, but *I* do! Almost every day I lay an egg; and with my eggs pancakes are made for the children, and they like pancakes so much that they would gladly eat them every day. Understand, then, that I am cleverer than you."

"Mew, mew, mew," said Pussy-cat, who had heard the Cock and Hen talking. "It is really I who am the cleverest," said she. "If I did not kill all the rats and mice, then those wicked animals would come and eat up all the butter and cheese and all the bread and cake, so that the children would have to go to school without any luncheon and would sit there and starve! That is the reason the children and I are such good friends. They give me milk and let me sit on their laps.'

"Bow, wow, wow!" said the Dog. He had put his head out of the kennel when he heard how Pussy was boasting. "How do you think things would go if I didn't watch over the house night and day? So I am surely the most important one on the farm."

Just then up came the farmer, who had overheard everything.

"You are all kind and useful," said he. And he scattered corn to the Cock and Hen, and gave Puss a saucer of milk, and the Dog a bone to gnaw.

Then they were all happy and satisfied and stopped disputing.

EMILIE POULSSON.

The Farmer and the Birds.

Mr. and Mrs. Brown Thrush thought themselves very fortunate when they found a large brush heap in which they could make their nest. But one day, after the nest was finished and the eggs were laid, Mr. Thrush heard some news which made him change his mind.

"Oh! my dear," he said to his wife when she came home after her daily exercise, "we have made a mistake. This brush heap, that we thought was such a good place for our nest, is to be burned to-morrow! What shall we do? Our eggs will all be ruined!"

"Oh, no!" said Mrs. Thrush, "they will not be harmed. I will watch for the master to-morrow and show him that I have a nest here, and he will not burn it up. Have you not noticed how many birds there are on the place? The master never allows any one to hurt them. In fact, the red birds and mocking birds, who stay here all winter, tell me that he puts food where they can get it when they can find none themselves."

"Then," said Mr. Thrush, "perhaps he *will* spare our nest. You can try, at any rate."

So the next day, when the master came near the brush heap, Mrs. Thrush flew to a tree growing close by, and then back to her nest again, several times.

"Robert," said the master to the man who helped him on the farm, "see that thrush! She acts as if she had a nest in that brush heap. Yes, she has! I can see it. It will not do to burn the brush now, for that would destroy her nest; and yet I need to plough this ground for the late corn that I want to raise. I know what we can do. Get four long sticks from the woodpile and we will move the brush away."

Robert brought the sticks; then, by placing themselves on opposite sides of the brush, crossing the sticks and putting them under the heap, the two men moved it to a little distance.* After that the horse was fastened to the plough and the ground was ploughed.

Then the farmer and his man planted the corn. They marked off the ground into squares of four feet each, made a hole at each corner of the squares, put three or four kernels of corn into each hole, drew the earth over the corn with a hoe and pressed it down with the foot to make it firm, so that it might keep moist longer after the next rain. Meantime, Mrs. Thrush, anxious to cover her eggs, had flown back to the nest as soon as the men had left the brush heap; and she sat looking contentedly on at their work.

Some days later a rainstorm came. The bird's eggs did not get wet, however, for these were kept warm and dry under the mother's wing; but the raindrops trickled down into the earth and gave the kernels of corn a drink. After drinking the water the kernels began to swell. They kept swelling more and more until at last a baby leaf burst the skin, pushed its way up and came out of the ground. The little leaf was folded tightly at first, but after a while it spread itself out. Then the stalk began to grow longer; and by and by another leaf came on the opposite side of the stalk. The third leaf grew on the same side of the stalk as the first; and on which side do you suppose the fourth leaf came out?

---

* A fact.

THE FARMER.

"On the same side as the second—just as it is in our weaving!"

Yes. And now can you tell me why the corn did not have two leaves instead of one at a time?

"When we soaked a kernel of corn and cut it open, we found only one baby leaf in it, besides the food for the baby plant to eat until it could feed itself from the earth and the air. So it could not make more than one leaf at a time."

You are right. But I should have told you that the corn was making roots at the same time that it made stalk and leaves, so that it had roots by which to suck in food from the earth, and leaves by which to suck in food from the air; and with all this food it grew very fast. The master took care that the weeds should not choke it.

As soon as the corn was up a few inches, the master directed Robert to go over the ground with a harrow. This destroyed all the weeds that had started at the same time as the corn. Then Robert ploughed the ground in again, but was careful not to throw the earth on the young corn. After that the farmer kept the weeds from growing by using the cultivator once in a while until the corn was as high as his shoulder; then it was strong enough not to need his help any more.

While the corn was still growing, Mrs. Thrush heard one day a queer little hammering sound in the nest; and she said to her husband: "Oh! now our eggs are ready to hatch. I am so glad! But I must help the little ones to come out of their shells!"

So, with the mother's help, the shells were broken and the little birds came out. Then began a busy time for the parent birds. The nestlings had great appetites, and Mr. and Mrs. Thrush brought them many a bug and worm which would have hurt the farmer's corn and other crops if the birds had not eaten them. The parent birds thus helped the farmer who had been so kind to them.

When the corn was large enough the tassels came and the ears of corn began to grow. The tassels are bunches of long, silky fringe, and each ear has a tassel hanging out of its husk. A husk is made of several large, thick leaves; these are folded around an ear of corn and keep it from being spoiled by the wet or eaten by squirrels or crows while it is growing.

Mrs. Thrush taught her little ones to fly, after which they could catch worms and bugs for themselves. When they were old enough they left the nest, but they stayed on the farm. And when the crop was ripe and the farmer was gathering it so that it could be stored in the barn for winter use, the thrushes sang their prettiest songs, as if to thank the farmer for saving their lives before they were hatched.

JOSEPHINE JARVIS.

Cobden, Ill.

Little Gustava.

Little Gustava sits in the sun,
Safe in the porch, and the little drops run
From the icicles under the eaves so fast,
For the bright spring sun shines warm at last;
    And glad is little Gustava.

She wears a quaint little scarlet cap,
And a little green bowl she holds in her lap,
Filled with bread and milk to the brim,
And a wreath of marigolds round the rim;
    "Ha! ha!" laughed little Gustava.

Up comes her little gray coaxing cat,
With her little pink nose, and she mews, "What's that?"
Gustava feeds her—she begs for more;
And a little brown hen walks in at the door;
    "Good day!" cries little Gustava.

She scatters crumbs for the little brown hen.
There comes a rush and a flutter, and then
Down fly her little white doves, so sweet,
With their snowy wings and their crimson feet.
    "Welcome!" cries little Gustava.

So dainty and eager they pick up the crumbs.
But who is this through the doorway comes?
Little Scotch terrier, little dog Rags,
Looks in her face, and his funny tail wags.
    "Ha! ha!" laughs little Gustava.

"You want some breakfast, too?" and down
She sets her bowl on the brick floor brown;
And little dog Rags drinks up her milk,
While she strokes his shaggy locks, like silk;
   "Dear Rags," says little Gustava.

Waiting without stood sparrow and crow,
Cooling their feet in the melting snow.
"Won't you come in, good folk?" she cried,
But they were too bashful and stayed outside,
   Though "Pray come in!" cried Gustava.

So the last she threw them, and knelt on the mat
With doves and biddy and dog and cat.
And her mother came to the open house-door:
"Dear little daughter, I bring you some more,
   My merry little Gustava."

Kitty and terrier, biddy and doves,
All things harmless, Gustava loves;
The shy, kind creatures 'tis joy to feed,
And oh! her breakfast is sweet indeed
   To happy little Gustava!

CELIA THAXTER

Houghton, Mifflin & Co.

THE HEN AND CHICKENS.

To the Teacher:—

With city children such subjects as this call for much illustration. A young chicken was once the pet and delight of a city kindergarten. Sometimes it is practicable to take the children to see a "Good Mother Hen" and her brood. At any rate, pictures of the common animals and farmyard scenes may be had for the trouble of collecting, and, if mounted on cardboard, will be useful for a long time.

THE TALK.

We have talked about the little birds who fly in the air and live in the trees. Now let us talk of some other friends who are dressed in feathers and have wings, but who are larger and live on the ground. Can you guess who these friends are? We shall find them if we go to the farmyard.

(If the children name the inhabitants of the farmyard, the hen and chickens will surely be mentioned. In comparing the hen and smaller birds, note particularly the hen's heavy body and short wings, and consequently feeble flight, and the strong toes for scratching.)

What kind of a noise does the hen make? Does she lay eggs? Build a nest? Not a snug, pretty nest as the little birds do. Usually the farmer gives her some hay in a box or barrel when she wants a nest; but sometimes the hen chooses a place herself up in the hayloft in the barn, where it is all dark and quiet, or perhaps she finds a sheltered place in the field among the grasses which will hide her safely.

When she has laid ten or twelve eggs, she sits on the nest day after day and night after night. She will scarcely leave the eggs to get what she needs to eat and drink. How long do you think she sits there? Twenty-one days. And after all this time what happens? One of these days the hen hears a faint little tapping and then a cracking noise, and one of the eggshells breaks and out comes a tiny, weak chicken! And soon another breaks its shell and comes out, and so on until, instead of ten white eggs lying in the nest, there are ten cunning little chickens nestling in the hay and cuddling under the mother hen's soft feathers.

The chickens are dressed in very soft, fine feathers, called down. This down is often bright yellow. As the mother hen walks about with her dear little chickens she seems to say: "This is why I was willing to sit still so long on those eggs of mine. Isn't this joyful?"

When the farmer sees the happy mother hen, he is glad, too; but he is afraid the chickens will get tired if they follow her everywhere. So he puts the mother hen into a nice coop. The chickens run in and out of the coop, and their mother watches them and calls to them if any danger is near. When she calls them, or when anything frightens them, they run into the coop and cuddle under her wings. Don't you know how glad you are to run to your mother when your are hurt or frightened or in any trouble? I suppose the chickens feel as safe and comfortable with the mother hen's wings over them as little children do in their mother's arms.

When night comes the mother hen clucks to her chickens and they creep under her wings to sleep. By and by when they are big enough, they will roost on perches at night and run about all day, scratching and pecking, finding insects and worms and seeds to eat, as the other big fowls do. But while they are little their mother watches them and takes care of them night and day.

"Where do the little chickens run
  When they are afraid?
Out of the light, out of the sun,
  Into the dark, into the shade,
  Under their mother's downy wing,
No longer afraid of anything."

TEACHER'S READING.

Winners in Life's Race (Chaps. VI, VII),	*Arabella Buckley*
The Song of Life (Chaps. IV, VI),	*Margaret Morley*
Hen Music ("Wood Notes Wild"),	*Simeon Pease Cheney*
Chickens,	*Gail Hamilton.*
Explanation and Play of "Beckoning the Chickens,"	*Froebel*

For the Children.

The Clucking Hen ("Aunt Effie's Rhymes").	
Snowball ("Stories for Kindergarten and Home"),	*M. L. Van Kirk*

STORIES.

The Lost Chicken.

Peepsie was lost—Peesie, the one little chicken which Mrs. Crackle, his mother, was trying to raise; and Mrs. Crackle was very lonely and sad. She stepped about the farmyard, lifting up her feet very slowly and looking in every nook and corner and calling, "Cluck, cluck," in a loud, anxious way.

The old barn cat washed every one of her kittens over twice as soon as she heard the distressing news, so as to be sure that none of her babies was lost. The cows called their little bossy calves close to them, and every sheep sought out her own lambkin, glad enough to hear it call, "Ma-a! Ma-a!" All the mothers told their children again and again not to stray away lest they should get lost, like poor little Peepsie.

In the meantime Mrs Cackle, having looked everywhere in the farmyard and having made sure that Peepsie was not there, started off to search outside. The first place to which she went was the hayfield. The grass was cut and spread out to dry. Mrs. Crackle thought Peepsie might be hiding under it, so she began to look and to call. There! What was that? Something moved, and Mrs. Cackle rushed after it. Was it her chicken? Listen and you shall hear. Mrs. Cackle soon saw the little thing plainly as it went across a bare place in the field, and she immediately stopped running. It was a baby, surely: not half so big as Peepsie, however, and with a long thread of a tail stretching out behind it. "Why, it is only one of Mrs. Field-mouse's children," said Mrs. Cackle in disappointment, and as she turned back to tell Mrs. Field-mouse, she met that mother coming to find her child. Mrs. Field-mouse could not tell where Peepsie was, but had seen a company of two-legged little folks going down the lane a short time before; so Mrs. Cackle thanked her and passed on.

The lane led past the orchard. Hark! Mrs. Cackle heard a faint cry. "Can that be Peepsie?" she thought, and into the orchard she went, guided by the sound. There, under one of the apple trees, lay another baby; but, alas! this was not Peepsie either, although it had feathers and a bill and two legs, and its chirp still sounded something like Peepsie's to Mrs. Cackle, even when she was so near. But when this baby moved it hopped on both legs at once, while Peepsie, of course, used his legs quite properly, one after the other.

Mrs. Robin, the baby's mother, circled watchfully about while Mrs. Cackle stood near the little one. "Peepsie lost?" chirped Mrs. Robin when the poor hen told her story. "Oh, how worried you must be! But I am sure he is not in the orchard, for my mate and I have been about here all the morning, teaching our little ones to fly, and we should have seen him."

Poor Mrs. Cackle decided that she would go on farther down the lane to look for her stray darling; and the happy Robin family continued their flying lesson, though Mrs. Robin felt very sorry about Peepsie and kept a sharp lookout for him.

Down the lane went Mrs. Cackle, but before she had gone very far she met Mother Duck. Now Mother Duck had gone out so early from the farmyard that she had not heard of Peepsie's being lost, and when Mrs. Cackle told her she said: "Alack! Alack! But perhaps, friend Cackle, your Peepsie has been with my children this morning. I'll call the whole company here and you may see for yourself." So Mrs. Cackle looked at all the long train of little folks which was following Mother Duck. One by one they filed past her, but alas for Mrs. Cackle! she knew at the first glance at each one that it was not Peepsie; for, instead of Peepsie's sharp-pointed bill, Mother Duck's children had broad, flat bills which Mrs. Cackle thought must be very difficult to eat with, and instead of pretty, slender, separate toes useful for scratching, these little folks had their toes joined together by a sort of skin; and then they walked so awkwardly— at least, so Mrs. Cackle thought. "My Peepsie is not there," she said to Mother Duck. "You are sure, are you?" replied the Duck, "because if you are not, we could go to our pond and *then* we could tell; for all my own children can swim, and I believe yours are like yourself—very timid about water." Mrs. Cackle *was* sure, however, so she said "Good-bye" and "Thank you" to Mother Duck, and turned back toward the farmyard, while "Mother Duck and her family large" went to their pond. "For," said the web-footed mother, "the very sight of a hen always makes me feel so glad that I can swim! I want to get into the water immediately and enjoy the use of my powers."

Unhappy Mrs. Cackle returned to the farmyard more worried than when she had started out. She now felt almost certain that some harm had happened to Peepsie. At the farmyard gate, however, she saw the farmer's little girl coming toward her.

Little Bess stooped and put her hands to the ground, and out ran the lost Peepsie—a wee bit frightened but not at all hurt. "There's your baby, Mrs. Cackle," said Bess; "I took him into the house to make a little visit, but mother said you would be lonely, so I have brought him back."

After that, whenever Peepsie disappeared, Mrs. Cackle used to go and cluck near the kitchen door, and then Bessie would let Peepsie go back to her; and Mrs. Cackle used to say to herself: "I do not wonder that she likes my baby, for when Peepsie was lost and I saw Mrs. Field-mouse's child and Mrs. Robin's and Mother Duck's, I certainly found that there was not one of them like *mine!*"

EMILIE POULSSON.

Pe-wee's Lesson.

In a large farmyard, in one of the whitest coops, Pe-wee lived with his mother. Pe-wee was a soft, downy little chicken; his feet were of the yellowest, and his eyes sparkled so that they made you want to look at them all the time, they were *so* bright; and then he had such a cunning way of winking, and of keeping one eye shut for a long time, while he looked all about with the other. Pe-wee had a good mother who loved her little chicken very dearly and watched closely that everything was for his comfort. When the little fellow was awakened by the crowing of the king of the farmyard, he would take a peep from under his mother's wings and watch the great sun grow smaller the higher up it came in the sky, and then he would look at the grass so refreshed after its night's bath.

"Everything is so lovely in this world," thought Pe-wee, while eating his good breakfast of moistened meal; "is there any other chicken so happy as I?"

One day some new neighbors—very young people with their mother—came to live close by; they were noisy, but so good-natured that Pe-wee longed to make their acquaintance; he was certain that he should like them. The mothers soon were fast friends; and although one was a duck, their friendship, as well as that of their children, progressed famously. They would have long talks and many pleasant walks together, and all went well until one warm morning they came to a pool of water; the little ducks, with their mother, at once jumped in, and were soon floating gracefully on the top of the water. Pe-wee wanted a merry time, too; he would not attempt anything like swimming, for he had never seen his mother swim, but he ran along to the water's edge, and, putting his wee feet in, enjoyed the coolness. But the ground on which he stood sloped very gently, and it must have been a little slippery, for Pe-wee felt himself sliding very slowly but surely toward the deep water. Poor, frightened little Pe-wee! He could only call a few times very feebly "Peep, peep!" and when his mother turned to look, she saw her baby certainly going to his death. Oh! how fast she ran to the water's edge, flapping her wings and crying piteously.

Mother Duck, seeing the trouble, swam quickly to the spot and gave Pe-wee a push toward the bank with her broad beak, which sent him up on the dry grass. Pe-wee followed his mother home, walking very quietly and very slowly; indeed, he could not have walked fast, for he was water-soaked and stiff. I think the old hen knew this, for she was a most thoughtful mother; and I think, too, she was sorry for her child, who never uttered a peep the whole way. As they neared home, the mother turned and said: "Never forget, my child, that *some* are made to go on the *water*, and *some* to stay on *dry land!*"

When supper was finished, our little friend stood apart, thinking and winking. The feathered people were all going to bed; first one hen and then another, with a loud cluck, cluck, would fly to a bar of her own choosing, and settle herself for the night. The flowers in the distance seemed tired, too; some had even closed their cups; and the summer breeze was rocking them gently to sleep; the buzzing insects were gone, and the sun was fast going. Still little Pe-wee stood there, his face toward the sunset.

"It is bedtime," said his mother; "but tell me first what my little chick is thinking of?"

Pe-wee went slowly to his mother, and just before hiding himself under her sheltering wing, he said: "I was thinking, dear mother, that *some* are made to go on the water, and *some* to stay on dry land."

"Stories for the Kindergarten and the Home."

The Story of Speckle.

Her name was Speckle because her white feathers were speckled all over with black. She had just as many eggs in her nest as you have "merry little men" on your hands, and her nest was in a wooden box in the barn. The box was filled with hay, so it was soft and warm for the eggs to lie on. There was something soft and warm *over* the eggs, too. What do you think that was? Why, Speckle herself! There she sat on the nest, having stepped in very carefully, so as not to break the eggs.

All day she stayed there; and even when the cows and horses came into the barn, and the other hens went to roost for the night, Speckle sat as still as ever, caring for nothing but to keep the eggs warm.

The next morning, before the farmer came to the barn, Dobbin, the big horse, poked his nose out of his stall and neighed to Speckle.

"I never saw you there before," said he. "What are you doing?"

"I am keeping my eggs warm," said Speckle cheerily.

"Moo-o!" said the old red cow. "Are you not in a hurry to get out into the fields where the new grass is so fresh and green?"

"Oh, no!" said Speckle. "I would not leave my eggs. I must stay here and keep them warm."

By and by the farmer came into the barn.

"Why, is that little Speckle?" said he, walking up to the corner where the box was. Speckle had never been afraid of the farmer before, but now she felt so anxious about her precious eggs that she made a queer noise in her throat and bristled up her feathers.

"There, there," said the farmer kindly, stepping away. "I won't touch your eggs. Don't be afraid of me;" and he went about his work in the barn.

The cows were milked and turned out to pasture; the horse was harnessed to the cart and went out to do his day's work.

The barn was very quiet. Speckle was left alone, but only for a short time. Fritz, the farm dog, strolled in, and looked at her with surprise.

"The rest of the hens are having their breakfast," said he. "Little Phœbe is giving them a regular feast of corn. Hurry, or you will not be in time!"

"I cannot go," said Speckle, though she was really very hungry. "I must sit here and keep my eggs warm."

Fritz was so astonished that he did not know what to say.

"I suppose I shall have to go sometime," said Speckle, "for I must not starve; but I can get along for a while yet."

Fritz put out his paws and stretched himself, and then lay

SPECKLE AND THE SWALLOW.

down on the sunny barn floor to think; but it was so comfortable that he fell asleep instead.

Not long after some swallows flew into the barn, and one of them, swooping down with a sudden dive, came so close to Speckle that her swift wings fanned the patient sitter. Speckle was startled, but only for an instant, for the swallow folded her wings and rested on the edge of the box, looking at Speckle in a friendly way.

"I know why you sit there," she said. "Isn't it a beautiful secret,—the secret of the eggs? My mate and I have almost finished mending our nest—one we found up high there—and I shall soon have some eggs to keep warm just as you have."

Twittering thus the swallow seized a wisp of hay and darted away, evidently feeling too busy to make a longer visit.

Speckle looked after her, with bright eyes, but the swallow was soon out of sight in a dim corner far above Speckle's head.

The hours passed and it was night again. Speckle had only been off her nest once to get a little food and water when she was so hungry and thirsty that she could not wait any longer. Her legs felt very stiff and cramped, and it seemed strange to her to be sitting there on a nest all by herself, instead of being on the perch in the henhouse with her friends. But she was contented and glad, and felt that there was nothing in the world that could make her leave her precious eggs.

The next day little Phœbe came running into the barn.

"Where are you, Speckle?" said she, peering about in the corners. "Oh, here you are, you dear thing! Father said last night that you had a nest here. I've brought you some breakfast and a nice little pan of water."

Speckle really did not know how to say "thank you," but she felt like it, I assure you, not only that day but many times after, for little Phœbe came every day and brought corn or meal and filled the little pan with fresh water, leaving them very near to the wooden box so that Speckle had only to hop out to get them, and could be back again on her eggs in a trice, instead of having to look all about for something to eat.

The old kind of life, when Speckle had run about the farm all day and roosted on the perch at night, seemed long past; and it was now three weeks that she had been living in this new way—sitting on her nest night and day and with kind little Phœbe bringing her what she needed to eat and drink.

And now at the end of the three long weeks—twenty-one days—a most wonderful thing happened.

Speckle heard a faint little sound which seemed to come from the eggs beneath her breast. It was certainly like the sound of an egg shell being broken. Speckle listened and waited. Soon she actually felt something moving beneath her and then she knew instantly what had happened. Do you know?

A little chicken had come out of one of the eggs. It had been growing inside the shell all the twenty-one days, until, being ready for life in the world, it had broken its shell and crept out! Before long there were several others fidgeting about in the nest, as one after another they broke open the pretty white houses in which they had lived so long; and at last there were ten cunning baby chickens covered with bright yellow down, stepping about on their wee bits of legs and staring at the new world with round, black eyes.

Speckle could scarcely contain herself for joy. All these pretty creatures were hers—her very own! She began to cluck softly—a little song she had never sung before and yet knew perfectly from the love in her heart. And the little chickens as they listened, nestling under their mother's soft breast, chirped in answer; and though all they said was "peep, peep," it made Speckle happy to hear them.

After she had cuddled them long enough and they were ready to take a walk, Speckle started out as proud and happy as a hen could be. Fortunately the barn was not far from the house, or it would have been too long a walk for the chickens. What a walk that was! Speckle found something to cluck about every step of the way, and the chickens looked in wonder at all the strange new things. They found it a great comfort to keep calling to their mother and to run very close to her many times.

On the way from the barn to the house they met the farmer driving old Dobbin. Speckle chuckled loudly to the chickens for fear one might get in the road and under the horse's feet. This attracted the farmer's attention.

"Ho, ho! Speckle! That's a fine brood, upon my word," said he, counting the ten.

Dobbin said nothing, but rolled his eyes around toward Speckle with an expressive glance which meant as much as the farmer's kind words.

Speckle led her yellow train on toward the farmhouse. The pasture was on one side of the road and Speckle chose to walk on that side, hoping that some of the cows would see her. Yes! Lady Jane, the oldest, and the leader of the herd, was standing near the bars. Again Speckle clucked very loudly to her chickens, for she was afraid they might run into the pasture. Lady Jane looked up from the tender grass she was cropping. *She* made no attempt at speaking, any more than Dobbin had, but by the way she put out her head and took several deep breaths, and switched her tail, Speckle knew that Lady Jane noticed her chickens with due astonishment and admiration.

But Fritz, the dog, was more surprised than either the horse or the cow, for he had only been on the farm a short time, and these were the first baby chickens he had ever seen. He thought it must be that Speckle had found a whole troop of canary birds like the pretty creature which lived in the cage and which Phœbe loved so much. So off he ran ahead of Speckle, barking loudly. The chickens were greatly frightened at this noisy monster, and ran to their mother—in front of her, behind her, and under her—in their panic; but she clucked soothingly and presently succeeded in quieting them. So when Phœbe opened the door to see what Fritz was barking at, Speckle and her brood were walking quite properly across the dooryard, and Fritz stood wagging his tail and looking up into Phœbe's face, as if to say: "There! Are you not glad I called you?"

Phœbe shouted with surprise and delight. She was soon close to Speckle and was so quiet and gentle that Speckle could not be afraid of her very long, and even the chickens forgot to be afraid when Phœbe brought a nice pan of meal for them.

While they were eating this, the farmer came up carrying a new coop. He set it down under a cherry tree.

"O father! is that for Speckle?" asked Phœbe.

"Yes, it is for Speckle," said the farmer. "She would trot those chickens all over the farm if I did not put her into a coop."

So, before Speckle knew what was going on, she found herself looking out between the slats of the coop. She called anxiously to her chickens, and though they ran about wildly for a little, they soon found their way into the coop and under her wings. They rested there a few minutes, but dear! dear! there was so much to see outside and they were such lively little creatures that before long they were out again. Speckle watched them and talked to them all the time, stretching her head away out between the slats of the coop and calling the little ones back if they were running away.

Suddenly a bird passed by, flying low, and Speckle looked up in alarm lest it might be something to hurt her chickens. Again the bird passed, and this time Speckle saw that it was her friend the barn swallow, the one who had spoken to her when she was sitting on her eggs.

"Look, look! Look, look!" called Speckle in great joy, delighted that the swallow should see her treasures; and the swallow twittered as joyously in return, for she, too, had glad news to tell.

"Happy, happy, happy!" she chirped. "Long I sat on my nestful of eggs; now it is a nestful of birds."

And away she darted to the barn, whither she had been flying,—as full of rejoicing over her baby swallows awaiting her return as Speckle was over her yellow darlings.

EMILIE POULSSON.

THE BEE, I.

To the Teacher:—

"Live bees in kindergarten!" Yes; all the difficulties—and they *are* many —can be, have been, surmounted, and bees have been kindergarten guests for a day or more. Some lived on a large branch of blossoms in a box covered with glass on one side and netting on the other, and some in a glass jar with netting over the top and with only a flower or two, or perhaps a wet lump of sugar for solace.

THE TALK.

When we talked of the farmer we spoke of many creatures who live on the farm—some with four feet (children name them), some with two feet. Now we will look at some tiny little creatures, smaller than the cows, smaller than the sheep, smaller than the hen, smaller than the chickens, smaller than the birds, smaller than the butterflies, although, like the birds and butterflies, they can fly. Can you think of any living things so small? (Lead the children to name all the insects they can, and then produce the bees.)

Bees are so small that we shall need to use our eyes well to find out much about them. Let us listen now to what each child tells us. (Question individual children.)

How does the bee move? What can the bee do? What kind of a noise does the bee make? How many legs has it? How many wings? How many feelers? What is its body covered with? Very many soft, fine hairs so that it is like plush or velvet. What colors does the bee wear? Do you see that the bee's body shows three distinct parts? (head, thorax, abdomen—the *fact* not the *names* for the children). How many parts were there to the butterfly's body?

Now some one with *very* sharp eyes may tell where the wings and legs grow. Sharp eyes can find out many things. Where did the butterfly's wings and legs grow? The wings and legs of insects always grow from the middle part of the body.

Has the insect a backbone? No; its body is made in a different way. Who will be "Sharp Eyes" this time and look carefully at the back part of the bee's body? What did you see at the back part of the butterfly's body? These rings remind us of the caterpillar from which the butterfly grew. The bee has just as wonderful a story as the butterfly; for, just as the butterfly grows from a caterpillar, so a bee grows from a little white thing, like a caterpillar, which does not look at all like a bee, and which has no wings, no feelers and not even any legs. It does not need legs, for it stays in one place, never crawling about for food as the caterpillar does, for some of the older bees feed all these white babies as long as they will eat. Then they cover them over with wax and leave them to change into perfect bees.

Do you remember how wet and crumpled the butterfly was when it first came out of its chrysalis? And how it had to straighten and dry its wings before it could fly? Even this the bee does not do for itself, for some of the older bees stroke and pet and feed it until it is strong enough to fly and to work.

TEACHER'S READING.

The Fairy Land of Science (Chaps. IX, X), - - - *Arabella Buckley*
The Origin of Species (Vol. I), - - - - - - *Darwin*
Ants, Bees and Wasps, - - - - - - - - *Lubbock*
An Idyll of the Honey Bee (" Pepacton and Other
   Sketches "), - - - - - - - - *John Burroughs*
Pastoral Bees (" Locusts and Wild Honey "), - - - *John Burroughs*
Telling the Bees, - - - - - - - - - *Whittier*
Paradise Lost (Book VII), - - - - - - - *Milton*
To the Humble Bee, - - - - - - - - *Emerson*
The Honey Makers, - - - - - - - *Margaret W. M'rey*
The Bee People, - - - - - - - - *Margaret W. M'rey*

For the Children.

A Little Dark Nursery Underground, } (" Littl Folks in Feathers
Nurseries for Baby Insects,   }   and Fur "', *Olive Thorn Miller*
'It is the May-time," said the B.. , (M:nr e's Third Read.r").

STORIES.
The Rhyme of the Little Idle Boy.
(From the French.)

And have you heard about the boy—
  (A very little boy indeed)—
Who did not wish to work at all,
  Or go to school or learn to read?

Oh! slowly, slowly did he walk,
  And heavy seemed his little book,
As through the daisy fields he went
  And past the merry, clattering brook.

Above his head there flew a bee.
" O Bee," the boy said, " won't you stay
  And show me how you fly so high,
And talk with me, and laugh and play? "

Then, scarcely pausing, said the bee:
" Dear child, no time have I to waste.
The North Wind long has kept me back,
  And now to work I gladly haste.

" Already I am laden, see!
  With honey for the honeycomb;
The lilac cups more nectar hold,—
  'Twixt hive and flower I ever roam."

Away then flew the downy bee,
  That joyous day of early spring.
A swallow passed the little boy,
  And brushed his cheek with waving wing.

She floated in the sunny air
  And called aloud in happy song:
" Rejoice! Rejoice! The spring is near! "
  So rang her message, clear and strong.

The child looked up with brightening face:
" O Swallow! I remember you!
You are the bird who carries joy;
  O Swallow, make me happy, too.

" Do come and play with me awhile! "
  " Fain would I," said the swallow then.
" For I have flown so fast and far;—
  But farther must I fly again,

"For many wait with eager heart
   To hear the message that I bring;
And I must bear it faithfully
   And herald now the dawn of spring.

"My happy news I sing abroad,
   Then — oh, what joyous work to do!—
My pretty nest, my home, to build;
   Indeed, I cannot play with you."

The swift-winged swallow flew afar,
   The child lagged on with footsteps slow;
And —yes! I have to own—he cried,
   But then he was so small, you know."

A dog who heard the steps approach
   Came stalking from his kennel door;
But pitying the crying child,
   All growls and barking he forebore.

"Good doggie," said the lonely child,
   "I am so very sad to-day;
The bees and birds all have to work—
   They will not come with me to play.

"I do not like to work at all,
   I do not care to learn to read;
O doggie dear! If I were you,
   I then could always play indeed!"

Old Stentor looked upon the child
   Whose dimpled fingers stroked his hair
"What, little one? Did you not know
   That even dogs in work must share?

"Not only all the livelong day
   I watch my master's home and farm,
But while he sleeps without a fear,
   My work it is to guard from harm.

"And more, my little one; for see
   Where yonder at the heavy plow
The faithful horse our master serves;—
   From year to year he works as now.

'The wool produced by yonder sheep,
   Your mother, singing, spins at home.
When all are cheerily at work
   Will you, a little idler, roam?

"The busy bee gives honey sweet,
  The swallow carries joy alway;
By some one's work all pleasure comes;
  Will you do nothing, then, but play?

"Oh no! Go, little one, to school;
  We dogs can never learn to read,
But *you* will be a man some day!
  To be a man is grand indeed!"

The child had listened eagerly
  To wise old Stentor as he spoke;
The words, "You'll be a man some day!"
  A brave and manly spirit woke.

He clasped old Stentor's shaggy neck
  And kissed the honest doggie's face;
And, with the book held proudly now,
  Ran off to school at happy pace.

All eagerness some work to do,
  Light hearted o'er the road he sped;
And reached the school. * * * When autumn came
  You cannot think how well he read!

EMILIE POULSSON.

Edith and the Bees.

One beautiful morning last June, a sweet little girl thought she would go out in the garden and pick some flowers for one of her playmates, who was sick and obliged to stay shut up in the house this fragrant summer morning. "Tommy shall have the most beautiful flowers in the garden," thought Edith, as she took her little basket and pruning scissors, and ran out into the garden. She looked like a lovely fairy or a sunbeam, flitting about the rosebushes. I think she was the most exquisite rose in all the garden herself. Her heart was full of thoughts of Tommy, while she worked away busily. "I wish I knew something that would please Tommy more than anything else!" she said to herself. "I would love to make him happy!" and she sat down on the edge of a beautiful fountain to think.

While she sat there thinking, two dear little birds began to take their bath in the lovely, sparkling water that rippled and danced in the sunshine. They would plunge into the water and

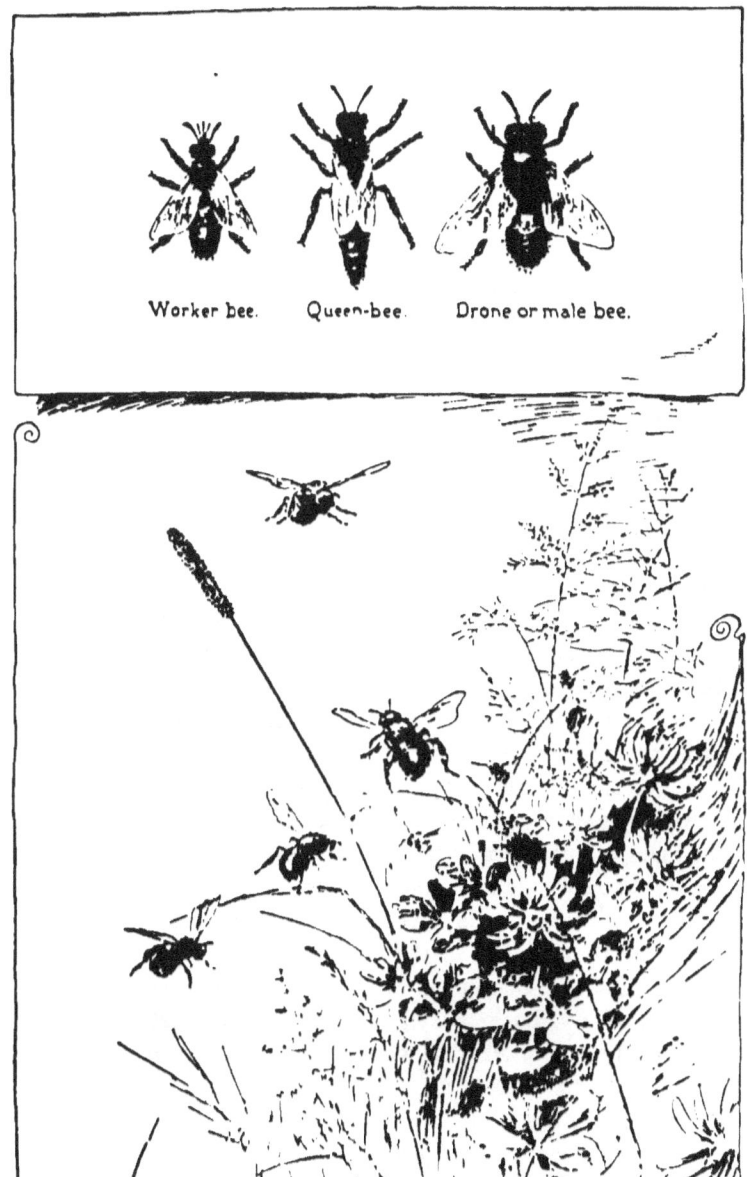

BEES GOING MARKETING.

come out dripping, perch on the side of the fountain for a moment, and plunge in again. Then they would shake the bright drops from their feathers and fly away singing sweeter than ever. Edith thought the little birds enjoyed their bath as much as her baby brother did his.

When they had flown away to a distant tree, Edith noticed a beautiful pink rosebud, more beautiful than any she had yet seen. "Oh, how lovely you are!" she cried; and, running to the bush where it was, she bent down the branch, that she might examine it more closely, when out of the heart of the rose came a small insect, and stung her pretty cheek. The little girl began to weep loudly, and ran to her father, who was working in another part of the yard. "Why, my little girl!" said he, "a bee has stung you." He drew out the sting, and bathed her swollen cheek in cool water, at the same time telling her many interesting things about the wonderful little bees.

"Do not cry any more, my child," said her father, "and I will take you to see a kind gentleman who keeps many hives of bees."

"Oh, thank you!" cried Edith, brushing away the tears. "I will run and get ready now."

The beemaster, as everybody called the old man who kept the bees, was very glad to show his little pets, and to tell Edith all he knew about them. He led her to a hive, made wholly of glass, so that she might watch the bees at their work.

"There are three kinds of bees in every hive," said the gentleman. "That large bee in the middle is the queen bee. She is the most important bee in the hive. She has a sting, but seldom makes use of it. Those busy little bees are the worker bees. It was probably a worker that stung you this morning, my little girl," said the beemaster.

Edith thought she did not like the worker bee as well as the others; but when she heard what industrious little workers they are, and how they take all the care of the young bees, build the cells of wax, and bring in the honey, she felt much more affection for them.

"What do the bees do in winter, when there are no flowers from which to gather honey?" inquired Edith.

"They sleep during the long, cold winter days, and awaken when the warm spring returns," replied her kind instructor.

"Now," said Edith's father, "we had better go, or you will not get to see Tommy to-day."

Then the little girl thanked her new friend for telling her so much about his interesting pets, and promised to come and see him as often as she could.

"O father!" cried Edith, as they walked homeward, "I am almost glad that the naughty little bee stung me this morning, for now I shall have something amusing to tell Tommy."

HELEN KELLER.

NOTE. This story was more complete in its details of bee life, but a few paragraphs have been omitted as being an unnecessary repetition of what has already been given in the talk

E. P.

THE BEE, II.

TO THE TEACHER:—

Many objects besides the bee itself will be useful for illustrating this talk,—flowers which show the pollen, a lump of wax, a wax candle, a wax doll, and best of all, a little feast of honey—honey in the comb, by all means.

THE TALK.

Young Bees in the Brood-comb.

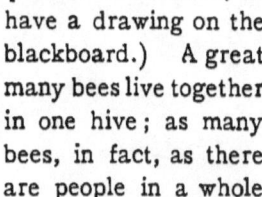

Where do bees live? In beehives. Yes, and there are wild bees which live in the woods, in hollow trees; but when farmers and other people keep bees they provide beehives—large wooden boxes—for them to live in. (Show picture of beehive, or have a drawing on the blackboard.) A great many bees live together in one hive; as many bees, in fact, as there are people in a whole city,—from 20,000 to 60,000. One bee in each hive is different from the others and is called the queen bee. She lays all the eggs, and you should see how carefully the other bees watch and tend her! The queen cannot even feed herself, but would starve to death with honey right beside her if there were no bees to feed her! Some of the bees are called drones, and others workers. When the queen flies out of the hive the drones go with her, and when she is at home the working bees attend to her.

What kind of work do you think such little things as bees can do? Yes, they can gather honey, but they can do many other things. They take care of the queen and the thousands of babies, and they make bee-bread to feed to them; they make thousands of wax cells in which they store their honey; they keep the hive clean, and, if it gets too warm inside, some of them stand at the doorway and fan fresh air into the hive with their wings! They drive away strange bees or wasps or snails or any other creatures which try to get into their hive. Do you wonder how they can tell which are the strange bees that do not belong to their hive? Some of the wise men think it is by touching each other's feelers. Whenever two bees meet they always touch each other's feelers. Perhaps that is the same for them that talking is for us.

Do you know what they have to protect themselves with when troubled? A sharp little thing called a sting. It hurts very much to be stung, but a bee will not sting any one who does not trouble or frighten it in some way.

Did you ever taste honey? Bees are such hard workers that they make a great deal of honey, and so *we* often have some. When we take honey from the hive, enough must be left for the bees through the winter, or else we must give them syrup to live upon until the spring flowers come. After the bee has eaten all the honey it wishes from the flowers, it gathers more to take home to the hive. The honey for the hive is carried in a little bag which is inside the bee's body, and which the bee can empty into one of the wax cells. It takes a great many journeys from hive to flower and from flower to hive before a bee can fill even one cell.

How does the bee get honey (or rather the nectar which it makes into honey) from the flowers? With its long tongue, which is something like the butterfly's tongue. Bees get something else from the flowers besides honey—the yellow powder called pollen. You have seen it on pussy willows and lilies. In the spring, bees are very anxious to get the fresh pollen. Going into a flower for honey, the bee gets covered with the yellow powder, but soon brushes it off with its feet and packs it away in little baskets to carry it home. You would not have thought that the bee always carried two baskets, would you? But there they are on its hind legs, and you can see them very plainly when they are full of the yellow pollen. Sometimes the bees fill their baskets so full that they can scarcely fly with their heavy load

In the hive the pollen is mixed with honey, forming what is called "bee-bread," and fed to the baby bees.

You remember that the bee had a tiny bag in which to carry honey, as well as two baskets for carrying pollen. Besides the bags for honey and baskets for pollen, the bee has eight pockets on the under side of its body, out of which it gets the wax for building its cells. Just think! A bag for honey, baskets for pollen, and pockets for wax.

The cells which the bee builds are pure white and of very pretty shape—six-sided. The bees never make a mistake. They do not make some cells square and some round and some with five sides; but always make their cells six-sided. All the cells which are built together make a honeycomb. What tools do the bees have? Only their jaws (mandibles) and feet. For what are the cells used? For storing honey and for the babies to live in. When a cell is full of honey the bee covers it over with wax. When we have honey to eat, it is sometimes in the comb and sometimes strained; that is, all the wax is taken out of it.

Do we use wax for anything? Ask your mamma if she has a piece in her workbasket, and what she does with it. Do you not remember that the cobbler uses it, too? Candles are made of wax sometimes—little ones for Christmas trees and big candles, too. And have any of these little girls wax dolls? Their pretty wax heads were also made of the bees' wax.

Try to remember the busy little bees the next time you play with your wax dolls, and whenever you eat honey.

HOMES FOR THE BEES.

TEACHER'S READING.

Half-hours with Insects, - - - - - - - - *Packard*
Nouvelles Observations sur les Abeilles, - - - - - - *Huber*
Treatise on the Honey Bee, - - - - - - - *Langstroth*
Rhoecus, - - - - - - - - - - *Lowell*
The Bee, - - - - - - - - - *Emily Dickinson*
The Bee, - - - - - - - - - - *Vaughn*

For the Children.

Buz, - - - - - - - - - - - *Maurice Noel*
The Bees' Pockets ("Kindergarten Stories and Morning Talks"), - - - - - - - - - - *S. E. Wiltse*

STORIES.

A Narrow Escape.

The time came when Buz and Hum, two young bees, were allowed to try their wings.

"Follow me," said a friendly older bee; "I can spare time to fly a little way; and when I stop, you stop, too."

"All right," cried Buz, trembling with excitement.

Hum said nothing, but her wings began to move, almost in spite of herself.

Away went the bee, as straight as a line from the mouth of the hive, and away flew Buz and Hum after her; but at first starting they both found it a little difficult to keep quite straight, and Buz knocked against the board to begin with, and nearly stopped herself, as she had not learned how to rise.

The older bee did not go far, and lit on the branch of a peach tree which was growing against a wall hard by. Buz came after her in a great hurry, but missed the branch and gave herself a bang against the wall. Hum saw this, and managed to stop herself in time; but she did not judge her distance very well either and got on the peach tree in a scrambling sort of way.

"Very good," said their friend, as they all three stood together;

"you will soon be able to take care of yourselves now; but just let me see you back to the hive."

So off they flew again, and alighted on the board in a very creditable manner.

"Now," said the bee, "I shall leave you; but before I go let me advise you, as a friend, not to quit the garden to-day; there are plenty of flowers, and plenty of opportunities for you to meet with 'Experience,' without flying over any of the four walls."

"Who is Experience?" asked Buz and Hum together

"Oh! somebody to whom you are going to be introduced, who will teach you more in a day than you could learn from me in a week. Good-bye." So saying, she disappeared into the hive.

"Isn't it too delightful?" exclaimed Buz to Hum. "Flying! why it's even more fun than I thought!"

"It is," said Hum; "but I should like to get some honey at once."

"Of course," replied Buz, "only I should like to fly a good way to get it."

"I want to fill a cell quickly," said Hum.

"Oh yes, to be sure! What a delightful thing it will be to put one's proboscis down into every flower and see what's there! Do you know," added Buz, putting out her proboscis, "I feel as if I could suck honey tremendously; don't you?"

"Yes, yes," cried Hum, "I *long* to be at it; let's be off at once."

So away they went and lit on a bed of flowers.

Hum spent the day between the hive and that bed, and was quite, quite happy; but Buz, though she, too, liked collecting the honey, wanted to have more excitement in getting it; and every now and then, as she passed to and from the hive, a lovely field of clover, not far off, sent forth such a delicious smell, as the breeze swept over it, that she was strongly tempted to disregard the advice she had been given, and to hurry off to it.

At last she could stand it no longer; and, rising high into the air, she sailed over the wall and went out into the world beyond.

And so she reached the field of clover, and, flying quite low over the flowers, was astonished to see how many bees were busy among them—bumblebees without end, and plenty of honeybees, too; in fact, the air was filled with the pleasant murmur that they made.

"To be sure," said Buz to herself, "this is the place for me! Poor, dear old Hum! I hope she is enjoying herself as much as I am. I don't mean to be idle either, so here goes for some honey."

Buz was very diligent indeed and soon collected as much honey as she could carry. But by the time she had done this she found herself close to the farther end of the clover field, and while resting for a moment, before starting to carry her load to the hive, she noticed a little pond in the corner. Feeling thirsty after her hard work, she flew off to take a few sips; but just as she reached the pond and was in the act of descending, a light gust of wind caught her and turned her half over, and before she could recover herself she was plunged far out into the water!

Poor Buz! She was a brave little bee, but this was a terrible accident; and after a few wild struggles she almost gave herself up. The water was so cold, and she felt herself so helpless in it; and then the accident had happened so suddenly, and taken her so utterly by surprise, that it is no wonder she lost courage. Only for a moment though; just as she was giving up in despair the hard and seemingly useless work of paddling and struggling with all her poor little legs at once, she saw that a bit of stick was floating near her, and with renewed energy she attempted to get to it. Alas! it was all she could do to keep her head above water; as for moving along through it, that seemed impossible, and she was tempted to give up once more. It was very hard though; there was the stick, not more than a foot away from her; if she could only reach it! At any rate she was determined it should not be her fault if she was unsuccessful; so she battled away harder than ever, though her strength began to fail and she was becoming numbed with the cold. Just as she made this last effort another gust of wind swept over the pond, and Buz saw that the stick began to move through the water, and to come nearer and nearer to her. The fact was that a small twig sticking up from it acted as a sail, though Buz did not know this. And now the stick was quite close, almost within reach; in another moment she would be on it. Ah! but a moment seems a long time when one is at the last gasp, as poor Buz was.

Would she be drowned after all? No! Just as she was sinking she touched the stick with one little claw, and held on as only drowning people can; and then she got another claw safely lodged, and was able to rest for a moment. Oh! the relief of *that*, after such a long and ceaseless struggle!

But even then it was very hard to get up on the stick, very hard indeed. However, Buz managed it at last, and dragged herself quite out of the cold water.

By this time the breeze was blowing steadily over the pond, and the stick would soon reach the bank; but Buz felt very miserable and cold, and her wings clung tightly to her, and she looked dreadfully forlorn.

The pond, too, was overshadowed by trees; so there were no sunbeams to warm her. "Ah!" thought she, "if I can manage to drag myself up into the sunshine and rest and be well warmed, I shall soon be better."

Well! the bank was safely reached at last; but Buz, all through her life, never forgot what a business it was climbing up the side. The long grasses yielded to her weight, and bent almost straight down, as if on purpose to make it as up-hill work for her as possible. And even when she reached the top it took her a weary while to get across the patch of dark shadow and out into the glad sunlight beyond; but she managed to arrive there at last, and crawling on the top of a stone which had been well warmed by the sun's rays, she rested for a long time.

At last she recovered sufficiently to make her way, by a succession of short flights, back to the hive. After the first of these flights she felt so dreadfully weak that she almost doubted being able to accomplish the journey, and began to despond.

"If I ever do get home," she said to herself, "I will tell Hum all about it, and how right she was to take advice."

Now whether it was the exercise that did her good, or that the sun's rays became hotter that afternoon, cannot be known, but this is certain, that Buz felt better after every flight. When she reached the end of the clover field, she sipped a little honey, cleaned herself with her feet, stretched her wings, and, with the sun glistening brightly on her, looked quite fine again. Her last flight brought her to the top of the kitchen-garden wall. After resting here, she opened her wings and flew gaily to the hive, which she entered just as if nothing had happened.

MAURICE NOEL.

Slightly altered from "Buz," Henry Holt & Co., New York.

Solomon and the Bees.

When Solomon was reigning in his glory,
    Unto his throne the Queen of Sheba came—
(So in the Talmud you may read the story)—
    Drawn by the magic of the monarch's fame,
To see the splendors of his court, and bring
Some fitting tribute to the mighty King.

Nor this alone: much had her Highness heard
    What flowers of learning graced the royal speech;
What gems of wisdom dropped with every word;
    What wholesome lessons he was wont to teach
In pleasing proverbs; and she wished, in sooth,
To know if Rumor spoke the simple truth.

Besides, the Queen had heard (which piqued her most)
    How through the deepest riddles he could spy;
How all the curious arts that women boast
    Were quite transparent to his piercing eye;
And so the Queen had come—a royal guest—
To put the sage's cunning to the test.

And straight she held before the monarch's view,
    In either hand, a radiant wreath of flowers;
The one, bedecked with every charming hue,
    Was newly culled from Nature's choicest bowers;
The other, no less fair in every part,
Was the rare product of divinest Art.

" Which is the true, and which the false? " she said.
    Great Solomon was silent. All amazed,
Each wondering courtier shook his puzzled head;
    While at the garlands long the monarch gazed,
As one who sees a miracle, and fain,
For very rapture, ne'er would speak again.

" Which is the true? " once more the woman asked,
    Pleased at the fond amazement of the King;

"So wise a head should not be hardly tasked,
  Most learned Liege, with such a trivial thing!"
But still the sage was silent; it was plain
A deepening doubt perplexed the royal brain.

While thus he pondered, presently he sees,
  Hard by the casement—so the story goes—
A little band of busy, bustling bees,
  Hunting for honey in a withered rose.
The monarch smiled and raised his royal head;
"Open the window!"—that was all he said.

The window opened at the King's command;
  Within the rooms the eager insects flew,
And sought the flowers in Sheba's dexter hand!
  And so the king and all the courtiers knew
That wreath was Nature's; and the baffled Queen
Returned to tell the wonders she had seen.

My story teaches (every tale should bear
  A fitting moral) that the wise may find
In trifles light as atoms of the air
  Some useful lesson to enrich the mind—
Some truth designed to profit or to please—
As Israel's King learned wisdom from the bees.

JOHN G. SAXE.

Houghton, Mifflin & Co.

Mrs. Flyaway.

(A Story of Ants.)

Once upon a time there lived in a big, brown house a very dainty little lady. They called her Mrs. Flyaway because she never wanted to stay at home.

The little person looked as if she had been polished, for she was very black and very shiny. She had two tiny, gauzy wings and six legs, so that she could walk quite fast for her size. She was very small, indeed—not half an inch long.

In fact, she was an ant and lived in an ant-hill.

A great many other ants lived in this same house—almost as many ants as there are leaves on a tree—so many that you could not count them.

The brown house stood in the middle of a beautiful green field and above it was an elm tree through which the wind sang all day and all night, so you see it was a very pleasant place to live in.

Perhaps the brown house wouldn't have seemed big to a boy or girl, but it was grand indeed for the little ants, and they were very proud of it, because they had built it all themselves. It doesn't seem possible that little ants could build a house, does it? But I will tell you how they did it.

Of course they had to begin with something very small, so they chose a blade of grass. Think of beginning to build a house with a blade of grass!

This blade of grass was standing very straight and stiff under the elm tree, and one little ant who was a mason said, "I will make some mortar, and then with it I will cover the blade of grass to make a stout pillar. This will be the beginning of our house." He found some soft earth and sticky clay with which he mixed a little water and tiniest bits of grass and wood. He kneaded this with his feet until it was a thick plaster, which he stuck on the blade of grass. Of course it took him a long time to cover the whole grass blade, but he worked hard and was very patient.

When the other ant masons saw what he was doing, they all went to work with a will and did just the same to other blades of grass.

The big Sun looked down and smiled on them when he saw how hard they worked. "I will help them," he said; and smiling more brightly than ever he baked their pillars hard and dry.

When the pillars were done the ants built arches across them, back and front, right and left, over and over, until a roof was stretched across. The good-natured Sun smiled down once more and then the roof also became hard and dry and strong.

Day after day the busy ants worked. They made more pillars above the first ones, and threw more arches over them until they had built a house big enough for all to live in. It had long, winding passages everywhere under the arches, and tiny little rooms opening into the passages. Over all this they put a covering of earth, with oh! so many doors and windows in it; and then the house was done.

One morning little Mrs. Flyaway went hastily out of one of the doors. Naughty Mrs. Flyaway! She was going to run away. She wanted to see that beautiful green world that lay all about.

She had not got very far when three or four other ants went tumbling out of the doors and windows and ran as fast as they could after her.

These little ants were not quite as pretty as Mrs. Flyaway; they had no lovely gauzy wings. They were very patient and industrious, however, and worked hard all day for the Flyaways (there were other Flyaways besides the one we know) ; and working hard for other people is much better than being only beautiful to look at, isn't it?

You see three kinds of ants lived in this one house. There were the Mr. Flyaways, who had four wings and were very grand, the Mrs. Flyaways who had two wings, and the dear little workers who hadn't any wings at all.

When the worker ants caught up to our Mrs. Flyaway, one of them said, breathing very hard through the breathing pores in his sides, "O my dear friend, what a run so early in the morning! You must come right back home. Why, what would we poor workers do, if we let the Flyaways leave us?"

"Yes," said another, "pretty soon you will have some little baby ants, and we have made room for them in the big, brown house. If you don't stay there you will have no home for them." So, coaxing and teasing, they got Mrs. Flyaway back to the house.

But their troubles were not over then, for either this Mrs. Flyaway or some other was always trying to run away. The workers were more than busy keeping them at home and finding enough food for them.

One beautiful day, in spite of all their care, Mrs. Flyaway was lost. They had just given up searching for her, when who should come running toward home but that dear little lady herself.

"Come," she cried in great excitement. "Come! See what I have."

They all ran after her as fast as possible, and what do you think she showed them, carefully hidden under a leaf? Twenty little eggs!

"See!" said Mrs. Flyaway joyously, "My little baby ants will come out of these eggs."

Mrs. Flyaway might have been called Mrs. Stay-at-home after this, for, would you believe it? she never wanted to run away any more! She just felt like staying at home and watching those eggs day and night. So she took off her pretty little wings and laid them aside, knowing that she wouldn't need them any more.

"Yours will be the first babies this year," said somebody.

"They won't be babies at all if we aren't careful," said one experienced old ant.

The little mother looked very anxious.

"We must get them in out of the dew;" the same ant added, "those tender little eggs can not stand the cool, damp night air." At this the ants went to work, and before the sun went down the eggs were all in the brown house.

Everybody was up early next morning to take the eggs out again and spread them in the sunshine. At noon time the eggs had to be changed again and put under a plantain leaf because the sun grew too warm. You can imagine that all this kept them very busy, morning, noon and night.

One morning when Mrs. Flyaway woke up, she felt something moving. She looked down, expecting to see a little ant. But what do you think had come out of the eggs instead? Twenty little grubs—little fat things with no legs and no wings. Mrs. Flyaway was very much surprised at first and a little disappointed, but she soon grew to think they were the most beautiful babies a mother ever possessed.

Oh! how much they did eat. Why, it took twenty workers besides their proud little mother to find enough honey-dew for them to eat, and to protect them from heat and cold.

The grubs were not to be grubs always. Before many days passed they spun themselves silky cocoons, rolled themselves up tight and went to sleep, looking like twenty little barleycorns. They slept so many days that their mother became quite anxious "Isn't it time to wake them?" she said.

"Just about time," said a little worker. "You know we will have to cut open the cocoons. The babies will not be able to get out unless we do." Now the ants who attended to this did not have any scissors or knives, but they had something which answered just as well. Teeth? No, but mandibles—parts of their mouths which they use for all such work. With these mandibles the ants cut a hole in each cocoon.

You would never guess what came out of those cocoons! Grubs do you think? No, indeed. Twenty little full-fledged ants—some Flyaways and some workers—came out, rubbing their eyes and yawning.

"Well," exclaimed their mother in the wildest excitement, "those babies have caused me continual surprise ever since I first saw the eggs, but this is the greatest surprise of all."

ADA COOK.

FLOWERS.

To the Teacher:—

Flowers are always welcome and appropriate in kindergarten, and those children are fortunate whose teacher brings to them these pretty chronicles of each season as it passes. It is not necessary to have a great bouquet; even one flower will give the children pleasure.

For this talk a plant with buds and blossoms would be best. Pansies, nasturtiums and other flowers which show the "honey streaks" will be necessary. Let the children taste the nectar at the bottom of the flowers—lilacs, clover, etc. If flowers are easily available, ask the children to bring some to talk about during the week.

THE TALK.

(Recalling the interesting little workers talked of last week, the children's thoughts can be naturally directed to flowers. Let the children name all the kinds of flowers familiar to them, and tell of what colors and of what shapes they are and which of them are fragrant.)

What kind of flowers did you see in the winter? Where did they grow? In doors. Why? What kinds did you see in the early spring? What kinds have we in kindergarten to-day? Where did they grow? What helped them to grow? (Sunshine and rain and the earth in which they were planted.) Would this flower grow (holding up a cut flower) if I should plant it? Why not? What do the roots do for the plants? Is it pure water which they drink? No, it has soaked through the ground and taken what the plants need from the soil.

When this juice soaks up from the roots it goes into another part of the plant. What part is that? The stem. And from the stem where does it go? Into the little stems, into the leaves and into the flowers. Do you remember what we call this juice of the plant? It is called sap. We spoke of it when we were talking about trees; and we had maple sugar in kindergarten because maple sugar is made of sap. When we have cut flowers and put them in water, the water takes the place of sap for a little while.

Let us look at one of the kindergarten plants and tell all its parts. The roots under the ground, then the stems, then the leaves and flowers. Little plants have all these parts, just as

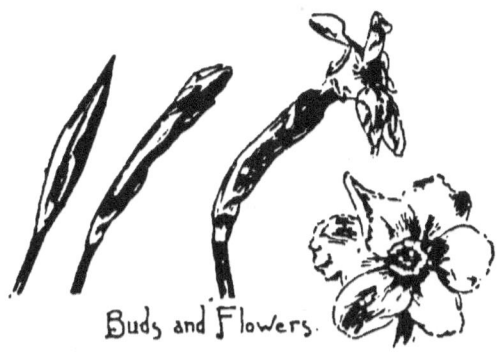
Buds and Flowers.

big trees have. Isn't it wonderful that all this could come from one tiny seed? (The children will be ready to tell of the kindergarten seed planting and its results.)

Do you remember what we found on the trees early in spring, before we could see any leaves? Leaf-buds. And what do we find on the plant before we can have any flowers? Flower-buds, of course. (Show bud.)

At first the bud is very small indeed, having within it only the beginning of a flower; but it grows and grows, and by and by the bud opens and the flower unfolds itself. Just before the bud opened, the pretty flower was packed and folded in the bud about as closely as the butterfly with his big wings was packed in the chrysalis. Flowers are so beautiful and so sweet that everybody loves them. Even if they were good for nothing but to be beautiful and sweet we should be glad to have flowers grow; but they are useful besides.

Certain little creatures with baskets on their legs and a bag inside the body would not know where to go to market if it were not for the flowers. What do bees get from flowers to put into their baskets? Pollen for bee-bread. What do they carry home in their bags? Can you think of any other insect which sips honey from flowers? How do the bee and the butterfly get the honey from the deep flower-cups? Many other insects like honey, too.

(Show some flowers having streaks or veins on the petals, and call attention to these lines.)

Who would think these lines were of any use? It seems as if they were only to make the flower prettier; but they really are of use to the bees. When a bee lights on a flower, it sees these streaks and knows that they point to the place where the flower keeps its honey. Isn't that interesting? It is a sign which says to the bee: "This way for honey!"

But the most wonderful use of the flower is still to be told. What do we plant in order to have flowers? Seeds. But where do seeds come from? (Some of the children may remember that certain fruits contain seeds; if so, trace back to the blossom.)

Ah! it is the flowers which do the great work of seed making. The flowers which are not plucked but which remain on the plants seem to fade away; but it is not the whole flower, it is only the pretty petals which fade and drop off. The other parts (point out the pistil and stamens to the children,) stay on the plant and finally make the seeds. What kind of seeds would this flower have made if it had stayed on the plant? And if we planted those seeds what would grow? Each flower makes its own kind of seeds; and no other kind of seed can grow into just that particular kind of flower. Now would you like to know what the flowers say? A lady (Susan Coolidge) tells us in some pretty verses:—

> The red rose says: "Be sweet,"
> And the lily bids: "Be pure,"
> The hardy, brave chrysanthemum,
> "Be patient and endure."
> The violet whispers: "Give,
> Nor grudge nor count the cost."
> The woodbine, "Keep on blossoming
> In spite of chill and frost."

WHICH DO YOU LIKE BEST?

TEACHER'S READING.

Botany,	*Gray, Hooker, Newell, Youmans*
How to Know the Wild Flowers,	*Mrs. W. S. Dana*
Flowers and their Pedigree,	*Allen*
Flower Object Lessons	*Le Maout*
Life of a Primrose ("Fairy Land of Science"),	*Arabella Buckley*
Wild Flowers and Where they Grow,	*Amanda B. Harris*
Song of Life,	*Margaret Morley*
The Sensitive Plant,	*Shelley*
Little Flower People,	*Hale*
Hymn to the Flowers,	*Horace Smith*
Flowers,	*Hood*
The Question,	*Shelley*
To the Rhodora,	*Emerson*
Chorus of Flowers,	*Leigh Hunt*
Nature and the Poet,	*Keats*
To a Mountain Daisy,	*Burns*
Flower in the Crannied Wall,	*Tennyson*
A Lay of the Early Rose, The Deserted Garden,	*Mrs. Browning*

For the Children.

St. Elizabeth and the Roses } ("Kindergarten Stories and
Baby Calla } Morning Talks"), — *S. E. Wiltse*

STORIES.
What They Did.

"O mamma!" cried Carrie Edwards as she entered the dining room, where a basket of choice flowers stood upon the center table, "where did they come from?" "They are yours, my dear," her mother answered. "Your father called at Mr. Brown's greenhouse this morning, and he sent them to you. He said that last winter, when his little boy was hurt at school, you cared for him until help came from home. It seems he never forgot the act; and so he has sent you this bouquet, with his kindest regards."

Carrie's face flushed with pleasure.

"I had almost forgotten about it," she said. "Little Willie Brown fell from his sled while coasting, and his arm was broken. I only picked him up and held him till others came. But these flowers are such beauties! It seems a pity that all their sweetness should be wasted on me. There, mamma, I have it! I met the minister on the street a moment ago, and he looked so sad. Frank is still very sick, they say, and takes scarcely any notice of what is going on about him. He is so fond of flowers, you remember, mamma. Last summer, when he called with his father, my pink rosebush was in full bloom, and I gave him one. He was delighted with it; and I saw him, when he thought no one was looking, caress it lovingly. May I share my flowers with him?"

"Yes, dear, if you like. They are yours to dispose of as you please."

A little later the minister's wife said, coming into her boy's room, "Frankie, darling, see what Carrie Edwards has sent you."

The lad opened his eyes, and a smile of joy lighted his face.

"For me?" he whispered.

"Yes, dear," Mrs. Voorhees answered; "the man who brought them said Miss Carrie sent them."

The boy held them to his lips, and inhaled their sweetness with a pleasure his mother rejoiced to see.

"Don't take them away," he whispered.

"You shall have them right here, dear."

Then he closed his eyes, and, with his face buried in the flowers, lay for a long time so quietly that his mother thought he had fallen asleep.

"Mamma!" he suddenly whispered.

"Yes, Frank."

"I have been thinking of Tommy Brown around the corner. You know he has to sit all day long in that little smoky room while his mother washes; for he cannot walk a step. May I share my flowers with him?"

"If you wish."

Tommy Brown sat by the window, in his mother's bare little room, gazing at the noisy scene across the street. His mother had been busy washing all day, and was tired and cross. Tommy could scarcely see through the window panes, so thickly were they covered with smoke and dust. The scene outside could not be called an interesting one, but there was so little to divert Tommy's mind that he strove his best to keep watch of what went on in the street. But it was hard work to peer through the steamy, grimy window. He sighed, then took his little hand and tried to clean the dirt from the pane. What he saw made him forget the smoke and the boys across the street; for he got a glimpse of a man bearing in his hand a bouquet of flowers.

"Oh!" he gasped, "how glad I am I saw them. I wonder how they happened to come down this street?"

A knock sounded at the door.

"For Tommy, from Master Frank," said a voice.

"Not the minister's boy?" cried Mrs. Brown.

"The same, ma'am. He had a gift to-day, and he was always one to share a blessing with others."

"O mother!" was all Tommy said. Then he sat very quietly for an hour or more, very carefully fingering each tiny blossom, with his eyes full of untold happiness. After all, it was such a good world to live in, when he was remembered by a sick boy, and such a boy as Frank Voorhees.

A moment later he cried: "What was that? Oh! yes, I know, it is little Bessie, upstairs. She has been alone all day while her mother is out working, and she is growing tired, I reckon. Why couldn't I spare her half of my flowers? I ought, if Frank Voorhees could spare them for me. Mother," Tommy said, "would you mind going up stairs to little Bessie's room with part of these flowers?"

Tommy's mother would usually have minded such a trip as this very much, but the gift of flowers had softened her heart. A few minutes later Mrs. Brown stood by little Bessie's cot; where the child was wasting her strength in tears.

"Here's some flowers Tommy sent to you, and the minister's sick boy, Master Frank, sent them to him."

The child gave a cry of joy and gathered the flowers to her bosom. "I never saw such beautiful flowers before," she said.

Only a few flowers! But what little missionaries of love they proved! SELECTED.

The Plant Household.

A certain household well I know,
 The prettiest ever seen,
And at its head in fairest robes
 There sits a dainty queen;
While all the upper servants dress
 In livery of green.

The cooks and those who with them work
 Are clad in dingy brown.
" No fancy dress for us! " they say,
 " A sober colored gown
Is better far for work like ours
 Than all the green in town.

" For we must toil beneath the ground,
 And hard we work indeed,
That Lady Flower and all the rest
 May have the food they need.
To choosing and preparing it
 We must pay strictest heed."

" And we," the upper servants say,
 " Must carry it with care

And see that every member has
    A full and proper share.
Thus day by day we gladly work
    To serve our Lady fair."

And Lady Flower sits up aloft
    In robes of rainbow hue,
All perfumed sweet and gold bedecked
    And gemmed with diamond dew.
Was never royal lady yet
    More wondrous fair to view.

And yet like all her servitors
    This little lady gay
Leads not a life of idleness,
    But works from day to day;
And in her task of making seeds
    She gives her life away.

                          EMILIE POULSSON.

Clytie.

Clytie was a beautiful nymph who lived among the woods and streams. Her golden hair was the color of the cowslips in the brook, and her robe was of pale green—a color she loved because it belonged to the young leaves, and to the grass in spring. Sometimes as she sat in the meadow beside her favorite stream, where the field flowers grew so tall as to half hide her, she seemed almost like a flower herself. She loved, as she sat there, to feel the wind blow her hair about, and to keep her face turned up to the sun, as a flower turns in the direction whence comes all its light and warmth. The hot noon never drove her indoors for shelter; side by side with the violets and lilies she rejoiced in the sun's caressing warmth, and grew stronger and more beautiful day by day.

Early in the morning, fresh as the dawn itself, she would come through the dewy grass to a hilltop, whence she could see the first pink flush come into the sky; then waiting till the shining edge of the sun appeared over the hills, she would greet him as he flooded all the world with light.

All day, as she roamed the woods or dipped her white feet in the waters of the streams, she could see him mounting higher and higher in the sky, or going down towards the western horizon. If clouds came across his face, she drooped and looked unhappy, but if a sudden shower came down upon her she laughed with glee, because she knew then that the sun would soon show himself again. As the afternoon shadows lengthened she would gather up her flowers—the narcissus or the great yellow lilies she had found—slowly mount the hill from which she could look towards the west, and settling herself into a comfortable nook in the rocks, would watch the great sun go slowly down out of sight, leaving a golden train of brightness behind him. Then, as the flowers closed their petals and sank to sleep, she brushed softly through the leaves, and soon was sleeping as peacefully herself, in her cool and quiet bower.

So the days of this sun-loving maiden were passed. She seemed a creature made to live in the light of the sun, and to grow under its beams, as do the flowers. Apollo, the great sun god, who looks down upon mortals, had seldom seen anything so beautiful, as he moved over the wide fields, and because she was so flower-like, and because she so loved the sunbeams and showers, he determined that she should never die like other mortals, but that she should become a flower, golden-colored like her hair, and like the sun that she so loved to look upon. The leaves are pale green, and the flower, standing high upon its stalk, turns its face to the sun. It is said that as the sun moves slowly across the sky, the flower turns its face from east to west, and for this reason it is called the sunflower.*   F. H.

The Indian Legend of the Trailing Arbutus.

On the south shore of Lake Superior, in the vicinity of the Pictured Rock, grows to perfection that dearest and sweetest of all wild flowers, the arbutus, the plant that the most skillful florist, the plant that the tender, loving touch of woman, even, cannot cause to grow in hothouse or garden.

---

* Heliotrope means sunflower, but no one knows just what the Greek flower was.

From time to time, while sitting by the camp fires in the evening, I have been told of the creation of many animals and birds by the great Mannaboosho and his captains the Manitos. And this is the legend as told me, of the origin or creation of the arbutus :—

It was many, many moons ago there lived an old man alone in his lodge, beside a frozen stream in the forest; his locks and beard were long and white with age. He was heavily clad in fine furs, for all the world was winter,—snow and ice everywhere; the winds went wild through the forests, searching every bush and tree for birds to chill, chasing evil spirits o'er hill and vale, and the old man went about searching in deep snow for pieces of wood to keep up the fire in his lodge. In despair he returned to his lodge, and sitting down by the last few dying coals, he cried to Mannaboosho that he might not perish. And the winds blew aside the door of the lodge and there came in a most beautiful maiden. Her cheeks were red and made of wild roses; her eyes were large and glowed like the eyes of fawns at night; her hair was long and black as the raven's, and it touched the ground as she walked; her hands were covered with willow buds; her bonnet was a wreath of wild flowers, and her clothing of sweet grasses and ferns, and her moccasins were white lilies, and when she breathed the air of the lodge it became warm.

The old man said :—

"My daughter, I am glad to see you; my lodge is cold and cheerless, but it will shield you from the tempest of the night; do tell me who you are, that you dare to come to my lodge in such strange clothing? Come, sit here and tell me of thy country and victories, and I will tell thee of my exploits, for I am Manito."

He then filled two pipes with tobacco, that they might smoke as they talked, and when the smoke had warmed the old man's tongue he said :—

"I am Manito. I blow my breath, and the waters of the river stand still."

The maiden said :—

"I breathe, and flowers spring up on all the plains."

The old man said :—

"I shake my locks, and snow covers all the ground."

"I shake my curls," said the maiden, "and warm rains fall from the clouds."

The old man said:—

"When I walk about, the leaves fall from the trees; at my command the animals hide in their holes in the ground, and the birds get up out of the water and fly away."

The maiden said:—

"When I walk about, the plants lift up their heads, the trees cover their nakedness with many leaves, the birds come back, and all who see me sing. Music is everywhere."

And thus they talked, and the air became warm in the lodge. The old man's head dropped upon his breast and he slept. Then the sun came back, and a bluebird came to the top of the lodge and called: "Say-ee, say-ee, I am thirsty;" and the river called back: "I am free; come and drink."

And as the old man slept, the maiden passed her hands above his head, and he began to grow small; streams of water ran out of his mouth, and soon he was a small mass upon the ground, and his clothing turned to green leaves; and then the maiden, kneeling upon the ground, took from her bosom the most precious white flowers, and hid them all about under the leaves; then she breathed upon them and said: "I give thee all my virtues and my sweetest breath, and all who would pick thee shall do so upon bended knee."

Then the maiden moved away through the woods and over the plains, and all the birds sang to her, and wherever she stepped, and nowhere else, grows the arbutus.

C. E. BELKNAP.

The Little Plant.

In the heart of a seed
  Buried deep, so deep,
A dear little plant
  Lay fast asleep.

" Wake! " said the sunshine
" And creep to the light."

"Wake!" said the voice
   Of the raindrops bright.

The little plant heard,
   And it rose to see
What the wonderful
   Outside world might be.

KATE L. BROWN

In " American Teacher."

"O Daffy-down-dilly! so brave and so true,
I wish all were like you;
So ready for duty in all sorts of weather
And showing forth courage and beauty together."

"Come, my love, and do not spurn
From a little flower to learn.
Let your temper be as sweet
As the lily at your feet;
Be as gentle, be as mild,
Be a modest, simple child."

"Whatever mine ears can hear,
Whatever mine eyes can see,
In nature so bright with beauty and light
Has a message of love for me."

SUMMER.

TO THE TEACHER:—

The subject of the seasons comes up so many times that the children will surely be ready with a good deal of conversation. Therefore the outline of this talk is very simple, first merely taking a look backward and forward to review the seasons and to notice that each brings special joys; and then calling out the children's reminiscences of summer.

THE TALK.

Did any of you meet Jack Frost, when you came to kindergarten this morning? No, I am sure you did not. The warm sunshine has chased him away long before this. When will Jack Frost be here again? In the winter. Tell something more about the winter. What season came after winter? What did spring bring? Summer is coming now. (Question as to the characteristics of summer and compare with those of spring.) We have spoken of winter, spring and summer, and there is one more season, the season when the birds fly away to warmer lands, when the leaves change from green to red, yellow and brown, when the farmer gathers his harvest in for the winter, and when the flowers have made their seeds.

Surely, you remember that all this was in autumn. Who can name the four seasons now? Do they all bring us something beautiful? (Show the children that we could have no spring if it were not for winter, no autumn if we had had no summer.) If it were summer all the year, what should we miss?

Here is a little verse about the seasons:—

    Spring, Summer, Autumn, Winter,
     All are beautiful and dear
    Spring, Summer, Autumn, Winter
    Make a joyous, varied year.

(Lead the children to contrast the seasons so that they will notice how much pleasure comes from the variety afforded by the change of season.)

What do you think the farmer will be doing all summer? Hoeing and weeding in the cornfield, potato field and garden, gathering peas, beans, and other vegetables, picking cherries, berries, and other early fruits.

What does the farmer do with all these things? Sends or takes them to market, so that city people who have no fields and gardens can buy fresh fruits and vegetables.

In some of the farmer's fields we should see only grass growing. What will the farmer do with that? (Describe haymaking, and let the children tell what animals eat hay. Speak of summer rains, thundershowers and rainbows.)

What are you children going to do this summer? Are you coming to kindergarten? No, it will be vacation. Those who expect to go away during the summer vacation may tell where they are going.

(The talk may be concluded with an imaginary trip to the seashore, some children enacting the waves running up on the shore and then retreating, other children pretending to play in the sand and others imitating crabs, etc., on the shore.)

TEACHER'S READING.

Pepacton,	*John Burroughs*
A Vision of Sir Launfal,	*Lowell*
A Midsummer Night's Dream,	*Shakespeare*
They Come, the Merry Summer Months,	*William Motherwell*
Summer (Journal),	*H. D. Thoreau*
Thank God for Summer,	*Eliza Cook*
Summer Wind, A Summer Ramble, An Evening Reverie,	*Bryant*
Al Fresco,	*Lowell*
Grasshopper and Cricket,	*Keats*
Grasshopper,	*Leigh Hunt*
Summer Woods,	*Mary Howitt*
Rain in Summer, A Day of Sunshine,	*Longfellow*

AT THE SEASHORE.

STORIES.

How the Beans Came Up.

Alice May was a little city girl who lived in a brick house which was just like all the other houses on the street, except that some of them had gardens in front, while Alice's house had but a tiny strip of green grass.

When the warm spring days came, and all the people along the street were planting their flower seeds, Alice longed for just one little seed that she might plant it, and perhaps some day have a blossom all her own. And one day, when "Uncle Peter," as she called the good old scissors grinder, came along, she told him all about it.

"So you want some seeds, do you?" said he. "Where would you plant them?" "Oh! just here, in this corner by the step," said Alice, "where they would get the warm sunshine, and I could water and watch them every day."

"Well, how will these do?" said Uncle Peter, drawing a handful of Lima beans from his pocket; "I'm taking some home to plant myself, but I guess I can spare you these if you want them."

"May I have them? Oh, thank you, Uncle Peter! I'll plant them right away, and take just the best care of them." And as Uncle Peter trudged off, he saw Alice digging holes with a little stick, dropping the beans in and covering them with earth. Then she had to wait for them to come up; it seemed a long time. Every morning the first thing she did was to run out on the doorstep to see if there were any little green sprouts, such as she could see in the gardens all along the street. One morning she found—what do you think? No little sprigs of green, but five beans, all split open, out on the ground! "Dear me," she thought, "I didn't plant them deep enough!" So she took a handful of earth and patted it down hard over each bean. But in two or three more days, there they were again, five beans, split in halves, on top of the ground. Alice covered them again, and yet again, for they came peeping up four or five times. Then, after a while, they did not come up any more: there was nothing for Alice to look at but the brown earth.

One morning Uncle Peter came to see how the beans looked, and Alice told him all about it; how they did not send out any green shoots, but just popped up themselves, and how they had not appeared at all since she last covered them. "Dig down and see what you find," said Uncle Peter. Alice found the little beans, all dried and withered; and Uncle Peter said: "You see they are good for nothing now. After you planted them, they sent down little roots to hold themselves firmly in place and pushed themselves up out of the ground. If you had waited, you would have seen two little green leaves grow from between the halves of each bean, and then two more, and they would have kept growing till you would have had some nice little vines by this time. But it isn't too late to try again. Come home with me and I'll give you some more beans. This time just plant them and let them alone."

Alice did as she was told. Before many days the beans popped up, and this time she did not cover them at all, but waited and watered them, and the sun shone on them, and they sent up first one pair of leaves, then another, and another, till they were little vines, ready to climb. Then Uncle Peter came and set some poles for them to twine around, and they liked it very much. They climbed and climbed, and soon Alice saw some white blossoms on her bean vines. She did not pick them, but waited to see what would come of them.

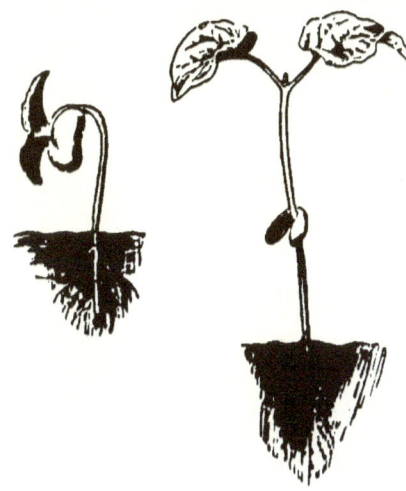

By and by the blossoms dropped off, and some tiny bean pods grew in their places; and oh, how fast they grew!

At last, one day, before Jack Frost came, Alice found that her beans were ready to pick. So she picked them and took them in to her mamma, who cooked them for dinner. There were enough for all to have a taste—her papa and mamma, and all the brothers and sisters; and they thought the beans were very nice.

The next year Alice planted some more beans, and this time she did not cover them up when they popped out of the ground, but waited for the green sprouts to appear; and there was time for ever so many beans to grow and ripen before the frost came.

F. E. MANN.

From " The Woman's Journal," Boston, Mass.

Mabel on Midsummer Day.

PART I.

" Arise, my maiden, Mabel,"
    The mother said; " Arise,
For the golden sun of midsummer
    Is shining in the skies.

" Arise, my little maiden,
    For thou must speed away
To wait upon thy grandmother,
    This livelong summer day.

" And thou must carry with thee
    This wheaten cake so fine,
This new-made pat of butter,
    This little flask of wine.

" And tell the dear old body
    This day I cannot come,
For the good man went out yester-morn,
    And he is not come home.

" And more than this, poor Amy
    Upon my knee doth lie;
I fear me with this fever pain
    The little child will die!

" And thou canst help thy grandmother;
    The table thou canst spread,
Canst feed the little dog and bird,
    And thou canst make her bed.

" And thou canst fetch the water
    From the lady-well hard by;
And thou canst gather from the wood
    The fagots brown and dry.

"Canst go down to the lonesome glen,
　　To milk the mother ewe;
　This is the work, my Mabel,
　　That thou wilt have to do.

"But listen now, my Mabel;
　　This is midsummer day,
　When all the fairy people
　　From elf-land come away.

"And when thou 'rt in the lonesome glen,
　　Keep by the running burn,
　And do not pluck the strawberry flower
　　Nor break the lady fern.

"But think not of the fairy folk
　　Lest mischief should befall;
　Think only of poor Amy,
　　And how thou lov'st us all.

"Yet keep good heart, my Mabel,
　　If thou the fairies see,
　And give them kindly answer
　　If they should speak to thee.

"And when into the fir wood
　　Thou go'st for fagots brown,
　Do not, like idle children,
　　Go wandering up and down

"But fill thy little apron,
　　My child, with earnest speed;
　And that thou break no living bough
　　Within the wood, take heed.

"For they are spiteful brownies
　　Who in the wood abide,
　So be thou careful of this thing,
　　Lest evil should betide.

'But think not, little Mabel,
　　Whil'st thou art in the wood
"Of dwarfish, wilful brownies,
　　But of the *Futher* good.

"And when thou goest to the spring
 To fetch the water thence,
"Do not disturb the little stream,
 Lest this should give offence.

"For the queen of all the fairies,
 She loves that water bright;
I've seen her drinking there myself
 On many a summer night.

"But she's a gracious lady,
 And her thou need'st not fear;
Only disturb thou not the stream,
 Nor spill the water clear."

"Now all this will I heed, mother;
 Will no word disobey,
And wait upon the grandmother
 This livelong summer day."

PART II.

Away tripped little Mabel,
 With the wheaten cake so fine,
With the new-made pat of butter,
 And the little flask of wine.

And long before the sun was not
 And summer mist had cleared,
Beside the good old grandmother
 The willing child appeared.

And all her mother's message
 She told with right good will,
How that her father was away
 And the little child was ill.

And then she swept the hearth up clear,
 And then the table spread,
And next she fed the dog and bird,
 And then she made the bed.

"And go now," said the grandmother,
 "Ten paces down the dell,
And bring in water for the day,—
 Thou know'st the lady-well"

The first time that good Mabel went,
  Nothing at all saw she
Except a bird, a sky-blue bird,
  That sat upon a tree.

The next time that good Mabel went,
  There sat a lady bright
Beside the well,—a lady small,
  All clad in green and white.

A courtesy low made Mabel,
  And then she stooped to fill
Her pitcher at the sparkling spring,
  But no drop did she spill.

"Thou art a handy maiden,"
  The fairy lady said;
"Thou hast not spilt a drop, nor yet
  The fairy spring troubled!

"And for this thing which thou hast done
  Yet mayest not understand,
I give to thee a better gift
  Than houses or than land.

"Thou shalt do well whate'er thou dost,
  As thou hast done this day;
Shalt have the will and power to please,
  And shalt be loved alway."

Thus having said she passed from sight,
  And naught could Mabel see
But the little bird, the sky-blue bird,
  Upon the leafy tree.

"And now, go," said the grandmother,
  "And fetch in fagots dry;
All in the neighboring fir-wood
  Beneath the trees they lie."

Away went kind, good Mabel,
  Into the fir wood near.
Where all the ground was dry and brown
  And the grass grew thin and sere.

She did not wander up and down,
   Nor yet a live branch pull,
But steadily of the fallen boughs
   She picked her apron full.

And when the wild-wood brownies
   Came sliding to her mind,
She drove them thence, as she was told,
   With home thoughts sweet and kind.

But all that while, the brownies
   Within the fir wood still,
They watched her how she picked the wood
   And strove to do no ill.

" And oh! but she is small and neat,"
   Said one; " 'twere shame to spite
A creature so demure and meek,
   A creature harmless quite! "

" Look only," said another,
   " At her little gown of blue;
At her kerchief pinned about her head,
   And at her little shoe! "

" Oh! but she is a comely child,"
   Said a third; " and we will lay
A good-luck penny in her path,
   A boon for her this day—
Seeing she broke no living wood
   No live thing did affray!

With that the smallest penny
   Of the finest silver ore,
Upon the dry and slippery path,
   Lay Mabel's feet before.

With joy she picked the penny up,
   The fairy penny good;
And with her fagots dry and brown
   Went wandering from the wood.

" Now she has that," said the brownies,
   " Let flax be ever so dear,

'Twill buy her clothes of the very best,
　　For many and many a year! "

" And go now," said the grandmother,
　" Since falling is the dew,
Go down unto the lonesome glen,
　　And milk the mother ewe."

All down into the lonesome glen,
　　Through copses thick and wild,
Through moist rank grass, by trickling streams
　　Went on the willing child.

And when she came to the lonesome glen,
　　She kept beside the burn,
And neither plucked the strawberry flower
　　Nor broke the lady fern.

And while she milked the mother ewe
　　Within this lonely glen,
She wished that little Amy
　　Were strong and well again.

And soon as she had thought this thought,
　　She heard a coming sound
As if a thousand fairy folk
　　Were gathering all around.

And then she heard a little voice,
　　Shrill as the midge's wing,
That spake aloud,—" A human child
　　Is here; yet mark this thing,—

" The lady fern is all unbroke,
　　The strawberry flower unta'en!
What shall be done for her who still
　　From mischief can refrain? "

" Give her a fairy cake! " said one;
　" Grant her a wish! " said three;
" The latest wish that she hath wished,"
　　Said all, " whate'er it be! "

Kind Mabel heard the words they spake,
　　And from the lonesome glen

Unto the good old grandmother
Went gladly back again.

Thus happened it to Mabel
On that midsummer day;
And these three fairy blessings
She took with her away.

'Tis good to make all duty sweet,
To be alert and kind;
'Tis good like little Mabel
To have a willing mind.

MARY HOWITT.

The Story of a Breeze.

Once upon a time a little Breeze who had been playing all day with the leaves and flowers, said to himself: "O dear! I'm of no use at all. I do nothing but play. I mean to ask the great strong Wind if I may go with him to-morrow and help him in his work."

So the Breeze was waiting in the early morning when the Wind started on his daily journey over the earth. When he came rushing through the tree where the little Breeze had played for so many long days, he heard a soft voice like the rustling of leaves, saying: "Please, dear, strong Wind, may I go with you and help you to-day?" The Wind was in a great hurry, and said as he rushed along: "Why, yes, my dear, if you really wish to help." This made the Breeze so happy that he darted on, dancing and fluttering over the grass, and still keeping ahead of the Wind.

Soon they came to such a queer building! It was quite high and had a large thing on one side that looked somewhat like a wheel. In the doorway stood a man talking with another man outside. Said the man outside; "Well, Mr. Miller, is my flour ready? Our bread is all gone and we have no more flour, and the children must have something to eat."

"I'm so sorry, Mr. Smith," said the Miller, "but the Wind has not been blowing for two days, and you know the mill cannot grind the wheat unless the Wind turns the wheel.".

At this the little Breeze rustled briskly forward and came right down close to the man's face, whispering to him that the Wind—the good, strong Wind—was coming very soon to turn the great wheel of the mill.

When the miller felt the Breeze upon his face, he said joyfully: "I declare! I really felt a Breeze! I think the Wind is going to blow."

By this time, the great wheel was turning round and round. The Breeze knew that everything would be all right now, so again he started on, as light-hearted as ever, to be the messenger of the Wind.

The next place they came to was a little village by the seashore. On a landing at the water's edge stood a woman with a baby in her arms, and a little boy and girl by her side. They were looking out over the wide sea, which was very smooth and beautiful. But the woman looked sad, and the little girl was crying. What do you think they were looking for? Why, the papa was a fisherman, and he had been out upon the water for a week, and the mamma knew that he did not have enough food to keep him from being very hungry during that long time; and as his boat was a sailboat, she knew that he could not get home unless the Wind came to help him

The little Breeze saw in a moment what the trouble was; so he kissed the little girl on her cheek and dried the tears that sparkled there, lifted the golden curls on the baby's head, and gently cooled the mother's aching brow, whispering in her ear that the Wind was coming.

Then the little boy said: "O Mamma! I see waves on the water!" So the Breeze knew that the Wind was bringing the father's boat home to the dear ones waiting on the shore. He stayed to see the mother smile and the children clap their hands at the sight of the white sail that was now coming rapidly towards them from far out on the water.

Next the Wind and the Breeze came to a large city. How beautiful everything looked! The Wind said to the Breeze: "Your work is here; they need you more than they do me in the city." And in another moment he was gone, and the Breeze had not even had time to ask what he was to do.

The houses were beautiful and large. Some were made of stone, some of marble, and some of brick; and all had parks and gardens around them. The Breeze saw some children playing; so he stopped to have a little fun with them. He tossed their kites, waved their flags, and led them a merry chase after the hats of the little girls. Then he helped the Sun to dry some clothes that were hanging in a yard. In a short time he came to a part of the city where the air was very close and hot. He saw a great many people working in shops and mills. He saw how warm and uncomfortable they were. So he flew in at the doors and windows and cooled the tired workmen till they forgot their weariness and thought only how nice it was to be able to work for their dear ones at home.

Again the Breeze went on his way; and soon he came to another part of the city where the houses were crowded—oh, so closely together! There were no nice yards here, no lace curtains at the windows for the little Breeze to play with, and the children did not seem to be so merry as those he had seen in the park. They just sat on the sidewalk and steps, the only places they had,—with no kites, no flags, no pretty playthings,—and the little girls had no hats at all!

"I'll just peep in the window and see what kind of homes these children have," thought the Breeze. So he went in through an open window and what do you suppose he saw? On a bed lay a dear little girl whose face was deeply flushed and who tossed from side to side moaning pitifully: "O Mamma! I'm *so* warm!" But the mother was too busy to stop and comfort the child; she had to do washing every day so that she could earn money to get the little one and herself something to eat. So the Breeze fanned the hot face and brushed the damp air from the little brow till the child dropped asleep feeling comfortable and happy, and smiling as she slept.

"She must be dreaming of the angels," said the Breeze, as he gave her a good-bye kiss. And so ended the day; but the Breeze still keeps on untiringly in his helpful and cheering tasks, proving a blessing wherever he goes.

MATTIE McROY.

SUNSHINE.

To the Teacher:—

The most auspicious and inspiring time for a talk upon sunshine, is on one of those brilliant days when the universe seems flooded with its radiance. The effects of a lack of sunshine can be strongly impressed upon the children by planting the ever-useful bean in a pot and keeping it in a closet or other dark place. Let them see what a pale, sickly plant it becomes, in comparison with plants grown in sunlight. Draw the parallel between the plant and the child, as to the necessity of sunlight for healthy, vigorous growth.

If the fact of the sun's standing still and the earth's turning and taking us away from the light is spoken of, it can be illustrated with a candle for the sun and a ball for the earth; or by letting the children "play" it in a very simple manner; and the following verse is offered as the sun's answer to "Good Morning, Merry Sunshine," where this way of dealing with the subject is preferred. (See Froebel's explanation of "The Little Boy and the Moon," quoted elsewhere.)

THE SUN'S ANSWER.

I never go to sleep, dear child,
   I'm shining all the night,
But as your world goes turning round
   It takes you from my light.
And when it brings you back again
   You find me waiting here,
To shine a bright "Good morning" down
   On all the children dear.

E. P.

In many kindergartens the spectrum is represented by colored papers arranged on a chart. Besides this, let us keep a prism or prisms hanging in the window, so that the children may have ever before them the mystery and wonder of the real spectrum in all the ethereal radiance of its blended colors.

THE TALK.

There is something in this room which came in so softly that no one could possibly hear it. You can all see it. Can you guess what it is? (Give the children suggestions, more or less definite, according to their skill in guessing.) It came a long way; it can come into the room even when the door is shut; it is out of doors, too, as well as in our room; it is bright—it is yellow—it is warm We say "Good morning" to it very often.

Where did the sunshine come from? It *is* a long way from the sun down to us, is it not? What shape is the sun? Can you show me? Let us sing "This is the way the sunshine comes down."

Where is the sunshine falling besides in our kindergarten? On the home where mamma is, on the shop where papa works, on the farmer's fields, on the great ocean where the ships are sailing.

(Try to give an impression of the sun's greatness by thus drawing out that its beams reach far and wide, over city and country, over land and sea.)

Can we always see the sun? What hides it sometimes? Did you know that the sun is always shining, whether we see it or not—even in the night time? Our world turns round, and so takes us away from the light, but the sun is shining just as brightly as ever. That is a wonderful and beautiful thing to think of, is it not?

What is the sunshine doing all day long? Giving us light, warming the air and the ground, helping plants and animals to grow, taking water (vapor) up into the sky, and in every way making the world more beautiful and more glad

(Speak of the sunshine at different seasons of the year. This point and all the work of the sunbeams has been dwelt upon in other talks, so that much should be drawn from the children on this whole subject. Remind the children of the glazier as the one whose work gives us our windows through which sunlight enters our homes, schools, etc. Play the "Light Bird.")

Would you like to catch a sunbeam? Can we catch it in our hands and keep it? No, but I have a glass by which we can find out something very beautiful about the sunbeams. (Show the prism, and hold or fix it in the sunlight.) What do you see? Tell me all the colors you can see.

(Repeated observations of the spectrum will be needed before the children can distinguish all the colors.)

Have you ever seen a rainbow? Where was it? Do you

THE RAINBOW.

remember what the weather was, whether it was rainy weather or bright weather? It must have been both at once! For we never have rainbows in the sky except when the sun shines while it is raining. The raindrops show us all the colors which the sunbeams hold, just as this prism shows them. We can sometimes see the rainbow colors in soap bubbles, too, or in water which stands in the sunlight.

Can you find each one of the rainbow colors in the room?

TEACHER'S READING.

Explanation of "The Light Bird," etc.,	*Froebel*
The Sun,	*C. A. Young*
Sun, Moon and Stars,	*Agnes Giberne*
The Fairyland of Science (Chap. II),	*Arabella Buckley*
Forms of Water,	*Tyndall*
Modern Chromatics,	*Rood*
Hymn before Sunrise in the Vale of Chamouni,	*Coleridge*
Address to Light,	*Milton*
A Day of Sunshine,	*Longfellow*
Sunshine,	*Mary Howitt*
To the Rainbow,	*Campbell*
Man and Nature, } The Prospect, }	*Mrs. Browning*
The Church Windows,	*Herbert*
The Thunderstorm,	*Emily Dickinson*
The Light of Life,	*Mrs. Gatty*

For the Children.

The Dawn Princess ("Stories for Kindergarten and Home").

STORIES.

The Wind and the Sun.

The blustering Wind was stalking up and down an open field one day, rejoicing aloud in his great strength. "Oh, I am strong, indeed!" he roared. "I breathe, and the grasses bow down before me. I wave my hand, and the reeds and the bushes bend or snap. I can break even the stout tree branches, merely by taking hold of them. "Oh, yes; I am strong! Who is stronger?"

As he stopped and his rough, roaring tones died away, a gentle voice said: "I am strong, too. Perhaps stronger than you; who knows?"

"Who is that?" roared the Wind.

"It is I, the Sun," said the same mild voice.

"*You* strong!" said the Wind. "You! with your soft ways and gentle smiles! Can you move mighty windmills? Can you, with a few touches, raise the wild waves upon the ocean? Can you break the strong oak, the king of the forest?"

"I am strong!" said the Sun again. "I can do many things that you cannot do. Shall we try our strength? Yonder comes a traveler, wearing a heavy cloak. Let us see which of us can force him to lay it aside, and agree that the one who does, shall be called the stronger."

The Wind could not help giving a pleased whistle at this easy task, for he thought that he should probably get the traveler's cloak off by one strong gust.

"You may make the first trial," said the Sun.

Away went the Wind. He met the traveler near the middle of the field and began to tug at the cloak. It flapped about a little, and the traveler fastened it more securely. The Wind tugged again and howled fiercely. The traveler took the edges of the cloak in his hands and wrapped it closely about him. Again the wind puffed and pulled and tugged. The bottom of the cloak fluttered, but the man only held it more and more closely about him. "Who would have thought there was such a wind to-day?" said the traveler, as he struggled on.

The Wind kept trying for some time, but without success; and he was quite ready to give up when the Sun claimed his turn.

"I don't see how you can do anything at all!" said the Wind; "for my angriest howls and my roughest pulls have only made him hold his cloak the more tightly."

"I had not meant to try that way," replied the Sun. "Anger and roughness are not what I shall use." Then the Sun smiled down upon the traveler. Not a sound was heard; but softly, steadily, silently, the Sun kept shining. The traveler, who had been using all his strength to keep his cloak about him, now found the air quiet again, and walked on more easily. Soon he loosened his hold of the cloak. The Sun kept on shining, softly, steadily, silently; and the traveler began to think his cloak too thick, so he unfastened it and threw it open. Still the Sun kept on shining, softly, steadily, silently.

At last the traveler said: "How strange! A little while ago I felt that I could not hold my cloak too closely, and now I am glad to throw it off entirely." So saying he took off his heavy cloak and sat down under a tree to cool himself in the shade.

And the Wind saw and acknowledged that the quiet Sun was indeed powerful and had won the title of "the stronger;" for without noise, without bluster, without anger, the Sun had succeeded in making the traveler take off his cloak, when the Wind had found it impossible.

Retold by E. P.

The Sunbeams.

"Now, what shall I send to the Earth to-day?"
   Said the great, round, golden Sun.
"Oh! let us go down there to work and play,"
   Said the Sunbeams, every one.

So down to the Earth in a shining crowd,
   Went the merry, busy crew;
They painted with splendor each floating cloud
   And the sky while passing through.

"Shine on, little stars, if you like," they cried,
   "We will weave a golden screen
That soon all your twinkling and light shall hide,
   Though the Moon may peep between."

The Sunbeams then in through the windows crept
   To the children in their beds—
They poked at the eyelids of those who slept,
   Gilded all the little heads.

"Wake up, little children!" they cried in glee,
   And from Dreamland come away!
We've brought you a present, wake up and see!
   We have brought you a sunny day!"

EMILIE POULSSON.

"*The Kindergarten.*"

The Story of the Morning-Glory Seed.

A little girl one day in the month of May dropped a morning-glory seed into a small hole in the ground and said: "Now, morning-glory seed, hurry and grow, grow, grow until you are a tall vine covered with pretty green leaves and lovely trumpet flowers." But the earth was very dry, for there had been no rain in a long time, and the poor wee seed could not grow at all.

So, after lying patiently in the small hole for nine long days and nine long nights, it said to the ground around it: "O ground, please give me a few drops of water to soften my hard, brown coat, so that it may burst open and set free my two green seed-leaves, and then I can begin to be a vine!" But the ground said: "That you must ask of the rain."

So the seed called to the rain: "O rain, please come down and wet the ground around me so that it may give me a few drops of water. Then will my hard, brown coat grow softer and softer until at last it can burst open and set free my two green seed-leaves, and I can begin to be a vine!" But the rain said: "I cannot unless the clouds hang lower."

So the seed said to the clouds: "O clouds, please hang lower and let the rain come down and wet the ground around me, so that it may give me a few drops of water. Then will my hard, brown coat grow softer and softer until at last it can burst open and set free my two green seed-leaves, and I can begin to be a vine!" But the clouds said: "The sun must hide, first."

So the seed called to the sun: "O sun, please hide for a little while so that the clouds may hang lower, and the rain come down and wet the ground around me. Then will the ground give me a few drops of water and my hard, brown coat grow softer and softer until at last it can burst open and set free my two green seed-leaves, and I can begin to be a vine!" "I will," said the sun, and he was gone in a flash.

Then the clouds began to hang lower and lower, and the rain began to fall faster and faster, and the ground began to ge wetter and wetter, and the seed-coat began to grow softer and softer, until, at last, open it burst!—and out came two bright green seed-leaves, and the morning-glory seed began to be a vine!

MARGARET EYTINGE.

"*St. Nicholas.*"

The Water Bloom.

A child looked up in the summer sky
Where a soft, bright shower had just passed by;
Eastward the dusk rain-curtain hung,
And swiftly across it the rainbow sprung.

"Papa! Papa! what is it?" she cried,
As she gazed with her blue eyes opened wide
At the wonderful arch that bridged the heaven,
Vividly glowing with colors seven.

"Why, that is the rainbow, darling child,"
And the father down on his baby smiled.
"What makes it, Papa?" "The sun, my dear,
That shines on the waterdrops so clear."

Here was a beautiful mystery!
No more questions to ask had she,
But she thought the garden's loveliest flowers
Had floated upward and caught in the showers—

Rose, violet, orange marigold—
In a ribbon of light on the clouds unrolled!
Red of poppy and green leaves, too,
Sunflower yellow, and larkspur blue.

A great, wide, wondrous, splendid wreath
It seemed to the little girl beneath;
How did it grow so fast up there,
And suddenly blossom, high in the air?

She could not take her eyes from the sight;
"Oh, look!" she cried in her deep delight,
As she watched the glory spanning the gloom,
"Oh, look at the beautiful water bloom!"

CELIA THAXTER.

Houghton, Mifflin & Co.

THE MOON AND STARS.

To the Teacher:—

"When a child first sees and contemplates natural objects whose being he is still unable to grasp, he believingly accepts true as well as false explanations from grown-up people; and he finds both equally easy and equally difficult whenever he tries to grasp one or the other, if on any occasion both relate to the way to look at any given object. And so, no doubt, to begin with, a child is not helped in his view and grasp whether he be taught to know the moon as a man or as a beautiful, bright, swimming ball; whether the stars be pointed out to him as golden pins, or burning lights, or as sparkling suns which look so small because they are so far off. *But while the first explanation is, in spite of its apparent liveliness, a dead one, the latter bears within it the foundation of a living, further development, that may lead to inner and more thorough insight.*"

(From Froebel's explanation of "The Little Boy and the Moon," in Mother's Songs, Games and Stories.)

THE TALK.

(Question the children upon the observations called out by the talk upon "Sunshine" and lead them to tell what else is seen in the sky.) Is the moon alone? What does she have for company? Can we see the moon and stars every night? No; they are sometimes hidden by the clouds just as the sun is, but they are in the sky night and day, even when we do not see them.

How many of you have seen the moon? What color is it? Does it always look round? (Have pictures which show the full moon, new moon, etc., and explain, if the children are ready for such explanation, that we can only see the moon when it is made bright by the light of the sun only the part which *shines*, though the whole moon is in the sky all the time. Tell the children Jean Ingelow's verse in which the child says:—

"O moon, in the night I have seen you sailing
And shining so round and low.
You were bright, ah! bright, but your light is failing
You are nothing now but a bow."

Speak of the Indian's way of counting time by so many "moons," and of our word "month.")

Which *looks* larger, the moon or the stars? Are there many stars? More than even the wisest man knows. Are the stars beautiful? Are they useful? (Explain how "the traveler in the dark" on land or sea can guide his course by the stars as well as see by their light. Remind the children of the star story of Christmas tide, if they do not mention it. Frequent use of songs about the moon and the stars will direct the children's thoughts to the heavenly bodies, and the subject should be recurred to after a little time has elapsed, as the children will then be more ready with questions and their own observations. Artificial lights furnish material for another talk; lights at home, street lights and the lighthouse with its work of mercy.)

TEACHER'S READING.

Explanation of "The Child and the Moon," etc.,	*Froebel*
The Expanse of Heaven,	*Proctor*
Easy Star Lessons,	*Proctor*
Wonders of the Moon,	*Guillemin*
Among the Stars,	*Agnes Giberne*
The Firmament,	*Ruskin*
Child's Dream of a Star,	*Dickens*
The Will o' the Wisp,	*Mrs. Gatty*
The Spacious Firmament on High,	*Addison*
Hymn to the Moon,	*Ben. Jonson*
Self Dependence,	*M. Arnold*
To the North Star,	*Bryant*
The Light of Stars,	*Longfellow*

For the Children.

The Waning Moon,	*Celia Thaxter*
The Wind and the Moon,	*George MacDonald*
The Legend of the Great Dipper ("Kindergarten Stories and Morning Talks")	*S. E. Wiltse*

LITTLE LINDA.

STORIES.

Linda and the Lights.

Linda was a little child who was very fond of looking up into the sky. She lived in a small village near the sea, for her father was a fisherman. Linda liked to play down by the sea, digging wells in the sand, making sand hills or sand pies, or gathering the pretty shells which the waves brought to her; but she would sometimes leave all this play and sit quietly on a big rock, looking at the wide blue sea and the wide blue sky,—the sea dotted with the white sails of the ships, and the sky with white clouds.

As she looked at the clouds, she used to say over a little verse that someone had taught her:—

> "White sheep, white sheep,
> On a blue hill,
> When the wind stops
> You all stand still;
> When the wind blows
> You walk away slow—
> White sheep, white sheep,
> Where do you go?"

She often fancied that the cloud masses did look like snowy sheep and lambs roaming over a broad blue field.

At night, too, Linda loved to look up into the sky. When the full moon came out in all its round, silver splendor, throwing such floods of brightness everywhere, she wondered whether anything could be more beautiful. When she saw the tiny new moon—crescent-shaped, timid, lovely—glimmering out among the stars, she wondered the same about that, and sang with delight:—

> "O mother, how pretty the moon looks to-night!
> She was never so cunning before!
> Her two little horns are so sharp and so bright,
> I hope she won't grow any more."

As she sang the whole pretty song, Linda would imagine herself up in that "bright cradle," rocking and floating in some wonderful way, and coming home down the glowing curve of a rainbow.

Then there were the starry nights when the whole dark sky was spangled with sparkling, twinkling lights. Linda always looked for the Dipper and for the North Star to which it pointed. Her father had told her of some sailors who would have been lost on the sea if they had not had the North Star by which to guide their boat home, so she loved the stars for this, as well as for their beauty.

While Linda was still a little girl, her father went on a long sea voyage and Linda and her mother went to live in the city. The noisy streets, the houses crowded close together—everything was strange to Linda, and she missed the shining, rolling sea, and the rocks and the sand; but at night when she stood at the window to look at the sky, as she always did before getting into bed, she said joyfully: "O mother! the sky is just the same here anyway! There is the moon, and over there the Dipper, just as I used to see them!" Her mother smiled to think that Linda should be so surprised at finding the same sky, and told her, as she tucked her into bed, that the beautiful sky was all over the world. "And the same moon and the same stars?" asked Linda. "The same moon shines for all, dear," said her mother, "but when father has sailed far to the south, he will see some stars which we never see here. One cluster which he will see is called the Southern Cross, because the stars make a cross, just as here some stars form the Dipper."

The next day, before Linda had seen much of her new surroundings, a storm set in. All day the sky was dull and dark with clouds, and at night there was not a star to be seen. Linda was turning away from the window in disappointment when she heard a rattling sound outside, and a strong light flashed into the room. Looking out again, Linda saw a man right at the side of the house and on the level with her window, and the light came from a lamp which was fastened to the house, and which he had just lighted.

In a moment he was down on the sidewalk and hurrying across

the street with his little ladder on his shoulder. Linda looked after him with great interest. She could see only a little way into the darkness of the stormy night, but soon another light flickered through the mist half-way up the block, on the other side of the street. Linda ran to the window in the next room, from which she could see farther;—yes! there was another light beyond, and there, still another! "O mother! Isn't it beautiful? See the lights! Did you know there were lamps in the street? And mother, see how light the lamp outside makes my room! I shall not need any other light to go to bed by. Are they lighted every night, mother?" "Not in this city," answered her mother. "Here they are only lighted on stormy nights, and nights when there is no 'moon,' as we say—that is, when we cannot see the moon."

The next night was also stormy and Linda was quite ready to go early up stairs, to see the street lamps lighted.

Soon she saw a light far down the street,—then another nearer,—and yes! that was the rattle of the ladder against the house; and there suddenly, was the lamplighter himself, right beside her window again! Linda clapped her hands and laughed outright, and what do you think? The lamplighter looked up at the window and smiled at her.

This was the beginning of an acquaintance. Linda called him her lamplighter, and was always on the watch for him on dark nights. She had many questions to ask him about the city lights; and from what he told her of their number, and from noticing herself how many street lamps there were everywhere about, Linda began to see what a great work it was to light a whole city. She did not forget the moon and stars, though, even when she did not see them. She would look from the street lamps up to the clouded sky, realizing more and more the power and beauty of the far-off heavenly lights—the millions of sparkling stars, and the wondrous moon which, with its glorious, silvery radiance, could light not only the whole city as no lamps could, but sea and land far and wide besides.

EMILIE POULSSON.

THE WEAVER.

On this and the following subjects of Wool, Cotton, Linen and Silk, the suggestions to the teacher and "The Talks" are combined.

(Sing some of the Trade Songs, and then ask the children what kind of work their fathers do. Let each trade be represented by a child, and by one whose father works at that trade, as far as possible. Unless in the region of silk, cotton or woolen mills, the weaver will usually not be mentioned by the children. To bring out the necessity of his work, the teacher and the other children play that they need new clothes, and ask each of the tradesmen in turn to make some cloth. Each tradesman tells what he *can* do, but owns that he cannot make cloth.)

Just think! with all these workmen there is not one who can make clothes for us! What shall we do? Some one must have made the cloth for all these clothes we have! Let us see if we can find out how it is made. (Take coarse material of any kind—cloth, toweling, flannel—and let the children ravel out some, and discover that it is made of threads. Now how are these threads put together? If the children do not find out from the cloth that the threads are woven, a coarse piece of ingrain carpet will show it very plainly. After seeing the "under and over" in a coarse fabric, the children should be shown that the finer fabrics are made of woven threads, too.) All the cloth from which clothes are made has been woven of some kind of thread. Can you guess the name of the workman who weaves the threads together?

Did you notice that the threads in the cloth run two ways—some up and down, and some left and right? Do you see how that is like a paper mat with the strings woven through it? (The warp and woof, the separation of the alternate threads, and the way the shuttle, carrying the thread, is passed through, and this thread pushed down, can all be shown very well with a large weaving mat—one with narrowest strips is best.

Let the children name all the articles they can upon which the weaver has worked, and lead them to notice that heavy carpets and finest linens and silks are the products of the loom.)

As for the threads which the weaver uses—"*that* is another story."

TEACHER'S READING.

Description of Loom,	*Encyclopædia*
Silas Marner,	*George Eliot*
The Betrothed,	*W. Scott*
A New England Girlhood,	*Lucy Larcom*
Spinning Wheel Song,	*J. F. Waller*
Sheep Shearing (from "The Seasons"—Spring),	*Thomson*
The Unused Loom ("New Lights on Old Paths"),	*Charles Foster*
The Emperor's New Clothes,	*Hans Christian Andersen*
The Weaver's Song,	*B. W. Proctor*
My Sunflower's Fan,	*"St. Nicholas," 1879*

For the Children.

New Work for Pense ("Each and All"),	*Jane Andrews*
What Happened to Muslin ("Stories for Kindergarten and Home"),	*M. L. Van Kirk*
Cloth and Paper Story ("Kindergarten Stories and Morning Talks"),	*S. E. Wiltse*

STORIES.

A Visit to the Weaver.

"Annie," said a lady to a little girl who was visiting her, "would you like to go with me to the weaver's to-day?"

"Oh, yes!" said Annie, "I should like it very much. I never saw a weaver at work."

So they set out. As they were walking along, the lady told Annie the story of "John's Trousers," so that by the time they reached the house of Mrs. James, the weaver, Annie knew not only where the wool came from, but also what had to be done to it before it was ready for weaving. Now, there are carding mills and cloth mills in which the carding and spinning and weaving are done by machinery; but the weaver whom Annie was going to see wove in the same way that John's mother and sisters did when they made his trousers.

The story had taken so much time that they reached the weaver's house soon after it was ended.

"Good morning, Mrs. James," said the lady; "I have brought a little friend to see you weave, if you have no objection."

"No, indeed," said Mrs. James; "I shall be very glad to show her how the work is done. Have you ever seen a person weave, little one?"

"Only in kindergarten," replied Annie. "We weave there; but we weave mats with paper, or leather, or flannel list, or braid, or tape. I never saw anyone weave cloth or carpet."

"I never saw any kindergarten weaving," said Mrs. James, "but I can show you how my loom works. The warp, as we call the yarn that is stretched on this frame, is first wound around that great beam overhead and then drawn tightly on the loom. We always measure three or four yards more than we want for a piece of cloth because some of the length is taken up in the weaving.

"Why, there are two sets of threads," said Annie.

"Yes; half of the threads go through one set of loops and half through the other," said Mrs. James.

"Oh! I see," said Annie; "and that thing that is full of yarn is your shuttle, isn't it?"

"Yes. Now see what happens when I press down one of these treadles with my right foot," said Mrs. James.

"Oh!" exclaimed Annie quickly, "half the threads are lifted up, and you throw the shuttle with your right hand so that it goes under those threads and over the others. That is like our weaving—only we have to lift up our strips one at a time, instead of all together. No do you press down the other treadle with your left foot?"

"Not yet; the cloth would be too open if I did not draw the 'strip,' as you call it, close up to the last one I put in. See!

I pull this bar toward me and it pushes the strip closely in place. In carpet weaving it is really a strip that is put through."

"We push our strips up close, too," said Annie, "but we use our fingers instead of a bar."

"That would do very well for paper weaving," assented Mrs. James, "but not for making cloth or carpets."

"No," said Annie, "I see that; for you pulled the bar very hard and used more strength than you could with your hands alone. What comes next?"

"I press down the other treadle with my left foot, as you said, and throw the shuttle with my left hand," said Mrs. James; "then, the threads that the shuttle went over before are lifted up, so that the shuttle can pass under them this time."

"And then you pull up the bar again, don't you?" asked Annie.

"Yes," answered Mrs. James. "And now I will show you how much I can do in ten minutes. I have been working slowly so that you might see how the work was done, but now you shall see me *really* work!"

Then Mrs. James made the shuttle fairly fly back and forth for a while, and Annie watched her with wonder, making her own little feet and hands go just as Mrs. James did hers, though not so fast.

After that Annie and her friend thanked Mrs. James for all her kindness and said "Good-bye."

JOSEPHINE JARVIS.

Cobden, Ill.

John's Trousers.
(*A True Story.*)

More than a hundred years ago our country was at war with another country called England, thousands of miles away. One morning, just after the war had begun, John told his mother that the troops were out and that he must join them early the next day.

"What shall we do?" exclaimed the patriotic mother; "John *must* have a new pair of trousers, and we haven't a bit of cloth in the house!"

A WEAVER AT HER LOOM.

"Nor any yarn, either!" added Deborah, "I used the last in weaving the cloth for Charlie's jacket."

"Something must be done," said the mother. "Perhaps we can get the trousers made, even if we have to spin and weave them. Let us try our very best!"

"Charlie and I will cut the wool," said Mary, the youngest girl.

"I am afraid you cannot catch the sheep," said the mother. "They are in the pasture."

"We'll take some salt," said Mary. "We can coax them with that."

When they reached the pasture, Mary pointed out a black sheep and told Charlie to hold the salt toward it. Charlie did so and the sheep came running to him at once. While the sheep was licking the salt, Charlie put his arm around its neck and held it still while Mary cut off some of its wool with the shears. Then they caught a white sheep and sheared some of its wool in the same way. With this black and white wool in the basket which she carried, Kate ran back to the house so that her mother and Deborah might begin carding it at once. Mary and Charlie kept on with their shearing—first a black sheep and then a white one—until plenty of wool had been cut.

After the wool is cut from the sheep, it is usually washed and dried; but now there was no time to spare for that process. The cards used were blocks of wood nearly square, with a handle and slanting iron teeth. The wool was combed by these cards until it was made into soft, long rolls, when it was ready for spinning.

After Kate and Mary came back from the shearing, they said they would do the carding so that their mother and Deborah could commence to spin. They owned two pairs of cards, and had borrowed an extra spinning wheel from a neighbor.

As soon as yarn enough was spun the loom was prepared, and the weaving of the cloth begun. They all took turns at the loom, and, when the cloth was made, all helped in the sewing; so that by working all night the trousers were finished in good season, and put in the bundle which John's mother packed for him the next morning.

JOSEPHINE JARVIS.

Cobden, Ill.

WOOL.

(A picture of sheep, some wool in its natural state, worsteds colored and white, very coarse white flannel, other woolen goods, the eraser, the worsted balls, and cotton and silk for contrast, would be a good equipment of objects for this talk. Like the cow, the sheep is less familiar to our city children than its products, so we take the products as the starting point.

Exercise the sense of touch, distinguishing wool by its roughness. Let the children find out which articles of their clothing are of wool.) At what season do we wear woolen clothes most? Why? They keep us warmer. Yes, the heat of our bodies is kept in better by woolen clothing than by any other. Can you think of other things which are made of wool? Blankets, carpets, etc.

(Fringe out the coarse flannel to show the threads of which it is woven, and untwist the threads to show the hair-like fibers. The children will see the similarity to the "raw wool" better with undyed material; afterwards speak of the dyeing. I have seen a good color exercise in this connection, the teacher showing alternately white worsted, then worsted of some color, and asking what must have been the color of the dye used.

Having traced the woolen clothes, etc., back to the wool, ask where the wool grew. Describe the washing and shearing of the sheep, not forgetting to tell the children that the sheep would shed much of the wool anyway and are more comfortable without it for the summer season.)

STORIES.
How a Little Boy Got a New Shirt.
(From the German.)

There lived one time a poor widow who had seven children, and all must eat; so the poor mother had to go out to work all day, and only in the winter evenings could she spin and weave shirts for her children, that they might not go naked. Each child had but one shirt, and when the largest had outgrown his, it went to the next in size. So it happened that the shirt that came to the youngest was always so thin that the sun shone through it.

The youngest child was a happy little fellow four years old, who had a wondrous love for animals and flowers. Whenever he saw a lamb he ran to find fragrant leaves to feed it; when he found a young bird that had fallen from the nest he carried it home and fed it until it was grown, then let it fly away. He was fond of the spiders, too, and when he found one in the house he would carry it out of doors, saying: "This little creature shall also live." But one time his little shirt had become so thin and old that it fell from his body, and as it was summer and his mother must go to her day's work, she could not make him another. So he ran about just as the dear God had made him.

One day as he was hunting for berries in the forest, he met a Lamb which looked kindly at him and said: "Where is your little shirt?" The little boy answered sadly, "I have none and my mother cannot make me one till next winter. But no, the new one will be for my oldest sister and mine will be an old one. Oh, if I only once could have a new shirt!" Then the Lamb said: "I am sorry for you, I will give you my wool and you can have a new shirt made of it." So the Lamb pulled all his wool off and gave it to the little boy.

As he now passed by a thorn bush with his wool, the Bush called, "What are you carrying there?" "Wool," said the little one, "to make me a shirt." "Give it to me," said the

SHEARING THE SHEEP.

Thorn Bush, "I will card it for you." The boy gave his wool to the bush, which passed his thorny branches to and fro and carded the wool most beautifully. "Carry it carefully," cried the Bush, "so that you do not spoil it."

So he carried the soft rolls along carefully till he saw the web of a Spider, and the Spider sat in the middle of it and called to him, "Give me your wool, little one. I will spin the threads and weave them. I see already how it is." Then the Spider began and worked busily with his little feet, and spun and wove the finest piece of cloth you ever saw, and gave it to the child, who trotted merrily along with it till he came to a brook, and there sat a great Crab which called out: "Where so fast? What are you carrying there?" "Cloth," said the little boy, "for a new shirt." "Then you come to the right one," said the Crab. "Let me take your cloth." And he took it and with his great shears he cut out a little shirt very nicely. "There, little one," he said, "all that remains to be done is to have it sewed."

The boy took it and went on sadly, for he was afraid that even then he could not have his new shirt till winter, when his mother would have time to sew. But pretty soon he saw a little Bird sitting on a bush, and the Bird twittered, "Wait, little one, let me make your shirt." So the Bird took a long thread and flew back and forth, working with his little beak, till the shirt was sewed together. "Now," said the Bird, "you have as nice a shirt as one could wish."

And the little boy put it on and ran happily home to show it to his sisters and brothers, and they all said they had never seen a nicer one.

Translated by LOUISE STUART.

"*Kindergarten Magazine.*"

Molly's Lamb.

Ever and ever so long ago, when grandma was only little Molly Ray, she was one day going through the sheep pasture, when she saw a wee lamb lying under a tree, too weak even to cry "baa-a."

"Oh! you poor little thing," she cried, "where is your mother?" and then she took it up in her arms and looked about the field to see whether the mother-sheep would not come to her; but the sheep all went on eating grass just as if nothing had happened; so grandma, not knowing what else to do, walked on slowly toward the house with the little wee lamb wrapped snugly in her blue checkered apron. On the way she met her brother Ned, and showed him what she had found.

"It's a poor little stray," he said. "You take it up to the house, Molly, and give it some warm milk, and maybe it will come to life again; it's almost gone, but mother will know what to do." So grandma trudged back to the house as fast as she could go.

"See, mamma, see!" she cried, as she burst into the kitchen where her mother was at work; "some bad mamma-sheep has gone off and left her lammie, and it's so hungry it can't walk!"

Great-grandmother was, no doubt, used to this sort of thing, for she at once set aside her work and brought an old basket from the shed, and with some soft flannel made a warm bed for the lamb; then, while grandma tucked it snugly in, she warmed some milk which the half-starved creature sucked greedily from her finger; after eating, it grew stronger and stood up, giving a plaintive "baa-a" that went straight to grandma's heart.

"You dear little thing!" she cried, "you haven't any really true mamma now; but I will be a mamma to you, and will love you and take care of you just as nice—you'll see!"

And when she asked her father about it, he said yes, that the lamb should be hers, and when it grew into a big sheep she should have all the wool for her winter coats and stockings. But grandma did not care about that part of it; she only thought of it as it was then—a dear, woolly little playmate, all her own— and she loved it so well and was so gentle with it that it soon learned to love her, and would come at her call and follow her all about the farm; and she took such good care of it that it grew very fast, and its coat became so soft and fine that the birds loved to come and carry off bits of it to line their nests with.

One warm spring day, grandma's father said to her: "The sheep are to be sheared to-day, Molly, and you had better see that your lamb is there, for it is quite time that she was rid of her winter coat."

Molly did not quite like the idea of her pet losing its snowy wool, but she knew that hot summer days were coming, when the lamb would be much more comfortable without it; and then the men were always gentle and never hurt the sheep.

So after breakfast grandma called her lamb, which was now almost as large as a sheep, and they went out to the pasture and down to a stream, where she found that the sheep had all been driven into a little pen beside the water, from which the men took them, one by one, and washed and cleaned their shaggy coats in the water;—for they had become quite gray, and were all tangled and burry—then they took a great pair of shears and cut off all the wool.

Grandma's lamb had a very short bath, for its wool was already quite clean, and it did not mind having its wool cut very much, either, which was a great relief to grandma; and when it was all off she gathered it up in her apron and showed it to her lamb, telling it that the wool that had kept it warm the past winter would keep her warm next winter. And so it was, for grandma's mamma took it to her spinning room one day, and after combing it out very carefully, grandma watched her make it into long rolls which she hung across the great spinning wheel; then she took one in her hand and held it close to the spindle, turning the big wheel with her hand. Whirr! went the wheel round and round, turning roll after roll into nice, fine woolen yarn; then, winding it up on the spindle, her mamma brought out a buzzy little reel that wound it into great skeins, and there it was ready to make into balls of soft stocking yarn. How soft and pretty it was! And whenever grandma sat down to knit, as she did in the long winter evenings, she thought of her dear little lamb in the warm fold, and was so glad she had found it in time that cold spring morning.

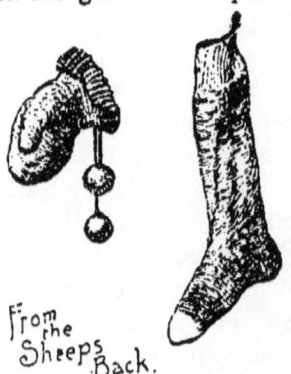

From the Sheep's Back.

Stories for the Kindergarten and the Home.

Sequel to an Old Story.

Mary had a little lamb,
  Which grew to be a sheep;
The wool upon its back became
  Too thick and warm to keep.

Then Mary's sheep did with the rest
  Down to the brookside go,
And soon again it well could boast
  " A fleece as white as snow."

The shearer came, and with his shears
  Cut off the heavy wool,
Till every sheep was shorn at last
  And all the bags were full.

The wool that came from Mary's sheep
  Was spun and woven, dears,
And made into a nice warm coat
  That Mary wore for years!

EMILIE POULSSON.

COTTON.

From the Cotton Field.

(Show specimens of calico and other cotton goods. Contrast with woolen and let the children find whether their dresses, aprons, etc., are cotton or woolen.)

Who made the cotton cloth? What kind of threads did the weaver use? (Ravel enough cloth for the children to distinguish that the threads are cotton.) Cotton cloth is made of cotton threads, just as woolen cloth is made of woolen threads.

What are woolen threads made of? What do you think cotton threads are made of? (Show cotton batting. Do not call it "cotton wool," as that would be a confusing term.) Where did the wool grow? Now the cotton grew in a very different place. (Show the seed-pod, or boll of the cotton plant.) Where do you think this grew? Yes, on a plant. The soft, fluffy cotton is just the covering which Mother Nature has wrapped about the seeds of the cotton plant. (Describe the plant and show picture of cotton field.)* Did you ever see cotton growing? It grows

---

* "Every year, in March or April, the seeds are planted. In a week or ten days the plants show themselves. By the last of June they begin to bloom. In the morning, when the blooms open, they are of a light cream color; later in the day they change to a deep pink. They die and fall off the second day, and then the bolls begin to form. They grow very fast, and become as large as a small egg."

When the seeds are ripe, the hot sun bursts the bolls open and shows the beautiful, snow-white cotton within. Then (about the middle of September) "the picking goes on. The fields are alive with busy workers. After that the cotton must be packed into bales to be sent away."

only in the warm countries. Tell me some other things which grow in the warm countries. Yes; oranges, lemons, bananas— all these need very hot sunshine. The cotton fields must be a beautiful sight when the seed-pods burst open and show the bunches of snowy cotton. Men, women and little boys and girls work in the hot fields picking these bunches from the cotton plants. The cotton then has the seeds taken out by a machine. After that it is sent to the mills and spun into threads; and then our good friend the weaver goes to work and weaves the threads into cotton cloth for Johnny's waist and Susie's apron, for papa's shirts, and mamma's dresses, and many other useful things. Doesn't it seem strange that some of our clothes come from the sheep and others from the cotton plant?

STORIES.
Machinery Magic.

Some years ago a great cotton exhibition was held in Atlanta. All the machines for ginning (taking out the seeds), spinning and weaving cotton into cloth were shown in one building. In a field near by, the cotton itself was growing.

One morning some of this cotton was picked in the field and carried into the hall, where it was twisted into thread, woven into cloth and made into suits, which were presented to some gentlemen, and worn by them on the evening of the very same day.

Holmes' Third Reader.

Cotton Field Stories.

The sun shone with great heat upon a certain cotton field one bright noontide. The people who had been working there all the morning had gone to get their dinners, and the Cotton Plants had the field entirely to themselves. Now if ever plants talk together I should think it would be at just such times, shouldn't you? times when no people are near them? And so,

"As I was saying yesterday," began one Cotton Plant, "it

would be a satisfaction to known where the cotton goes after it is picked from our bolls."

"Why, it goes to the cotton-gin," said a Plant near the edge of the field.

"Oh! yes, I know; but I mean *after* that, when it really gets out into the world. I have heard something about the cleaning and the spinning and weaving, and the strange changes that are made in the cotton; but I should like to know more."

"Tweet, tweet," said a sweet voice near. "I can tell you something."

"Who is that?" whispered the Cotton Plants.

"Tweet, tweet," said the same voice. "I am only a little bird. My wing is hurt, or I should be far away in the pleasant Northern land now. Last year I was there."

"Indeed!" said the Cotton Plants. They themselves always stayed in one place and preferred it, but they thought that the creatures who could move about were very wonderful.

"Yes," continued the little bird, glad to have found listeners.

> "I was there, yes! there, with my mate so dear,
> And our days were glad with love and cheer.
> Happy of heart and swift on the wing
> Naught did we do but carol and sing.
> We caroled with rapture, but soon, oh! soon
> A deeper joy gave a sweeter tune.
> For my mate and I, in a tall, green tree,
> Built the prettiest home that you e'er did see.
> Such a cosy home! Such a precious nest!
> But the brood it held—Ah! that was the best!"

"That is a very pretty song," said the Cotton Plants. "But did you say you could tell us something about what becomes of our cotton?"

"Tweet, tweet; that I can!" said the bird. "When my mate and I were ready to build our nest we had to search well for the materials. One day we were flying near the window of the house in which lives the family for whom we often sing, and there we saw the mother and little Nellie sewing. Pretty soon we heard little Nellie's mother say that the birds would like some threads to weave into their nest, and Nellie threw a bunch of long strings out of the window. Oh, they were so fine and

PICKING THE COTTON.

strong! And—now I suppose you will think this the best part of my story!—those fine, strong threads were made of cotton from cotton plants. I am sure of it, for I heard Nellie's mother telling her the whole story. So that is what becomes of part of your cotton; Nellie and her mother sew with it and give some to the birds for nest making."

The Cotton Plants had listened eagerly and now thanked the little bird for his pretty story,—"As pretty as your songs," said they, "and that is high praise. Come and tell it to us again sometime."

"Gladly," answered the little bird. "Truth to tell, I am somewhat lonely at times, far away from my friends in the North, and I shall be happy to visit you."

While the bird was telling his story, some of the Sunbeams which were playing about the field had drawn near to listen, and now they began to speak.

"We know something about cotton," said they. "Often and often have we heard the women say that there was nothing like the sunshine for bleaching cotton cloth; and often have we bleached it. But that is not all, for we not only bleach the cotton cloth—yards upon yards of it—but there is scarcely a day that we do not, with the wind's help, dry many things that are made of it, when they have been washed and hang clean and wet upon the line."

"Yes, indeed," said a little Breeze, rustling among the Cotton Plants. "The Sunbeams and I often work together at drying clothes, and most of them are made of cotton cloth—dresses, aprons, underclothes, stockings, sheets and pillowcases. Surely, Cotton Plants, you may feel that you are very useful, for people would scarcely know how to get along without the cloth which is made from your cotton."

"These are delightful stories," said the Cotton Plants, nodding to one another, smiling as the Sunbeams danced among them, and spreading out their leaves for the breeze to play with. "Now we can grow with more pleasure than ever before. Thank you, good friends; come again and tell us these stories often."

Soon after this the workmen came back into the field. With them came a gentleman and his two children. The Cotton

Plants, of course, did not talk any more then, but oh, how they listened! for they soon found that what they heard was of special interest. It was more of the same story which the little Bird had begun and the Sunbeams and the Breeze had continued. The gentleman was talking with his children about what becomes of the cotton after it is taken from the field; and he not only spoke of cotton thread and cotton cloth, but of cotton batting for comforters and quilts, of cotton which doctors use, of cotton cord and cotton lamp wicks, and of still other things made of cotton; more than you or I could remember! He told, too, of old, worn-out cotton rags being changed into beautiful paper—paper out of which books are made, paper for letters to be written upon, and paper of beautiful colors—"the very paper, Teddy, out of which were made the squares of folding paper and the weaving mats and strips which you used to have in kindergarten," he added, smiling down at the little boy.

Teddy and his sister were looking with much wonder at the cotton plants, half expecting to see some of the things which their father mentioned sprouting out somewhere upon them; and they treasured long afterward the cotton boll and spray of leaves which were given to each of them as they went away from the field.

You may believe that the Cotton Plants were full of wonder and joy. They had even ventured to say to the gentleman, as they had said to the Bird and the Sunbeams and the Breeze, "Thank you, good friend. Come again and tell us these delightful stories often." But the gentleman, far from understanding a word, had not even seemed to know that they were speaking. So the Cotton Plants contented themselves with telling the story to one another whenever they talked together.

The little Bird kept his word and came again and again, as did also the Sunbeams and the Breeze; they were always ready to tell the same stories they had told before, of what becomes of the cotton, and the Cotton Plants were as happy as the day was long. And surely it is no wonder that the Cotton Plants were pleased to know that they were of so much use in the world, is it? For what is better worth being glad about than that?

EMILIE POULSSON

LINEN.

The children will probably have difficulty in distinguishing cotton and linen, though the latter is colder to the touch.

Speak of the superior durability of linen and its usefulness in bandaging, etc. Flaxseed should have been planted, so that a plant would be ready to illustrate this talk.

The process by which the raw material is converted into the finished linen, and, indeed, the whole subject-matter for a talk on linen or on paper, are presented effectively in Andersen's story. For the children the details of manufacturing processes are unimportant, and descriptions of them would be tedious; but it is different with the chief steps in such transformations as from the flax plant to linen, and from rags to paper. A visit to a paper mill would stimulate the teacher's interest.

Flax.

STORIES.

The Flax.

The Flax was in full bloom; it had pretty little blue flowers, as delicate as the wings of a moth, or even more so. The sun shone, and the showers watered it; and this was just as good for the Flax as it is for little children to be washed and then kissed by their mother. They look much prettier for it, and so did the Flax.

FROM FLAX TO PAPER.

"People say that I look exceedingly well," said the Flax, "and that I am so fine and long that I shall make a beautiful piece of linen. How fortunate I am; it makes me so happy, it is such a pleasant thing to know that something can be made of me. How the sunshine cheers me, and how sweet and refreshing is the rain; my happiness overpowers me, no one in the world can feel happier than I am."

"Ah, yes, no doubt," said the Fern, "but you do not know the world yet as well as I do, for my sticks are knotty;" and then it sang quite mournfully—

> "Snip, snap, snurre,
> Basse lurre:
> The song is ended."

"No, it is not ended," said the Flax. "To-morrow the sun will shine, or the rain descend. I feel that I am growing. I feel that I am in full blossom. I am the happiest of all creatures."

Well, one day some people came, who took hold of the Flax and pulled it up by the roots; this was painful; then it was laid in water as if they intended to drown it; and, after that, placed near a fire as if it were to be roasted; all this was very shocking. "We cannot expect to be happy always," said the Flax; "by experiencing evil, as well as good, we become wise." And certainly there was plenty of evil in store for the Flax. It was steeped, and roasted, and broken, and combed; indeed, it scarcely knew what was done to it. At last it was put on the spinning wheel. "Whirr, whirr," went the wheel so quickly that the Flax could not collect its thoughts. "Well I have been very happy," he thought in the midst of his pain, "and must be content with the past;" and contented he remained till he was put on the loom, and became a beautiful piece of white Linen. All the Flax, even to the last stalk, was used in making this one piece. "Well, this is quite wonderful; I could not have believed that I should be so favored by fortune. The Fern really was not wrong with its song of

> ' Snip, snap, snurre,
> Basse lurre.'

But the song is not ended yet, I am sure; it is only just beginning. How wonderful it is, that after all I have suffered, I am made something of at last; I am the luckiest person in the world—so strong and fine; and how white, and what a length! This is something different to being a mere plant and bearing flowers. Then, I had no attention, nor any water unless it rained; now, I am watched and taken care of. Every morning the maid turns me over, and I have a shower bath from the watering pot every evening. Yes, and the clergyman's wife noticed me, and said I was the best piece of Linen in the whole parish. I cannot be happier than I am now."

After some time, the Linen was taken into the house, placed under the scissors, and cut and torn into pieces, and then pricked with needles. This certainly was not pleasant; but at last it was made into twelve garments of that kind which people do not like to name, and yet everybody should wear one. "See, now, then," said the Flax; "I have become something of importance. This was my destiny; it is quite a blessing. Now I shall be of some use in the world, as every one ought to be; it is the only way to be happy. I am now divided into twelve pieces, and yet we are all one and the same in the whole dozen. It is most extraordinary good fortune."

Years passed away; and at last the Linen was so worn it could scarcely hold together. "It must end very soon," said the pieces to each other; "we would gladly have held together a little longer, but it is useless to expect impossibilities." And at length they fell into rags and tatters, and thought it was all over with them, for they were torn to shreds, and steeped in water, and made into a pulp, and dried, and they knew not what besides, till all at once they found themselves beautiful white paper. "Well, now, this is a surprise; a glorious surprise, too," said the Paper. "I am now finer than ever, and I shall be written upon, and who can tell what fine things I may have written upon me. This is wonderful luck!" And sure enough, the most beautiful stories and poetry were written upon it, and only once was there a blot, which was very fortunate. Then people heard the stories and poetry read, and it made them wiser and better; for all that was written had a good and sensible meaning, and a great blessing was contained in the words on this Paper.

"I never imagined anything like this," said the Paper, "when I was only a little blue flower, growing in the fields. How could I fancy that I should ever be the means of bringing knowledge and joy to men? I cannot understand it myself, and yet it is really so. Heaven knows that I have done nothing myself, but what I was obliged to do with my weak powers for my own preservation; and yet I have been promoted from one joy and honor to another. Each time I think that the song is ended; and then something higher and better begins for me. I suppose now I shall be sent on my travels about the world, so that people may read me. It cannot be otherwise; indeed, it is more than probable; for I have more splendid thoughts written upon me than I had pretty flowers in olden times. I am happier than ever."

But the Paper did not go on its travels; it was sent to the printer, and all the words written upon it were set up in type, to make a book, or rather, many hundreds of books; for so many more persons could derive pleasure and profit from a printed book than from the written paper; and if the Paper had been sent about the world, it would have been worn out before it had got half through its journey.

"This is certainly the wisest plan," said the written Paper; "I really did not think of that. I shall remain at home, and be held in honor, like some old grandfather, as I really am to all these new books. They will do some good. I could not have wandered about as they do. Yet he who wrote all this has looked at me, as every word flowed from his pen upon my surface. I am the most honored of all."

Then the Paper was tied in a bundle with other papers and thrown into a tub that stood in the washhouse.

"After work, it is well to rest," said the Paper, "and a very good opportunity to collect one's thoughts. Now I am able, for the first time, to think of my real condition; and to know one's self is true progress. What shall be done with me now, I wonder? No doubt I shall go still forward. I have always progressed hitherto, as I know quite well."

Now it happened one day that all the paper in the tub was taken out, and laid on the hearth to be burnt. People said it could not be sold at the shop, to wrap up butter and sugar, because it had been written upon. The children in the house stood round the stove; for they wanted to see the paper burn, because it flamed up so prettily, and afterwards, among the ashes, so many red sparks could be seen running one after the other, here and there, as quick as the wind. They called it seeing the children come out of school, and the last spark was the schoolmaster. They often thought the last spark had come; and one would cry, "There goes the schoolmaster;" but the next moment another spark would appear, shining so beautifully. How they would like to know where the sparks all went to! Perhaps we shall find out some day, but we do not know now.

The whole bundle of paper had been placed on the fire, and was soon alight. "Ugh," cried the Paper, as it burst into a bright flame; "ugh." It was certainly not very pleasant to be burning; but when the whole was wrapped in flames, the flames mounted up into the air, higher than the flax had ever been able to raise its little blue flower, and they glistened as the white linen never could have glistened. All the written letters became quite red in a moment, and all the words and thoughts turned to fire.

"Now I am mounting straight up to the sun," said a voice in the flames; and it was as if a thousand voices echoed the words; and the flames darted up through the chimney, and went out at the top. Then a number of tiny beings, as many in number as the flowers on the flax had been, and invisible to mortal eyes, floated above them. They were even lighter and more delicate than the flowers from which they were born; and as the flames were extinguished, and nothing remained of the paper but black ashes, these little beings danced upon it; and whenever they touched it, bright red sparks appeared.

"The children are all out of school, and the schoolmaster was the last of all," said the children. It was good fun, and they sang over the dead ashes—

"Snip, snap, snurre,
Basse lurre:
The song is ended."

But the little invisible beings said: "The song is never ended; the most beautiful is yet to come."

But the children could neither hear nor understand this, nor should they; for children must not know everything.

HANS ANDERSEN.

The Flax Flower.

Oh, the little flax flower!
  It groweth on the hill,
And, be the breeze awake or 'sleep,
  It never standeth still.
It groweth, and it groweth fast;
  One day it is a seed
And then a little grassy blade
  Scarce better than a weed.
But then out comes the flax flower
  As blue as is the sky;
And "'tis a dainty little thing,"
  We say as we go by.

Ah! 'tis a goodly little thing,
  It groweth for the poor,
And many a peasant blesseth it
  Beside his cottage door,
He thinketh how those slender stems
  That shimmer in the sun
Are rich for him in web and woof
  And shortly shall be spun.
He thinketh how those tender flowers
  Of seed will yield him store,
And sees in thought his next year's crop
  Blue shining round his door.

Oh, the little flax flower!
  The mother then says she,
"Go, pull the thyme, the heath, the fern,
  But let the flax flower be!
It groweth for the children's sake,
  It groweth for our own;

There are flowers enough upon the hill,
  But leave the flax alone!
The farmer hath his fields of wheat,
  Much cometh to his share;
We have this little plot of flax
  That we have tilled with care."

Oh, the goodly flax flower!
  It groweth on the hill,
And, be the breeze awake or sleep,
  It never standeth still.
It seemeth all astir with life
  As if it loved to thrive,
As if it had a merry heart
  Within its stem alive.
Then fair befall the flax field,
  And may the kindly shower
Give strength unto its shining stem
  [illegible]

                MARY HOWITT.

SILK.

From the Silk-worm.

Silkworm cocoons can usually be obtained and should always be shown during this talk. Sewing silk, ribbons and pieces of silk will also be needed. See whether the children remember where wool and cotton and linen came from, and who were the chief workers in the manufacture of the goods. That the beautiful, shining silk can be traced back to so small a creature as the silkworm, is always a delight to children. The following stories and verses will supply the points for a talk upon silk, especially if the subject is taken up after cotton, wool, and linen.

STORIES.
The Life of a Silkworm.

Once there was a baby Caterpillar who found himself on a broad, green leaf, in a mulberry tree; and on the stems between the leaves were pretty, yellow-white berries, very much like the raspberries that you city children see in the grocery stores in the summer. This little Caterpillar lifted his brown head up and stretched himself and looked all around him; and he thought: "Well! this is a very nice place to be in!" Then he crawled all around the leaf and went underneath it. While he was underneath he thought he would have a little fun; so he held on with his fore feet, and swung back and forth, and then drew himself up again, and had a grand time.

The warm summer winds played in and out through the branches of the trees, whispering to each other and rocking the leaf on which the baby Caterpillar was crawling, until at last he

IN THE SILK FACTORY.

began to feel tired, and rolled himself into a ring and took a little nap; for caterpillars never sleep very long at one time. When he woke up he was very hungry. He did not know what to eat, so he thought he would taste a piece of the leaf on which he was lying, for it looked extremely nice. When he bit into it, it tasted so very good that he kept on eating till the whole leaf was gone. Then he traveled down the stem and found another leaf that he thought he would like; and he curled himself up on that to rest before commencing to eat again. He kept on in this way for a long time—eating and resting, eating and resting —till he grew so big and fat that his clothes were too tight for him and he felt very uncomfortable. So Mother Nature went to work and made him a new suit. It was just like his old one, only a little larger, and he was very much pleased with it. But he ate so *much* and grew so *very* fast that Mother Nature had to make him two or three new suits, and he began to grow tired of wearing the same kind of clothes all the time and of crawling around and eating the same kind of food. He had tried eating one of the nice looking berries one day, but it had made him very sick.

Now when Mother Nature found that he was getting so fretful, she said to him: "Well, my dear, what is the matter with you? You are not the same contented little Caterpillar you were a few weeks ago. What is it? What do you want?"

And the Caterpillar said; "Oh, I don't know, I'm sure—but I am *so* tired of crawling around on these leaves! I wish I could fly away!"

"H'm!" said Mother Nature, "that's the trouble, is it? Very well, dear; you are quite right. All my caterpillars have that feeling sooner or later. Only be patient a little longer and you *shall* fly."

"*I* fly!" said the Caterpillar; and he looked at his clumsy body and thick feet, and then at a butterfly with gorgeous wings just passing over his head. He was so amused and laughed so hard that he almost rolled off the leaf.

"Well," said Mother Nature, "wouldn't you like to fly?"

"Oh, yes," said the Caterpillar, "I would, indeed! but wings, Mother Nature; I have no wings!"

"Don't be troubled about the wings, little Caterpillar," Mother Nature answered. "That is for me to attend to; and I generally bring all things right in the end, when I undertake them."

So she taught the Caterpillar how to spin, and then how to choose a good, firm twig and fasten his thread to it; and the Caterpillar went back and forth, and back and forth, with his thread, till he made himself a nice hammock. Then he was very much pleased, and thought: "This is great fun; I like this spinning and weaving." And he worked so hard that he forgot all about eating. He spun on and on, and wound the thread around and around, until he became so dizzy that when he stopped he did not notice at first that he was in the dark. But when he found himself completely wrapped about, with no way of escape, he called; "O dear Mother Nature! I've shut myself in. How shall I ever get out?"

And Mother Nature said: "Oh! you are all right, dear Caterpillar. Go to sleep now and rest; I will tell you how to get out when the proper time comes."

So, as the Caterpillar was very tired and sleepy, he thought this was the best thing he could do. He took off his clothes (for it was very warm in the little cradle he had spun for himself), and tucked them all down at his feet, and then lay down to take a good sleep.

Every time the wind blew and shook the twig, the cradle swung back and forth, rocking the Caterpillar into a still sounder slumber. After he had been asleep a long, long time, he was awakened one day by a great shaking of his cradle; and, as he was only half awake, he thought: "Oh, those threads which I spun must have broken!" After that there came another shake, and Mother Nature called: "Wake up! Wake up! It is time to come out!"

And the Caterpillar said: "How shall I get out? It is dark in here, and I'm very stiff from being so long in one position."

"Force your way out," answered Mother Nature. So he made a little round hole right at his head, and pulled himself through.

"I don't call *this* flying!" said he. "I believe that I'm just the same clumsy Caterpillar that I was before."

"Oh, no, you are not," said Mother Nature.

Then the Caterpillar opened his eyes very wide and looked at his feet and did not know what to say, for they were changed entirely; and, while he was wondering, he felt something growing looser and looser all around his body. "Oh!" thought he, "I'm falling to pieces!" and he caught hold of his old cradle with his feet and hung on quite frightened, shutting his eyes and shaking all over. After he had hung there for a little while he grew quieter; and finally he heard Mother Nature saying gently: "My dear Moth!"

He looked up. "You don't mean *me*," said he; "I'm a Caterpillar!"

But Mother Nature answered, "No, not now. Do you not remember? You wanted to fly; so while you were asleep in that cradle I changed you into a moth. Now you have wings and can fly!"

And sure enough he really *had* wings—beautiful wings! They had been rolled around his body when he first came out, but now he began to wave them back and forth, and soon they were dry and strong.

Then away he flew, fluttering gaily over the green fields; for now he did not have to crawl about slowly and live upon mulberry leaves, but could fly wherever he chose, sipping honey from the beautiful flowers.

NETTIE FLEMING.

The Silkworm.

Silkworm on the mulberry tree,
Spin a silken robe for me;
Draw the threads out fine and strong,
Longer yet—and very long;
Longer yet—'twill not be done
Till a thousand more are spun.
Silkworm, turn this mulberry tree
Into silken threads for me!

All day long, and many a day,
Busy silkworms spin away;
Some are ending, some beginning.
Nothing thinking of but spinning!

Well for them! Like silver light,
All the threads are smooth and bright;
Pure as day the silk must be,
Woven from the mulberry tree!

Ye are spinning well and fast;
'Twill be finished all at last.
Twenty thousand threads are drawn
Finer than the finest lawn;
And as long, this silken twine,
As the equinoctial line!
What a change! The mulberry tree
Turneth into silk for me!

MARY HOWITT.

The Goddess of the Silkworm.

Once upon a time the Chinese people dressed chiefly in the skins of animals, but these began to grow scarce and the question arose as to what the people should do for clothing.

According to the old stories the answer was found in this way. Hoangti, the third emperor of China (2600 B. C.), had a wife named Si Ling Shi, and Si Ling Shi, who must have been a thoughtful woman, and interested in the welfare of the people, began to try to find some material which should take the place of the animal skins.

Nothing did she find, however, even with much thought and searching, until one morning when she was walking as usual in the beautiful palace garden among the mulberry trees.

Si Ling Shi had probably often seen the silkworm cocoons there before, but on this day as she looked at the loose, filmy outside webs of the cocoons, the idea came to her that a fabric which could be used for clothing might be made out of these delicate threads. Many earnest people had to give a good deal of thought to the work, and many trials had to be made, but at last the way was found. The threads were wound off from the cocoons, twisted together and woven, and thus was made the shining, rustling stuff which we call silk.

The people were so grateful to the wise, observant and ingenious Si Ling Shi for her discovery, that they ever after called her the "Goddess of the Silkworm." E. P.

ALPHABETICAL INDEX.

A Barnyard Talk..........................324
A Boston Thanksgiving Story...........93
Adventure, The Minnow's 242
A Kitten Rhyme........................145
A Lesson of Faith......................307
An All-the-Year-Round Story..........113
A Narrow Escape.......................356
An Autumn Song........................48
An Old-fashioned Rhyme................30
An Old Story, Sequel to...............419
Ant, The Dove and the.................80
Ants, A Story of (Mrs. Flyaway).......361
Apple-Seed John........................59
Apple, The Sleeping....................7
Apple Trees, The Four.................256
Arbutus, The Indian Legend of........375
A Surprise............................274
A True Pigeon Story....................81
A True Story of a Dog.................180
Autumn.................................45
Autumn, Birds in.......................11
Autumn Song, An........................48
A Visit to the Weaver.................408
A Wise Old Horse......................151

Baby Buds' Winter Clothes, The........47
Bag of Winds, Odysseus and the........69
Baker, The............................82
Bakery, Nero at the...................88
Barn, Christmas in the................119
Barnyard Talk, A......................324
Basket, The Flower....................106
Beans Came Up, How the................382
Beauty, Such a........................317
Bee I, The............................344
Bee II, The...........................354
Bees, Edith and the...................348
Bees, Solomon and the.................360
Bird, Child and.......................290
Birds.................................282
Bird's Christmas, The.................125
Birds in Autumn........................11
Birds, Lisa and the....................13
Birds' Nests..........................292
Birds, The Farmer and the.............325

Bird Thoughts.........................16
Birthday Cake, Teddy's................88
Birthday, Froebel's...................279
Birthday, Song for Froebel's..........281
Birthday, Washington's................197
Blacksmith, The.......................201
Boston Thanksgiving Story, A..........93
Boy Got a New Shirt, How the Little..414
Boy, The Rhyme of the Little Idle....346
Boys, The Chestnut....................49
Breeze, The Story of a................390
Brook and the Water Wheel, The.......237
Butterfly, The........................302
Butterflies, Some Common..............306

Cake, Teddy's Birthday.................88
Cake, The Johnny......................85
Camp, The Logging.....................19
Carpenter, The........................25
Cat, The.............................140
Caterpillar, The......................313
Chestnut Boys, The....................49
Chicken, The Lost.....................333
Chickens, The Hen and.................331
Child and Bird........................290
Children, The Cobbler and the.........189
China Rabbit Family, The...............86
Christel, The Dream of Little.........111
Christmas.............................117
Christmas in the Barn.................119
Christmas, The Birds'.................125
Cleverness of a Sheep Dog.............178
Clock, The............................33
Clock Told Dolly, What the............36
Clothes, The Baby Buds' Winter........47
Clytie...............................374
Coal.................................214
Cobbler, The.........................181
Cobbler and the Children, The.........189
Colors, The Nest of Many..............297
Common Butterflies, Some..............306
Constant Dove, The....................80
Cornwallis' Kneebuckles, Lord.........172
Cotton...............................420
Cotton Field Stories..................421

Cow, The...................157	Go Sleep Story, The...............115
Cow that Lost her Tail, The..........161	Gustava, Little....................329
Crane Express, The..............14	Haarlem, The Little Hero of......232
Cycle, The Dandelion.............69	Helpers, Spring and Her............265
	Hen and Chickens, The............331
Dandelion, How West Wind Helped....65	Hero of Haarlem, The Little.........232
Day, Mabel on Midsummer's.........384	Honest Woodman, The...............22
Day, St. Valentine's...............191	Horse, The......................148
Day, Thanksgiving................90	Horse, A Wise Old................151
Deeds of Kindness, Little............27	Horse that Fed his Friend, The......156
Did, What They...................371	Household, The Plant..............373
Discontented Pendulum, The.........41	How Frisk Came Home.............176
Dog and the Kitten, The............180	How Patty Gave Thanks............94
Dog, Cleverness of a...............178	How the Beans Came Up...........382
Dog, The........................174	How the Little Boy Got a New Shirt ...414
Dog, A True Story of a.............180	How West Wind Helped Dandelion...65
Dolly, What the Clock Told..........36	
Dove and the Ant, The............80	Idle Boy, The Rhyme of the Little....346
Dove, The Constant................80	Immortal Fountain, The............222
Do What You Can.................235	Indian Legend of the Arbutus, The...375
Dream of Little Christel, The........111	
	Jack and Jenny Sparrow............385
Echo, The Story of................257	Jack Frost and his Work............104
Edith and the Bees................348	Jet, My..........................144
Escape, A Narrow.................356	John, Apple-Seed..................59
Express, The Crane................14	Johnny Cake, The..................85
	John's Trousers...................410
Fairy's New Year Gift, The.........138	
Faith, A Lesson of................307	Kindness, Little Deeds of............27
Family, Spotty's...................146	Kind Old Oak, The.................48
Family, The China Rabbit...........86	Kitten Rhyme, A.................145
Fantail Pigeon, The................76	Kitten, The Dog and the............180
Farmer, The......................321	Kneebuckles, Lord Cornwallis'......172
Farmer and the Birds, The.........325	Lamb, Molly's....................416
Fed his Friend, The Horse that......156	Legend of the Arbutus, The.........375
Fishes...........................239	Lesson of Faith, A................307
Five Peas in a Pod.................53	Lesson, Pe-wee's..................336
Flax, The........................426	Life of a Silkworm, The............434
Flax Flower, The..................432	Linda and the Lights..............404
Flower Basket or Loving and Giving..106	Linen............................426
Flowers..........................366	Lisa and the Birds.................13
Flyaway, Mrs.....................361	Little Boy Got a New Shirt, How the..414
Fountain, The Immortal............222	Little Christel, Dream of............111
Four Apple Trees, The.............256	Little Deeds of Kindness............27
Friend, The Horse that Fed his......156	Little Gustava....................329
Frisk Came Home, How............176	Little Hero of Haarlem, The.........232
Froebel, Friedrich.................276	Little Idle Boy, The Rhyme of.......346
Froebel's Birthday, Song for........281	Little Plant, The..................377
Frost and his Work, Jack...........104	Little Servants...................108
Fruits...........................3	Little Worm that was Glad to be Alive.272
	Little Yellow-wing................289
Gift, The Fairy's New Year.........138	Logging Camp, The................19
Give Thanks, To Whom shall we.....219	Lord Cornwallis' Kneebuckles.......172
Goddess of the Silkworm, The......437	Lost Chicken, The.................333
Golden Touch, The................211	Lost her Tail, The Cow that.........10
Goody Two Shoes.................184	

Mabel on Midsummer's Day............384
Machinery Magic......................421
Maple Tree's Surprise, The...........259
Meeting of the Winds, The............269
Milk Told me, The Story the..........160
Miner, The...........................209
Minnow's Adventure, The..............242
Molly's Lamb.........................416
Moon and the Stars, The..............401
Morning-glory Seed, The Story of a...399
Mouse, Santa Claus and the...........122
Mrs. Fiyaway.........................361
Mr. Stickleback......................247
My Jet...............................144
Nahum Prince,........................205
Narrow Escape, A.....................356
Neptune..............................236
Nero at the Bakery....................88
Nest of Many Colors, The.............297
Nests, Birds'........................292
Nest, The Sparrow's..................300
New Year, The........................131
New Year Gift, The Fairy's...........138
North Wind at Play....................71
Oak, The Kind Old.....................48
Odysseus and the Bag of Winds.........69
Old-fashioned Rhyme, An...............30
Old Horse, A Wise....................151
Old Story, Sequel to an..............419
Patty Gave Thanks, How................94
Pearl and her Pigeons.................79
Peas in a Pod, Five...................53
Pegasus..............................154
Pendulum, The Discontented............41
Pe-wee's Lesson......................336
Philip's Valentine...................191
Piccola..............................129
Pigeons, The..........................73
Pigeons, Pearl and Her................79
Pigeon Story, A True..................81
Pigeon, The Fantail...................76
Plant Household, The.................373
Plant, The Little....................377
Play, North Wind at...................71
Pod, Five Peas in a...................53
Prince, Nahum........................205
Psyche's Task.........................57
Pussy Willow.........................262
Rabbit Family, The China..............86
Rhyme, A Kitten......................145
Rhyme, An Old-fashioned...............30
Rhyme of the Little Idle Boy, The.....34
Rocky, Stony and.....................230

Sandpipers, The......................290
Santa Claus and the Mouse............122
Scarecrow, The.......................296
See, Wait and..........................7
Seed, The Story of a Morning-glory...399
Seeds.................................51
Seeing Shoes Made....................187
Servants, Little.....................108
Sheep Dog, Cleverness of a...........178
Shirt, How a Little Boy Got a New....414
Shoes Made, Seeing...................187
Silk.................................434
Silkworm, The........................438
Silkworm, The Goddess of the.........439
Silkworm, The Life of a..............434
Sleeping Apple, The....................7
Smith, Vulcan the Mighty.............206
Snowflakes...........................220
Solomon and the Bees.................360
Some Common Butterflies..............306
Song, An Autumn.......................48
Song for Froebel's Birthday..........281
Sparrow, Jack and Jenny..............285
Sparrow's Nest, The..................300
Speckle, The Story of................337
Spotty's Family......................146
Spring...............................263
Spring and Her Helpers...............265
Squirrels, The Thrifty...............101
Stars, the Moon and the..............401
Stickleback, Mr......................247
Stony and Rocky......................230
Stories, Cotton Field................421
Story, An All-the-Year Round.........133
Story, A True Pigeon..................81
Story of a Breeze, The...............390
Story of a Dog, A True...............180
Story of Echo, The...................257
Story of a Morning-glory Seed, The...399
Story of Speckle, The................337
Story, Sequel to an Old..............419
Story, The Boston Thanksgiving........93
Story, The Go-Sleep..................115
Story the Milk Told me, The..........160
Story, The Wake Up...................113
St. Valentine's Day..................191
Such a Beauty........................317
Suggestions..........................212
Summer...............................379
Sun, The Wind and the................396
Sunbeams, The........................398
Sunshine.............................393
Surprise, A..........................274
Surprise, The Maple Tree's...........259

Tail, The Cow that Lost Her...... 161	Washington's Birthday..................107
Talk, A Barnyard......................324	Water, I............................316
Task, Psyche's.........................57	Water, II...........................227
Teddy's Birthday Cake..................88	Waterbloom, The....................400
Thanks, How Patty Gave................104	Water Wheel, The Brook and the......237
Thanks, To Whom shall we Give......219	Weaver, A Visit to the... 408
Thanksgiving Day......................90	Weaver, The.........................407
Thanksgiving Story, The Boston........93	West Wind Helped Dandelion, How....65
They Did, What.......................371	What the Clock Told Dolly.............36
Thoughts, Bird.........................16	What They Did.......................371
Thrifty Squirrels, The.................101	Willow, Pussy........................261
Touch, The Golden...................213	Wind, The............................62
To Whom shall we Give Thanks?......219	Wind at Play, North...................71
Trees................................253	Wind and the Sun, The...............396
Tree, The............................259	Wind Helped Dandelion, How West....65
Trees, The Four Apple........ 256	Winds, Odysseus and the Bag of........69
Tree's Surprise, The Maple............250	Winds, The Meeting of the............269
Trousers, John's.....................410	Winter...............................98
True Pigeon Story, A..................81	Winter Clothes, The Baby Buds'........47
True Story of a Dog, A................180	Wise Old Horse, A...................151
Two Shoes, Goody....................184	Wood.................................17
Valentine, Philip's...................191	Woodman, The Honest..................22
Valentine's Day, St..................191	Wool................................413
Visit to the Weaver's, A..............408	Work, Jack Frost and His.............104
Vulcan the Mighty Smith...... ...206	Worm, The Little....................272
Wait and See...... 7	Year, The New......................131
Wake Up Story, The.................113	Yellow-wing, Little...................258

www.ingramcontent.com/pod-product-compliance
Lightning Source LLC
Chambersburg PA
CBHW032008300426
44117CB00008B/941